MINDSCAPES

Political Ideologies Towards the 21st Century

ROGER GIBBINS
University of Calgary

LOLEEN YOUNGMAN
University of Calgary

McGraw-Hill Ryerson Limited

Toronto   New York   Auckland   Bogotá   Caracas
Lisbon   London   Madrid   Mexico   Milan   New Delhi
San Juan   Singapore   Sydney   Tokyo

MINDSCAPES:
POLITICAL IDEOLOGIES TOWARDS THE 21ST CENTURY

CAN©OPY

ISBN: 0-07-552611-5

1 2 3 4 5 6 7 8 9 10 BBM 5 4 3 2 1 0 9 8 7 6

Printed and bound in Canada
Care has been taken to trace ownership of copyright material contained in this
text. The publisher will gladly take any information that will enable them to rectify
any reference or credit in subsequent editions.

Sponsoring Editor: Gord Muschett
Developmental Editor: Norma Christensen
Production Editor: Liba Berry
Production Coordinator: Nicla Dattolico
Cover Design: Dave Hader/Studio Conceptions
Typesetter: Pages Design Ltd.
Printer and Binder: Best Book Manufacturers

Canadian Cataloguing in Publication Data

Gibbins, Roger, 1947–
    Mindscapes: political ideologies towards the 21st century

Includes bibliographical references and index.
ISBN: 0-07-552611-5

1. Political science. 2. Ideology. I. Youngman, Loleen. II Title.

JA83.G52 1996   320.5   C95-933278-2

Contents

Acknowledgments

This work attests to the dictum that good scholarship is often collaborative scholarship. The book project first emerged in the early spring of 1994, when our initial and still very tentative prospectus was enthusiastically embraced by McGraw-Hill Ryerson. Once launched, the project drew into its web a large number of co-authors from the Department of Political Science at the University of Calgary: Jodi Cockerill, Boris DeWiel, Ron Hallman, Michelle Honkanen, Butch Kamena, Jennifer Stewart-Toth and Fred Wall all put in long hours on individual chapters, and in reading the seemingly never-ending drafts of other chapters. In some cases their work stretched over months, indeed years, and in other cases was compressed into intense, nerve-racking sprints as we responded to inexorable deadlines with a life of their own. Throughout, valuable research assistance was provided by others: John Soroski compiled much of the material on early patterns of ideological thought in western democratic states, and Heather Bala's assistance spanned most of the ideological themes tackled in the book. The assistance of these people went far beyond being useful; it was of critical importance. Valerie Snowdon, administrative assistant with the Department of Political Science, cheerfully turned around draft after draft; without her professional anchor, the project might still be mired in a muddle of inconsistent and incomplete drafts. Chris Gibbins, Judi Powell and John Soroski pulled together most of the artwork. The reviewers recruited by McGraw-Hill Ryerson provided a wealth of critical commentary, most of which we were able to address with good spirits and a reasonable measure of success. They include Mark Charlton (Trinity Western College); Derek Cook (University College of the Cariboo); Pierre A. Coulombe (University of New Brunswick); D.W. Daycock (University of Manitoba); Bruce Foster (Simon Fraser University); Michael D. Henderson (York University); Henry Jacek (McMaster University); J. Paul Johnston (University of Alberta); Paul Kopas (University of Saskatchewan); Ingrid Makus (Brock University); Peter McCormick (University of Lethbridge); Stefania Miller (McMaster University); Richard Noble (University of Winnipeg); Richard A. Nutbrown (University of Waterloo); and Jonathan Rose (Queen's University). Finally, we would like to thank the Social Sciences and Humanities Research Council of Canada, whose research grants supported the more general research projects of which the present book constitutes an important part.

Any book on political ideologies will inevitably be contentious. This is particularly so in the current environment where the lines between scholarship, social commentary and political activism are becoming increasingly blurred. We are particularly grateful, therefore, to have had the chance to work with a group of colleagues, and in a departmental setting, in which freewheeling ideological debate was the norm, where it was seen to be an essential component of scholarship. In this book, we have not attempted to settle ideological disputes as much as bring them to the surface so that students can appreciate the complex dynamics of contemporary ideological debate. At the very least, we have learned that there are few simple answers, and if readers can come away with the same conclusion, our basic objective will have been achieved.

CHAPTER ONE

The Nature of Ideologies

*The history of mankind is the history of ideas. For it is ideas, theories and doctrines
that guide human action, determine the ultimate ends men aim at, and the choice
of the means employed for the attainment of those ends. The sensational events
which stir the emotions and catch the interest of superficial observers are merely the
consummation of ideological changes.*

LUDWIG VON MISES

*The field of politics always presents the same struggle. There are the Right and the
Left, and in the middle is the Swamp.*

AUGUST BEBEL, 1906 Congress of the German Social Democratic Party

The term "ideology" may initially strike readers as abstract and esoteric, remote
from everyday experience. Yet, if we reflect for a moment, it is striking how
prominently ideological terms figure in media coverage of political events, classroom
discussions and conversations among family and friends. Note how often politicians
are described as conservatives or liberals, and how many people in our social circle
use ideological terms to describe themselves as conservatives, environmentalists, feminists, liberals or nationalists. In short, ideological terms and concepts percolate
throughout our political discourse and daily lives, sometimes with breathtaking effervescence. A recent one-page article in *National Review*, for example, managed in only
a few paragraphs to bring into play conservatism, feminism, liberalism, populism,
right-populism and socialism, along with elitism, racism, sexism, statism, and paleo-conservatism![1] There is no avoiding the conclusion that the political world is ideologically charged, and that political dynamics flow along ideological channels and
grooves.

It is not surprising, then, that "ideology" is one of the truly big words in the social
sciences. It brings into play a multitude of conventional "isms"—communism, conservatism, fascism, liberalism and socialism, to name but a few—along with a growing number of emergent "isms," including environmentalism, feminism and
populism.[2] Even if we restrict our gaze to a single ideology, such as feminism or liberalism, the scope of the subject matter is vast, as subsequent chapters will show.
Moreover, ideologies have a broad temporal and geographical reach, and as they
move through both time and space they can be dramatically transformed. For exam-

ple, the nature of liberalism has changed substantially since its emergence at the time of John Locke in the seventeenth century, and conservatism will be different in Canada or the United States than it will be in Poland or Thailand. The study of ideologies is also approached from a wide range of methodological perspectives; political philosophers grapple with the substantive cores of ideologies, while survey researchers determine whether the belief systems of mass publics coalesce into recognizable ideological patterns. Finally, and because ideologies carry a great deal of normative content, their analysis inevitably involves debate over the characteristics and values of the "good society," over the ends we should pursue and the means we should use in doing so. No area of political science is as morally charged as the study of ideologies.

Indeed, the study and understanding of political ideologies can be a very complex challenge. This chapter tackles the challenge by first providing a brief terminological history, then moving to a more detailed working conceptual definition of what we mean by an ideology. We identify characteristics shared by a broad range of ideologies, and thereby establish criteria through which ideologies can be distinguished from similar and, at times, related phenomena. With that backdrop in place, we turn to a number of conceptual tools that are useful for thinking about ideologies, for mapping ideological "mindscapes" and for understanding the role ideologies play in moulding political identities. This entails discussion of two of the most elementary yet widely used ideological concepts, "left" and "right." In this context we also discuss how ideologies differ from political philosophy, public opinion and political culture. The concluding section addresses the basic architecture of subsequent chapters, and outlines how they will enable us to sketch in the ideological terrain of western democratic states as we approach the twenty-first century.

A BRIEF HISTORY OF THE TERM

The word *"idéologie"* was coined by the French scholar Antoine Destutt de Tracy (1754–1836) to mean the "the science of ideas." Tracy and his colleagues, known as *idéologues*, designed a system of education based on this science of ideas, one that was intended to achieve a number of political goals. The new science drew from John Locke's epistemology, and more specifically, from Locke's claim that we begin our lives with minds that are blank slates, which then acquire ideas through sensory experience. Tracy took this assertion a step further and argued that it is possible to trace ideas to their experiential sources; different experiences, he expounded, would account for different ideas (Ball and Dagger 1995), an assertion that helped ground the later study of ideologies in material interests. The *idéologues* hoped that the study of ideology would contribute to the enlightenment of society by demonstrating that many ideas—for example, metaphysical religion—are the result of error or superstition. Education, therefore, was seen as a remedy for "ideological distortions" (Larrain 1979:33). In this sense, Tracy reflected the broader Enlightenment theme that science and reason, not faith and religion, should provide the foundation for political thought and our understanding of the "good society."

Tracy and his colleagues upset the traditional elites of French society by attacking commonly held beliefs. Napoleon Bonaparte, in a bid to gain support from the church and social elites, publicly denounced ideology in 1812 as "sinister metaphysics" (Ball and Dagger 1995:6) out of touch with practical politics. It was Napoleon who linked the term to impractical dreamers and their theories. (The *idéologues* also provided a scapegoat for his military failures.) The term, then, took on a pejorative meaning, which it often maintains to this day. As Terence Ball and Richard Dagger (1995:6) explain, Napoleon "declared the new science to be nothing but a mask to cover the subversive political plans of his opponents and critics." Karl Marx later used the notion of ideology to refer to any line of thought that was independent of reality, and thereby at variance with his materialist conception of history. In this way, religions could be seen as ideologies.

Jorge Larrain (1979:33) notes that the *idéologues* accounted for ideological distortions with respect to underlying "passions, superstitions, individual interests, religious prejudices or man's necessary self-alienation." Marx used the term "ideology" similarly. For Marx, ideology referred to the political usage of systems of ideas, including religions, and in particular to their use by ruling classes to legitimize the political order. By presenting hierarchical society as the natural order, Marx argued, ideology supports oppression. At the very least, it conceals the domination of the ruling class by promoting a "false consciousness." Just as Napoleon claimed the "science" of ideas was a mask for subversive activity, Marx claimed that belief systems like liberalism were masks for the exploitation of one class by another (Goodwin 1982:18–19).

Karl Mannheim is generally identified as a key figure in a further revision of the term. Mannheim agreed with Marx that there is a connection between ideas and social class, but applied the term more widely than Marx by arguing that *all* social groups—not just the dominant class—produce ideas that are peculiar to their experience. Mannheim called the study of the social origins of ideas the "sociology of knowledge." In *Ideology and Utopia* (1936), Mannheim advanced two conceptions of ideology—the particular and the total. The particular conception refers to the values and beliefs of a particular group, and generally implies opposition. When someone suggests, for example, that conservatives, feminists or liberals are "ideological," it is seldom meant as a compliment. Mannheim's total conception of ideology is less pejorative, and "refers to the characteristic ways of thinking of an entire class or society or historical period, such as medieval society or the modern age" (Ball and Dagger 1995:7–8). This second conception stretched the term to mean an entire worldview, and within this context Mannheim proposed that all thought may be ideological, affected by the social context of the thinker. If this is so, and it is by no means generally accepted as such (Parekh 1973:67–74), it would be impossible for the scholar to stand fully outside ideology and be completely objective. Mannheim's total conception alerts us to the possibility that a single ideological perspective may be so pervasive, so dominant, that we become almost oblivious to its presence and fail to recognize the extent to which it shapes our understanding. As Chapter 2 suggests, contemporary liberalism may be such an ideological perspective.

Ideology remained a largely pejorative term into the 1960s, and was typically defined as "both the distortion of thought by interest—public or private, consciously or unconsciously known—and the study of such thought" (MacRae 1961:64). As Max Skidmore (1993:11) notes, "The early association of ideology with totalitarian movements probably accounts for the tendency on the part of some to view it solely as an instrument of dictatorial propaganda." Certainly there is no question that the mid-century experience with fascism and nazism, and with the totalitarian excesses of Soviet communism, gave ideologies a very negative connotation. However, and as Skidmore also notes (1993:11), "A more sophisticated understanding of the term leads to the recognition that ideology is a feature of all societies and has a powerful effect in every one of them." It is tempting, then, to study all belief systems objectively as belief systems, and to avoid debates over which is right and, by implication, why others are wrong. (This line of thought is pursued at length in Chapter 12.) Behaviourist students of ideology from the 1960s on favoured this more analytic perspective, one that this book adopts when, for example, we examine the interplay among conservative and liberal ideologies in the North American setting. At the same time, there are limits on neutrality and objectivity; fascism in Adolf Hitler's Germany was not "just another ideology," and some of the "ideologies at the edge" discussed in Chapter 10 will challenge everyone's tolerance. But the loss of neutrality is not necessarily to be mourned, for the intellectual excitement in the study of ideologies comes from the clash of ideas and perspectives. Indeed, to avoid intellectual combat is to miss what brings the study of political ideologies to life.

A WORKING DEFINITION

Given the complexity inherent in any discussion of political ideologies, it is important to ask at the outset what various ideologies have in common. For example, what reasons might exist for lumping together conservatism, environmentalism, feminism, liberalism and socialism as ideologies? How do we decide what to include within the ideological domain, and what distinguishes ideologies from political philosophies, public opinion, political culture or religion? There are, we would suggest, a number of characteristics that ideologies hold in common:

- Ideologies are *social constructions* rather than individual belief systems. We all have idiosyncratic belief systems; one person may believe that the fortunes of political parties are linked in some complicated way to the phases of the moon, while another may believe that governments respond to the passing concerns of the well-to-do while ignoring the pressing needs of the poor. However, unless these belief systems are shared, they are not ideologies. As John Plamenatz (1970:31) explains, "For beliefs to be ideological … they must concern matters important to the group, and must be in some way functional in relation to it: they must serve to hold it together or to justify activities and attitudes characteristic of its members." We not construct our own ideologies, but rather buy into preexisting ideological packages. Our personal experiences will affect the *degree* to which we buy in, and we will all add, perhaps inadvertently, our own colouration to the ideological packages we adopt, but in the final analysis ideologies are social phenomena.

- Ideologies are *normative blueprints* for the "good society," and they are blueprints based on a particular conception of human nature. They not only explain the political world by giving us a conceptual vocabulary and a simplified framework within which to think, but they also enable us to evaluate that world, in part by identifying the heroes and villains of political life. Kenneth Minogue (1985:33) maintains that an ideology is "an analysis which explains evil." In a similar vein, L. T. Sargent (1990:4) writes, "All ideologies attempt to organize our complex world into a pattern that will at least give some signposts to help the believer distinguish good from bad." Ideologies, therefore, provide a foundation of values and assumptions from which normative judgments can be made.

- Ideologies provide a guide to *political action*. As David Bell (1985:53) explains, "The force of an ideology is to tie an *idea* to a *will*." Although ideologies need not be exclusively political in character, they must be politicized to a significant degree to be considered an ideology. Astrology, for example, would not be an ideological framework because it does not provide a means by which the political world can be interpreted, nor does it provide a guide to political action. Religions are ideologies only to the extent that they have a secular focus and provide a guide for action in the political sphere. Feminism is an ideology because it offers an explanation of the political world, provides a set of values to be applied to that world and promotes a political program with immediate relevance to the direction of public policy.

- Ideologies have some measure of formal articulation. They are more than folklore or myths passed down by word of mouth. Ideologies find expression in written texts, and can therefore be studied in this form as well as through the tools of survey research.

- Ideologies have *carriers of the creed*—specific individuals who are identified with the particular ideology, play a significant role in its formal articulation and shape its evolution through time. Thus, if one wants to understand populism in the Canadian or American context, one listens to Preston Manning or Ross Perot, respectively. If one wants to understand various forms of feminism, one turns to such writers as Andrea Dworkin (*Letters From A War Zone*), Betty Friedan (*The Second Stage*), Catherine McKinnon (*Feminism Unmodified*), Kate Millet (*Sexual Politics*) or Naomi Wolf (*The Beauty Myth*).

- Ideologies have *considerable scope* and draw together a broad range of values and beliefs. They are integrative concepts with wide application, encompassing a considerable slice of the political world. (By contrast, a conviction that federal taxes are too high is too narrow to be an ideology, no matter how widely shared and formally articulated this belief might be.) In this sense, Robert Lane (1962:355) discusses how ideologies provide a useful context for new political information, although he also draws a distinction between *contextualizing*, of which he approves, and *ideologizing*, of which he does not approve: "The difference centers on the need to confirm the pattern of ideas employed in the process; if the event is used and needed to support an emotionally involved theory or interpretation, the tendency is toward ideologizing."

- Ideologies are characterized by a significant measure of internal consistency or attitudinal *constraint*. Their components are woven together by logic and/or common values, and if one buys into part of the ideology, there is considerable pressure to accept the rest. As Milton Rokeach (1960:295) says about belief systems, "We organize the world of ideas, people, and authority basically along lines of belief congruence. What is not congruent is further organized in terms of similarity to what is congruent." Ideologies are most internally consistent when they are formally articulated, and the consistency may break down among people who accept their underlying values but are not familiar with the texts. For example, the fiscal conservatism of Canada's Fraser Institute displays greater coherence than the populism expressed by a caller to a radio hot-line program.

- Ideologies have some *durability*; they must have stood a reasonable test of time. Thus, new political ideas propagated by a single contemporary personality or social movement are seldom considered full-blown ideologies. They are at best *latent* ideologies until they have demonstrated a capacity to move through time and space.

Ideology Defined

An ideology is a **socially constructed** and **transmitted** system of **political beliefs** with some significant measure of **formal articulation**, **scope**, **internal consistency** and **durability**. As such, it provides both a **normative framework** for understanding the political world and a **practical guide for political action**.

Different ideologies, of course, vary with respect to the characteristics identified above. Take, for example, the difference in *formal articulation* between Marxism and populism. There is an immense and global literature on Marxism, one anchored by such "sacred texts" as Marx and Engels's *The Communist Manifesto* (1848). On the other hand, the literature on populism is much thinner and is less accessible to the casual reader; there are few, if any, "sacred texts" which set forth its basic principles and values. Populism, therefore, is less formally articulated than Marxism, and may quite appropriately find its most common forms of expression through such vehicles as talk shows and the rhetoric of election campaigns. In fact, populism is so loosely articulated that a reasonable debate could be held on whether it constitutes an ideology in the conventional meaning of the term.[3]

Or consider the contrast between feminism and nationalism in terms of *scope.* Feminism can provide a very sweeping ideological orientation. At one level, it offers a framework for thinking about the nature of economic and political institutions, and provides at least a rudimentary theory of the state. At another level, the determination of some feminists to eliminate the barrier between the public and private spheres, and the phrase "the personal is political," carries feminism into the most intimate aspects of human relationships. Therefore, certain branches of feminism offer many individuals a comprehensive framework that informs many, and perhaps most, areas of their lives; in some cases, it even offers "internal liberation" (Ball and Dagger 1995:208). By contrast, nationalism has a narrower scope. It speaks to the nature and boundaries of the national community, to the relationships between that community and its neighbours, and perhaps to the appropriate distribution of power and legitimacy among ethnic, linguistic and religious groups within the national community. However, it is mute with respect to interpersonal relationships and, unlike feminism, generally provides little insight into the way in which power is, and should be, organized across a myriad of social relationships. (The more extreme forms of ethnic nationalism may be an exception in both cases.) Thus the ideological scope of nationalism is more restricted than the scope of feminism.

This discussion of feminism brings another caveat to mind—various ideologies also differ considerably in their *internal consistency*. As you will see in Chapter 5, feminism as a global concept embraces a wide range of quite discrepant ideological and public-policy perspectives. This diversity, however, should not suggest that feminism is somehow "less ideological" than environmentalism or nationalism. Indeed, much of the ideological richness it has to offer comes from the variety of feminist thought, and from the ideological debate that takes place within the feminist tent.

We must also note that not all "isms" are ideologies. To take some obvious examples, racism, ageism and sexism do not fit the definition offered above, and federalism is generally seen as an institutional approach to government which only rarely takes on ideological tone or content. The American Civil War and the more recent Canadian constitutional experience show that intense debate can erupt over the specific form that federalism takes: Should it be relatively centralized or decentralized?; Should it formally recognize the equality of, or differences among, constituent units? However, federalism is seldom on the table as an ideological concept to be defended or attacked, although even here there have been exceptions. Debates over American federalism in the 1780s and 1790s certainly verged on ideological form; the opponents and proponents of Quebec nationalism have seen federalism as an ideological concept to be attacked and defended (Trudeau 1968); and the European proponents of a federal union have promoted federalism for more than its instrumental value—it has been advocated as the principled foundation for the "good society." A final example of the difference between "isms" and ideologies is provided by totalitarianism. Although we have had totalitarian states, their ideological foundations have not been provided by totalitarianism as such. Nor has totalitarianism been lauded as an exemplary model of government, even by its practitioners. Rather, totalitarianism has been the consequence of the marriage between state institutions and such ideologies as communism or fascism.

Ideologies differ in the extent to which they find institutional expression within state structures. In some cases, they are deeply embedded within those structures and may even find formal constitutional expression, which has been the case in many totalitarian states. Additional examples are provided by the explicit separation of church and state in the United States Constitution, an expression of liberal values, and by the Australian requirement for national referendums to ratify constitutional amendments, an institutional embodiment of populist values. Other ideological perspectives may yet lack constitutional or institutional expression, and may therefore challenge the established order. In this respect, the 1970s campaign for the Equal Rights Amendment (ERA) in the United States was an unsuccessful attempt to provide constitutional reflection for feminist values, whereas the 1982 insertion of the gender-equality provisions in the Canadian Charter of Rights and Freedoms was a successful attempt to do the same. In the latter, ideological values were embedded in both the constitution and the institutional structures of the federal state (Pal 1993).

Ideologies further vary in the extent to which they have organizational champions in the political arena. Environmentalism and feminism provide examples of ideological perspectives that have strong organizational voices in the domestic arenas of western democratic states. Groups like Greenpeace, the Sierra Club, and Earth First! advocate environmentalist principles, and champion both domestic and international causes. The National Organization of Women (NOW) and the National Action Committee for the Status of Women (NAC) do the same for feminist principles

Definitions of "Ideology"

An extensive literature has grown up around the study of ideologies, and embedded within this literature are scores of definitions. The following are some useful examples which correspond to some degree with our own:

Ideology is a pattern of beliefs and concepts (both factual and normative) which purport to explain complex social phenomena with a view to directing and simplifying socio-political choices facing individuals and groups. Julius Gould, "Ideology," in Julius Gould and William L. Kolb, eds., *A Dictionary of the Social Sciences* (New York: The Free Press of Glencoe, 1964), 315.

[Ideology is a] logically coherent system of symbols which, within a more or less sophisticated conception of history, links the cognitive and evaluative perception of one's social condition—especially its prospects for the future—to a program of collective action for the maintenance, alteration or transformation of society. Willard A. Mullins, "On the Concept of Ideology in Political Science." *American Political Science Review* 66 (1972), 510.

An ideology is a system of collectively held normative and reputedly factual ideas and beliefs and attitudes advocating a particular pattern of social relationships and arrangements, and/or aimed at justifying a particular pattern of conduct, which its proponents seek to promote, realize, pursue or maintain. Malcolm B. Hamilton, "The Elements of the Concept of Ideology," *Political Studies* 35 (1987), 38.

Political ideology is a form of thought that presents a pattern of complex political ideas simply and in a manner that inspires action to achieve certain goals. Max J. Skidmore, *Ideologies: Politics in Action*, 2nd ed. (Toronto: Harcourt Brace Jovanovich, 1993), 7.

An ideology is a fairly coherent and comprehensive set of ideas that explains and evaluates social conditions, helps people understand their place in society, and provides a program for social and political action. Terence Ball and Richard Dagger, *Political Ideologies and the Democratic Ideal* (New York: Harper Collins, 1995), 9.

Ideology is a form of social analysis which discovers that human beings are the victims of an oppressive system, and that the business of life is liberation. This view may be held at any level of sophistication from densely academic treatises to graffiti on walls. Kenneth Minogue, *Alien Powers: The Pure Theory of Ideology* (London: Weidenfeld and Nicolson, 1985), 37–8.

in the United States and Canada, respectively. Other ideological perspectives may have a weaker organizational voice, although this is not always associated with the weakness of the perspective itself. We argue, for instance, that liberal values are thoroughly embedded and entrenched in North American political life even though it is difficult to identify organizational voices for liberalism in the political arena.[4] It should be stressed, however, that ideologies are not to be equated with the social movements which often provide ideologies with their voice in the political arena. Although social movements may draw heavily from ideological roots, there is an important distinction between a set of political ideas and its organizational manifestation.

In summary, it is not easy to come to grips with the vast range of ideas encompassed by contemporary political ideologies. Nor is it easy to come to grips with ideologies as analytical concepts. The following section presents a number of conventional ways in which people use ideological styles of thought. We begin by briefly mapping the ideological space of contemporary western democratic states, and then explore how "left" and "right" have come to be widely used as an ideological shorthand in those states.

Ideology as a Negative

There is no question that ideological terminology often carries negative, even pejorative connotations in popular discourse. To describe someone as "an ideologue" is seldom meant to be flattering; it is meant to convey a description of someone with extreme ideas only loosely connected to reality. An ideological style of thought is generally considered to be inflexible, uncompromising and dogmatic. For example, to label someone as an "ideological feminist" is to imply that she is unreasonable and closed to contrary evidence or argumentation. In a society where individuals pride themselves on being open to a plurality of ideas, it is perhaps not surprising that ideologues are frowned upon. (Whether the individuals who do the frowning are open to new ideas themselves is another matter!)

It must be emphasized, therefore, that our use of ideological terms and labels is quite different. We do not assume that ideologies are unreasoned constructions, or that ideologues are themselves unreasonable. Ideologies are an inevitable feature of the political landscape, and for most people they serve a useful role. However, this does not mean that we consider all ideological perspectives to be equally valid or attractive. Neither should the reader make any such assumption. There is a huge difference between understanding a particular ideological perspective and endorsing it.

CONCEPTUAL TOOLS FOR THINKING ABOUT IDEOLOGIES

Given the complexity that surrounds a discussion of political ideologies, what conceptual template might we apply to bring some order to our thoughts? Perhaps ideologies can best be seen as maps for the political terrain. Both maps and ideologies are abstractions that provide a simplified picture of a more complicated reality, and therefore help us make sense of a world that might otherwise overwhelm us with its complexities. Ideological maps identify the most prominent features of that terrain and suggest a route by which to reach goals and objectives. In some cases, the map may be well developed, resembling an atlas that covers the world and provides more detailed information than most people are likely to use. In other cases, the map may be rudimentary, doing little more than tracing out major "highways" and "landmarks." But all ideological maps provide a means by which individuals and social movements orient themselves in the political world, and thereby they also provide a guide to political action. To extend the analogy one last step, the thinkers who articulate the ideological patterns that shape our political world can be compared to the cartographers who tried to map the physical world for early explorers. Just as the latter tried to provide visual maps for a complicated and, to some degree, unknown physical reality, so the propagators of ideological thought try to provide us with mental maps for our own explorations of the political world.

Mapping Ideological Space

The ideological terrain of western democratic states has been fundamentally transformed over the past few centuries. Indeed, the ideological winds that blow across the contemporary political landscape are very different even from those that shaped the events surrounding the Second World War, and there is little reason to expect either the pace or extent of ideological change to moderate as we move into the twenty-first century.

One of the ideological anchors of the twentieth century was put into place by the Russian Revolution in 1917 and the subsequent establishment of the Soviet Union. The initial success of communism established the basic ideological polarity between socialist and liberal-democratic states that was to dominate the international landscape for most of the twentieth century. Although the divide between East and West was temporarily bridged in the Second World War, when both sides faced the military threat of fascism, the bridge was not to survive victory by the Allied powers. With the onset of the cold war in 1945, the bipolar ideological landscape was frozen; both the decolonization movement in the southern hemisphere and the explosive growth in the number of players in the international community were played out against the backdrop of this larger ideological divide. The Soviet blockage of Berlin in the late 1940s, the Korean War in the early 1950s, the erection of the Berlin Wall and the Vietnam War were landmark events in the ideological struggle between East and West. The cold war divide, moreover, rippled through domestic debates within western democracies over the extent and desirability of the welfare state. In Europe, the domestic debate pitted powerful parties from the democratic left against their more conservative opponents. In North America, the debate largely took place under the umbrella of liberalism, as we will see in Chapter 2, and addressed the reach of the welfare state and the appropriate degree of government intervention in economic affairs.

The North American debate over the early emergence of the welfare state was played out against the backdrop of the Great Depression in the 1930s. In the post-war period in the United States, it coincided with, but was not greatly shaped by, the communist witch-hunts of Senator Joseph McCarthy in the early 1950s. With the exception of the McCarthy episode, an admittedly big exception, the 1950s and early 1960s were times of ideological tranquility in *domestic* North American politics. As Barbara Goodwin (1982:23–4) explains, this tranquility was shattered by the mid-1960s:

> [T]he Civil Rights, Black Power, Women's Liberation, Student Power, and Anti-Vietnam movements of the 1960s and 1970s in the States showed that ideology and conflict could not be excluded from politics forever. Left-wing thinkers ... sought to expose the covert ideological premises of liberal-democratic thought and institutions and others demonstrated that even the most empirical studies were in fact guided by theoretical presuppositions which could not themselves be empirically established but were *assumed* ....

The end of the cold war and the collapse of the former Soviet Union have now thawed the international ideological landscape, and to a significant degree have freed up ideological debate within states on both sides of the former divide. Socialist states and parties have been thrown into profound ideological confusion, and across the world the conservative end of the ideological spectrum has become very competitive terrain as groups try to position themselves relative to the market economy and the new world order. As we will discuss in Chapters 7 and 11, territory has declined in importance as a means by which people organize their political identities and priorities, with new space opening up for *transnational* ideologies such as environmentalism and feminism. Aboriginal movements have added another unique ingredient to a rapidly evolving ideological mix, one that is taking place against the backdrop of globalization. At the same time, while the old ideological polarities face increased competition, they have by no means been swept away. Impassioned debates continue to address the appropriate scope of the free market, the degree of state intervention to help the less fortunate and the relevance of national communities and political sovereignty in a global environment.

Perhaps the most important thing to recognize about the ideological space of contemporary western democratic states is that it is very crowded. If ideologies provide maps by which to navigate the political world, there are now a large number of maps from which to choose.[5] The ideological terrain is pluralistic rather than monolithic; individuals can choose to interpret the political world from the perspective of feminism, liberalism, nationalism or socialism, or any combination thereof. They may even select ideological perspectives that lack social support or sanction. For example, we may find strands of fascist thought within the landscape of western democratic states, as Chapter 9 will discuss. Individuals may also employ different maps depending upon the situation and the company in which we find ourselves. Both liberalism and feminism may provide appropriate maps for making sense out of the politically charged university environment, whereas nationalism and populism may operate better for understanding the ideological currents at work on the national political stage.

It is important, however, not to overstate the freedom that individuals have in the ideological domain. The variety of ideological perspectives often compete for our attention and loyalty, forcing us to choose. For example, do we present ourselves as conservatives or liberals, as nationalists or internationalists? In other cases, quite distinct ideological currents may reinforce one another, as did fascism and nationalism in Germany in the 1930s to produce, with anti-Semitism, the destructive ideological blend of nazism. In the contemporary world, and with more positive effect, the ideological tenets of feminism offer support for those of environmentalism, just as the tenets of populism are often woven into conservative orientations towards the state.

In summary, we confront an ideological world that is crowded, in flux and characterized by numerous convergences among ideological currents and streams. Given this complexity, it is not surprising that people turn to simple conceptual tools to bring order to the ideological world. Some of the most useful tools come from very basic forms of spatial orientation.

The Notions of Left and Right

One way to think through how ideologies work is to consider the simple terms "left" and "right." The two terms are not ideologies in and of themselves, and it is highly unlikely that left and right are used in identical ways by individuals in different countries or, for that matter, by different individuals in the same country. Nonetheless, the polarized left-right spectrum is a standard, indeed, a ubiquitous feature of ideological discourse in western democratic states. It began simply enough as a seating plan in the French National Assembly, following the French Revolution. Left and right provided a spatial orientation through which to sort out friends and foes according to who sat near whom. Over time, left and right became a means to sort out a vast array of policy options and political perspectives. The basic ideological distinction between left and right came to be anchored by differing conceptions about the appropriate role of the state in the economic order. Individuals and parties placing themselves on the left of this spectrum tend to favour a positive role for the state with respect to the regulation of the economy and the use of the tax system to redistribute income from the rich to the poor. Conversely, those on the right tend to favour a minimal role for the state in both respects. Historically, the left was associated with support for state ownership of economic enterprises, while the right was associated with support for private ownership, wherever possible, although this distinction is rapidly fading as support for state ownership weakens across the board. As figure 1.1 suggests, those in the middle of the left-right spectrum are likely to support some degree of public ownership, some degree of government regulation and some measure of income redistribution.

FIGURE 1.1: The Conventional Left-Right Spectrum

Left	Centre	Right
Full government ownership of the means of production		No government ownership of the means of production
Extensive government regulation		No government regulation
Extensive redistribution of income		No redistribution of income

Over time, the terms "left" and "right" have picked up additional ideological baggage to expand considerably their application in political discourse and debate. In current political discourse, the left has come to be associated with support for minority rights,[6] women's rights, gay and lesbian rights, environmental protection and foreign aid, whereas the right is now associated with military spending, neoconservatism and libertarianism, "family values," opposition to intervention by the state on behalf of minority interests and even fascism. Conventional, everyday usage within the North American context tends to equate the far left with socialism, the centre with liberalism and the far right with conservatism, although the ideological universe of all three belief systems is much more complex than this equation suggests. The middle of the spectrum is where we usually find the bulk of the population: those who support government ownership in special circumstances, such as public utilities; those who support a modicum of regulation while complaining about red tape; and those who support income redistribution so long as it does not cut too deeply into their own standard of living.

There are few political personalities, values or ideals that cannot, with some creativity, be placed on the left-right spectrum. As Daniel Bell (1985:57) explains, the terms "left" and "right" in modern usage "have long since frayed and lost their meaning, though the vocabulary, now primarily used as terms of abuse, still remains." In many respects, then, the spectrum is like a charm bracelet upon which different individuals can attach quite different assortments of beliefs and values. A good deal of confusion can therefore arise when people use the terms "left" and "right," or for that matter "liberal" and "conservative." One individual might describe himself as a conservative because he believes in a limited state, but then find that others wrongly assume he also has "conservative" tastes with respect to music, clothes and religious values. Another person may describe herself as a liberal with reference to her opposition to censorship in the arts, only to find that friends mistakenly interpret this label to mean that she also endorses an expanded role for the state in assisting marginalized citizens.

Exercise One: The Left-Right Universe

On a piece of paper, sketch out a conventional left-right scale ranging from one (far left) to seven (far right). Now, where would you locate yourself on this scale? Would you fall at three? At six? At four? (Remember, there are no correct answers!) If asked to do so, how would you explain your choice? How did you decide on which side of the scale to fall, and which number to choose?

Where would you locate your parents? Close friends? Major political parties and leaders? Your own position five years ago? Is there a consensus in your tutorial or class as to the location of leading political figures of the day?

As you use this scale, you will begin to appreciate its relational qualities. The scale enables us not only to locate ourselves in ideological space, but also to locate ourselves relative to other people and political objects, such as parties. Thus, we can see that we are "closer to" some objects than to others. Furthermore, we can use the scale to plot change over time. We can ask, for example, whether the Democratic party in the United States has "moved to the left" in recent decades, or whether the Canadian Liberal party has "moved to the right."

Admittedly, the scale is rudimentary, and the assignment of specific numerical values can be rough and ready at best. (Was former President George Bush a five or a six? Is Canada's New Democratic Party a two or a three, or even a four?) It may also be difficult to apply the scale to multidimensional players or objects. President Bill Clinton, for example, may be further "to the left" on domestic policy than on foreign policy, just as the Liberal government in Canada may be further "to the right" on economic policy than it is on social policy. In short, ideological consistency may be lacking among leaders and parties just as among voters. Nevertheless, the left-right scale can still be remarkably useful as a means by which to orient oneself on the political landscape, and to do so relative to other people and groups.

But what does it mean when individuals adopt an "ideological identification" in terms of right or left? Most simply, it means they use the terms "left" and "right" in political discourse. More substantively, it means that once we know how individuals locate themselves on the left-right spectrum, their position with respect to more specific issues can be predicted with reasonable accuracy. We know, for example, that individuals "on the left" are today more likely to support state intervention on behalf of minority interests than are people "on the right," whereas the latter are more likely to oppose employment-equity programs and gay rights. In some cases and among some populations, self-placement on the left-right spectrum is a powerful predictor of a wide range of social and political attitudes. For example, an extensive survey of senior university students in Australia, Britain, Canada, New Zealand and the United States (Nevitte and Gibbins 1990) found that self-placement on a seven-point left-right scale was strongly associated with student opinions on such matters as social welfare, employment quotas for women and minorities, tax policy, gay rights, income limits and the appropriate power for unions, minorities and women.

More commonly, however, the ideological constraint imposed by left-right iden-
tifications is quite limited. The scale provides a conceptual means by which to locate oneself and others on the political landscape, but its predictive power for more specific political and public-policy issues is modest. The ideological domains of left and right are generally little more than loose clusters of more specific ideological orien-
tations. For instance, we might find feminism, environmentalism and socialism all clustered to the left, but beyond such broad groupings, the ideological landscape is hardly neat and tidy. There will be right-wing environmentalists and feminists, and predispositions such as populism that cut across, rather than reinforce, the left-right divide. Ideological orientations do not intersect neatly like lines on a graph; they overlap and jostle about in the same attitudinal space.

We must also remember that the ideological content of left and right will vary across time. For example, left-of-centre Americans today bear only a loose family resemblance to left-of-centre Americans prior to the Great Depression and President Franklin Delano Roosevelt's New Deal in the early thirties. The concerns of the former with issues like gay and lesbian rights, pay equity and environmental protection would have been all but unknown to the latter. Ideological politics during the depres-
sion had a more limited scope, although it was by no means less intense as a conse-
quence. As he was running unsuccessfully for reelection in 1932, Republican president Herbert Hoover said that the election was more than a contest between two men, more than a contest between two parties; it was a contest between two philosophies of government. At the time, the primary question was the extent to which the government should intervene to help the victims of severe economic distress brought on by the collapse of world trade and domestic markets. Although today's presidential contests are certainly not without economic content, they tend to address an ideological agenda that is more diffuse.

Furthermore, it should be noted that the centre of the ideological spectrum will shift across time, and may shift even if the contents of left and right are relatively fixed. It could be argued, for instance, that the centre of ideological debate in North America moved to the left in the 1960s, a shift reflected in the "great society" policies of President Lyndon Johnson and the "just society" policies of Prime Minister Pierre Trudeau. More recently, it could be argued that the centre of ideological debate has shifted, or has been pulled, to the right by such leaders as Britain's Margaret Thatcher, American president Ronald Reagan and Canadian premiers Ralph Klein and Mike Harris.

Similarly, we must realize that the ideological content of left and right will vary across space. We must not assume that a left-of-centre Canadian shares a worldview with a left-of-centre Jamaican or New Zealander. While individuals living in different countries, but sharing an ideological self-identification, may have broad characteristics in common, they may take quite different stances towards specific public-poli-
cy issues, stances which are a product of national circumstance rather than common ideological principles. The ideological centre of gravity may also be quite different in Canada and New Zealand, or in Jamaica and the United States, even if voters in each country attach roughly the same meanings to left and right.

Exercise Two: Sorting Out Right and Left

Label each item on the following list "left," "right" or "can't say." Does your ideological labelling correspond with that of your friends or classmates? Where is there a strong consensus? Where are there points of disagreement?

Nuclear disarmament	Prayer in school
Minimum wage	Free trade
Agricultural-price supports	Public broadcasting
Foreign aid	Social security
Country-and-western music	Tougher immigration control
Military draft	Employment equity
Animal rights	Income tax
Work-for-welfare	Performance art
Right-to-life	Pollution controls
Gun control	Supreme Court
Feminism	Deficit reduction
Capital punishment	Tougher crime laws
Legalization of marijuana	Free speech
Populism	Body piercing
Alternative music	Recycling

In summary, although the notions of left and right are often ambiguous, they are widely used as ideological road maps in western democratic states. People may not have a common or precise understanding of the terms, but most are still willing and able to locate themselves on a five- or seven-point scale ranging from left to right.[7] Moreover, they are prepared to locate political objects, including parties and leaders, on the same scale, and to use left and right as rhetorical weapons in partisan debate. The left-right spectrum therefore provides not only a simple, convenient way of organizing political space, but also a guide to political action. At the same time, citizens also have a variety of more complex and nuanced ideological tools at their disposal for making sense out of the political world. Conservatism, environmentalism, feminism, liberalism and populism are only some of the options, which can either stand alone or be rolled into the conventional domains of left and right.

The Implied Polarity

The discussion of the left-right spectrum brings into focus the polarity implied in many ideological perspectives. For example, a person cannot be both left and right, and to drift towards one end of the spectrum is to drift away from the other. This polarity is by no means restricted to the left-right spectrum; it is present in the contrast between liberals and conservatives, capitalists and communists, nationalists and internationalists. It is almost as if polarity is intrinsic to ideological thought, and to the simplified maps of the political world that ideologies provide. At times, however, the polarity may be forced; thus, to fall too quickly into polarized patterns of thought is to impair our understanding of political reality. Take, for example, the case of environmentalism which, as Chapter 6 shows, is a full-fledged contemporary ideology with formal articulation, a political program and recognized carriers of the creed. But is there a polar opposite to the environmentalist position? More specifically, is there a clearly articulated *ideological position* that stands in specific opposition to environmentalism? Many people do not place much emphasis on environmental protection; there are also those who, if forced to decide, would choose economic development over environmental protection. But does this imply an underlying ideological dimension anchored at one end by environmentalism and at the other by its ideological negation? It probably makes more sense to think of environmentalism as a unipolar ideology. One can buy into the creed to varying degrees, but there is no polar opposite to environmentalism that has assumed ideological form.

Or take the case of feminism. Certainly, there are substantial numbers of people who resist or even reject the claims and values of feminism, and there is no question that feminism confronts significant opponents in the political arena. But does opposition to feminism assume an *ideological* form? Is there an antifeminist ideology? Here the answer is somewhat more complex, as there may be a patriarchal counterpoint which, while not strongly articulated in ideological terms, is nonetheless deeply embedded in social and political institutions. Yet, in other respects, it may not make a lot of sense to think of feminism in bipolar terms. It may be better to think of feminism as an ideological position that one can support or oppose, or be indifferent to, but with no assumption that opposition to feminism is an ideological position in the same way that support for feminism can be.

A final example of the polarity implied in many ideological perspectives is provided by populism. The polar opposite of populism, were one to exist, would be an ideology that supported the concentration of economic and political power in the hands of a few. However, there is no ideological support or rationale for such a position in contemporary western democratic states, even though some may adopt this position for other reasons, and even though fascist ideological support existed in the past. It is difficult, then, to think of populism in bipolar terms, for the opposing perspective is generally subterranean and lacks formal articulation.[8] Therefore, it may be best to think of some ideologies in terms of a continuum that measures the degree or intensity of support, but which is not bracketed by polarized ideological visions.

RELATED CONCEPTS

As we have seen, even simple ideological notions such as left and right can be complex in their application. This complexity can become confusing, or more confusing, if we fail to distinguish between ideologies and a number of seemingly similar, but nevertheless distinct, concepts.

Ideologies provide a structure for the way in which we see and think about the political world. However, structure is also implied in political philosophy, in the notion of political culture and, to some extent, in patterns of public opinion. It is useful, therefore, to examine how these concepts relate to, and differ from, political ideologies.

Political Philosophy

Political philosophy and political ideologies are often conflated, in part because the former often informs the latter. It is through political philosophy that many, and perhaps most, ideologies find their formal articulation. Still, important distinctions between the two concepts exist. First, political philosophy is a *discipline* rather than a program for action. Political philosophers maintain that they seek to understand, rather than to affect or transform political reality (Copleston 1983:25). Marx drew attention to this difference and subsequently rejected philosophy, although we would still consider him to be a political philosopher: "The philosophers have only interpreted the world, in various ways; the point, however, is to change it" (Marx 1845:145). In our terms, if not in his, Marx's commitment to change moved him from contemplation to action, and thus from philosophy to ideology.

As a result of its different orientation, the *practice* of political philosophy also differs from that of ideology. First, political philosophers continually subject their theories to further questioning. Their conclusions are open-ended, and often criticized by others within the discipline. Notably, however, such criticism does not place any political philosopher outside the discipline. By contrast, disagreement with the ideology's fundamental tenets is logically impossible for an adherent of any ideology. For example, if you do not believe that "class" is the most relevant category, you cannot be a socialist. Adherence to a particular ideology implies adherence to a particular, definitive view of political reality.

In *The Republic*, the first classic of political philosophy, Plato distinguished "knowledge" (*episteme*) from "opinion" (*doxa*), and censured the latter as being one step above ignorance. According to Plato, the lover of opinion contents himself with appearances and partial truths. The lover of knowledge, on the other hand, prefers to "consort with reality"; he is "guided by the truth … else he would be an imposter and have no share at all in true philosophy" (Grube 1974:147). Plato's distinction is retained today in the manner in which many use the terms "ideology" and "philosophy"; the latter, it is maintained, is closer to Plato's "knowledge." In some respects, the function of philosophy reaches beyond that of ideology. As Anthony Parel (1983:7) explains:

> The function of political philosophy is to distinguish between the good regime and the evil; to understand the relative importance of politics in the totality of human activities that go beyond politics; to criticize ideology and popular opinions in order to bring them more and more in conformity with the dictates of right reason; to analyze, prescribe, and interpret assumptions about human behavior.

Yet political philosophy can also be thought of as the attempt to find what is true and good within each ideology, but it is an attempt that brings its own constraints in terms of logical consistency and the rules of academic argumentation. While at times this attempt places the political philosopher outside the bounds of any particular ideology (Copleston 1983), political philosophy is more a subset of ideological discourse than its opposite. Political philosophers often contribute to ideological thought, within which their ideas are used, adapted and applied. Subsequent chapters will therefore include frequent references to political philosophy and philosophers, although our emphasis will be on how political philosophy has contributed to the evolution of ideological debate rather than upon the philosophical literature itself.

Political Culture

Social scientists often discuss the "political cultures" of different national communities, and at times different political cultures within single states.[9] We may hear, for example, that the political culture of one country is more participatory, democratic or deferential than the culture of another country, or that the political culture of the middle class is more likely to support participation in community life than is the political culture of the working class. But what is the connection, if any, between political cultures and ideologies? Are political cultures ideological constructs?

Although both political cultures and ideologies shape perceptions of the political world, the former are more comprehensive and loosely knit than the latter. Note, for instance, David Bell's definition (1995:105):

> Political culture consists of the ideas, assumptions, values, and beliefs that condition political action. It affects the way we use politics, the kinds of social problems we address, and the solutions we attempt. Political culture serves as a filter or lens through which political actors view the world …. [It] is the language of political discourse, the vocabulary and grammar of political controversy and understanding.

Bell points out that political cultures are often crystallized in symbols, such as Canada's Parliament and the Charter of Rights and Freedoms. Furthermore, they demarcate "the zone of appropriate action for government" and set other areas "beyond the realm of the legitimate" (Bell 1995:106). In these latter respects, there are clear similarities between political cultures and ideologies. Yet ideologies are more limited, coherent, formally articulated and focused on the search for solutions. Ideologies are action-oriented in a way that political cultures are not.

In most cases, and certainly within western democratic states, political cultures can best be seen as broad composites with many ideological components, rather than as ideological entities in and of themselves. As Mark Hagopian (1978:390) explains, ideologies are "explicit, often highly systematic patterns of political belief. Political culture, on the other hand, is the far more complex and diffuse set of political beliefs in a whole country."[10] For example, any complete description of Canadian political culture would have to note the pervasive nature of liberalism, the commitment to democratic values and processes, the salience of federalism, the growing recognition of cultural diversity and the force of both Canadian and Québécois nationalism. It would have to acknowledge the emerging challenge of conservatism and populism to established institutional practices. It would also have to incorporate the persistence of regional alienation, the ongoing tension between linguistic communities, the growing assertion of aboriginal rights and the transformative impact of immigration on social values. It is no wonder, then, that political cultures are more expansive and less internally consistent than ideologies. They weave together various ideological and nonideological strands into a complex, multihued national tapestry, and it would be a rare occurrence indeed for a national political culture to be adequately captured by a single ideology. Even in the heyday of the former Soviet Union, there was more to the political culture of the USSR than communism, although the latter was its central component.

David Bell also draws our attention to empirical evidence which shows that most people in western democratic states do not think about the political world in ideological terms. Because they do not display a great deal of principled consistency or coherency, Bell concludes that the broader notion of political culture better encapsulates the worldviews of the nonelite population. However, while most people may not think about politics in a consistent or coherent manner, this is not to say that their worldviews are unaffected by the ideological currents sweeping through the enveloping political culture. The "power" of ideological currents such as environmentalism or liberalism cannot be measured only by determining the extent to which they are accepted, holus-bolus, by individuals. Ideologies have the capacity to affect the way in which people see the political world without necessarily engendering consistent and coherent patterns of ideological thought within individuals. As we will discuss shortly, people may use ideological perspectives selectively, depending upon the circumstances in which they find themselves.

In this context, it is useful to think of political cultures as offering a wide variety of socially constructed ideological fashions in a way that is analogous to a store offering a variety of prescription eyeglasses. Citizens can shop among established brand names, looking for something that fits their own values and life experiences, just as they can browse among various styles of glasses, perhaps selecting different lenses for reading and driving. It is unlikely, however, that even the most open and pluralistic political culture will offer a complete range of ideological merchandise. Products without some minimal market appeal, or found to be offensive to the mainstream consumer, will be discontinued. This in turn opens up some room for specialty stores catering to ideological niche markets, including those discussed in Chapter 10. Such stores may not have a large clientele, but can survive if their own clientele is enthusiastic and loyal. It should also be noted that the "shopping behaviour" of ideological consumers may not parallel that of more conventional consumers. As Robert Lane (1962:425) explains, "The individual does not select an ideology as a person selects a new car; the processes, criteria, alternatives, expectations are largely, but not wholly, unconscious."

Political cultures are visually analogous to the core samples geologists use in the search for oil and minerals. It would be possible to take a core sample of a given political culture at a particular point in time, and then look for ideological "bands" within that sample (see figure 1.2). We might find, for example, a broad band of lib-

FIGURE 1.2: Ideological "Core Samples"

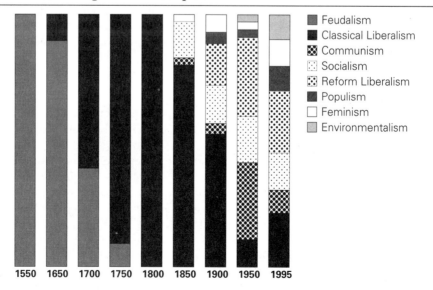

eral values and a narrower band of feminist values. Core samples of different political cultures taken at the same time could be compared, as could core samples of the same political culture at a different time. In the first case, we might find a broader band of socialism or populism in one culture than in another; in the second, particular bands may have been widening or narrowing with the passage of time. For instance, environmentalism might have been all but absent in ideological core samples taken early in this century, but today may constitute a relatively thick band within the political cultures of western democratic states.

In summary, while political cultures are not ideologies, they have important ideological components nonetheless. Moreover, the comparative analysis of political cultures across time and space provide valuable insights into the dynamics of ideological change. Thus, the concept of political culture provides a useful tool in thinking about ideologies and the role they play in the larger political process.

Public Opinion

The contrast between ideologies and public opinion is most evident in the narrow scope of the latter. We all have opinions about events, actors and issues in the political world, but these opinions are not necessarily woven into broader ideological patterns, nor are they necessarily reflective of such patterns. In a typical public opinion survey, a respondent might be asked what she thinks about health-care reform, gun control, deficit reduction, abortion, famine relief for Africa, capital punishment, and the prohibition of smoking in public places. The respondent might treat each question as a discrete issue, and not feel that her answer to one constrains how she should respond to others. Many social conversations take on a similar pattern as the discussion flows from one topic to the next, with only the occasional reminder that what was said over the first course of a meal might be inconsistent with what was said over coffee and dessert. Take, for example, a scene from Rick Salutin's political novel, *The Age of Improv* (1995: 50):

> It's one of those conversations which McLuhan licensed back in the 1960s. If you call the ideas "probes," they don't have to be consistent or add up to a real viewpoint. As long as each thought is a morsel with some taste, you're happy and move on to the next.

Good manners demand only that we have opinions; they do not demand that our opinions be woven into a coherent pattern.

Opinions, therefore, *may* be discrete and unconnected. However, it is when opinions begin to coalesce into relationships, when we begin to recognize the constraint that one opinion imposes on others, that ideological patterns begin to emerge. And indeed, this is precisely how survey researchers look for ideological patterns within the complexity of public opinion data. They look for opinions which "go together" by searching for statistical correlations among opinions on different topics. The emergent patterns are ideological in part because they display some significant degree of coherence and constraint, even though they may lack formal articulation or carriers of the creed. In this sense, opinions are the raw material from which ideological constructs might be formed.

The factors that impose order on clusters of opinions are largely social and organizational in character. To understand how such patterns are socially constructed, consider the religious opinions that individuals might hold about good and evil, life after death and the transcendent nature of morality. If we live in a social vacuum, we are free to construct our own, idiosyncratic religious paradigms. If, however, we participate in an organized religion, if we discuss religious beliefs with friends or relatives, if we read what others have written about religious principles and values, then we cannot escape the imposition of greater constraint. We learn that X goes with Y, and Q follows from P. In a similar fashion, we can predict the circumstances under which individuals are likely to face ideological constraint in the political realm. Those who are exposed to postsecondary education, are active in political organizations or display a personal interest in things political most likely construct reasonably coherent patterns of *ideological* thought. Conversely, those who are relatively withdrawn from political life are freer to construct their own idiosyncratic belief systems. If those systems depart from conventional norms, the individuals who hold them are unlikely to be exposed to conflicting information or to be active in forums in which their idiosyncratic beliefs might be challenged.

IDEOLOGIES AND PERSONAL IDENTITIES

Ideologies provide us with frameworks for thinking about the political world, a vocabulary for political debate and a means for evaluating leaders, parties, groups and ideas. At times, they may go further by providing a significant part of our personal identity. Ideologies offer costumes to wear as we present ourselves to the world. We may be environmentalists in one context, nationalists in another and conservatives in a third. Consider, for example, a young woman who defines herself as a feminist. This self-definition not only guides her actions within the political arena, but also makes a statement about her political identity and perhaps her personal identity beyond things political.[11] Of course, her identity may be anchored more by gender than by feminism, but it is the latter which politicizes gender and enables gender-based mobilization to occur within the political process.

In short, ideologies shape more than what we believe; they also shape how we see ourselves and how we position ourselves within the social world (Minogue 1985). As William Bloom (1990: 25–6) explains, "Insomuch as every identification is made with an external social actor, identification is … a social act as much as a private psychological one." Therefore, our personal identities can be seen, at least in part, as ideological constructs. What needs to be determined is the extent to which individuals use ideological elements to define themselves, remembering, of course, that we can draw upon a multitude of nonideological elements in constructing social and political identities. To the degree that ideological elements are used, we can ask how much they contribute to the construction of multilayered personal identities. To what extent and under what circumstances do people use ideological costumes to present an identity to the external world? One individual, for example, might weave together various, and not necessarily logically compatible, elements of environmentalism, nationalism and liberalism to create a uniquely blended political identity. Another individual might slip on the cloak of feminism when talking to co-workers and then shift to an emphasis on nationalism while travelling abroad.

The intensity of "ideological identities" may vary considerably from one individual to the next. For one person, feminism may provide an all-encompassing worldview, in which case personal identity is likely to be deeply rooted in her ideological affinity with feminism. As Ball and Dagger (1995:208) explain, "liberation ideologies" such as black liberation, gay activism and some forms of feminism may be very deeply embedded in personal identities. For another person, feminism may be activated only in particular situations; a man might present himself as a strong feminist within the context of a university seminar and yet, in another context, perhaps in conversation with friends or family, may never "think of himself" as a feminist. Where feminism is a situationally specific form of identification, it is unlikely to be deeply rooted. This also suggests that one can assume multiple identities, particularly if these identities are situationally specific. As mentioned above, it is possible to have a number of pairs of glasses, and to switch depending upon the conditions—different lenses work for reading, driving and the sun. The tough part comes if different and potentially conflicting identities are brought into play in the same situation, or if one identity is so "imperialistic" that it intrudes into all aspects of a person's life and crowds out other forms of identity. It may be the case, for example, that someone sees the world exclusively through the lens of environmentalism or feminism, and that other "optics" are employed only to the extent that they can be incorporated within the dominant perspective.

Exercise Three: Elements of Identity

Write a list of approximately fifteen terms that you might use to describe or define yourself. These could include any component that is important to you. For example, "I am . . . a woman, a Catholic, a liberal, a student, short, a parent, an environmentalist, young, middle-class, British Columbian, Canadian." If it is helpful, think how you might use a few words in a "personal ad" to describe yourself. Given that you are restricted to listing fifteen points, would you include your age, occupation, sexual preference or ethnicity? Your grade-point average, hair colour, partisanship, hobbies or family background?

Next, reduce the list to ten terms. How much of "you" is lost as you pare down the list? How did you decide which aspects of your identity to prune? Are the losses important or relatively inconsequential? Now reduce the list to only five items. Here again, how did you decide which aspects of your identity to prune? How difficult was the choice? Can you make any further reductions without losing the essential "you"? If you were restricted to only one or two terms, which would they be? Or would the choice depend upon the situation in which you found yourself?

As you can see, our personal identities are elaborate constructs that draw upon our physical features, social and economic status, religion, geographical location and political values. Given this complexity, we are all truly unique. At the same time, the components of our identities provide vital links with others in our social and political environments. Therefore, while our assembled identities may be unique, their components are not.

The impact of ideological identities on political behaviour may depend upon the options that are available within the political environment, and therefore upon the structure of political institutions. It is easier for an individual to act politically as an environmentalist if there are green parties in the electoral arena, or if the major parties have clearly differentiated policies with respect to the environment. Similarly, it is easier for someone to act on populist beliefs if the party system provides a champion for those beliefs, or if populist devices such as plebiscites and referendums are part of the institutional structure of the state. In the absence of such choices and opportunities, it may be very difficult to activate an ideological identification no matter how strongly that identification is held. Here, the electoral system can play a particularly critical role in determining the "opportunity structure" for ideological identities. In continental Europe, electoral systems based on proportional representation have opened up political space for green parties, space that is not found within the first-past-the-post, single-member constituency systems used in Britain, Canada and the United States. Hence, it is easier for Europeans to act as environmentalists within the electoral arena. It is also easier for environmental parties to emerge and survive, whereas in the North American context, environmentalism is brought under the umbrella of large, pluralistic parties which provide more limited grounds for ideological self-identification.

A key role played by ideologies with respect to personal identities is not so much in their creation as in their politicization. For example, an individual may feel a strong patriotic attachment to Canada or the United States, but it is the ideology of nationalism that politicizes that identification and suggests that it is an appropriate criterion by which to make political choices. Another person may think of her identity predominantly in gender-related terms, without that identity having any political consequences; it is feminism that politicizes the gendered identity. Or, in a third example, someone may recycle without seeing himself as an environmentalist; it is environmentalism that provides a means by which that behaviour can be located within an ideological perspective on the political world, and begins to link personal environmental behaviour to broader political choices and perspectives.

Erik Erikson (1959) points out that identity formation is an ongoing process that stretches from infancy to old age. We should therefore expect political identities to change over time. As Winston Churchill said, "If you're not a liberal at twenty, you have no heart, and if you're not a conservative at forty, you have no head." The causes for change are varied. Some will be life-cycle effects. For instance, acquiring a job, a family and a mortgage are events that can have a quite dramatic impact on self-identification. Other effects stem from changing circumstances that may be independent of life cycle. For example, people may drop or add identifications due to disenchantment with previous beliefs or associations; new social groups, occupations or interests may expose a person to issues and views that he has never considered, and consequently he may choose to adopt an additional identity, or to drop one previously held. It is easier, for instance, to be a feminist today than it was fifty years ago when feminism was not widely accepted. In short, we adjust our identities in response to changes in the social and political environments.

Of course, the process of adopting and adapting identities is not always conscious. Rarely do we get up in the morning and think, "From now on, I am defined by my union membership/gender/religion." Rather, the process is typically subtle as we begin to see the world differently: "I never realized how poorly women are treated in the workplace"; "I hate Joe's racist jokes"; or "There sure is a lot of litter around. We really should do something about this." As the ideological currents to which we are exposed slowly alter the ways in which we think, we begin to see the world in different ways and adjust our identities accordingly. This, in turn, raises the question as to how and why ideological currents change in the world around us. For this there are no simple answers. Political scientists such as Ronald Inglehart (1977;

1990) direct our attention to a fundamental shift in social values stemming from the increased material security of the postwar years, but we must also examine the complex and idiosyncratic evolution of particular ideological currents.

TO COME

Ideological thought began to take hold in western democratic states by the late 1700s and early 1800s, at a time when the values associated with liberalism were beginning to transform them. It is appropriate, therefore, that our examination of specific ideological currents begins in Chapter 2 with a detailed look at liberalism. This is followed in Chapter 3 with a discussion of conservatism, and in Chapter 4 by a discussion of socialism. In all cases, the ideologies are traced from their historical roots to their contemporary manifestations in public-policy debates within western democratic states. These three chapters provide an overview of the conventional patterns of ideological thought that have dominated western democratic states for a large part of the past two centuries. Although the respective ideological orientations of liberalism, conservatism and socialism will be discussed separately, it will rapidly become clear that the evolution of any one orientation has been shaped by conflict and competition among the three.

Chapters 5 and 6 examine feminism and environmentalism, two emergent ideological perspectives both of which have built upon and challenged more conventional ideological perspectives, and which have come to assume a prominent position on the contemporary ideological landscape of western democratic states. Chapter 7 explores nationalism and some of the factors challenging the territorial assumptions upon which nationalist ideologies rest. The discussion in Chapter 8 turns to traditional and contemporary forms of populist thought in North America, and explores the way in which populism can be located upon the ideological landscape.

The discussion of populism moves us from the core to the margins of contemporary ideological thought. This movement continues with the examination in Chapter 9 of fascism, an ideology that played an important role in shaping politics in the 1930s and 1940s, and which, unfortunately, has still not been completely dislodged from the ideological landscape of western democratic states. Chapter 10 looks at a number of contemporary examples of ideological extremism, and offers some explanation of why what seem to be radically different "ideologies at the edge" have many characteristics in common. Chapter 11 returns to the core of the contemporary political culture, and explores how our traditional understanding of citizenship is being transformed, and how that transformation is being shaped by ideological change. Finally, Chapter 12 addresses how, as both citizens and students of political ideology, we might handle the ideological diversity that characterizes contemporary western democratic states and that is bound to increase as we enter the twenty-first century.

NOTES

1. Florence King, "Who's got the elitist?" *National Review,* May 29, 1995, p. 72.
2. One of the newest ideological entrants is the "therapeutic ideology" described by Charles Sykes. As he explains (1992:37), "It often shares with the utopian ideologies of the twentieth century a faith in the limitless plasticity of reality and in the changeability of human nature."
3. For just such a debate, see Chapter 8.
4. The American Civil Liberties Union (ACLU) might be seen as an organizational voice for liberal values in the United States. To the ACLU, conservative Republicans would add universities, the news media and national cultural organizations.
5. Within the North American context, the argument has been made (Horowitz 1966) that Canadians have always been exposed to a larger number of ideological maps or options than have Americans.
6. Historically, the left was quite hostile to diversity and minority interests, both of which were difficult to reconcile with economic determinism.
7. There is extensive empirical debate about the proportion of the electorate who think in ideological terms. Perhaps the lowest benchmark was established by P. E. Converse (1964), whose analysis of American national surveys conducted in 1958 and 1960 concluded that only seventeen percent of the electorate displayed a coherent understanding of the liberalism-conservatism spectrum.
8. For a far from subterranean and very articulate defence of elitism, see Allan Bloom.
9. The conceptual frontiers of "political culture" were mapped by Gabriel Almond and Sidney Verba (1965, 1980).
10. David Bell (1995:108) makes a similar point: "A single political culture could comprise several ideologies; historically, the Canadian political culture has included the ideologies of conservatism, liberalism, and socialism."
11. In the case of radical feminism, the tenet that "the personal is political" makes the distinction between a personal and political identity more difficult to sustain than may be the case with other forms of ideological self-identification.

CHAPTER TWO

Liberalism:
The Individualistic Centre

A liberal mind is a mind that is able to imagine itself believing anything.
MAX EASTMAN

*The essence of the Liberal outlook lies not in what opinions are held, but in how
they are held: instead of being held dogmatically, they are held tentatively, and with
a consciousness that new evidence may at any moment lead to their abandonment.*
BERTRAND RUSSELL

*Liberalism is, I think, resurgent. One reason is that more and more people are
becoming so painfully aware of the alternative.*
JOHN KENNETH GALBRAITH

There is a great deal of confusion about liberalism in our popular culture. In everyday discourse, we use "liberal" to refer to those who are generous or open-minded. A large piece of cake is a "liberal helping," and a nontechnical program of study is a "liberal education." In political terms, we often classify liberals as people who hold moderate or slightly left-of-center positions. These usages of the term "liberal" are not incorrect; however, they do not refer to the *ideology* of liberalism. Instead, they capture dispositions and political leanings.

An ideology goes beyond mere dispositions. Ideologies are belief systems which shape our thoughts and influence our perception of the world. Although conservatism and socialism are also important, the ideology of liberalism is the *dominant* belief system in Canada and the United States. Its tenets are so pervasive, we often do not recognize that it is indeed an ideological belief system, a way of looking at the world. Instead, we tend to accept the liberal postulates as "givens" or "truths." Political and ideological disputes in Canada and the United States largely occur *within* the broad framework of liberalism, with conservatism, socialism and other ideologies adding "flavour."

The danger of this blanket acceptance of liberalism is that, in failing to recognize our beliefs as beliefs, we lose perspective; other ideological positions become difficult to understand or appreciate, making aspects of political dialogue and comparative study problematic. For example, European politics contain strong elements of conservatism and socialism—ideologies that differ greatly from liberalism. Without an understanding of diverse belief systems, it is impossible to truly understand the political dynamics in a comparative context. In a sense, Americans and Canadians can be seen as unilingual in a multilingual ideological world. We speak our mother tongue (liberalism) very well, and have even developed various dialects within the language. However, when it comes to other ideologies, we know only a few phrases.

The other difficulty with not recognizing the ideological nature of our belief systems is that we lack the ability to critically assess our beliefs. Broadening our knowledge and looking at the assumptions that underlie our perspectives allows us to understand why we feel the way we do about issues, and how we have reached certain conclusions. For some of us, a critical perspective allows us to question whether we truly do believe the "truths" that we have accepted throughout our lives. If we find that our experiences in life and perceptions of the world do not fit our ideological constructs, we must rethink our belief systems.

This chapter will examine liberalism by placing it within a broader ideological context. The tenets of liberalism will be outlined, and their political implications will be considered. The reader will then be able to compare liberalism with conservatism, socialism and other ideological perspectives in the following chapters. It may be surprising to some how pervasive liberalism is in our societies—most North American political debates can be captured within the parameters of liberal thought. Even issues containing definite conservative or socialist aspects have at their core a degree of liberalism.

We will examine the ideology of liberalism in four stages. First, we will discuss the social and political beliefs reflected in liberalism. Although liberalism consists of two dominant and often competing veins of thought—reform and classical liberalism—there are a number of beliefs that hold constant throughout liberal thought. This initial discussion will address both the normative and practical sides of liberalism, and will look at liberalism's scope and internal consistency. Second, we will trace the history of liberal thought. This will involve a discussion of the works of major liberal thinkers, political events shaped by liberalism and the evolution of liberal thought into its present forms. Third, we will outline the differences between reform and classical liberalism, and in so doing illustrate the broad range of contemporary liberal thought. Finally, we will examine the ideological terrain of liberalism heading into the twenty-first century.

Readers should note that this chapter does not attempt to cover the debates and controversies within liberal thought in exhaustive detail. Indeed, a series of books would be required to do justice to the vast literature that exists on the subject. Rather, the chapter modestly aims to provide an understanding of the basic tenets of liberal thought and the importance of liberalism as an *ideology*, both of which will assist the reader in future readings and research. In the same vein, the following chapters should also be seen only as introductions to broad bodies of thought.

Exercise One: Preconceptions About Liberalism

What are your preconceptions about liberalism? What views do you think liberals hold on the following issues: welfare programs; abortion; the free market; law and order; religion and the state; the role of women in society; gay and lesbian rights; affirmative action? What general leanings can you detect from your list? Do you think liberals are optimistic or pessimistic? Relativistic or absolutist? Egalitarian or elitist? Hold on to your list as you read the next section to determine if what you view as "liberal" fits with the ideology of liberalism.

BASIC TENETS OF LIBERALISM

All political ideologies start with general beliefs about human nature, and from these underlying assumptions fall conceptions of society, politics and economics. Beliefs about human nature colour all other perceptions, and are generally taken as "truths." There is a range of possible positions on human nature (Dolbeare and Medcalfe 1988:33). The highly optimistic view is that humans are good, rational and community-oriented. Within such a view, a person would look at the broader implications of her actions, and would cooperate with others to seek the common good. The highly pessimistic view of human nature is that humans are weak, emotional, self-centered and noncooperative. This leads to a state of conflict and unrest, a "war of all against all." Between these two poles—extreme optimism and extreme pessimism—lie many more tempered positions.

Liberals hold a moderately optimistic Lockean view of human nature. Humans are seen as rational but essentially self-interested creatures. This individualism means that cooperation will occur *if* it is in the self-interest of the individual.[1] Liberals have a great deal of faith in man's rational abilities; although they recognize the emotional side of humankind, they believe that reason will prevail over emotion. This rationality, and its ability to temper rash impulses, makes man capable of looking after himself. The liberal view is that rationality is a universal trait of humankind—all humans, regardless of race, class or sex, are rational, self-interested creatures. The exceptions are the mentally challenged, the insane and very young children.

A liberal also believes that humans are naturally competitive and acquisitive. This falls from the assumption of self-interest. Each rational self-interested individual seeks to improve her own lot in life; because resources are finite, individuals must compete to attain property. Given that humans can protect themselves, and are naturally driven to compete, liberals argue that humans should have the *liberty* to be competitive and look after their own interests. Paternal authority is not necessary, since self-interest ensures that all will protect themselves. As attempts to enforce cooperation and deter competition would be futile, the desirability of a paternal government is further reduced.

It may seem that this stress on liberty suggests that there is no need for government. However, liberals are not *that* optimistic, and do not embrace anarchism. Liberals recognize that competition can get out of hand, and that self-interest can lead individuals to infringe upon the interests of others. Thus, a degree of government is necessary to keep order and protect an individual's liberties from the coercion of other people. But how does one balance the need for government—a potentially coercive force—with the desire to protect individual liberty? Liberal theory holds that the ideal form of governance is a limited government that is accountable to the people. The legitimacy of government is seen to derive from the people; government and individuals form a two-way contract that each party must uphold: citizens consent to obey the government under penalty of law, and governments consent to uphold the individual rights and liberties of the citizens. Citizens are assured of equal rights to prevent the government from arbitrarily favouring some individuals over others in law. Liberals reserve the right to overthrow a "rebel" government that does not uphold its side of the contract. Thus, the powers of the state are constrained.

In addition to protecting liberties, the state, liberal theory espouses, is used to resolve the problem of collective goods. A collective good is something that all people have access to and benefit from, and for which one person's consumption does not limit another's. For example, national defence is a collective good. However, although all benefit, no *one* individual has the personal incentive to provide or contribute to the collective good, no matter how much he or she may support its provisions. In fact, each has the incentive to "free-ride": to not contribute to the good's creation, but to make use of the collective good when it has been provided. This "free-rider problem" makes collective action very difficult, and the result, in theory, is that many collective goods would not be provided within society, or would not be provided to an optimal degree. The taxation powers of government are therefore used to address this problem by forcing all individuals to contribute to the creation of the good. We all agree to be taxed so that no one can free-ride. The point to stress is that liberals do recognize a need for government on two levels, individual protection and collective goods, but in general wish to constrain the powers of government in order to protect liberty.

The emphasis on liberty also explains the liberal's attitudes about property. Property rights have always been an important aspect of liberal thought. This is understandable in light of the liberal belief that humans are naturally competitive and acquisitive, and should have liberty to pursue these ends. If all are competing for goods, the ultimate distribution of goods in a perfect world will depend upon the efforts of the individual: she who works hard will acquire a great deal of property; she who is lazy will acquire very little. It is argued that property should be distributed according to merit—if the dedicated worker's property is taken away and given to the lazy or less efficient worker, there is no incentive for hard work and efficiency. The system of basing rewards on effort is known as *meritocracy*, and liberals believe it provides the best motivation for individuals. The underlying assumption, however, is that all people start on a level playing field, that there are not some people who have economic, social or natural advantages over others. There are disputes within liberalism as to what constitutes an equal starting position, although the belief that rewards should be allocated according to merit remains solid within liberal thought.

Liberal support for capitalism also derives from assumptions about the competitive nature of humans. Capitalism is seen as the best available economic system. In addition to supporting meritocracy, capitalism is believed to foster progress and change. Liberal optimism leads to *meliorism*, the belief that society can positively change and evolve through human endeavour. Human rationality allows us to progress and continually improve our abilities and circumstances; the free market best allows this progress. Thus, the move from agrarian to industrial society was celebrated by liberals, as was the move from industrialism to the technological and postindustrial age. However, most liberals acknowledge that there may be problems with capitalism, and therefore accept some limitation on the free market. For example, laws to control fraud are considered acceptable and necessary limits to the dangers of rampant individualism. Of course, the amount of restraint deemed acceptable varies: to what degree should health, safety and environmental protections extend, for example? Yet despite internal debates on such issues, all liberals share a basic level of support for the free market system.

Important Terms Defined

Meritocracy: government by, or educational and/or social-status advancement of, the most intelligent or talented members of a society

Meliorism: the theory that the state of the world (being neither good nor evil) can be improved by human endeavour

Laissez-faire: the philosophy or practice of avoiding planning, esp. the doctrine of avoiding government controls in economic affairs.

Source of definitions: Webster's Dictionary

The liberal's assumptions concerning human rationalism leads to an interesting attitude towards law. Rational individualists do not obey laws out of a sense of morality or justice, but rather out of self-interest (Qualter 1986:215). A liberal prefers to live in a society that is governed by law rather than live in anarchy, and although it may be in his immediate self-interest to break the law, the liberal realizes that in the long term his interests are best served through the preservation of lawfulness. Because of this interrelation between law and rationality, government is necessarily limited in the regulations it can place on society and the economy: laws commonly believed to be contrary to individual self-interest will not be respected. There is a parallel here to the emphasis that liberals place upon social and moral liberty, an emphasis that also follows directly from their belief in a rational human. Many social and moral quesitons are seen as private, and outside the reach of government. Thus, the state does not control or limit public morality; instead, individuals use rationality to guide their choices in the social and moral spheres. A high degree of personal liberty ensures that the government does not encroach unnecessarily upon the moral lives of individuals, and prevents citizens from viewing the government as tyrannical.

The Achilles' Heel of Liberalism?

One area liberal theory fails to address with complete success is morality. Liberalism does not subscribe to a faith in broad, unchanging principles, but instead recommends examining issues from a rational perspective. Thus, issues are seldom black or white, good or bad. For many, this flexibility is one of the liberal ideology's chief advantages. However, some people are uncomfortable without an objective moral order to which they can turn. Rogers M. Smith (1994:662–3) notes that this discomfort can weaken support for liberal principles:

> [Liberalism] suggests that most if not all the prevalent forms of religious doctrine, and, hence, the church organizations built in their name, rest on shaky if not clearly false intellectual foundations. But in place of these systems of value and meaning, so profoundly important to millions ... liberalism offers only a relatively uncertain and mundane vision of enhanced comfort, freedom, and understanding in this life .... [Many] are daunted by the fact that after it discredits many of the religious notions they have used to guide their lives, modern liberalism provides only rather general standards on the forms of meaning they may then embrace. Instead, it bestows upon them the dubious blessing of having great freedom to decide on the meanings they will pursue. That liberty has always been experienced as emancipating by some but as a crushing burden by others.

For those who dislike the flexibility of liberalism, the more defined moral positions of conservatism, socialism and even fascism may be appealing.

The basic tenets of liberalism can be summarized as follows:

- the human being is a rational and self-interested individual;
- liberty is necessary for humans to progress;
- humans rationally *choose* to form societies and follow laws;
- resources should be awarded according to talent and effort; humans will naturally compete to attain these rewards;
- government should be limited, and should not intrude into moral arenas; and
- the free market best allows humans to compete and progress; this free market applies not only to economics, but also to ideas.

Different schools of liberalism vary in their interpretation of these tenets, but all base their thought on individualism and liberty.

Exercise Two: Assessing Liberalism

To what extent do you agree with the basic tenets of liberalism? Do you believe that humans are individualistic, or that they are more community-oriented? Is change always progress, or can change represent regression? Does the free market motivate people to perform labor, or does it alienate them?

For most of us, these questions are difficult. The fact that not all of the basic tenets of liberal thought are taken to be gospel illustrates the limits of the ideology: although it provides the primary ideological underpinning for western democratic states (hence, the term "liberal democracies"), it *alone* does not structure our moral and social beliefs. Other important influences, including culture, religion and history, help to shape our values.

PLACING LIBERALISM IN THE BROADER IDEOLOGICAL CONTEXT

Chapter 1 introduced the left-right spectrum, a simple spatial model used to represent the economic positions of individuals, groups and ideologies. Those favouring an interventionist ("positive") role for the state in the economy fall to the left of the political spectrum, while those holding positions on the right of the spectrum argue in favour of a noninterventionist ("negative") state.[2] Ideologies are not located at specific points along the left-right spectrum, but rather occupy a range of positions. This inability to locate ideologies at a single point upon the spectrum reflects both the impossibility of confining ideological debates to the economic dimension, and the dynamic nature of political thought. If a political ideology was static (fixed at a single point along the spectrum), it would quickly lose relevance in the dynamic social world. The fact that a number of ideologies have received widespread social acceptance and support over the centuries illustrates not only the existence but also the utility of flexibility within ideological thought.

Liberalism occupies a broad central band on the left-right ideological spectrum (see figure 2.1). Recall that the left extreme of the spectrum indicates government intervention, ownership and control, while the right extreme emphasizes deregulation and private ownership. Thus, socialism occupies the spectrum beyond the left extreme of the liberalism range, while conservatism occupies the spectrum to the right.[3] One should note that the lines separating these three principal ideologies are not clearly defined. Policies that would be considered "left" in conservative thought may blend into right-wing liberalism, while moderate socialist positions may be shared by the liberal left—overlaps between the three dominant ideologies do exist. Moreover, the dynamic nature of ideologies allows the specific ideological bands to expand or contract with time. Policies that obviously fell into the socialist domain twenty-five years ago may now be part of the liberal left, or alternatively, debates that concerned right-liberals a century ago may be addressed by conservatives in present discourse. However, although ideological positions are not set in stone, their locations *relative* to one another on the left-right spectrum remain constant. It is also important to emphasize that although liberals may on occasion hold common policy positions with socialists or conservatives, the reasoning that liberals use to reach their positions is very different from that used by socialists and conservatives. As we will see in future chapters, the differences among liberalism, conservatism and socialism are best seen when we look beyond the one-dimensional left-right spectrum.

FIGURE 2.1: The Left-Right Spectrum

As figure 2.1 shows, the ideological range occupied by liberal thought is quite large. This allows for a great deal of internal debate; as noted above, almost *all* of the contemporary political debate within Canada and the United States falls within this liberalism band. Proponents of the left within the liberalism band are popularly referred to as "left-wing" or "liberals," while supporters of the liberal right are often described in everyday language as "right-wing" or "conservatives." (As we will see in the following chapter, ideological conservatism cannot be equated with right-wing liberalism). The Canadian and American ideological spectra are actually truncated on both ends, going only slightly beyond the liberalism band in each direction. Rarely do Canadians and Americans truly reach into the right and left extremes of political thought; given that liberal values are so embedded in our culture, it is not surprising that we often forget that political thought does extend beyond liberalism. That this was not always the case becomes quickly apparent when we examine the evolution of liberal thought and see that liberalism was a radical shift in belief from the preexisting feudal order.

The Ideology of Liberalism

- *scope*: Addresses questions of economic, social and political liberty. Addresses all issues excluding questions of personal morality.

- *internal consistency*: Argues that the role of government should be limited to the purpose of protecting the life, liberty and property of individuals. Divisions within liberalism largely revolve around the interpretation of liberty: *classical liberals* hold that liberty refers to absence from coercion, whereas *reform liberals* argue that liberty requires the ability to act. These different interpretations lead to different roles for government.

- *durability*: Liberalism has enjoyed intellectual and political support for over three centuries. Classical liberalism dominated the ideological landscape of the nineteenth century, while reform liberalism has structured debate in the twentieth century.

- *normative framework*: Humans are rational, egocentric individualists. Government and law should be designed to draw on these traits and maximize the potential of individuals, while at the same time advancing the interests of society as a whole. Progress and evolution are the goals of society.

- *practical guide for political action*: Issues are seen as they affect personal liberties. Policies should be designed to minimize the infringement upon economic (free market) and social liberties; such policies will in turn naturally advance the welfare of society as a whole. The focus is on individual rights and social progress, rather than upon issues of morality. Rights ensure that individuals are protected against both a positive government and the rampant, competitive individualism of their fellow citizens.

- *formal articulation*: Isaiah Berlin, *Four Essays on Liberty*; Thomas Jefferson, *The American Declaration of Independence*; F. A. Hayek, *Law Legislation and Liberty*; John Locke, *The Second Treatise of Government*; John Stuart Mill, *On Liberty*; Adam Smith, *The Wealth of Nations*; *Equity*; *The Financial Post*; *The New Republic*.

THE EVOLUTION OF LIBERAL THOUGHT

Liberal thought emerged with the movement from feudalism to capitalism. During the Middle Ages, the western world was divided into feudal states and aristocrats and royalty provided the small government of the day. Democracy, a primary liberal belief, was not an important political concept for two reasons. First, it was believed that rulers had been ordained by God. The doctrine of the divine right of kings established the monarchy's legitimacy; the aristocracy was in turn selected by the monarchy, with titles passed down through generations. The absolute right of kings extended to property; royalty retained the right to seize property from citizens, and the landed class held property only by the prerogative of the king. Second, gross inequalities between the landowning aristocrats and the labouring classes would have made notions of democracy seem utopian in the extreme. Labourers were largely illiterate and poor, while landowners enjoyed access to education and wealth. This aristocratic monopoly over literacy and wealth essentially prevented the emergence of ideological alternatives to feudalism. With the poor lacking the ability to read, write or own books, an ideological alternative would have had to emerge either from within the elite or through a new learned class. Thus, hierarchy was not challenged by those at the bottom of the pyramid; rather, it was understood to be a natural human condition.

One of the reasons for the resignation of the labouring class is the role played by religion, and in particular the idea of divine right, in legitimizing the feudal system. The other reason the system was accepted was the prevailing conservatism held by all segments of the system. Society was understood by everyone to be a collective, organic whole. The serfs needed the landowners in order to have access to agriculture, which provided for their basic needs. The landowners were dependent upon the serfs, who paid the landowners in food, labour and military service. The landowners accepted a responsibility to the serfs, known as benevolent paternalism or *noblesse oblige*, and ensured that the serfs were able to sustain a basic level of economic welfare. Thus, the feudal society was ideologically conservative, based upon hierarchy and collectivism (Qualter 1986:206).[4]

Feudalism was undermined in the late Middle Ages, when communities began to trade goods. Capitalism led people to abandon the feudal estates and form cities, which facilitated trade (Hayes et al. 1956:651). A monied class of merchants and bankers emerged which did not have *inherited* hierarchical status, but attained power and status through their wealth. This wealth allowed for the proliferation of literacy and the written transmission of new ideological ideas. Slowly, this "middle class" began to reject the notion that hierarchy was a natural human condition, and argued in favour of what was then a radical concept: basic human equality. Status and power could be *earned* by anyone, it was believed; an individual's social position was not limited to his father's.

This "early conception of liberalism" was furthered by the idea of natural rights, which asserts "that all men are created equal and that governments derive their just powers from the consent of the governed" (Sabine and Thorson 1973:673). Each individual has intrinsic rights to which he is morally and legally entitled.[5] This notion of natural rights is evident in the work of Thomas Hobbes. Hobbes's *Leviathan* (1651) advanced the notion that humans are naturally individualistic and competitive, and that government and society are the creation of humankind, rather than natural conditions. The natural right of self-preservation, which all humans hold equally, drives individuals to join together to form societies and thereby legitimizes government. The role of government, Hobbes argues, is to protect humans from each other, thus allowing every individual to seek his own conception of "the good life." However, this government does not need to *provide* "the good life" for its citizens, nor will it serve to protect one person's "good life" from the malice of another. Government merely maintains order and keeps society from becoming a "war of all against all." One's life is protected, but what the individual does with that life is up to him.

Although Hobbes did not advocate a liberal democratic state as seen in the twentieth century, he is a key figure in the development of liberalism for a number of reasons. First, the introduction of the rational individualist is vital to the liberal conception of humanity. Second, Hobbes introduced the notion of rights before duties. According to Hobbes, the right of self-preservation trumps all other factors. In the organic state, one is obligated to consider the social effects of actions before all else; in the individualistic (liberal) state, social duties are subordinate to self-preservation. Third, Hobbes introduced the ideas of consent and contract. Rather than perceive government legitimacy as deriving from divine authority, Hobbes argues that sovereignty arises from the people, who form a contract with each other to consent to the will of the sovereign.

Many of these concepts became politically salient with England's "glorious revolution" of 1688. Part of the motivation for the revolution was dissatisfaction with arbitrary rule. The overthrow of the monarchy (James II) supported the notion that sovereignty derives from the citizens rather than from God. People desired equality of right, in the form of government that impartially enforced law upon all citizens, regardless of rank. Property rights—that is, the protection against the arbitrary loss of property—were also desired. These concepts are expressed in John Locke's revolutionary *The Second Treatise of Government* (1690), which attacks the concept of the divine right of kings. Locke recommended an expansion of citizen rights and limitations upon government. He also introduced property to liberal theory, arguing that a main function of government was to protect individually owned property. Thus, while Hobbes's government was enjoined to protect humanity's *one* natural right (self-preservation), Locke's government served to protect *three* natural rights: life, liberty and property.

Locke and Hobbes also differ in the limits placed on government. Hobbes advanced the notion that humans contract *with each other* to create and obey the laws of an absolute sovereign, whereas Locke advocated a two-way contract between the government and the governed. If a government failed to meet its obligations to protect and rule impartially, that government could be overthrown by a majority. It should be noted that Locke was more democratic and liberal than many of his predecessors; he argued for majority rule, political tolerance, equality of right and freedom from enslavement. However, like most thinkers of his day, Locke did not advocate full democracy; political rights remained limited to the relatively small propertied class, which, in practice, comprised only white adult males.

The impact of the liberal thought advanced by Hobbes and Locke was reflected in the American (1776) and French (1789) Revolutions. Evidence of liberalism in the American Revolution appears in Thomas Paine's influential *Common Sense* (1775), and in Thomas Jefferson's *American Declaration of Independence* (1776). The liberal thought of the French Revolution is expressed in the *Declaration of the Rights of Man and Citizen*, adopted by the National Assembly in 1789. All three documents emphasize the rule of law, limited government and the consent of the governed. The concepts of individual rights and personal liberty were central to eighteenth-century liberalism; in particular, individuals were afforded religious freedom, freedom of speech and thought and the right to oppose the government. It is important to note that liberty in early liberalism was understood to mean freedom from external restraint, or what today is referred to as "negative liberty."

Selected Portions of The Declaration of the Rights of Man and Citizen

ADOPTED AUGUST 26, 1789, BY THE FRENCH NATIONAL ASSEMBLY

The representatives of the French people, organized in National Assembly, considering that ignorance, forgetfulness or contempt of the rights of man are the sole causes of the public miseries and of the corruption of governments, have resolved to set forth in a solemn declaration the natural, inalienable, and sacred rights of man, in order that this declaration, being ever present to all the members of the social body, may unceasingly remind them of their rights and their duties: in order that the acts of the legislative power and those of the executive power may be each moment compared with the aim of every political institution and thereby may be more respected; and in order that the demands of the citizens, grounded henceforth upon simple and incontestable principles, may always take the direction of maintaining the constitution and the welfare of all. In consequence, the National Assembly recognizes and declares, in the presence and under the auspices of the Supreme Being, the following rights of man and citizen.

1. Men are born and remain free and equal in rights. Social distinctions can be based only upon public utility.

2. The aim of every political association is the preservation of the natural and imprescriptable rights of man. These rights are liberty, property, security, and resistance to oppression.

4. Liberty consists in the power to do anything that does not injure others; accordingly, the exercise of the natural rights of each man has for its only limits those that secure to the other members of society the enjoyment of these same rights. These limits can be determined only by law.

11. The free communication of ideas and opinions is one of the most precious of the rights of man; every citizen then can freely speak, write, and print, subject to responsibility for the abuse of this freedom in the cases determined by law.

Selected Portions of the American Bill of Rights

ADOPTED SEPTEMBER 25, 1789, BY CONGRESS, RATIFIED BY THREE-FOURTHS OF THE STATES, DECEMBER 15, 1791

ARTICLE I
Congress shall make no law respecting an establishment of religion, or prohibiting the free exercise thereof; or abridging the freedom of speech, or of the press; or the right of the people peaceably to assemble, and to petition the government for a redress of grievances.

ARTICLE II
A well regulated militia, being necessary to the security of a free State, the right of the people to keep and bear arms, shall not be infringed.

ARTICLE V
No person shall be held to answer for a capital, or otherwise infamous crime, unless on a presentment or indictment of a grand jury, except in cases arising in the land or naval forces, or in the militia, when in actual service in time of war or public danger; nor shall any person be subject for the same offense to be twice put in jeopardy of life or limb; nor shall be compelled in any criminal case to be a witness against himself, nor be deprived of life, liberty, or property, without due process of law; nor shall private property be taken for public use without just compensation.

The concepts of political and social liberty were accompanied by an emphasis on economic liberty in the form of a free market. Capitalism was advocated, while the former mercantilist system was seen as flawed. Capitalism promoted meritocracy (earned wealth), while the feudal-mercantilist system granted wealth on the basis of hierarchy and privilege. Adam Smith's *The Wealth of Nations* (1776) argues that human needs would naturally be served by a free, competitive marketplace. Smith's views on the appropriate role of the state in the liberal society illustrate the extreme minimal state. Essentially, Smith felt the state should serve only three purposes: 1) to provide national defence; 2) to maintain law and order (by promoting justice and protecting property rights); and 3) to ensure the minimum supply of collective goods, such as infrastructure and education. Thus, Smith advocated only a limited role for government in the economy; namely, to enforce contracts made between firms and to protect property rights. Tariff barriers, price-fixing and monopolies—conditions that were previously enforced by governments—were to be abandoned in favour of international free trade.

By the nineteenth century, the liberal state was increasingly industrialized, and a number of problems relating to capitalism arose. Of particular importance was the emergence of economic oligarchies and the highly visible urban poor. Many felt that liberalism was failing to ensure that all citizens had equal liberties, for poverty effectively restricts freedom. John Stuart Mill expanded the concept of liberty to include the freedom to *perform* an action (what is now referred to as "positive liberty"). In a utilitarian view, a state in which all citizens are guaranteed a minimum standard of well-being is preferable to a state that allows a minority of citizens to hold a maximum standard of living at the expense of the masses. Clearly, if wealth is concentrated within a small segment of society, the "greatest good for the greatest number" is not ensured. Thus, Mill advocated a degree of wealth redistribution through taxation. This change in the conception of liberty, and the redistribution policies that follow, represent a significant break from classical liberalism. Indeed, Mill is considered a pioneer of reform (or social-welfare) liberalism (Dickerson and Flanagan 1995:102). Mill is also distinct from Hobbes and Locke in that he based his support for liberalism on utilitarian concerns, rather than upon the notion of natural rights.

Mill broke with the classical liberal tradition in two additional ways; first, in his support for democracy, in particular by advocating the extension of the franchise to women and the poor; second, in his promotion of personal and political liberties. It is this latter break with traditional classical liberalism that leads some to classify Mill as a libertarian thinker.[6] Mill's essay *On Liberty* (1859) states that although society may restrict actions that affect others, it has no right to regulate actions that impact the individual alone. Choice of religion, or attire, or association are examples of such individually oriented actions. Of course, the effects of actions are not always clear: does suicide impact the individual alone, or do its effects extend to others? Mill argued that actions have social consequence only when they have a decisively negative effect upon the liberty of others.

Mill's notions of positive liberty were fully brought into nineteenth-century liberal thought by Thomas Green, who espoused that liberty is not only the absence of legal or political barriers, but also the absence of social and economic barriers. Thus, liberty requires the ability or power to *perform* an action, rather than just the abstract permission to do so. The practical barriers to true liberty, Green said, are ignorance and poverty (Qualter 1986:100). To reduce these barriers, Green advocated the creation of a "welfare state" to provide a minimum education and standard of living to all citizens. Such an equalization of opportunities would require government intervention and the redistribution of wealth through taxation. Taken together, the views of Mill and Green form the basis of reform liberal thought.

While classical liberalism was the dominant western ideology of the eighteenth and nineteenth centuries, reform liberalism has served to expand the ideological terrain of the twentieth century (Dickerson and Flanagan 1995:105). An important reform liberal thinker of the latter period is economist John Maynard Keynes. In his *General Theory of Employment, Interest and Income* (1936), Keynes expounded that the problems of the free market, so manifest during the Great Depression of the 1930s, could be remedied by government spending. Keynes's thesis was that the problems of capitalism were due to the natural swings in the business cycle: periods of prosperity followed by periods of economic recession. He recommended that governments manage the economy by running deficits during the recessionary period of the business cycle then paying the resulting public debts with the surplus wealth generated during the expansionary period of the business cycle. The impact of Keynesian economics can be seen in the American New Deal, and the growth of the Canadian welfare state under Prime Ministers Mackenzie King, Louis St. Laurent, Lester Pearson and Pierre Trudeau. However, although Keynesian economics enjoyed almost hegemonic status in the thirty-five years following the end of the Second World War, it has come under strong ideological attack in the 1990s.

Liberal Economic Theories

Traditionally, classical and reform liberals have differed in the economic theories they advance. Classical liberals prefer the laissez-faire (noninterventionist, free market) principles of Adam Smith, whereas reform liberals advocate the degree of government intervention necessitated by the economic theory of John Maynard Keynes. History has shown problems with both theories. The laissez-faire system was characterized by unstable markets and high levels of urban poverty. Such large inequities in wealth made any faith in equality of opportunity under a laissez-faire system appear Pollyannish, if not duplicitous. For its part, Keynesian economics has proven its inability over the past two decades to deal with simultaneously high levels of inflation and unemployment, or what has been termed "stagflation." The challenge for liberal economists is to find the optimal market system—no small task! Neither Smith nor Keynes appear to equip us theoretically for a global economy characterized by huge national disparities in wealth and massive transnational corporate entities.

Liberalism has successfully dominated the ideological terrain of Canada and the United States. Reform liberalism defines the left wing of the liberalism spectrum, while classical liberalism defines the right. When British settlers, fleeing religious persecution, arrived in the Americas in the early seventeenth century, they did not establish feudal societies; instead, they favoured a liberal society that emphasized the importance of rights, negative liberty and a free-market economy. As Louis Hartz argues in *The Founding of New Societies* (1964), the settlers represented a "liberal fragment" of Europe that did not have to compete with a preexisting conservative culture. Both Canada and the United States were therefore founded upon liberal democratic principles, and liberalism enjoyed a virtual monopoly within the ideological space of the two countries. However, liberalism, like all other political ideologies, is not static. It evolves in response to altered social conditions, changing political circumstance and the emergence of new strands of political and social thought. The discussion will now turn to a more detailed analysis of the debates between classical (right) and reform (left) liberalism, followed by an assessment of liberal ideology as it enters the twenty-first century.

TWO BRANCHES OF LIBERALISM

Liberal thought places great emphasis on liberty. Liberals believe that society progresses as greater liberties are ensured. However, disputes have arisen within liberal thought as to what "liberty" means. In addition, varying definitions of "equality" fracture the liberal ideology. These two factors have led to a division of liberalism into two dominant branches: classical and reform liberalism. It is the distinction between classical and reform liberalism that sets many of the parameters of "right" and "left" in Canadian and American ideological debate, although it would be foolhardy to suggest that conservatism and socialism have no effects on those elements. Reform liberalism emerged approximately 200 years after classical liberalism, and caused the liberal ideology both to expand and fragment. It arose from reconceptualizations of liberty and equality, and we shall therefore look at each of these two concepts in turn, presenting first the classical liberal view and then the reform liberal modification.

Liberty

All liberals agree that individuals should have the freedom to pursue their own ends. But what exactly does freedom mean? The freedom to attend university may be limited by one's ability to pay tuition. The freedom to play NBA basketball is limited by one's talent. And so on. Not all liberties can be actualized by all people. This leads to two conceptions of liberty: freedom from restraint ("negative liberty") and freedom to act ("positive liberty"). These two conceptions have very different political and public-policy implications.

What is Freedom?

free·dom *n.* enjoyment of personal liberty, of not being a slave nor a prisoner .... liberty in acting and choosing ... - *Webster's Dictionary*

The only freedom which deserves the name is that of pursuing our own good in our own way, so long as we do not attempt to deprive others of theirs or impede their efforts to obtain it. - John Stuart Mill

Almost every moralist in human history has praised freedom. Like happiness and goodness, like nature and reality, the meaning of this term is so porous that there is little interpretation that it seems able to resist. - Isaiah Berlin

Freedom's just another word for nothing left to lose. - Janis Joplin

Freedom and not servitude is the cure for anarchy; as religion, and not atheism, is the true remedy for superstition. - Edmund Burke

It is by the goodness of God that in our country we have those three unspeakably precious things: freedom of speech, freedom of conscience, and the prudence never to practise either of them. - Mark Twain

---

Negative liberty—"freedom from"—is the opportunity to act, or the absence of human interference with the opportunity to act. Negative liberty does not ensure that Jane has the resources to own a business, but it does ensure that the law does not restrict her from owning said business. Thus, negative liberty is freedom from the control of law, and exists when government power does not prevent a person from participating in an action.[7] Negative liberty can take two forms. The first accrues when an area of activity is not legally defined or controlled. For example, we do not have laws governing the type of clothing we wear; attire is left to our own discretion, as long as we wear something. Second, negative liberty can take the form of political rights. Freedom-of-expression laws, freedom from religious persecution, and, in the United States, the right to bear arms, are all examples of negative liberty. In such cases, the freedom of individuals is unconstrained by the state.[8] Clearly, there is an infinite supply of negative liberty, since it depends only upon the willingness of others (and of the state) to stay out of one's affairs. For example, *all* citizens can be guaranteed freedom of religion without requiring the creation of expensive social programs or a redistribution of wealth and resources.

Since its conception, liberalism has posited a degree of restraint on negative liberty, for full negative liberty would lead to a state of anarchy. A large number of debates within liberalism concern the tension between negative liberty and order. Order refers to the use of governmental power to restrict the social and political freedoms of individuals in an effort to protect the "public good." There are two purposes of order: it can be used to keep individuals from harming others (a rights-based justification) or to keep individuals from harming themselves (a morality-based justification). The former is more consistent with liberal theory. Liberalism demands a watchdog government; the question is at what point does the government cease to act as a watchdog and begin to infringe upon individual rights. For example, censorship of pornography restricts individual freedoms in an effort to prevent the exploitation of women and children. Some argue that this is a necessary social protection, whereas others feel that freedom of expression is a more important value.

Like all good things, both negative liberty and order need to be tempered. Negative liberty, taken to the extreme of anarchy, can lead to the economic and physical exploitation of the many by the few. In a system where there are no labour laws, what would prevent employers from taking advantage of their workers? In a society where murder is legal, what would deter murder from becoming the norm? On the other hand, order, in extremes, can lead to authoritarianism or dictatorship. A government could force its citizens to be "free," arguing that it knows society's best interests. For example, government could control what occupations you are allowed to enter, what area of the country you live in, even who you marry and how many children you have. In China, couples with more than one child face economic penalties so severe that extreme poverty is almost inevitable—a strong deterrent to having large families.

Positive liberty requires that the power of the state be harnessed to ensure the ability of an individual to do something; individuals are granted "freedom to." Positive liberty works to equalize opportunities by reducing barriers to freedom. This involves the use of state power to reduce the economic liberty of some in order to increase the positive liberty of society as a whole. For example, the government does not prevent Bob from attending university (thus he has negative liberty), but he lacks the funds necessary to meet the tuition requirements. If the government were to provide university education to all interested applicants free of tuition fees, Bob would have the freedom to attend university. This would require, however, that other taxpayers be "forced" to pay for his education. Positive liberty therefore has a practical emphasis upon government redistribution and the welfare state, and often requires a Robin Hood approach—taking wealth from the rich, and giving it to the poor. This increases the freedom of the poor to achieve their goals. Unlike negative liberty, positive liberty has a finite supply as it relies upon the availability and redistribution of resources.

Liberty, both positive and negative, can be considered in three primary spheres: politics, economics and private life. An example of negative liberty in the political sphere is the right to run for election. Positive liberty would recognize that election campaigns are costly to run, and would require limitations on campaign spending, or perhaps even state-funded campaigns. Negative liberty in the economic sphere is illustrated by capitalism: all people can set up businesses and compete freely. Positive liberty is seen in the form of small-business grants, and regulations preventing monopolies or oligopolies. The right to abortion might be seen as an example of negative liberty in the private sphere; state provision of abortion services would be the accompanying example of positive liberty.

There is an obvious tension between negative and positive liberty. By definition, negative liberty entails a minimal state, with a narrow range of powers and restricted taxation powers. Positive liberty requires a larger state, as resources, particularly wealth, are redistributed across the population; this requires broader taxation powers for the government, thus infringing upon property rights. Classical liberals favor negative liberty. However, reform liberals argue that negative liberty is unequal in its effects—not all individuals are able to take advantage of negative liberty due to the existence of unequal resources and opportunities. It is this differing conception of liberty that leads to the difference between reform and classical liberals in their conceptions of equality.

Equality

The range of possible equalities can be seen as a continuum, one that is related to the distribution of resources. At one end of the continuum lies equality of result. In this situation, all individuals have equal wealth, power and status. At the other extreme sits inequality, or hierarchy. Here, social, political and economic resources are unevenly distributed, with a majority of resources held by a minority of the people.

FIGURE 2.2: Equality Continuum

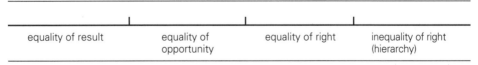

equality of result	equality of opportunity	equality of right	inequality of right (hierarchy)

Liberalism does not concern itself with either of the two extremes; both are considered unacceptable. Equality of result violates the principle of meritocracy, and thus deters competition and progress. By placing some people on better footing, and particularly when that better footing may be the consequence of inheritance, inequality also denies meritocracy. Liberals agree that all individuals should be placed on the mythical level playing field so as to ensure fair competition. Then, according to the meritocratic principle, those who work hard are rewarded for their efforts. The question within liberalism is what exactly constitutes equal footing.

The equality debate within liberal thought can be understood as a debate between *equality of right* and *equality of opportunity*. The classical liberal position is that equality of right is sufficient to ensure an equal starting position. Equality of right refers to the equalization of legal and political rights. Beyond this, the state has no role in ensuring social or political equalities. It is accepted that inequalities will result under this system, but these inequalities are assumed to be a measure of merit. Classical liberals do not feel that inequalities between classes, races or genders are so large as to dilute the effect of a meritocratic system. In other words, it is believed that anyone can get ahead if they try hard enough. This is often referred to as the "Horatio Alger myth," named after rags-to-riches stories popular in nineteenth-century America. It should be noted that equality of right refers to the political equalities of *individuals* regardless of distinguishing features, and does not necessarily include the specific protection of *groups* such as women, racial minorities, homosexuals or the physically challenged. Law in such a liberal universe is blind to such differences between individuals, and presupposes that they are largely inconsequential, or that "matter doesn't matter" (a liberal-feminist slogan).

Thus, classical liberals argue that one merely has to look at the results (output) that an individual produces to assess her merit—the idea that a tree shall be judged by its fruit. However, reform liberals argue that to do so gives unfair advantage to certain classes, races and sexes. If one assesses merit by comparing the outputs of the "privileged" to the outputs of the "disadvantaged," the differences between the groups are reinforced: the rich get richer and the poor get poorer. Reform liberals feel that efforts should be made to ensure that everyone starts from an equal point and that none are advantaged by their class, race or gender. They believe that if everyone has an equal opportunity to compete and meet with success, the true merit of individual efforts can be measured and compared in a fair manner.

Equality of opportunity exists when mechanisms are created to ensure that all individuals have the same access to the tools necessary for achieving a goal. For example, most modern democratic states provide equal access to public education, whereas past societies have limited education to the elites.[9] The redistribution of wealth through social programs is another means to equalize opportunities; for example, welfare programs ensure that all citizens have a minimum standard of living. It should be clear that the concept of equal opportunities is strongly linked to the idea of positive liberty: with equalized opportunities, we all have equal freedom to perform activities and achieve meritocratic goals.

Reform liberals support equality of opportunity, arguing that equality of right does not protect against discrimination. Direct discrimination occurs when an individual or agency overtly disfavours certain social groups. For example, the pre-1961 policy of denying status Indians the vote in Canada was direct discrimination. On the other hand, systemic discrimination is defined as the unintended discrimination against a group throughout society or a set of institutions. For example, if a group cannot achieve equal educational levels, they are at a disadvantage in the meritocratic system. Systemic discrimination against blacks in the American education system was addressed in the 1954 landmark U.S. Supreme Court case, *Attorney General v. School Board of Topeka*.[10] Discrimination, by limiting access to resources, prevents "disadvantaged" individuals from achieving results comparable to the results from "advantaged" individuals. The result is that the meritocratic system fails to recognize and reward *all* forms of merit, and thus breaks down.

Many reform liberals advocate that special measures must be taken to protect against the effects of systemic discrimination. One such means is affirmative action programs, which give preference to disadvantaged groups when all other factors are equal.[11] One mechanism used for affirmative action is the establishment of quotas designed to reflect the population weight of a group or bloc. For example, if women constitute fifty percent of the qualified applicants to a law school, women as a group may be allotted fifty percent of the available spaces.[12] Affirmative action has been a controversial issue, partly because quotas recognize groups or blocs of people rather than individuals (Rae 1989:81). Most reform liberals see affirmative action as a temporary measure that can be discarded once all social groups have equal access to the meritocratic system. Opponents of affirmative action have seized upon this point to argue that such programs have therefore outlived their usefulness, because women have clearly improved their social position. However, as Margaret Wente (1995: D7) notes:

> While women are moving fast toward job and income parity, blacks aren't. While women are well-represented in middle management and the professions, blacks aren't. In the United States, affirmative action is no longer about gender, although gender gets a polite nod in every discussion of the issue. It's about race.

Overall, affirmative action is a divisive issue in the liberal left; many who support other reform liberal policies have difficulties with affirmative action.

Exercise Three: Levels of Equality

What form of equality do you favor? Most people accept some level of equality—particularly pertaining to law. What type of society would result, for example, if legal rights varied with social position? Discrimination is also an equality issue: the popularity of the slogans "Equal pay for equal work" and "Equal pay for work of equal value" suggest that society generally does not approve of wage differences on the basis of race, gender, age or physical ability. The question of equality focuses largely on *how much* equality is desirable in society.

Use university admissions to work through different conceptions of equality. Equality of right would ensure that everyone is allowed to apply for admission to publicly funded universities. Of course, that does not mean that all are admitted. Some students lack the grade-point averages required for admission. Others cannot afford the tuition charged by the universities. In effect, two groups are denied access to the university: below-average students and the financially challenged. To ensure equality of opportunity, the university would have to install mechanisms to overcome these inequalities in wealth and grade-point averages. For example, tuition fees could be waived for the poor, and the grade-point–average qualifying standard could be eliminated. Which policy, if any, would you favour? Why?

It is apparent that equality of opportunity presupposes equality of basic political rights. However, some opponents of reform liberalism argue that equality of opportunity gives greater rights to the disadvantaged groups in society, and thereby undermines equality of right. Thus, considerable tension exists between the liberal left and right over the desirability of equality of opportunity. This tension is accentuated by different views of the state. Equality of opportunity requires a much greater role for the state than equality of right requires: in the former, the state functions to redistribute wealth and resources, and to create and run programs that are accessible to all citizens. An example of this is public education: all adult citizens, regardless of whether or not they have school-age children, must pay for public education through tax dollars.

Another tension between reform and classical liberals exists due to the infringement placed on negative liberty by government programs inspired by reform liberalism. An example of the negative liberty versus equality of opportunity tension is access to medical care. Universalized access to medical care requires government involvement, either through regulation or funding. Recall that the classical liberal is highly supportive of negative liberty. The positive use of the state to expand access to medical care can be seen as an infringement upon negative liberty: taxation reduces economic liberty, while regulation limits the liberty of hospitals, insurance companies and physicians within the free market. The intended result is greater social equality: all citizens, regardless of race, class or gender, have equal access to medical care. Reform liberals feel the increase in equality merits the decrease in liberty. Classical liberals take the opposite view.

Classical liberals are defined by their desire to return to a smaller state, and by their opposition to any policies that would create a larger state. The "four Ds" of classical liberalism are *downsizing, deficit reduction, deregulation* and *decentralization*. Downsizing refers to the reduction of government bureaucracy and costly red tape; in other words, classical liberals wish to streamline government to make it more efficient. Deficit reduction requires that governments attempt to balance their budgets, by increasing taxes or, more popularly, by reducing spending. Spending can be reduced by cutting social programs, or by eliminating universality (access to all, regardless of wealth) and targeting programs. The third D, deregulation, calls for greater negative liberty, or less government intervention in all aspects of society. In the economic realm, this could mean a relaxation of environmental or employment standards. As might be suspected, classical liberals support privatization—the reentry of publicly owned corporations into the private market. Finally, decentralization refers to the transfer of decision-making and program administration to the lowest possible level of government (what the Europeans term "subsiduarity"). Again, this leads to attacks on universality, since provinces or states may choose to discontinue or limit programs. The overriding theme of these four positions is the retreat of the government, and the return to a minimal state.

Reform liberals are characterized by their efforts in the social sphere. In particular, reform liberals are known for their attacks on poverty, racism, sexism and homophobia. Social policies designed to address these issues are often universal in scope.[13] To address social issues, reform liberals require a larger state; employment policies, social welfare programs and other such goals require significant bureaucratic control and regulation. The theme of reform liberalism is to seek greater equality for all individuals. This is a much more difficult position than that of classical liberalism: whereas government reduction is a clear-cut goal, with a defined end point, social equality is an ambiguous and potentially unending goal. Originally, reform liberalism sought to equalize only great inequalities in wealth. Over time, however, race, gender and sexual orientation have been added to the reform-liberal equality agenda. And with every issue added to the agenda, the potential for opposition increases. As Stephen Amidon (1994:10) notes, reform liberalism is often stereotyped as overly "permissive," or as "just another lifestyle." This incomplete and inaccurate picture of reform liberalism is, of course, useful to its political opponents.

In summary, the classical liberal supports equality of right and negative liberty on most issues. This ensures a minimal role for the state. The reform liberal supports equality of opportunity and positive liberty on most issues. This requires an expanded role for the state. The classical liberal position defines the right wing of liberal thought, whereas reform liberalism defines the left. Having distinguished between the two branches, we shall now briefly examine two less dominant developments in liberal thought: *neoliberalism* and *libertarianism*. As you shall see, these offshoots force us to consider liberal thought along two dimensions, rather than along the single left-right dimension that distinguishes reform and classical liberalism.

Exercise Four: Testing Liberal Views

Are you more supportive of reform or classical liberalism? Take the following test and note whether you "agree" or "disagree" with each statement. Remember, these questions examine your political beliefs; there are no right or wrong answers.

1. Most social services, including medical care, are best met through the free market.

2. The costs of gun control and gun registries outweigh the potential benefits.

3. Racism and sexism will not disappear on their own; we must use the state to address these problems.

4. We need to eliminate poverty and racism to solve social problems.

5. Unemployment insurance programs undermine meritocracy by reducing incentives to work.

6. The greatest problem facing Canada and the United States as we approach the twenty-first century is public debt.

7. Without government regulation, the environment will be destroyed by the business interests.

8. Deregulation will not lead to a significant relaxation of labour standards.

9. The low number of women and minorities in the legislatures of Canada and the United States is proof of systemic discrimination.

10. Social programs can be administered most efficiently by the individual provinces and states.

Score one point for each "agree" on questions 1, 2, 5, 6, 8 and 10, and one point for every "disagree" on questions 3, 4, 7 and 9. Low total scores suggest reform liberal leanings; high scores indicate classical liberal leanings.

Neoliberalism

During the 1950s and early 1960s, reform liberalism enjoyed great success. Postwar affluence allowed governments to establish social programs and pursue an expansion of civil liberties without having to impose inordinately high taxes on the populace. However, public support for reform liberalism began to wane in the 1970s.

Growing public debt, unemployment and inflation made many people conclude that the large state was incapable of meeting the needs of society. It was argued that the modern welfare state, by attempting to be all things to all people, was in fact failing to fully meet the needs of any. There were three reactions to this perceived failure of reform liberalism, each involving some degree of shift to the right. First, support for classical liberalism grew. This movement to the right had many policy implications, but remained within the bounds of liberalism. Second, interest in conservatism developed, with neoconservatism and the New Right emerging as political forces. And third, some former reform liberals chose to become more "pragmatic" about their liberalism. This final category comprises the neoliberals.

Neoliberalism combines classical and reform liberalism in a unique way. Rather than blending or moderating the two liberalisms, neoliberalism combines the *extremes* of both views. Defining themselves as "realistic liberals," neoliberals hold the economic beliefs of a classical liberal and the social and political beliefs of a reform liberal (Sargent 1990:99). Neoliberals simultaneously advocate a free economy, which requires a smaller state, and extensive social and political equality and liberties, which require a larger state. To achieve both ends, neoliberals believe that government must recognize its limitations, and aim its efforts at meeting the needs of those who really require its help. Thus, a neoliberal can be expected to oppose universal social programs, such as Canada's former family allowance program, which gave all parents a financial subsidy, regardless of the family's income. The neoliberal agenda was advanced in New Zealand in the late 1980s: spending was cut, but the government remained committed to "progressive" social policy.

Although neoliberalism fits within the broader liberal framework, it deviates in some significant ways. Most important is its emphasis on the community interest (Dolbeare and Medcalfe 1988:70). While neoliberals do not fully reject individualism, there is a strong social emphasis not found in the two dominant liberal branches. The classical liberal wishes to promote individual self-interest; reform liberals seek to reduce social inequities and protect civil liberties so as to allow for the better promotion of individual self-interest. In contrast, neoliberals base political action on the national interest, and wish to use the government to benefit society. This belief in a "common good" fits better with conservatism than liberalism. Also, neoliberals have less optimism regarding human nature than reform and classical liberals (Dolbeare and Medcalfe 1988:73); this, too, suggests a leaning towards conservatism. Ultimately, however, "[n]eoliberals stress that they are concerned with getting the system to work rather than with ideology" (Sargent 1990: 99). The emphasis in neoliberalism is on efficiency: pragmatically reaching social goals, while recognizing and respecting fiscal constraints. Neoliberals can be seen as holding an intermediate position between classical and reform liberalism on the left-right spectrum, with less support for individualism than the two dominant schools. This positioning is captured in figure 2.3.

FIGURE 2.3: Two-Dimensional Map of Ideological Space

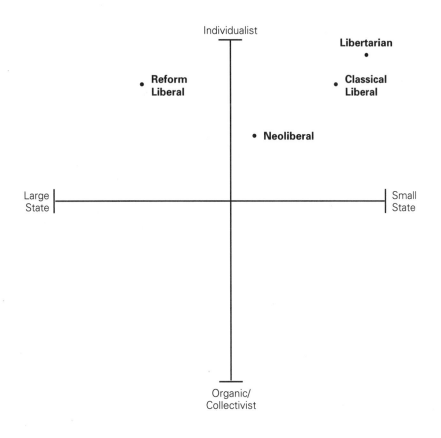

Libertarianism

Libertarians are strong individualists who believe that the role of government should be limited to the protection of individuals in their person and property. In a libertarian state, there would be no laws governing "moral" issues (such as drug use, pornography, gun control and prostitution) and no welfare state. Libertarians are "pure" capitalists, and support full international free trade. Liberty is valued above all other principles. Not only are the reform liberal uses of the state eschewed, so also are the more modest classical liberal restraints on the economy. Some libertarians even recommend replacing liberal democracy with an anarchist society (Sargent 1990:177).

Anarchy: Eliminating Imposed Order

Anarchy exists when society is without any form of government. Rather than through an overriding state, society functions through the existence of voluntary social organizations. Anarchists feel that states are coercive and unnecessary, and that a stateless society is a feasible alternative. Opponents of anarchy argue that society would break down without imposed order. Others claim that the absence of a state would leave mankind unprotected against tyrants. Anarchy is advocated not only by libertarians, but also by some socialists known as "social-anarchists."

The libertarian perspective is increasingly important on the liberalism landscape, since it "has nearly doubled its number of supporters in one decade" (Maddox and Lilie 1984:155). David Futrelle (1995:20) writes that "libertarianism may in fact be the wave of the future. American politics, like it or not, is in the midst of libertarian revival." Libertarians are frequently young, highly educated, middle-class whites (Maddox and Lilie 1984:96). Part of the appeal of libertarianism is its simplicity: reduce government to its smallest possible role. To do so, however, might entail more losses than gains. Putting aside the impact that libertarianism might have on moral issues such as the legalization of drugs and the sex trade, there are other areas in which eliminating government involvement would have profound social consequences. For example, what would be the effect on the environment of an uncontrolled free market, completely unfettered by environmental regulations? It is best to see libertarianism as an ideological position that influences politics on an issue-by-issue basis; few citizens would truly advocate a full libertarian state. In terms of ideological space, libertarianism is more individualistic than the other liberal positions, and falls to the right of classical liberalism (see figure 2.3).

The limits of the left-right spectrum in representing ideological positions can be understood by considering a popular libertarian topic: the legalization of drugs. Recall that the left-right spectrum reflects attitudes towards economic liberties. This places both classical liberals and libertarians to the right of the spectrum. However, drug laws concern social and moral liberties rather than economics. On this debate, reform liberals tend to support drug legalization (or at least decriminalization) and align with libertarians. Does this mean we can expect that libertarians will coalesce with classical liberals on all economic issues and reform liberals on all social issues? In a word, no. Consider the issue of gun control. Libertarians, as expected, oppose such restrictions. However, in this matter, they draw their support from the right of the political spectrum: classical liberals typically oppose gun control, whereas reform liberals support restrictions on firearms. Clearly, not all political issues can be captured in one-dimensional ideological space.

Exercise Five: Liberal Policies

Consider the following policy issues: affirmative action, affirmative gerrymandering, gun control, women in combat, free trade and censorship. Do you associate some with reform liberalism (or the political left) and others with classical liberalism (or the political right)? Are there inconsistencies between the policies supported by classical liberals? By reform liberals? Is one ideology more "pure" than the other in practice?

LIBERALISM AND POLITICS IN THE 1990s

The presentation of the liberal spectrum divided between reform liberalism on the left and classical liberalism on the right may suggest that there is a polarity in Canadian and American politics. This is not the case; the polar differences between the two branches of thought are not reflected in society. This point can be illustrated by looking at both popular and party support for the differing ideological positions.

Liberalism and the Public

As one might suspect from considering the political dispositions of friends and family, individuals are rarely "pure" reform or classical liberals. Some people hold more intermediate positions, not fully agreeing with either extreme. Others combine aspects of the two branches according to the issue; for example, supporting classical liberalism with respect to economics and reform liberalism with respect to social issues. Unlike ideologies, individuals are not required to be consistent in their beliefs, and this can lead to contradictory political positions. (Inconsistencies are often easy to see in other people, although they are less identifiable in ourselves!) For example, an individual can support both the pro-life movement and the death penalty without noticing the conflict between his principles. Contradictory values are also discernible at the aggregate level. Pollsters often find that the public desires both sharp reductions in government spending and an increased number of state-provided social programs, particularly when such programs might benefit the individual being polled.

What conclusions can one draw from this failure of the public to maintain "ideological purity"? Are the ideological models flawed? Is the public ignorant of ideology? Both explanations are plausible, but the inconsistencies can be accounted for by a number of possible factors. First, ideology is only one of the factors contributing to an individual's political views. Other important factors include moral and religious beliefs, life experiences, and personal needs and interests. Furthermore, the role of ideology in determining individual issue positions varies: some people may use ideological principles to formulate their positions, while others may simply use ideology to justify their existing beliefs. The left-right–liberalism model does not attempt to account for nonideological factors. Second, recall that the left-right–liberalism spectrum should be seen as a range of ideological positions. Discussion of reform and classical liberalism is a discussion of the poles, or outer extremities, of this spectrum. Between left and right lies a middle ground within which the majority falls. This majority may lean to the left on some issues, and to the right on others, or alternatively may seek a compromise position on all issues. Finally, ideological inconsistency within the public may be exaggerated. Public opinion polling typically aggregates data—we hear that fifty percent of the public supports issue A, while sixty-two percent oppose related issue B. It is not necessarily the case that at least fifty percent of the population is ideologically inconsistent; in this example, it is possible that only twelve percent have given inconsistent responses. Thus, the presentation of survey results can be misleading.

Although the public can be distributed between the reform and classical liberalism camps, the distribution is not constant. Popular support may shift left or right at different times. Perceptions of support may also depend upon the issue being emphasized. If someone looks solely at support for social programs, she may suspect that the public leans to the left; however, if she looks only at support for deficit cutting, she may be led to believe that the public leans right. To look for changes in perceptions, she must compare support for various issues over time. Statistically significant changes in support for policies, if consistent over time, indicate true shifts in ideological positions.

Storm Clouds on the Liberal Horizon

Over the past few years, the public opinion climate has become less hospitable to reform liberalism. Voters have expressed increased distress with tax levels, public debt and the cost of social programs. Note, for example, the following statistics:

- In a survey conducted in November 1994, fifty percent of Canadians said they were *very* concerned about the size of the federal government's deficit, and thirty-three percent said they were *somewhat* concerned. In 1989, only thirty-one percent were very concerned (The Gallup Poll, December 5, 1994).

- When asked whether taxes were too high or about right, seventy-seven percent of Canadians in a 1993 poll said that they were too high. This is an increase from seventy-two percent across five polls in the 1980s, seventy percent across two polls in the 1970s, and fifty-eight percent across two polls in the 1960s (*The Gallup Report*, April 30, 1993).

- American tax sentiment is more stable than the Canadian case, and also less negative. In surveys conducted from 1976 to 1989, American respondents were asked if the amount of federal income tax they had to pay was too high, about right or too low. Virtually no one said too low, while the proportion saying too high was sixty percent in 1976, sixty-eight percent in 1977, seventy-one percent in 1980, seventy-two percent in 1982, sixty-four percent in 1984, sixty-two percent in 1985, sixty-one percent in 1987, fifty-seven percent in 1988 and fifty-eight percent in 1989. (Floris W. Wood, ed. *An American Profile: Opinions and Behavior, 1972–1989* (Detroit: Gale Research, 1990) 753.

Liberalism and Party Politics

Ideological inconsistencies also occur within party politics. Although parties may lean left or right, they remain highly flexible. Merely examine party names and this becomes apparent. For example, is Canada's Progressive Conservative Party truly conservative, or even classical liberal? Some would argue that the Progressive Conservative governments of Brian Mulroney were more centrist than right-wing. To understand the failure of political parties to accurately reflect their party labels, it is important to understand the role of ideology within party politics. Truly competitive parties seek election above all else—winning elections is the reason for their existence. Ideology is primarily a tool for attracting votes: the voter understands the rhetoric of ideology, and votes for the party whose ideological position along the left-right spectrum is closest to her own. A party's ideological position is not written in stone, and the parties typically move along the left-right spectrum to find the position at which they might receive the maximum electoral support (Downs 1957).

Under some conditions, parties may find it to their advantage to adopt an ambiguous ideological position so as to draw support from a maximum range of potential supporters. For example, the Liberal Party of Canada covers a broad range of ideological space, and appears to benefit from its large centrist position.

FIGURE 2.4: Unimodal Voter Distribution

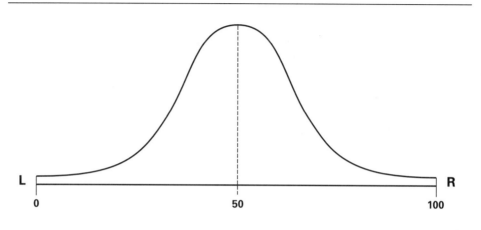

Downs (1957) argues that when voters are distributed unimodally (normal bell-shaped curve), the parties will converge to the position of the "median voter" (the exact midpoint of the voter distribution), while maintaining some more extreme views to appease their more extreme supporters and to distinguish themselves from the other parties. If the median voter shifts position (that is, if social views move either to the left or to the right), the parties follow. If society shifts to the right, for example, a party will also shift to the right, even though it is called labour, or liberal, or democratic. Thus, a party name may accurately reflect the party's ideological leanings at the time of its conception, but provides little insight into the party's present-day position.

Typically, a party's platform (the proposals it advances when running for office) is more ideologically coherent than its actual policies when it is in government. However, party platforms themselves can be internally contradictory. This often occurs as a consequence of the coalition-building process within the party. Parties are aggregates of diverse interests, and must attempt to balance and reflect those interests within the party platform. The Democratic party in the United States, for instance, is described as a "coalition of minorities." Within its platform it must appeal to a number of "minority" interests—for example, the interests of women,[14] blacks, trade unions, Catholics and homosexuals. The result is a platform that is ideologically scattered, but which nevertheless serves the party's electoral interests quite well. Canada also has a history of "brokerage politics," when parties attempted to balance regional and social cleavages *within* the party itself. For decades, the federal Liberals were relatively successful at balancing religious, linguistic and regional concerns, thus limiting the support for third parties.

Overall, this flexibility in party positions is often considered one of the virtues of liberalism: rather than being painted into ideological corners, liberal politicians can consider what is best, given all the variables at hand. Stephen Amidon (1994:10) writes:

> Whereas conservatism finds its essence in unwavering truisms revealed in the church or annunciated by secular authority, liberalism holds that the human intellect, working in concert with other free minds, can solve problems as they occur. The great document of liberalism, the U.S. Constitution, was committed to the principle of human freedom, but not dogmatic about its forms, leaving free the possibility of consensual change. Indeed, the founders would be horrified by the canonical regard American gun enthusiasts hold for the Second Amendment's right to bear arms, as if this were an eternal edict rather than a sensible means of dealing with the (now vanished) problem of maintaining a militia.

Of course, flexibility can also provide ground for political opportunism: "A Liberal does whatever works, or whatever the situation demands, or whatever will get him elected..." (Coyne 1995:A16).

In summary, political parties and the electorate both vary in their positioning on the left-right spectrum, with the former following the latter. Over time, shifts along the spectrum can be dramatic. But if this is so, what does the future hold?

THE FUTURE OF LIBERALISM

It is clear that liberalism is and will remain the dominant ideology of Canadian and American politics. The basic tenets of liberal thought, particularly the concepts of individualism and meritocracy, have become the accepted doctrine of the North American political culture. Very little political debate occurs beyond the range of liberalism, and it is doubtful that this will change significantly in the near future. However, the distance between reform and classical liberalism is becoming larger and more polarized over time. Although the two dominant branches of liberal thought are based on the same fundamental principles, they draw radically different conclusions with respect to matters of public policy, and are increasingly hostile to each other's goals. A number of factors will encourage this division in coming years.

The economy will play a large role in the future conflict between the left and right wings of liberalism in two ways. First, economic issues are a clear point of division between left and right. Reform liberals advocate an expanded welfare state to promote a greater level of social equality and to ensure a minimum standard of living for all citizens. Classical liberals emphasize debt- and deficit-cutting over welfare spending, and oppose dramatic redistributions of wealth through taxation. Not surprisingly, some of the support for left and right can be be explained with demographics. People who benefit from the welfare state often favour the left; people who pay for the welfare system often favour the right. Of course, this generalization does not give the whole picture: there are many "haves" who support the left, and many "have-nots" who support the right. However, there is a relationship between demography and issue support; thus, we can expect that factors such as the aging population, increasing racial diversity, the growing number of women in the work force, high divorce rates and the ever-increasing gap between rich and poor, will all have an impact upon ideological debate in Canada and the United States.

> ## Exercise Six: The Effects of Demography
>
> How do you think that our changing demography will affect the ideological debates of the next fifty years? Are there demographic groups that you associate with one end of the spectrum or another? Are these associations based on your own experience, literature you have read or on stereotypes? How much do your own demographics characteristics (age, race, gender, class, religion, ethnicity, location) affect your views on various issues?

Liberalism debates in the future will also be affected by the *state* of the economy. When the economy is poor, such as it was in the late 1980s and early 1990s, there is a greater emphasis on cutting spending, tackling debt-and-deficit problems and generally tightening the belt. Thus, society shifts to the right on economic issues. When the economy is strong, equality-seeking measures are less likely to be seen as social luxuries. The shift to the right in the last two decades may be followed by a return to a more centrist position should economic growth or at least stability return.

Of course, economic issues are only one part of the left-right picture. Social issues are growing in political importance due to the popular perception of social degeneration. Those who argue that society is "breaking down" cite as evidence such things as increasing crime rates, high divorce levels, the large number of single-parent families and teenage pregnancy. There are two popular positions on social degeneration. The first, supported by the left, feels that the causes of social degeneration are to be found in inequality and the associated problems of sexism, racism, the rise in urban poverty and the poor economy, and thus that the cure is to be found in more aggressive state action. The left argues that inequalities should be addressed through affirmative action programs, welfare spending and an emphasis on education. The second, supported by the right of the left-right spectrum, argues that the causes of social degeneration are to be found in loss of "morality" or "family values," and that the cure is to be found in rolling back the state. We shall examine this second position further in the following chapter.

Overall, support for left and right in Canada and the United States can be expected to fluctuate with the state of the economy, shifting demographics and general social stability. As these fluctuations occur and the debates continue, it is likely that the divide between left and right will enlarge. In fact, the distance between the two poles is already so large that liberalism as an ideology has split into two separate ideologies, each with its own normative framework, political agenda, internal consistency and durability. These two ideologies will continue to distinguish and define themselves over the next fifty years, with socialism and conservatism adding further complications to the Canadian and American political debates.

NOTES

1. The opposite position to individualism—collectivism—will be discussed in Chapter 3.
2. "Negative" describes the role of the state. A noninterventionist state is "negative," while an interventionist state is "positive." These terms have no normative values.
3. As we will see in upcoming chapters, there are important variations within socialist and conservative thought.
4. Max Weber argues that religion, formerly used to justify feudalism, was also used to legitimize the accumulation of wealth. See Max Weber, *The Protestant Ethic and the Spirit of Capitalism*. London: Unwin, 1985.
5. Not all liberal thinkers support the idea of natural rights. One important critic is English jurist and philosopher Jeremy Bentham (1748–1832).
6. John Stuart Mill wrote on a wide variety of subjects, ranging from economics to electoral law. Because of the breadth of his scholarship, it is difficult to classify him as entirely utilitarian or libertarian.
7. Of course, the legal acceptance of an act does not ensure its social acceptability. Often, social coercion is as much a determent as is the law. For example, the success of the pro-life movement in some states has placed many single pregnant women in a Catch-22 situation: abortion is seen as immoral, and raising children alone is seen as both irresponsible and a burden on society.
8. These are not pure examples of negative liberty. Freedom of expression excludes hate literature and slander, for example, while the right to bear arms faces similar limitations.
9. Note that many do not feel that equal access to education results in equal quality of education.
10. In this case, the Supreme Court ruled that although blacks and whites were afforded equal access to education, the quality of education in the "black" schools was lower than that of the "white" schools. In the view of the court, separate schools could not by their nature be equal. As a result, the court ordered the desegregation of the school system. Over time, this has evolved to an active integration of schools, with minority students being bussed into "white" schools.
11. In some forms, exact equal ability is not required; rather, a minimum standard must be met. For example, fire fighters must complete a rigorous physical exam. Biological differences between the sexes place men at a physical advantage. A possible affirmative action policy is the hiring of women who pass the minimum standard, despite the fact that male applicants may exceed the women's physical capabilities.
12. It is uncertain which population should be represented: the general population, the university population, the percentage of total applicants or the percentage of qualified applicants (Rae 1989:80). The final option was arbitrarily chosen for the purposes of the example.
13. Many reform liberal policies have been pursued through the courts. However, recent trends suggest that the court system cannot always be expected to advance the reform liberal agenda.
14. Of course, women are not a minority in society; however, "women's issues" are often relegated to minority status.

CHAPTER THREE

Conservatism: The Organic Right

Good order is the foundation of all things.

EDMUND BURKE

Conservatism is the politics of reality.

WILLIAM F. BUCKLEY, JR.

Conservative, n: A statesman who is enamoured with existing evils, as distinguished from the Liberal who wishes to replace them with others.

AMBROSE BIERCE

Although liberalism has successfully captured most of the ideological terrain in Canada and the United States, we still hear references to contemporary "conservatives." As mentioned earlier, this usage often refers to one's political disposition or degree of cautiousness, rather than to the *ideology* of conservatism. An individual is said to be conservative if she opposes radical change; some authors suggest that the term "conservative" can refer to anyone who seeks to maintain the status quo. In this sense, a conservative in the former Soviet Union would wish to prevent the quick dismantling of the communist system (Ball and Dagger 1995:93). Clearly, "resistance to change" is too broad an idea to define conservatism. In addition, many people who identify themselves as conservatives do not merely wish to maintain the status quo; rather, they seek to revert to a previous social or political arrangement, such as the classically liberal state that existed prior to the Great Depression.

Given such wide variety in the application of the term, it is not surprising that there is confusion about what "properly" constitutes a conservative. Indeed, there are writers who argue that conservatism does not constitute a true ideology. George H. Nash (1976: xi–xii) writes:

> I doubt that there is any single, satisfactory, all-encompassing definition of the complex phenomenon called conservatism, the content of which varies enormously with time and place. It may even be true that conservatism is inherently resistant to pre-

55

cise definition. Many right-wingers, in fact, have argued that conservatism by its very nature is not an elaborate ideology at all.

The definitional problem exists partly because of the nature of conservatism. Conservatives tend to define themselves and their political programs by what they *oppose* rather than by what they support (Dolbeare and Medcalfe 1988:145). Thus, their political views can depend upon the current state of liberalism. Often, it is opposition to the liberal agendas of the day that provides the policy content of the conservative agenda.

Yet, despite the variations and fluctuations within conservative thought, a definable conservative ideology does exist. One can identify a core set of political beliefs that are distinctly conservative in nature. These beliefs are broad in scope and contain a reasonable degree of internal consistency; inconsistencies in right-wing policies tend to appear when conservative views are combined with views drawn from liberalism. The conservative ideology is socially constructed and transmitted; indeed, conservatism is strongly identified with a sense of community, and conservative views are often advanced by community organizations such as the church. Conservatism is formally articulated by intellectuals, journalists and public figures, and its durability is impressive: conservative thought has existed as long as that of liberalism. Finally, conservatism has a clear normative framework, which provides a guide to political action. Although conservatism primarily manifests itself in Canada and the United States as a reaction to liberalism, it is in fact greater than this. Conservatism is a distinct ideology rather than merely a reactive set of political dispositions.

Like liberalism, the ideology of conservatism contains within itself two distinct schools of thought—classical (organic) and individualist conservatism. The two have varied in prominence over time, and occasionally seem to differ more than they converge. But again, as with liberalism, conservative thought embraces a number of constant beliefs which can be seen as the foundation of the ideology. The two schools of conservative thought build on this foundation in unique ways, and the result is that the same basic beliefs lead to divergent policy positions. Contemporary manifestations of conservative thought draw on these two schools in varying degrees.

How relevant is the conservative ideology in contemporary Canadian and American political thought? As noted in Chapter 2, support for the free market and a reduced role for the state (deregulation, decentralization, downsizing, deficit reduction and privatization of services) are features of classical liberalism, although these views are often labelled "conservative" in everyday discourse. Thus, many political issues can be captured within the framework of liberalism and individualism. However, the ideology of conservatism does contribute to our current political debates in a variety of ways. This often occurs on an issue-by-issue basis; that is, conservative beliefs may factor into a single political debate, yet fail to strongly influence broader currents of social thought. While "true" conservatives do exist in our society, the dominant ideological belief system remains liberal individualism. In the context of Canada and the United States, it is therefore best to think of conservatism as an ideology that serves to complicate and alter the substance of liberal questions, rather than present a true alternative to liberalism. The resurgence of conservative thought in recent decades adds complexity to the already muddy liberal terrain.

This chapter will begin by outlining the tenets of the conservative ideology, noting its differences from liberalism. The discussion will then distinguish organic and individualistic conservatism, and illustrate how the latter differs from classical liberalism. With a basic understanding of the beliefs of conservatism in hand, we shall explore the history of the ideology, and subsequently discuss the impact of conservative thought on contemporary Canadian and American political discourse. Finally, the challenges and possibilities facing conservatism as we approach the twenty-first century will be examined.

Exercise One: Preconceptions About Conservatism

What are your preconceptions about conservatism? What views do you think conservatives hold on the following issues: welfare programs; abortion; the free market; law and order; religion and the state; the role of women in society; gay and lesbian rights; affirmative action? What general leanings can you detect from your list? Do you think conservatives are optimistic or pessimistic? Relativistic or absolutist? Egalitarian or elitist? Hold on to your list as you read the next section to determine if what you view as "conservative" fits with the ideology of conservatism.

BASIC TENETS OF CONSERVATISM

Melvine Thorne (1990:8) writes that conservatism has two fundamental ideas at its core. The first is that "human nature is unchanging and unalterable ... mixed of both good and evil." The second is that "there exists an objective moral order." These two ideas are common to all strands of conservative thought. In addition to these basic building blocks, conservatives of all stripes hold a number of other views in common. It will be apparent, however, that many of these views find their source in the two fundamental ideas identified by Thorne.

Recall that the liberal ideology posits that man is a rational creature. This rationalism, it is argued, allows humanity and society to progress to the point of near perfection. The liberal's optimism about human nature is not found in the conservative ideology. Instead, conservatism is pessimistic about the potential of humankind (Williams 1991:165), for the conservative believes that the human capacity for rationality is limited:

> Man is not only a rational being; he is also passionate. Irrational drives and impulses are constantly at war with his rational judgement. Left to his own devices, a man would soon come to grief by the unruliness of his passions, destroying both himself and others in the pursuit of evil purposes. Rational self-interest is very far, therefore, from providing an adequate guide to action (Watkins 1964:32–3).

This negative view of human nature leads to very different political positions than those held by liberals. If humans are rational, it follows that they will be able to thrive under a minimal state. Thus, liberals support a watchdog (minimal) state that allows individuals to grow and develop freely. However, if humans are vulnerable to irrationality and subject to dangerous impulses, the state must step in to provide stability and control. In the classic political tension between liberty and order, the conservative favours order. This allows for a more expansive, and at times even authoritarian, role for the state than does the liberal watchdog conception.

It is distrust of human rationality that leads conservatives to be wary of radical change. They believe that those institutions and practices that have withstood the test of time illustrate their value by their longevity, and should not be reworked unnecessarily. This is not to say that conservatives abhor change and seek a static state. Conservatives accept the dynamic nature of society, but feel that change should be gradual. Evolution, rather than revolution, is the conservative position. Or, to put it more parochially, "If it ain't broke, don't fix it." This distrust of the new and faith in the old leads to a "reverence of tradition" (Sargent 1990), and a reluctance to reform existing institutions.

The reverence of tradition and distrust of rationalism also stem from the conservative belief in "an objective moral order, the belief in the real existence of universal, eternal principles of right and wrong" (Qualter 1986:222–3). Unlike liberals, who maintain a distinction between the public and moral spheres, conservatives are willing to use the state to ensure that private morality conforms to this objective order. The objective moral order exists independent of our knowledge of it; many feel that this order is created by God (Thorne 1990:38). Given man's imperfect ability to use reason, the moral order may not always be understood. However, a guide exists in tradition, which is "the accumulated wisdom of generation after generation and of numerous societies" (Thorne 1990:42). Thus, "things that have always been, have established their authority to continue to be" (Qualter 1986:223). Preference is given to the status quo and to custom rather than to the trial and error of change.

Reluctance to change is evident in the conservative's distaste for large-scale attempts to perfect society. It has been said that conservatives see politics as the "art of the possible." In other words, government should not vainly attempt to attain perfection; instead, it must do what is practical and necessary. Geraint Williams (1991:161) writes:

> Conservatives have traditionally avoided doctrines or programmes, on the basis that adequate political policies are always responses to circumstance rather than blueprints for the future, and that their ideology is neither reactionary nor utopian, but practical. Thus policies may and should change, but the values towards which they are directed should remain constant.

This skepticism towards broad social planning and "blueprints for change" is discernible in the strong conservative opposition to socialism, and particularly communism. Pessimism about human rationality leads to a distinct conservative view regarding the role of the state. On one hand, a strong state is required to ensure the maintenance of order and authority. At the same time, a "big government" state that uses its power to shape and transform society is eschewed. The socialist concept of "state planning" is inconceivable in conservative thought. It should also be apparent that conservative perspectives on this matter differ greatly from those of liberals, who promote a minimal state with regard to order, yet accept a stronger state to promote progress and greater social equality. Clearly, optimism and pessimism about human nature lead to very different views of the state.

Another important tenet of conservatism is the idea that society is an organic (or collective) whole, rather than simply an aggregation of individuals. Within this whole there exist differences between individuals, but all persons are interdependent. A good analogy is a living organism, which has brain cells, cardiac cells, muscle cells and so on (Qualter 1986). The importance of each individual cell varies; for instance, the body has fewer brain cells than skin cells, and skin cells can be replaced. However, each type of cell is essential to the continued existence of the being, and the being is essential to sustain the cell. Thus, the individual is dependent upon the society, just as society is dependent upon the existence of different types of people. This organic notion of society differs greatly from the liberal individualist view, which pictures each person as an autonomous agent.

These different images of society hold important implications for the concept of equality. Under the individualist view, all humans must share, at the least, an equality of right. By seeing society as a delicate balance, the organic view may lead one to be more accepting of political and social inequalities, particularly if it is believed that these inequalities must be maintained to ensure the continuation of society in its present form.[1] Conservatives feel that a natural hierarchy exists, and that this hierarchy is a positive force in society. Inequality encourages the emergence of natural leaders, and this in turn leads to "wise government and a sound economy" (Eccleshall 1984:90). The privileged class is responsible both to guide and restrain the masses. Again, the conservative position is "realistic" as opposed to "idealistic"; conservatives maintain that inequalities are inevitable due to individuals' varying talents and efforts. Therefore, attempts to eliminate inequality are utopian.

The conservative acceptance of hierarchy gives economic power to the elites, but also entrusts in them responsibility for those lower in the social strata. The idea of *noblesse oblige*, or benevolent paternalism, is particularly important to classical conservatism. Although conservatives reject the eradication of inequalities, they do feel that the upper classes have an obligation to protect those who hold the lowest positions in society. Thus, conservatism has been linked with support for welfare programs, although many conservatives feel such programs should be provided by nongovernmental institutions. In addition, protecting the lower classes is not the same thing as creating social and political equality. Critics assert that conservatism is characterized by a "persistent tendency to glamorize social and political inequalities by endowing them with an aura of righteousness" (Ecceshall 1977:62).

The concept of the organic state, combined with the desire to maintain the status quo, has implications for liberty, as well. As Terence Ball and Richard Dagger (1995:98) note, the classical conservative position is that:

> [L]ike fire, freedom is good if it is kept under control and put to good use .... individuals should be free from obstacles to pursue their goals, but only when their goals do not threaten the social order; if they do, then their freedom must be limited.

Conservatives favour order over liberty, a preference which can require a strong paternalistic state. Their preference for order is strongly linked to the idea of an objective moral order. Thus, the state is used to ensure that particular moral values are upheld in society, and liberty is permitted only when it does not infringe upon these norms. This reluctant acceptance of liberty extends to the economy as well as to individual actions. Conservatives vary in their enthusiasm for the laissez-faire economy, with individualist conservatives being the most supportive of the free market (Eccleshall 1984:86).

Finally, the belief in the organic state leads to support for traditional social institutions, including the church and the family (Watkins 1964:33–4). Both the church and the traditional family are hierarchical, paternalistic units, and as such provide a model for the conservative state. The maintenance of such institutions, moreover, helps to maintain the social fabric and keep mankind's dangerous passions in check. Again, the conservative view of human nature combines with its organic view of society to support the preservation of "traditional" social structures. Although conservatives support a strong state with regard to national issues, they feel that issues of local concern should be left to local communities. Power is distributed, rather than concentrated, in a centralized state: "The traditional authority of churches, families, and other groups should be respected. In this way government will be strong enough to protect society, but not strong enough to smother the little platoons that make ordered liberty possible" (Ball and Dagger 1995:102). Failing to maintain civil society would create a vacuum which government would inevitably try to fill, and therefore strong private institutions provide a safeguard against the emergence of "big government" and social planning.

The basic tenets of conservatism can be summarized as follows:

- human rationality is limited and humankind cannot be perfected;
- society is an organic whole, with interdependent parts;
- liberty can be submerged for the sake of order;
- there are natural inequalities among individuals and thus inequality and hierarchy are accepted[2];
- change should occur gradually and naturally;
- an objective moral order takes precedence over public-private distinctions; and
- political power should be fragmented, rather than centralized.

The broad policy implications of these tenets include support for a strong state in some respects. However, they also encourage decentralization, a distaste for grand schemes and social planning and a "positive hatred for redistributionist schemes involving taxation...or, for that matter, anything in the way of mandated equality" (Nisbet 1985:129).

This disapproval of redistribution and taxation places conservatism at the right of the classic left-right economic spectrum. As with liberalism and socialism, the conservatism band on this spectrum is quite large, encompassing a variety of views and positions. And, like liberalism and socialism, conservative thought is not always clearly demarcated. Elements of conservatism blend into liberalism, and certain conservative views sound similar to those of socialists. These caveats aside, conservatism can be seen as right-wing, but as we saw in Chapter 2, not all of what is considered right-wing in the Canadian and American usage of the term can be classified as true conservatism.[3] For example, support for laissez-faire economics is captured by classical liberalism. One can identify conservatism most quickly by looking at attitudes towards morality rather than beliefs about economics.

As noted earlier, conservatism is often defined in terms of the desire to avoid change. Although this is not a full or accurate description of the ideology, it is important to stress the tendency of conservatives to defend the status quo, and at times to advocate a return to a previous order ("reaction"). Conservatives do not oppose *all* change, but do oppose certain modes of change—for example, revolution. Leon Baradat (1988:44) proposes a spectrum of attitudes towards social and political change. This spectrum may appear similar to the traditional left-right spectrum, but should be seen as an independent illustration of a more narrow political dimension:

Exercise Two: Testing Conservative Views

To what extent are you an ideological conservative? Take the following test and note whether you "agree" or "disagree" with each statement. Remember, these questions examine your political beliefs; there are no right or wrong answers.

1. Those of us who are better off have a responsibility to provide assistance for the less fortunate.

2. We should address inequalities in political and economic power through affirmative action programs.

3. It is important to condemn divorce, illegitimate childbirth and homosexuality in order to protect the family unit.

4. We need to crack down on crime if we are to solve social problems.

5. One person's actions, provided they affect only that individual, are of no concern to anyone else.

6. Social norms are relative, dependent on time and place; what was unacceptable 200 years ago is of no relevance to what is appropriate today.

7. Over time, humans will be able to eliminate poverty, intolerance, war...the problems we have suffered throughout history are progressively being eradicated.

8. The problem with today's society is that there is a lack of responsibility; individual needs are put before the needs of the family, the community and the nation.

9. The entrance of women into the work force has disrupted the natural balance of society, and has caused more harm than good.

10. Progress is inevitable, and we should do everything we can to hurry it along.

Score one point for each "agree" on questions 1, 3, 4, 8 and 9, and one point for every "disagree" on questions 2, 5, 6, 7 and 10. Low scores reflect little support for conservatism; high scores indicate strong conservative leanings.

FIGURE 3.1: Rate-of-Change Continuum

radical	"liberal"	moderate	"conservative"	reactionary
immediate change	rapid change	gradual change	maintain status quo	return to previous order

The conservative ideology can be seen as extending from the moderate position to the reactionary extreme. At the moderate position, conservatism overlaps with liberalism, although, as we shall soon see, the wide range of conservative thought and its overlap with liberalism clearly demonstrates that conservatism cannot be classified by this dimension alone. Other characteristics of conservatism stand in polar opposite to the views of liberal thinkers. The following section will examine the two dominant schools of conservative thought, and distinguish between the individualist conservative and classical liberal positions.

The Ideology of Conservatism

- *scope*: Addresses all issues, including questions of morality.

- *internal consistency*: Conservatism holds that there exists an objective moral order that should be upheld by government and society. Given man's fallible logic and susceptibility to whim, the maintenance of traditional social institutions is vital for the continuation of society. Divides within conservatism largely revolve around the role of government in the economy, and the use of government to provide social welfare.

- *durability*: Conservatism has enjoyed intellectual and political support for over two centuries.

- *normative framework*: Human rationality is limited. Government and law should recognize these limitations and acknowledge the latent wisdom in tradition. Conservatism seeks to preserve "what is ours," and thus varies between societies. Society is an organic whole, with natural inequalities among individuals. The interdependence of society requires that programs be regarded in a broad context, that their impact on society as well as on the individual be considered.

- *practical guide for political action*: Issues are seen as they affect society as a whole. Caution is emphasized; change should occur gradually and naturally, rather than being forced on society by government programs. Both citizens and government have duties to each other. Order and authority ensures that liberty does not progress to the point where it undermines the collective good.

- *formal articulation*: Edmund Burke, *Reflections on the Revolution in France*; Richard Weaver, *Ideas Have Consequences*; Russell Kirk, *The Conservative Mind*; Michael Oakeshott, *Rationalism in Politics*; *The Alberta Report*; *The National Review*; *Commentary*; *The Public Interest*.

TWO BRANCHES OF CONSERVATIVE THOUGHT

We have noted that all forms of conservatism hold a number of values in common, and it is these that distinguish conservatives from right-leaning liberals and myriad other ideological positions. However, these similarities cannot mask important distinctions within the conservative ideology. Conservatism has two dominant branches of thought. More recent developments in conservatism, such as neoconservatism and the New Right, tend to draw more heavily on one school or the other.

Classical and individualist conservatism share strong beliefs about human nature and the existence of an objective moral order. The differences in the two branches stem largely from the emphasis each gives to the organic conception of society. The organic state is of greater importance to classical conservatism than to the individualist school, and this leads to diverging social and economic policy positions. As Ball and Dagger (1995:114) write, "Contrary to the traditional [classical] conservatives, who stress the intricacy of society and the complexity of its problems, individualist conservatives are inclined to claim that social problems—and their solutions—are simple."

A strongly organic conception of society, combined with an acceptance of social inequalities, can lead to support for benevolent paternalism (*noblesse oblige*). Responsibility for the welfare of individuals is partially assumed by society, for society's strength and longevity depend upon the survival and maintenance of its units. This is the position of classical conservatism. As was witnessed in the United Kingdom in the middle of the twentieth century, classical conservatism can be associated with strong social welfare programs, including those which necessitate state intervention and redistribution of wealth. However, classical conservatives do not advocate such welfare programs to promote advanced levels of equality (such as those promoted in the welfare programs of reform liberal or socialist systems), but instead seek to meet basic human needs only. In Canada, conservatives who support social welfare programs have been labelled "red Tories." Red Tories have a strong belief in the community, and feel compassion and respect must be extended to the less fortunate in society. Red Tories are also associated with support for Canadian nationalism, as is evidenced in their support for such public institutions as the Canadian Broadcasting Corporation (CBC) and the Canada Council. There is also a willingness, on the part of red Tories, to use the powers of the state to protect that community.

Individualist conservatives place less emphasis on the organic state, and more on competitive individualism. Much of this support for individualism comes from faith in the free market economy, which allows for the natural emergence of elites. Unlike classical conservatism, which originally supported the aristocracy and hereditary elitism, the individualist view is similar to the liberal belief in meritocracy. However, the individualist conservative position has a stronger moral bent, as expressed in the view that "indolent people slither into poverty, while skillful and energetic individuals scale the heights of affluence and social status.... It is morally illegitimate, in this view, for government to distribute rewards in accordance with some principle of human need or the collective welfare" (Eccleshall 1984:86). It is important to stress that individualist conservatives do not deny the need for assistance to the very poor; however, they feel that responsibility for such programs lies *outside* government. Many also feel the disadvantages of the free market are exaggerated. For example, Ronald Reagan's idea of "trickle-down economics" rested on the belief that, left unencumbered, the free market would provide for all.

These differences in social and economic policy preferences lead to different roles for the state. The classical conservative supports a strong state, which exercises its authority, and guides both society and the economy when necessary. The individualist conservative sees a smaller role for the state; she supports using the state to provide order and moral guidance, but stops short of economic intervention.

The distinction between classical and individualist conservatism should be clear at this point. However, it may be easy to confuse individualist conservatism with classical liberalism. Indeed, with regard to the economy, these two perspectives are very similar. Recall that classical liberals support an unencumbered free market and a reduced role for the state in the economy and society. The differences between classical liberalism and individualist conservatism are most evident when we look beyond the economic dimension. Like all conservatives, individualist conservatives attach considerable emphasis to law and order. Whereas a classical liberal supports a watchdog state, the conservative is willing to extend state power in a paternalistic fashion when necessary, to protect social order, and at times to promote moral positions. A dramatic example is the buildup of arms in the United States under Ronald Reagan. Although the issue was multifaceted, one important aspect was Reagan's belief that communism was morally wrong, as was expressed in his description of the then–Soviet Union as "the Evil Empire." In this case, the conservative belief in an objective moral reality virtually necessitated an aggressive response to the perceived Soviet threat.

FIGURE 3.2: Individualist Conservatism

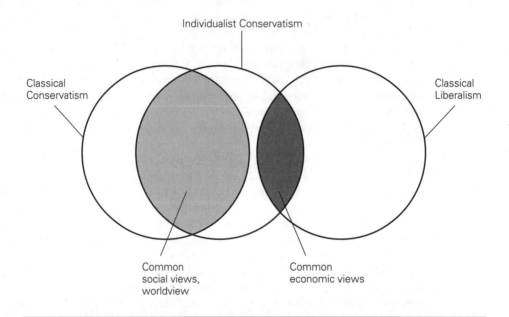

The individualism of the individualist conservative extends only to economic matters. On social issues, she reverts to a more organic and moralistic conception of society, whereas the classical liberal holds his individualist values and maintains support for the small state in all spheres. Similarly, the classical conservative maintains her organic view of the state in all areas. Individualist conservatives, moreover, remain pessimistic about human nature, whereas classical liberals maintain their moderate optimism. Thus, the individualist conservative position contains elements of both classical liberalism and classical conservatism, blending elements of the individualistic and organic views. However, allegiance to the core values of conservatism keeps the individualist conservative within the larger body of conservative thought. Although classical liberals and individualist conservatives may share policy positions on some issues, they arrive at the same place through a very different reasoning process. For example, classical liberals oppose an expanded welfare state because it infringes upon liberty, whereas individualist conservatives are concerned that the welfare state may lead to laziness and social breakdown.

FIGURE 3.3: Conservatism on the Ideological Landscape

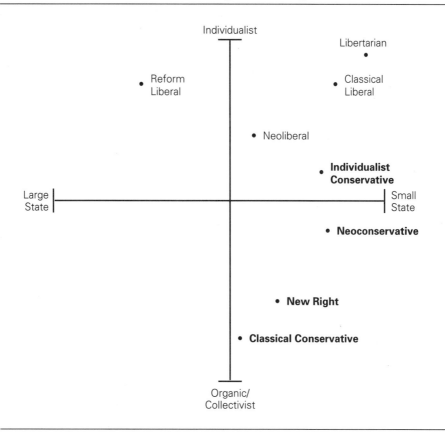

The positioning of the different ideological perspectives is more understandable when we locate each in two-dimensional ideological space (see figure 3.3). Recall that the positioning of the ideological variations is relative, and cannot truly be represented by a single point. Nonetheless, we can see from the diagram that the individualist conservative occupies a position that blends individualism and collectivism. In contrast, the classical liberal occupies a strongly individualist position, whereas the classical conservative occupies a strong organic location. On the left-right dimension, the classical liberal supports a minimal state. The individualist conservative is more willing to use the state, particularly for the maintenance of law and order. Finally, the classical conservative accepts an expanded state, not only for law and order but also to keep up social relief programs. Note, however, that the classical conservative's acceptance of a larger state does not approach that of the reform liberal.

Having distinguished between the two branches of conservatism, a question remains: how important are these branches to our political discourse? As stated earlier, conservativism has had much less impact on our society than liberalism. Conservatism tends not to exist in a "pure" form in Canada or the United States; it is hard, for example, to distinguish a strong classical conservative position in contemporary society. Instead, conservative values are often combined with liberal values on an issue-by-issue basis, adding moral perspectives to rational liberal debates. While there are certainly influential thinkers and political figures who hold consistent conservative ideological views, most who are identified as "conservative" actually hold a blend of conservative and liberal views. But before exploring the present state of conservative thought, it is helpful to examine conservatism's origins and evolution.

Exercise Three: Individualistic Versus Organic Values

For those raised in a society embedded with the individualistic values of liberalism, many of the organic values of conservatism may seem foreign. However, considering the organic perspective can increase our understanding of the political world. Conservatives are correct in pointing out that our social structure assumes a certain degree of interrelatedness. No one is an island. Consider a number of contemporary issues, such as gun control and welfare programs, from a community-oriented perspective. Does this lead to differ views than those you hold when examining the same issues from an individualistic perspective?

THE EVOLUTION OF CONSERVATIVE THOUGHT

The roots of conservatism are found in feudal society where individuals were arranged hierarchically, with status, money and power coming from birthright. European society in feudal times was organized pyramidally: a broad base of serfs, a narrower strata of aristocracy and at the tip of the pyramid, royalty. This hierarchy was believed to be ordained by God, as is seen in the doctrine of divine right of kings. As a preordained system, the hierarchy could not be challenged. One held his station for life, and accepted that station as part of a divinely inspired social order. However, the development of capitalism gradually led to the creation of a middle class, and with it the development of liberalism, whose individualist basis stood in sharp contrast to the organic feudal society. The organic-to-individualism shift was also occurring in the Church of England, where Puritans "challenged the hierarchical authority of the Tudor Church and State in the name of individual conscience" (Eccleshall 1984:96).

In France, strong individualism was an instrumental force in the French Revolution, which overthrew the monarchy and installed a republican government. The motto of the French Revolution—Liberty, Equality, Fraternity—invoked liberal principles that differed greatly from the feudal order. A strong vocal critic of the French Revolution was Edmund Burke, a British member of Parliament, who is often considered the father of classical conservatism. His work, *Reflections on the Revolution in France* (1790), both condemns the revolution and outlines the basic principles of early conservative thought. Burke argues that the French Revolution was dangerous in that its reliance on liberal ideology exaggerated the rational capacities of human beings. Burke saw his conservatism as anti-ideology (Watkins 1962:32) rather than as an ideology: it promised no great solutions or utopian outcomes, but instead was based on the true nature of humankind.

Burke asserts an organic view of society which rejects the French Revolution's goals of equality and individual rights. According to Burke, society is a partnership;

both the state and its citizens have duties that they owe each other. A defence of custom and tradition is also found in Burke's writings. Although he asserts that there is no one perfect form of government for all societies, Burke gives great support to representative government (with a limited franchise) and the maintenance of a "natural aristocracy," whose private-property rights would be respected. In addition, Burke suggests that the spheres of influence of family and church should be maintained to ensure that power and influence are distributed throughout society, rather than concentrated in the state (Ball and Dagger 1995:102).

The Words of Edmund Burke

- Liberty must be limited in order to be possessed.
- People will never look forward to posterity who never looked backward to their ancestors.
- For man is a most unwise and a most wise being. The individual is foolish; the multitude, for the moment, is foolish, when they act without deliberation; but the species is wise, and, when time is given to it, as a species, it almost always acts right.
- Custom reconciles us to everything.
- The march of the human mind is slow.
- We must soften into a credulity below the milkiness of infancy to think all men virtuous.
- I am not one of those who think that the people are never in the wrong. They have been so, frequently and outrageously, both in other countries and in this. But I do say, that in all disputes between them and their rulers, the presumption is at least upon a par in favour of the people.
- The only thing necessary for the triumph of evil is that good men do nothing.

Burke's writings were essentially a defence of what was then the status quo in Britain. This status quo was being undermined by changes in the economy and the church, and was being attacked by the ideology of liberalism. As discussed in Chapter 2, liberal views had come to dominate the political thought of the time, and conservatism sought to protect the existing order, or at least slow the pace of change. This wish to move glacially is different from the reactionary desire to return to a previous order.[4] However, conservative thought has, through its evolution, often contained an element of reaction, although reactionary views are at odds with traditional conservatism in at least two respects. First, the reactionary rejects *any* change, including cautious evolution. Second, the reactionary is often radical in style, advocating a quick and dramatic return to the traditional. The differences, then, touch on both the direction and pace of change.

As liberalism advanced through the nineteenth century, the feudalism of the past became increasingly romanticized in England. Poets such as William Wordsworth and Samuel Taylor Coleridge championed preindustrial society, and recommended a return to a more hierarchical system (Eccleshall, 1984:88). Conservative party leader Benjamin Disraeli asserted the idea of benevolent paternalism, arguing that conservatism benefitted not only the aristocracy, but also the working class. This classical conservatism dominated British conservative thought until the 1970s (Ball and Dagger 1995:106), when the individualist conservatism of Margaret Thatcher gained dominance.

Conservatism took a very different, more restricted form in North America. With the exception of French Canada, which contained a "feudal fragment,"[5] Canada and the United States were settled by "bearers of liberal individualism who have left the tory end of the spectrum behind them" (Horowitz 1991:161). Both countries were free from feudal history and aristocracy, and the lack of a hereditary aristocracy made organically based classical conservatism an awkward creed in the North American setting. Who should be the guiding elite when an aristocracy does not exist? One answer was to look to the propertied elite: those who were the best leaders could be expected to rise to the top of society through their efforts. This view was supported by the theory of social Darwinism, which "held that government assistance to disadvantaged people was undesirable because the human species was improved by the struggle to survive" (Dolbeare and Medcalf 1988:126). This individualistic conservative view is a sharp contrast to the benevolent paternalism of classical conservatives.

Due to different settlement patterns, however, the effect of classical conservatism has been greater on Canada than on the United States. One important factor was the movement of the United Empire Loyalists into Canada from the United States following American independence, in effect, sending the small American Tory fragment north. This strengthened conservatism in Canada, and weakened conservatism in the United States. In addition, the smaller population of Canada allowed the Loyalists to have greater intellectual and ideological impact than they would have had in the United States.

In Britain, conservatism became entangled with the welfare state after the First World War. Economic protectionism and social policy reforms were directed at enabling the government to improve the lives of, and thus meet its duties to, the very poor. Such policies were similar to the welfare state created in Canada and the United States, but in Britain they were "justified in the language of duty and compassion, rather than rights and freedoms" (Williams 1991:163). They also helped the Conservative party ward off, although not with complete success, a serious electoral challenge from the left-wing Labour party. As discussed in Chapter 2, the emergence of the welfare state and reform liberalism in Canada and the United States led to a polarization between classical and reform liberals, with the former often referred to as "conservatives." The welfare state also divided conservative thought. The welfare state was supported in principle by classical conservatives, such as Canada's red Tories, but opposed by individualistic conservatives.

Individualist conservatism shows greater faith in the free market economy than does classical conservatism, and as such is less supportive of social welfare. It is asserted that the free market system allows people to "help themselves"; although support for a strong state is maintained in other respects, it is argued that the state should limit its involvement in the economy. Until the cold war period, classical and individualist conservatives had few policy positions in common, but opposition to communism provided shared ground for the two branches of the right. The 1950s saw a revival of conservatism, as is evidenced by the McCarthy witch-hunts within the United States government. Senator Joseph McCarthy attempted to rout all communists from the government, and was willing to override civil liberties to do so.

Kenneth Dolbeare and Linda Medcalf (1988:128) write that both classical and individualist conservatives "viewed his efforts and the liberal reaction as a clear indication of just how serious and deep the problem of communism was. They saw a nation that was spiritually rotting from within, that faced an implacable foreign enemy, and that was dominated by a ruling group whose complacency made them blind to these twin dangers." Opposition to communism continued to play a strong role in holding together a conservative alliance until the end of the cold war.

Neoconservatism emerged in the mid-1960s as an intellectual movement that embraced and updated many of the individualist conservatist views. At the same time, classical conservatism remained a force, with writers such as George Will stressing the organic-society perspective. And finally, a more popular movement known as the New Right emerged. (Each of these strands of conservative thought will be examined later in this chapter.) Conservatism was both gaining strength and diversifying by the mid-1970s. As George Nash (1976:xv) writes:

> In 1945 "conservatism" was not a popular word in America and its spokesmen were without influence in their native land. A generation later these once isolated voices had becomes a chorus, a significant intellectual and political movement which had an opportunity to shape the nation's destiny.

The years 1979 and 1980 saw the election of two strong individualist conservative governments. The first was the Thatcher government in the United Kingdom, followed quickly by the election of Ronald Reagan to the American presidency. Throughout the 1980s, both countries dismantled much of the welfare state, and engaged in high levels of military spending in the face of the perceived communist threat.[6] In Canada, the election of the Progressive Conservatives in 1984, and the subsequent dropping of trade barriers and privatization of many government companies (Crown corporations), can better be seen as a revival of classical liberalism than of conservatism. As this shows, however, the line between individualist conservatism and classical liberalism was blurred greatly during this period, and the end of the cold war and the apparent defeat of communism makes the distinction even more problematic. Again, one must look at the moralistic reasoning that leads to particular policy positions, rather than to the positions themselves, in order to identify conservatism, and to distinguish it from classical liberalism.

RECENT TRENDS IN CONSERVATISM

A glance through the newspapers and magazines of recent years quickly confirms that there is a revival of interest in conservative thought. Some of this interest is directed at the economy, and tends to blend with classical liberalism. But more important is the attention given to the role of the state and the direction of society. It is in this realm of discussion that the true ideological conservatism can be distinguished. On some issues, modern conservatives are reluctant to move "forward"— the granting of equal rights to homosexuals, for example. On other issues, modern conservatives appear to be reactionary, wishing to return to a previous order distant in our collective memories. Thus, some conservatives wish to return to the 1950s-style traditional family, in which the mother remained at home, the father was the breadwinner and the children obeyed their parents. However, there is no single conservative position; rather, there are several which can be loosely grouped under the banners of neoconservatism and the New Right.

Neoconservatism

Neoconservatism might best be understood as a reaction to reform liberalism and the growth of the welfare state. The roots of neoconservatism were laid in the writings of intellectuals after the Second World War:

> Shocked by totalitarianism, total war, and the development of secular, rootless, mass society during the 1930s and 1940s, the "new conservatives" urged a return to traditional religious and ethical absolutes and a rejection of the "relativism" which allegedly corroded Western values and produced an intolerable vacuum that was filled by demonic ideologies (Nash 1976:xiii).

Neoconservatives sought a return to a "moral" state, and their roots in organic conservatism are evidenced in the emphasis on hierarchy, ethics and morality. Not surprisingly, neoconservatives were also known as "traditionalists."

Neoconservatism developed further in the 1960s, when the civil rights movement, feminism and the New Left increased social pressure for greater rights and social equality. Many of these demands met with success through legislatures and the courts, and the result of increasing egalitarianism was the attendant growth of the state. Neoconservatives saw the growth in egalitarianism as a threat to order and authority, and to individual freedoms such as property rights (Dolbeare and Medcalf 1988:130). Some of the impetus for neoconservatism came from divisions within the New Left movement, where anticommunists moved to the right of the movement and then into the neoconservative camp. Indeed, the term "neoconservative" was coined by an American socialist to refer to "right-wing hawkish social democrats," but has grown to incorporate "hard-line right-wingers," as well (Lipset 1988:33–4). At present, neoconservatism is supported primarily by "a powerful party of intellectuals" (Steinfels 1979a:7); prominent spokespersons include Irving Kristol, James Wilson, Seymour Martin Lipset, Nathan Glazer and Daniel Bell. Many of neoconservatism's leading proponents are university professors or media personalities who grew disenchanted with the political left. Neoconservatism lacks a grass-roots base, but it has nonetheless had significant influence among economic and political elites. The journal *The Public Interest* is an important forum for neoconservative thought.

While reform liberals attack the problems of market failure, neoconservatives address the issue of *government failure*. Government failure occurs when state programs designed to resolve one set of social problems create a new set of problems in their wake. Well-intentioned government programs, it is argued, may "seriously reduce expected benefits, produce negative consequences elsewhere or even cause the opposite to what was intended. This has been described as the Law of Unintended Consequences" (Ashford 1981:356). For example, generous social welfare programs may create a dependent clientele that lacks incentive to leave welfare lists. The neoconservative solution is straightforward: reduce government programs. Such an approach has been adopted by Progressive Conservative premiers Mike Harris and Ralph Klein.

Neoconservatism is most clearly defined by its opposition to using the state as a means to achieve greater social equality. Neoconservatives emphasize the conservative belief in natural hierarchy. They believe that the pursuit of equality through state power undermines order and authority, and threatens social liberty (Steinfels 1979b:179). Opposition to state-imposed equality leads to support for the laissez-faire market, distaste for affirmative action programs and demands for a less bureaucratized, more efficient welfare state—positions common to the classical liberal. However, note that:

> [N]eoconservatism also has incorporated more than a touch of organic conservatism. Its emphasis on the need for deference to authority, acceptance of traditional ways, and respect for moral, religious, and spiritual values is squarely in the organic conservative model (Dolbeare and Medcalf 1988:132).

Neoconservatism is similar to individualist conservatism in its basic values, and the two forms of conservatism often yield similar policy positions. But there are important differences. First, the neoconservative support for laissez-faire economics is more reluctant and cautious than that of individualist conservatives. Second, individualist conservatives place less emphasis on the organic state than do neoconservatives. Individualist conservatism draws significantly on classical liberalism, while neoconservatism incorporates larger parts of classical conservatism, and less classical liberalism.

FIGURE 3.4: Neoconservatism

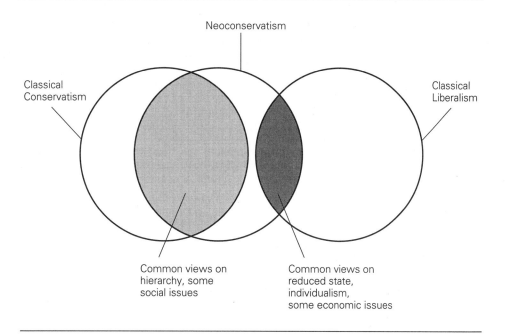

With respect to foreign policy issues, the neoconservatives are "hawkish." This was particularly evident during the cold war, when neoconservatives supported the buildup of arms under the Reagan administration. The differences between neoconservatism and individualistic conservatism also manifest themselves in the realm of domestic policy. Lipset (1988:34, 36) writes:

> [Q]uestions of affirmative action and meritocracy apart, almost all the neoconservatives remained liberals and Democrats on most domestic policy issues … almost all of the original neoconservatives have been supporters of the welfare state and continue to criticize Friedmanite free-market economics. Ironically, on a philosophical level the neoconservative position is closer to classic Toryism in British or Canadian terms.

The neoconservative support for social welfare takes on a unique form. For example, many neoconservatives support housing and education voucher systems,[7] which introduce free-market principles into the government provision of social welfare (Ashford 1981:356). Finally, as noted, the neoconservatives emphasize the need for order and authority in society.

To understand where neoconservatism fits in ideological space, refer to figure 3.3. On the individualist-collectivist dimension, the neoconservative holds an intermediate position; she is less individualistic than the individualist conservative, but the difference here is slight. The neoconservative displays much greater support for collectivism than the classical liberal. As noted in Chapter 2, classical liberals are often incorrectly labelled neoconservatives in the media because classical liberals and neoconservatives share some policy positions. However, the neoconservative's emphasis on morality and social hierarchy differs significantly from the classical liberal view. On the left-right dimension, the neoconservative leans strongly towards a small state, but this position is still tempered by the need for law and order, the desire for a more "moral" state and a commitment to a strong military.

Neoconservatism has had important political influence, and is popular among modern right-leaning intellectuals. However, it lacks strong public support. This may be attributable to its elite emergence and proliferation, and its emphasis on hierarchy. Modern conservatism has made its public effect largely through the New Right. It is to this manifestation of conservatism that we now turn.

The Neoconservative Mood

- Neoconservatives believe in the importance of economic growth, not out of any enthusiasm for the material goods of this world, but because they see economic growth as indispensable for social and political stability. - Irving Kristol

- Many of us are former liberals or socialists who think of themselves as people who are trying to restore the country to a kind of intellectual and spiritual health. - Midge Decter

- Let's face it: elitism lends life a patina it sorely needs. God may have loved the common people but He made far too many of them. - Florence King

---

The New Right

Neoconservatism is often confused in popular discourse with the New Right (also known as the "authoritarian right" or "religious right"). The positions of these two branches of conservatism are by no means identical. The New Right uniquely combines organically based social policies with individualist based economic policies. Supporters of the New Right combine support for the free market (requiring a negative state) with a strong family-values doctrine, which denies the liberal principle of individuality. The combination of conservatism and extreme individualism can lead to internal inconsistencies. The New Right, Patricia Marchak suggests (1988:13–4), can be seen as

> a somewhat contradictory set of beliefs which combine advocacy of minimal government, establishment of a completely free market, extreme individualism; and strong, centralized government, controlled markets, and a special concern for major economic corporations in the international market-place. The common core in this position is hostility toward democracy, the welfare state, unions, and collective bargaining.

Like neoconservatism and individualist conservatism before it, the New Right shares terrain with classical conservatism and classical liberalism. Yet, as figure 3.5 illustrates, there is a great deal of ideological terrain that is unique to the New Right, and that cannot be attributed to the traditional ideologies.

FIGURE 3.5: The New Right

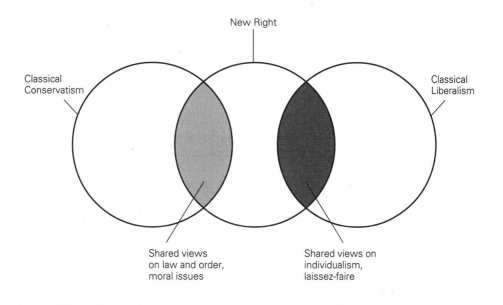

The New Right emerged as a political force in America between 1974 and 1975 (Crawford 1980); and was an important factor in the election of Ronald Reagan in 1980. Unlike the intellectually based neoconservatism, the New Right is a populist movement. There are two large bodies of support: religious fundamentalists and the disaffected lower-middle class (Dolbeare and Medcalf 1988:165). The distinguishing characteristic of New Right supporters is resentment. Its members feel that government programs "bleed" them of their rightfully earned dollars, and that excessive permissiveness has led to the moral deterioration of society. New Right leaders are often reactionary in their views, seeking radical changes rather than the slow evolution common to other branches of conservative thought.

If neoconservatism can best be seen as economic conservatism, then the New Right is defined by social conservatism. Much of the New Right movement focuses on social issues, such as abortion, pornography, women's role in society, the role of religion in the education system and the promotion of integrated schooling (Sargent 1990:97). The New Right feels the state's power can and should be used to promote a more moral state. American society in the 1950s is often held up as a model of the "best" society. Opposition to equality programs is based on a distaste for the ramifications of such programs rather than skepticism about their effectiveness. For example, proponents of the New Right argue that busing students disrupts communities. Encouraging women in the work force is seen to lead to the destruction of the family. Thus, it is believed that state power is being used to promote an immoral, overly relativistic society, and that in the future such power should be directed to different ends.

The traditional conservative belief in an objective moral order is perhaps best articulated today by the New Right movement. Not coincidentally, religious fundamentalists provide a large base of support for the New Right (hence the term the "religious right"); important New Right leaders include figures such as the Reverend Jerry Faldwell. This strong fundamentalist backing is witnessed in the New Right's support for prayer in school, instruction in creationism and home schooling. Strong opposition to feminism also emerges from the religious side of the New Right, where feminism is seen to undermine the traditional family unit, which is based on a hierarchy comparable to that of the Church. For similar reasons, New Right activists oppose homosexuality (and particularly its legal recognition), common law marriage and abortion. Each issue is seen as a sign that society is morally degenerating, and the solution is to impose greater social order by reversing existing permissive legislation.

Not all New Right supporters are drawn from the fundamentalist movement. The disaffected lower-middle class provides another substantial pool of support (Dolbeare and Medcalf 1988:165). Donald Warren (1976) refers to this segment of society as "middle American radicals," or MARs. For these people, the abiding issue is government spending and taxation. Tired of paying for social welfare programs, which are seen to benefit people other than themselves, MARs advocate a "rolling back" of the state and a restriction on taxation. This classical liberal economic stance is joined by a strong antagonism to both "big business" and "big labor" (Dolbeare and Medcalfe 1988:172); the former is seen as an ally of the large state, and the latter is viewed as coercive and undemocratic. Many New Right supporters thus support greater decentralization not only in the political arena, but also in the economic realm. More generally, it is important to stress the disaffected position of the non-fundamentalist New Right supporter. Warren (1976:1, 3) writes:

> Often MARs feel their problems stem from the rich and the government working together to defraud the rest of the country. They blame the situation on defects in the system such as bad taxes … The MAR consistently sees an unholy alliance growing between the liberal and minority establishment at his expense. White efforts to end racism have forced him to carry out good deeds, through his taxes, that he never felt compelled to institute. The burden falls on *his* shoulders ….

While the fundamentalist New Right supporter emphasizes the breakdown of social morality, the MAR looks at the impact of government programs upon *himself*. The common ground is the resentment felt, and the solutions sought.

However, the New Right's opposition to the big state ends with issues of law and order. The New Right is highly supportive of a stronger corporal state, seeing the legal status quo as "soft on crime." This leads to support for capital punishment and "three-strikes" felony legislation, and opposition to drug legalization. Moreover, the New Right's desire for order extends beyond the country in question. Its members are strongly patriotic and vigorous in their defence of democracy and capitalism: "Where mainstream conservatism is anti-communist, the New Right is nationalistic—which makes for a greater number of enemies abroad and a more aggressive stance against immigration at home" (Dolbeare and Medcalf 1988:179). Not surprisingly, the New Right's emphasis on morality and order attracts a number of extremists. Racist groups and antiabortion terrorists have emerged among the New Right, leading to a degree of public skepticism and media backlash (see Chapter 10 for further discussion). On the whole, however, these groups are marginalized and do not represent the broader New Right movement. Yet, even without the extremists element, the New Right continues to draw greater attention and public criticism than neoconservatism, something that may largely be attributed to the radical reactionary nature of the movement.

The New Right holds a distinct position in ideological space (see figure 3.3). It is more collectivist than neoconservative due to its emphasis on morality, but this collectivism does not extend to the responsibility-holding collectivism of the classical conservative. The New Right accepts a larger state than the neoconservative in order to promote and regulate a moral society, but like the neoconservative rejects large-scale social welfare programs.

The New Right Mood

- We believe in God and in the importance of the traditional family. We believe that the way to peace is to be stronger than any country that wants to conquer us. We believe in fiscal prudence, and in helping those—but only those, who truly cannot help themselves.... We care about the social and cultural index of this nation as well as the Consumer Price Index. - Richard Viguerie

- It may not be with bullets, and it may not be with rockets and missiles, but it is a war nevertheless. It is a war of ideology, it's a war of ideas, it's a war about our way of life. And it has to be fought with the same intensity, I think, and dedication as you would fight a shooting war. - Paul Weyrich

---

The New Right has received less than full support from more "traditional" conservatives, and indeed, many of its positions are antagonistic to those of classical and individualist conservatism. As a populist movement, the New Right rejects the importance of hierarchy in society, it does not embrace benevolent paternalism, nor does it exhibit the conservative preference for slow, evolutionary change. Alan Crawford (1980:7) writes that:

> [Traditional conservatives] regard the New Right as anti-intellectual, insensitive to questions of civil liberties, hostile to reforms, more concerned with using political processes for social protest than with improving the quality of life in America by informed public policy and ameliorative social programs. Because they believe New Right dominance could mean the end of responsible conservatism in America, the conservatives have viewed with encouragement and optimism the rise of the "neo-conservative" intellectual movement ....

Thus it is important to note that contestation and tensions exist within the conservative terrain, as they do in liberalism. It is also important to note that the New Right has received less support in Canada than in the United States. The Canadian right wing tends to emphasize classical liberalism and neoconservatism rather than the moralistic New Right positions. However, support for the New Right in Canada has been increasing since the late 1980s in the wake of growing populist and middle class discontent.

A Conservative's Lament

George Grant mourns the failure of Canadian conservatism in *Lament for a Nation* (1965:68):

> The impossibility of conservatism in our era is the impossibility of Canada. As Canadians we attempted a ridiculous task in trying to build a conservative nation in the age of progress, on a continent we share with the most dynamic nation on earth. The current of modern history was against us.

More recently, the tensions between classical conservatism and its modern, more individualistic variants are captured by Charlotte Allen (1995) in "A Conservative's Lament":

> Conservatives are supposed to stand for a love of tradition—hence their name—and also for a suspicion of government. If only it were so today. Although they talk a great deal about personal responsibility and ethics, most of today's conservatives refuse to support the traditional social and economic arrangements—small towns, extended families, generational roots, secure livelihoods, and respect for the land—that create the stability in which a sense of duty to others thrives .... there is very little about American conservatism nowadays that would be recognizable as conservative anywhere else ....

Allen recommends that conservatives address community issues such as the environment, family farms, consumerism, small business and peace. She writes:

> Burkeans of the world, unite. But keep in mind that some of your fiercest enemies are likely to be other people who mistakenly call themselves conservative.

CONSERVATISM AND POLITICS IN THE 1990s

The impact of conservatism on the Canadian and American political landscapes is detectable in general public sentiments and in the rhetoric of party politics. We shall examine each in turn.

Popular Support for Conservatism

An ideology is of little political relevance if it has no followers. Conservatism in Canada and the United States was a weak political force at best until the post–World War II period. Prior to 1945, the political right was largely dominated by classical liberals, rather than true ideological conservatives. The postwar period witnessed the emergence of conservatism, in both traditional forms and more modern manifestations. The ideological impact of conservatism became politically significant in the 1970s, and its influence continues to grow in the 1990s. Consequently, the political right has become a very congested terrain, particularly because the growth of conservatism developed alongside the reemergence of classical liberalism. As mentioned earlier, decentralization, deregulation, government downsizing and deficit reduction are all classical liberal policies. Although modern conservatives also support these principles, they alone do not demarcate the conservative ideology. The ideological impact of conservatism is best seen in the noneconomic areas, including social policy, antagonism to socialism and a broad set of issues relating to law and order.

The increased public support for conservatism in the last thirty years is attributable to a number of factors. First, bloodshed in Vietnam and Afghanistan intensified the cold war, and increased antagonism towards communism and socialism. Although the cold war is over, the hostility toward communism remains. If anything, it may even have intensified as the "triumph" over communism reinforces the belief that there is an objective moral order, which communism failed to meet. The new foe is unrestrained individualism, and attacks on liberalism in the 1990s have come to echo attacks on communism in the 1980s. As Lewis Lapham (1995:33) writes:

> In the absence of enemies abroad, the protectors of the American dream began looking for inward signs of moral weakness rather than outward shows of military force ... the authorities rounded up as suspects a motley crowd of specific individuals and general categories of subversive behaviour and opinion—black male adolescents as well as leftist English professors, multiculturalists of all descriptions, the liberal news media ... welfare mothers, homosexuals ...

A second factor contributing to public support for conservatism is the perception that society is deteriorating. Due to the entry of women into the work force, the growing number of single parents, rising divorce rates, increasing acceptance of homosexual and interracial relationships and myriad other factors, the modern family often bears little resemblance to the traditional 1950s-style family structure. At the same time, crime rates are seen to be rising. For example, a Canadian Gallup poll conducted in May 1994 found that fifty-four percent of the respondents felt the level of violent crime in their community had been increasing, and only four percent perceived a decrease.[8] Moreover, as figure 3.6 illustrates, such perceptions are not out of line with reality. Yet the point to stress is that many supporters of the conservative moral agenda attribute rising crime and disorder to increased permissiveness and relaxed moral standards. Individualism, they believe, has led to disaster, and the proper response is a return to hierarchical collectivism and greater social responsibility: ideas have consequences, and the conservative perception is that liberalism's ideas and their consequences have been negative (Viguerie 1981:19).

As noted in Chapter 2, economic turbulence has helped create a climate of fiscal restraint. In the face of debt, deficit, inflation and high unemployment levels, many social programs are seen as frills rather than necessities. This perception has led to a resurgence of classical liberalism. As this chapter argues, many conservatives adopt classical liberal views in the economic realm. Thus, a final factor contributing to the increasing support for conservatism is poor economic circumstance. It must be remembered, however, that in the absence of the moral convictions of a conservative, support for fiscal restraint is a classical liberal position.

FIGURE 3.6: Violent Crime Rates in Canada

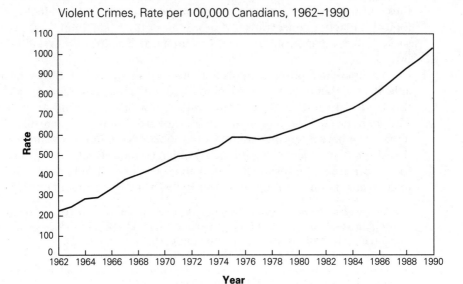

Violent Crimes, Rate per 100,000 Canadians, 1962–1990

Source: Rick Linden, ed. *Criminology: A Canadian Perspective*, 2nd ed. (Toronto: Harcourt Brace Jovanovich, 1992) 75.

Reactions to Social Change

The fact that North American social patterns have changed dramatically should not lead us to assume that all such changes have been seen in a positive light. Note, for example, the following public opinion snapshots.

- In 1977, thirty-eight percent of Americans thought a pregnant woman should be able to obtain a legal abortion if she wants it for any reason; by 1989, that proportion had only increased to forty percent.

- Across the 1970s and 1980s, between seventy and seventy-seven percent of Americans thought that sexual relations between two adults of the same sex was "always wrong." There was no systematic change over time in this proportion.

- A 1992 poll showed that sixty-one percent of Canadians opposed, and twenty-four percent favoured, marriages between people of the same sex (*The Gallup Report*, May 21, 1992).

- A 1994 Canadian poll showed that thirty percent agreed that homosexuals should be allowed to adopt children, up from twenty-five percent in 1988, whereas fifty-seven percent thought they should not be allowed (*The Gallup Poll*, November 1, 1994).

- In 1993, thirty-one percent of Canadians believed that abortions should be legal under any circumstances, fifty-six percent only under certain circumstances and ten percent illegal in all circumstances. The proportion supporting legal abortions under any circumstances had increased from twenty-three percent in 1975 and 1983 to twenty-seven percent in 1990. (*The Gallup Report*, August 2, 1993).

The American data comes from Floris W. Wood, ed. *An American Profile: Opinions and Behaviors, 1972-1989* (Detroit: Gale Research, 1990).

The factors leading to increased public support for conservatism suggest that conservatism in Canada and the United States exists largely in reaction to developments in liberalism, rather than as a stand-alone ideology. Not surprisingly, the conservative movement in both countries tends to be reactionary rather than cautious; conservatives seek a quick return to a moral order. For example, opponents of gay rights do not just wish to discontinue the advances of the gay rights movement, but also seek to reverse any gains that have been made. Supporters of the antiabortion movement in the United States seek to overturn the *Roe v. Wade* Supreme Court decision that legalized abortion. An intermediate position—for example, a more limited access to abortion services—is not considered acceptable by adherents of the antiabortion movement. The belief in an objective moral order thus limits the possibility for political compromise.

Has conservatism become an ideology strong enough to compete with liberalism in Canada and the United States? Arguably, it is has not. As explained earlier, many of the economic positions articulated by the right can be attributed to classical liberalism. Despite the growing attention to moral issues, collectivism does not appear to be replacing individualism as the dominant mind-set—citizens continue to emphasize rights and liberties, as opposed to duties. Support for a natural hierarchy is weak, and the belief in meritocracy remains strong. These factors suggest that conservatism should be thought of as an important influence on our liberal societies, rather than a strong contender for ideological hegemony.

Conservatism and Party Politics

Neoconservatism and the New Right lack formal political parties in Canada and the United States, but they have influenced the thinking of many political leaders as conservatism becomes more attractive to the public. Growing public frustration with taxation, crime and "deteriorating morality" has been recognized by party politicians of all stripes, and aspects of conservatism are emerging in political rhetoric. In his 1992 American presidential campaign, Democrat Bill Clinton appealed to "community development" and social responsibility, issues not typically addressed by a reform liberal. The 1994 Republican domination in elections for the House and Senate stemmed in part from the Republicans' "Contract with America," which included many New Right positions. In Canada, the 1993 federal election illustrated growing popular support for the Reform party, a populist party whose platform included planks on morality, law and order, and immigration. The neoconservative Alberta Progressive Conservative government under leader Ralph Klein continues to receive high levels of public support, and is presented as a model of fiscal restraint to other provinces. Ontario voters chose to follow Alberta's lead, electing Mike Harris's Progressive Conservatives in 1995 and apparently endorsing an explicit conservative policy agenda.

It is undeniable that there has been a swing to the right in recent years. But how conservative are the parties that have capitalized on this swing? Can their appeal be understood as an articulation of ideological conservatism, or is it best seen as support for classical liberalism? We will examine this question by looking at two national parties in the 1990s: the Reform Party of Canada, and the American Republican party. To detect the ideological conservatism of these parties, we must look beyond the values that conservatives share with classical liberals—fiscal restraint and private ownership—and examine their social and moral views.

In the 1993 Canadian federal election, the center-right Progressive Conservative government suffered the greatest defeat in its history, dropping from 169 seats to two. Part of this debacle is attributable to the party's loss of support in the province of Quebec, where the separatist Bloc Québécois captured fifty-four of the province's seventy-five seats. But the greater factor leading to its defeat was the loss of support from the political right, particularly in western Canada. This can best be understood by examining the spatial model below. If we look at the 1993 federal election on a single left-right dimension (thus ignoring the federalist-separatist dimension that accounts for the Bloc Québécois' success), the political parties can be represented as follows:

L				R
NDP	Liberals	PC		Reform

As noted, the electorate has experienced a shift to the political right in recent years, as support for classical liberalism and conservatism has increased. In response, all parties made moves toward the right. The Liberal party can still be seen as holding a centrist position, although some would argue that it too has moved to the right *since* its election, and the New Democratic Party (NDP) occupies a center-left position. The left of the political spectrum was largely ignored. Rather than following the electorate's shift to the right, the Progressive Conservative government maintained a center-right position. This opened the party to an "invasion from the right": the Reform party captured the classical liberal and conservative vote to replace, if only temporarily, the Progressive Conservatives as the party of the right (Flanagan 1995:163).

The right-wing position of the Reform party is clear, although its leader, Preston Manning, prefers not to see the party in ideological terms (Flanagan 1995:11). But of what exactly is the right-wing support composed? Can the Reform success be accounted for in classical liberal terms, or did neoconservatism, the New Right and other elements of conservative thought play a role? These questions can be answered by looking at two variables: the Reform party platform, and the voters. The Reform party platform is outlined in its "Blue Book," in which classical liberal economic principles—in particular, fiscal responsibility and a limit on taxation—are included. The policy manual does not suggest a neoconservative approach to social welfare programs, and the party's positions on moral issues cannot be fully classified as New Right:

> One item in the party's Statement of Principles affirms "the importance of strengthening and protecting the family unit," but beyond that the Blue Book gives a wide berth to all the contemporary issues of sexual politics, such as pornography, sexual harassment, reproductive rights, employment equity and pay equity, and homosexuality (Flanagan 1995:14).

The Reform party does take a strong stand on law and order issues, a conservative position. So where does the Reform party sit with respect to conservatism? The party demonstrates conservative tendencies, but cannot be classified as reflecting one particular branch of conservatism. Thomas Flanagan (1995:15) argues that this lack of consistency is due to the divergent views of the leader, Preston Manning:

Manning holds many opinions that most people would call conservative, but they are not supported by an overall conservative philosophy. He is not consistently and strongly conservative .... Rather, he is eclectic in his thinking, and has a tendency to embrace contradictory positions in the belief that they will be reconciled in some future synthesis. He is certainly not a socialist or even a liberal, but in ideological terms he could lead a centrist party with a favourable orientation to business. He could be a Democrat like Bill Clinton, talking about productivity, economic growth, international competitiveness, level playing fields, the knowledge economy, and job retraining.

The partisan loyalties of Canadian voters are highly flexible. Studies of the 1993 election suggest that the Reform party pulled most of its support from former Progressive Conservative voters. In particular, western Canadian voters favoured the Reform party. Flanagan (1995:161) maintains that the Reform party was successful in putting together a coalition of support:

> There were both middle-class and working-class Reform voters, and they could be found in both cities (especially suburbs) and rural areas. What held these disparate groups together? Probably a positive orientation towards the private-sector economy and traditional moral values, although this needs to be tested by further research.

It is the emphasis on moral values that suggests Reform voters had been influenced by conservative values.

The 1993 election results demonstrates a strong shift to the right in Canada, a shift that cannot be accounted for solely by a return to classical liberalism. The Reform party's success was due to its ability to organize a coalition of support from the various right-wing ideologies: classical liberals, neoconservatives and the New Right. This coalition does, however, lead to tensions within the party, with some activists wishing to pursue a more economic (classical liberal) agenda and others wanting to pursue a moral social platform. The economic liberalism of the Reform party attracted many classical liberals, but the moral agenda of the party may serve to alienate its more individualist supporters. How solid Reform's ideological coalition is remains to be tested in upcoming elections.

These Canadian events were paralleled to a degree in the American elections of 1994, which saw the Republican party form the congressional majority for the first time in forty years. Unlike its platform in previous elections, the Republican party adopted a specific, detailed party platform in 1994. Two aspects of that position stand out: first, the great emphasis on government downsizing, and second, the strong moral tone. The "inaugural address" by Republican House Speaker Newt Gingrich was described as follows: "The 'most painful problems' abroad in the land he identified as 'moral problems,' and toward the end of his speech he began to talk about bringing the United States more nearly in line with the kingdom of Heaven" (Lapham 1995:32).

This emphasis on morality clearly allows us to classify the Republican position as ideologically conservative. A large state is supported for the purposes of law and order, but not for the purposes of welfare and wealth redistribution. "Traditionalism" (the family, the church) is promoted. As with the Reform Party of Canada, the American Republicans drew their support from a variety of ideological positions on the political right. Gingrich became "the shared symbol of resentment binding together the several parties of the disaffected right—the Catholic conservatives with the Jewish neoconservatives, the libertarians with the authoritarians, Pat Robertson's Christian Coalition with the disciples of [white supremacist] David Duke" (Lapham 1995:32).

The Republicans' Contract with America

A conservative moralistic tone is evident in the Contract with America. Consider its mission:

> Like Lincoln, our first Republican president, we intend to act "with firmness in the right, as God gives us to see the right." To restore accountability to Congress. To end its cycle of scandal and disgrace. To make us all proud again of the way free people govern themselves.

The policy platform embedded in the Contract with America includes: the Fiscal Responsibility Act, which calls for a balanced budget/tax limitations and a legislative line-item veto; the Taking Back Our Streets Act, which is an anticrime package; the Personal Responsibility Act, designed to discourage illegitimacy and teen pregnancy by prohibiting welfare to teenage mothers; the Family Reinforcement Act, designed to reinforce the central role of families in American society; and the Citizen Legislature Act, which proposes term limits in order to replace career politicians with citizen legislators.

The true measure of a party's ideological conservatism is found in an examination of its rhetoric and platform. If the views espoused are consistent with some or all of the basic tenets of conservatism, then the ideology has had influence. The previous discussion indicates that the conservative ideology has made inroads into both Canada and the United States, in their political parties as well as in public opinion. However, conservative views remain tempered by larger liberal values. If conservatism is to have greater success in the future, the liberal values of meritocracy, liberty and rationalism must be replaced by faith in hierarchy, order and objective morality. The ideological challenge for conservatives is a large one indeed.

NOTES

1. Although many early conservative thinkers opposed a universal franchise (as did many early liberal thinkers), few conservatives would now reject basic equality of political rights. However, the failure of the Equal Rights Amendment (ERA) in the United States (see Chapter 5) indicates that resistance to full political equality remains in society.
2. As argued in Chapter 2, liberals accept inequalities if they are due to differences in effort and talent. (Recall the meritocracy principle.) Conservatives also permit social mobility (thus, institutionalized social positions, such as a caste system, are not advocated), but are more accepting of traditional social divisions.
3. Nor, for that matter, is "right-wing" necessarily the same in Canada and the United States.
4. A common stereotype of conservatism is that it advocates the return to a previous social arrangement. Although some conservatives hold such views, it is inaccurate to consider reaction a dominant force in conservative thought.
5. The "feudal fragment" theory of Gad Horowitz is not universally accepted.
6. The aggressive stance of Margaret Thatcher's Conservative government in the Falkland Islands war further justified high levels of military expenditures.
7. Voucher systems give parents the right to select a school for their child; the school collects its government funding according to the number of vouchers it receives. It is argued that competition between schools will lead to a higher quality of education.
8. *The Gallup Poll*, May 19, 1994.

CHAPTER FOUR

Socialism: The Organic Left

*Let the ruling classes tremble at a communist revolution. The proletarians
have nothing to lose but their chains. They have a world to win.
Workers of the world, unite!*

KARL MARX

*A revolution is not a dinner party, or writing an essay, or painting a picture,
or doing embroidery, it cannot be so refined …. A revolution is an
insurrection, an act of violence by which one class overthrows another.*

MAO TSE-TUNG

*Trade unionism is killing socialism in this country,
and it is time socialists did something about it.*

PAUL JOHNSON

In Canada and the United States, socialism has been the bogeyman of all ideologies. Associated with authoritarian communism in China, Cuba and the former
Soviet bloc, and with high taxation and big government in many western European
and Scandinavian countries, socialism attracts the ire of liberals and conservatives
alike. Expressions such as "better dead than red," and derogatory labels such as
"pinkos" illustrate the strong resistance to socialism, particularly in the United States.
And this resistance, of course, is linked to the military tension that existed between
the West and the socialist states for most of the past fifty years. While the cold war
may be over, its impact on the ideological landscape of western democratic states will
persist for generations to come.

It is perhaps not surprising, then, that of the primary political ideologies, socialism is sometimes difficult for contemporary North American students to grasp, and
therefore easy to discredit, fear or dismiss. The worldview of a committed socialist
differs greatly from that of a liberal, and many are unwilling or even unable to step
outside the dominant ideological paradigm of liberalism in order to come to grips
with socialist perspectives. However, socialism is not as foreign as it may seem.
Socialism, liberalism and conservatism all grapple with the issues of liberty, equality
and order. Furthermore, the tenets of socialism overlap substantially with those of
conservatism in some areas, and with those of liberalism in others. Although social-

ism is defined in part by opposition to liberalism, it draws from a similar conceptual foundation. As M. Patricia Marchak (1988:3) writes, liberalism and socialism "are the two sides of a single coin: one describing how the entire structure looks to one who accepts it and expects it to survive; the other, how it looks to one who rejects it and anticipates its demise." In terms of public policy, social democrats often agree with reform liberals, although the reasoning that brings them to similar policy positions is very different.

The resistance among American and Canadian students to an understanding of socialism may be due in part to the immense body of thought, literature and experience the ideology encompasses. Socialist thought ranges from hard-line communism to social democracy and the margins of reform liberalism; its proponents range from Karl Marx and V. I. Lenin to moderate social democrats such as former Canadian provincial premiers T. C. "Tommy" Douglas and Dave Barrett. As with any large body of thought, one is certain to find something or someone to which one objects. Moreover, the real-world experience with applied socialism is vast. Any belief system that can be applied to czarist Russia, postwar China and industrial communities in contemporary Italy must enjoy not only great range but also great flexibility; although Fidel Castro's Cuba and the British Labour party may share some principled points of departure, they differ far more than they converge. As with liberalism and conservatism, the same fundamental beliefs can lead to a wide array of policy positions, and this is never so clear as within socialism. In fact, the differences and antagonisms between socialism's two dominant schools—social democracy and communism—are so great that it is often hard to believe that they grew from the same ideological soil. It is for these reasons that the late American socialist Michael Harrington (1989:28) suggests that it is more appropriate to speak of socialism*s* than socialism.

While it may be difficult to attain, understanding socialism is important for a number of reasons. First, socialism is not without ideological importance in North America. There have been significant socialist movements and parties in Canada, and although socialism has had less impact in the United States, it has nevertheless played a role in the ideological debates that have shaped the American system. The New Left, for example, was an influential ideological force in the United States during the 1960s and early 1970s; in addition to bolstering socialist ideologies, it inadvertently encouraged the growth of American conservatism. Contemporary socialist thought contributes to many variants of feminism and environmentalism in both Canada and the United States.

Second, understanding socialism furthers one's appreciation of liberalism and conservatism. In particular, a greater knowledge of socialist thought allows us to identify some of the important differences between socialism and reform liberalism—differences that are often blurred in public-policy debates. Reform liberals have sometimes adapted and even adopted socialist policies, although the original spirit and intent of those policies have been altered by their placement within a liberal framework. In making these changes, the liberal left has undermined the larger socialist program: why adopt socialism, one may well ask, when all, or much of it, can be achieved within the liberal system? Yet, occasional policy similarities aside, the principled core of socialism differs greatly from that of liberalism. In many ways, socialism is more similar to conservatism than to liberalism. This may seem counterintuitive, considering the often-assumed locations of socialism and conservatism on opposing poles of the left-right spectrum, but socialism and conservatism share an emphasis on the political *community* that liberalism lacks. An appreciation of the tenets of socialism, therefore, allows for a better understanding of both conservatism and liberalism.

Third, a knowledge of socialist thought is vital for students with an interest in the broader international picture. It is particularly important that North American students not let their own ideological environment lead them to underestimate socialism's global appeal. At least until very recent times, socialism in its various forms was the dominant ideology outside North America (Levine 1988:3). For better or worse, communism has played a defining role in the political evolution of the twentieth century. The communist revolutions in China and Russia were truly monumental events, and communism remains a powerful ideological force today in China, Cuba, North Korea and Vietnam. Socialist thought in other forms, including liberation theology, continues to be an influential ideological current across the developing world. Social democracy, in many ways the most relevant branch of socialism for most readers, has also been a very significant influence on the world stage. Contemporary European politics clearly demonstrate that this variant of socialism is neither dead nor irrelevant, and as social democracy frees itself from the burden of the cold war, it may well broaden its base of popular and intellectual support.

Finally, it is premature to announce the demise of socialism even though opposing ideological perspectives may be in ascendancy. The currents of ideological change at work in the world are by no means unidirectional in their effect. While it is undoubtedly true that socialism has been buffeted by recent forms of ideological change, and by an enthusiastic embrace of the free market around the world, there are other ideological currents at work which may act to reinforce, rather than erode, the ideological perspectives associated with socialism. In short, an understanding of socialism may not only help the reader understand the ideological past, but may also provide some useful insights into the ideological future.

This chapter begins by outlining the basic tenets of socialist thought, and by comparing them with the tenets of liberalism and conservatism. After establishing these fundamentals, we will distinguish between social democracy and communism, showing how common ground in political principles has given rise to radically different ideological positions. In these contexts, the distinction between social democracy and reform liberalism will be discussed. The discussion then turns to the evolution of socialist thought, first in a non–North American setting, and then as socialist ideas began to wash ashore in Canada and the United States during the late-nineteenth and early-twentieth centuries. Of particular interest here is the relatively infertile soil that North America provided for socialist thought, and the impact of international politics on the reception given to socialist ideas. The discussion will conclude with the future of socialism.

Exercise One: Preconceptions About Socialism

What are your preconceptions about socialism? What views do you think socialists hold on the following issues: welfare programs; abortion; the free market; law and order; religion and the state; the role of women in society; gay and lesbian rights; affirmative action? What general leanings can you detect from your list? Do you think socialists are optimistic or pessimistic? Relativistic or absolutist? Egalitarian or elitist? Hold on to your list as you read the next section to determine if your initial understanding of socialism fits with the ideology of socialism.

BASIC TENETS OF SOCIALISM

We saw with liberalism and conservatism that the policy positions and general orientations manifest in an ideology fall from its underlying assumptions about human nature. This is also true of socialism. Socialists stand apart from liberals, and particularly conservatives, in that they hold a highly optimistic view of humankind. The socialist believes that given the right conditions, humans are socially oriented beings who have the potential to be cooperative, rational and community-interested. The key word is "potential." Socialists do not claim that humans are or must be such positive beings; in fact, they may at times act like the competitive individualist in the liberal worldview, or the impulsive personality in the conservative conception. However, they do not see human nature as fixed or constant, but rather believe it is malleable and that progress is possible. Like liberals, socialists believe that the human capacity for reason can make the world better. Thus, while conservatives recoil from the prospect of social engineering, socialists embrace it, believing that social institutions can be rationally designed to foster a cooperative community.

In this sense, there is a utopian, forward-looking tone to socialist thought that is largely absent from liberalism and conservatism. Leon Baradat (1994:180–1), for example, discusses the "socialist intent," which he defines as the "goal of setting people free from the condition of material dependence that has imprisoned them since the beginning of time." Socialists, then, seek to uncover our *true* selves, the compassionate and cooperative beings who are presently buried beneath and within dysfunctional institutions.[1] As Baradat explains, the socialist vision is truly utopian[2] in nature:

> [S]ocialism is much more than an economic system. It goes far beyond the socialization of the economy and the redistribution of wealth. It foresees a completely new relationship among individuals based on a plentiful supply of material goods. Its goal is a completely new social order in which human cooperation is the basis of conduct and productivity.

There is, then, a crusading tone to socialism that conservatism and liberalism lack. Canadian socialist Cy Gonick (1992:221) nicely captures the emotional and utopian aspects of socialism's appeal as follows:

> [P]eople do not just fight and give a big part of their lives to building a movement and a new society that promises fairer taxes, better wages and improved health care.

This is not what motivates the human struggle and neither does some abstract principle like equality. We have to relate to and address what people really do want—love, commitment and community—and show how fulfillment of these needs are utterly denied by capitalism and can only be realised through socialism.

It is not surprising, therefore, that we find frequent references to the "New Jerusalem," to the possibility of heaven on earth, in socialist texts and speeches. Many of the early socialist movements in Canada drew their leadership from the clergy, for whom socialism provided a secular extension of their religious beliefs. Their political goal was to improve the spiritual and *material* conditions of the secular world. The Social Gospel movement during the early decades of the twentieth century (Allen 1973) was decidedly religious in tone and socialist in its social policy objectives. As Michael Harrington (1989:266) explains more generally, socialism "deals with putting an end to the *unnecessary* evil of the world that is caused by economic and social structures."

Socialists argue that it is the *organization* of society that determines the state of human nature: humans meet the expectations of and are shaped by social and economic systems. Given the right circumstances, humans are by nature cooperative and selfless; put in the wrong circumstances, they are competitive and selfish. Liberalism and conservatism are flawed, socialists maintain, because they are based on an incomplete or inaccurate picture of humanity, one that does not allow it to reach its true potential. For example, liberalism bases its socioeconomic system (capitalism) on the conception of a competitive, self-interested human being. This assumption, socialists believe, locks the individual into that very description, and becomes a self-fulfilling prophesy. Because we expect people to act this a way, we design a system that ensures they will in fact exhibit these behaviours. The liberal system does not allow the cooperative, socially oriented side of human beings to emerge. This difference is linked to the different ideological perspectives on human nature discussed above. Because liberals and conservatives feel human nature is constant, they mould their systems to fit this nature. Socialists, however, feel that economic and social systems can be designed to encourage cooperation and community, that people are in control, not only of their individual destinies, but also of their social destinies. If forced to choose between "nature" and "nurture" as the dominant force in human affairs, socialists will choose nurture.

To create a cooperative and community-oriented system, one must do away with social arrangements that encourage self-interested, competitive behaviour, and replace them with arrangements that promote more "positive" qualities. Sounds simple enough. But what are the institutions that prevent the positive side of human nature from emerging? Socialists point first to the economic system, believing that how we meet our primary needs (food, shelter and clothing) has a greater impact on the form society takes than any other factor. In this sense, classical socialists are economic determinists who believe that the economic horse pulls the social cart.[3] There are clear differences, socialists assert, between systems which aim to meet the needs of all of society, and those which leave each man to fend for himself. To promote the socially oriented side of humanity, the economic system must be based on egalitarian principles designed to satisfy the needs of all in a fair and equitable manner. Distributive justice, rather than economic efficiency, is the principal concern, although socialists would reject the necessity of tension between the two. It should be possible, they would argue, to redistribute the fruits of the economic system in a way that promotes equality and social justice while not undermining the efficiency of the system itself.

If the economic system is to be based on more egalitarian principles, something has to be done about the unequal distribution of private property. It is not surprising, then, that socialism has entailed varying degrees of challenge to private property. It is also therefore not surprising that the propertied classes, those who have far more to lose than their chains, have been the most vigorous opponents of socialism. In the *Communist Manifesto* (1848), Karl Marx summed up the basic philosophy of communism in only four words: "Abolition of private property." Instead of private property, socialists advocate that at least the primary means of production should be publicly owned. Indeed, if there is a conceptual core to socialist thought, it is to be found in the principle of public (or social) ownership (Balcerowicz 1991:68; Levine 1988; von Mises 1981:211). Andrew Heywood explains (1992:104) that socialists criticize private property because it is unjust, because it breeds acquisitiveness and materialism and because it fosters social conflict between the haves and the have-nots. Vincent Geoghegan (1984:123–4) suggests that private property "makes individuals

---

Communism and Socialism

- The issue is Socialism versus Capitalism. I am for Socialism because I am for humanity. - Eugene Debs, Socialist party candidate for the American presidency, 1897 speech.

- There is little reason to believe that this socialism will mean the advent of the civilization of which orthodox socialists dream. It is much more likely to present fascist features. That would be a strange answer to Marx's prayer. But history sometimes indulges in jokes of questionable taste. - Joseph Schumpeter, *Capitalism, Socialism, and Democracy*, 1942.

- Property is exploitation of the weak by the strong. Communism is exploitation of the strong by the weak. - Pierre Joseph Proudhon, *What is Property?*, 1840.

- If the Labour Party is not going to be a Socialist Party, I don't want to lead it …. When you join a team in the expectation that you are going to play rugger, you can't be expected to be enthusiastic if you are asked to play tiddly-winks. - Aneurin Bevan, speech in 1956.

- Marxian Socialism must always remain a portent to the historians of opinion—how a doctrine so illogical and so dull can have exercised so powerful and enduring an influence over the minds of men, and, through them, the events of history. - John Maynard Keynes, *The End of Laissez-Faire*, 1925.

- Every Communist must grasp the truth: political power grows out of the barrel of a gun. - Mao Tse-tung, 1938.

- Discovering Marxism … was like finding a map in the forest. - Fidel Castro, 1971.

- To the masses the catchwords of Socialism sound enticing and the people impetuously desire Socialism because in their infatuation they expect it to bring full salvation and satisfy their longing for revenge. And so they will continue to work for Socialism, helping thereby to bring about the inevitable decline of the civilization which the nations of the West have taken thousands of years to build up. And so we must inevitably drift on to chaos and misery, the darkness of barbarism and annihilation. - Ludwig von Mises (1981:13).

so concerned with their own survival and prosperity that the public good is lost sight of and government becomes merely an instrument of class domination." The more extreme forms of socialism, such as communism, advocate the *abolition* of private property, but even milder forms advocate *restrictions* on private property. Social democrats, for example, long supported inheritance taxes designed to prevent the transfer of property across generations.

The materialist underpinnings of socialist thought does not mean, incidentally, that socialists neglect the arts. As Louis Patsouras and Jack Ray Thomas (1981:xix–xx) point out, "The Socialist quest for justice, equality, and fraternity, and to replace a world with varying degrees of inequality, injustice, and the attendance alienation, has a significant artistic-spiritual dimension that could not but attract many artists...." Not surprisingly, support for socialist principles has often been relatively high within artistic communities. Nonetheless, economics play the primary role in socialist thought.

Like conservatism, socialism is based on an organic conception of society, but the collectivist emphasis of socialism is much more pronounced. Andrew Heywood (1992:96) writes that "at its heart, socialism possesses a unifying vision of human beings as social creatures, capable of overcoming social and economic problems by drawing upon the power of the community rather than simply individual effort." Thus, where liberalism emphasizes and relies upon the individual, socialism emphasizes and relies upon the community. George Lichtheim (1970:4) maintains that the organic, community-centred nature of socialism "is rooted in sentiments as ancient and permanent as human society itself." By contrast, individualism is a "comparatively recent faith." But socialists do not simply contrast their values with the individualism of liberalism; they actively reject that individualism in favour of social order: "On the whole, socialism places society first, and points to the chaos and conflicts which may result from unbridled individualism, pleading for an ordered state in which the community, or some authority representing the community, would have the ordering of things" (Gray 1946:489). As Anthony Wright (1986:24) explains, this opposition to individualism, the foundational value of liberalism, is of fundamental importance for an understanding of socialist thought:

> It is the assault on individualism, the ideology of capitalism, that has been the common ground of socialist arguments. This ideological veneer concealed the character of capitalist exploitation. Its competitive, self-regarding values thwarted human cooperation and fraternity. It stunted the individual personality and destroyed the possibility of real community. It elevated private greed and ignored public need. The terms of this indictment are common to the whole range of socialist literature, though the presentation may vary.

Socialists, like conservatives, feel that each person has a responsibility to the larger whole, and that the larger whole has a responsibility to each person. However, conservatives accept and respect natural inequalities; duty is limited to ensuring that all maintain a minimal level of sustenance. In contrast, socialists eschew inequities, and it is here we find the source of socialist support for the cradle-to-grave welfare state. Social responsibility is not limited to bare sustenance, socialists maintain, but rather extends to the social well-being of all community members. If liberty is the cornerstone for liberalism and order functions similarly for conservatism, *equality* is the cornerstone for socialism. If forced to choose between liberty and equality, socialists are likely to opt for equality. Or, put somewhat differently, socialists see at least a modicum of equality as a precondition for liberty; liberty without equality is seen to be a hollow sham.

The egalitarianism of socialism is linked to a particular conception of liberty. Socialists argue that liberty is a social, rather than individual, property: either all are free, or none is truly free. As Theotonia dos Santos (1985:182) explains, the socialist conception of liberty, unlike the liberal conception, is embedded in the community: "Freedom is therefore the supreme ideal of socialism. By freedom should be understood the full development of the individual *through his community*" (emphasis added). The emphasis is also on *positive* liberty, or the ability to act. As noted in Chapter 2, positive liberty is conceptually linked to high levels of equality. Socialists go beyond equality of right or even equality of opportunity to favour equality of result, as is suggested in the Marxist slogan "From each according to his ability, to each according to his need." They maintain that the negative freedom associated with liberalism, freedom as the absence of constraint, is shallow and contradictory "because the liberty of the 'free' market undermines the freedom formally enshrined in social and political rights; the market produces poverty and poor individuals cannot be fully free" (Geoghegan 1984:116). This conception of freedom expands the political equality associated with liberalism into the economic realm, and to the pursuit of equality of result. This is an expansion that liberals tend to oppose because it entails too great a role for the state, too great a threat to private property, and because it ignores the important fact that individuals are free in law to allocate their talents, aptitudes and inclinations. Admittedly, socialists vary in the degree to which they support equality of result; for some, it means reducing but not eliminating class differences. Yet, regardless of its form, equality of result is a radical departure from the liberal system of meritocracy, and requires a very different and much more expansive role for the state.

The Primacy of Class

Part of what sets socialism apart from other ideological perspectives is the primacy it attaches to social class. While socialists are by no means blind to other forms of social differentiation, class is seen as the most important in any political analysis. James L. Marsh (1991:172–3) explains:

> The tendency now in leftist circles is to talk about racism, sexism, and class domination as distinct, co-equal forms of domination. This tendency is understandable in the light of the economism and reductionism of much of the Marxist left, but is finally not justified. Three models are possible here, a vulgar Marxist model that denies any autonomy at all to the sexual or racial domains, the three-sector model mentioned above, and a sophisticated Marxist model that asserts the dominance of class exploitation but allows autonomy to the other two spheres. The sophisticated Marxist approach is the best account ....
>
> Why is class domination ultimately more fundamental and overriding? It is more universal, extending over the United States and Western Europe as well as over the Third World in Africa, Asia, and South America, covering women and blacks and many men and whites. Class struggle is the most antagonistic of conflicts—fundamental cooperation is emerging between the sexes and the races but not between labor and capital. Racism and sexism we have rejected in principle but not capitalism.

Equality of result necessitates the redistribution of wealth, and therefore the state must have the capacity to redistribute income, wealth and property. How does this state allocation of resources fit with capitalism, free enterprise and economic competition? As one might expect, equality of result and capitalism blend like oil and water. The redistribution of wealth requires state intrusion into the economy: the state either removes resources from some and gives them to others, or ensures that the original distribution of property is equitable. Reform liberals are willing to do the former within the context of the free market system, and rely upon progressive income taxes as their primary instrument. Socialists, however, feel that private property by its very nature undermines communalism and cooperation. Systems that allow for the unequal accumulation of property create different classes of citizens, which negates social equality. According to socialists, this is particularly true when private property constitutes the means of production within the economy. For example, a person who owns a silver mine not only possesses that property, placing her at an unequal status, but also has the potential to create for herself greater wealth. Thus, she has a tremendous economic advantage over the rest of society. Control over the means of production is therefore a more significant source of social inequity than are minor forms of private property (such as a house or car).

For these reasons, socialists argue that the state should control at least the major means of production in a society. Nationalized corporations and industries reduce inequalities by giving every member of society an equal share in the means of production. Public ownership is advocated for another reason: socialist theory maintains that it allows the state to better control and plan the economy. Public control allows production to be structured so that it benefits all, rather than a few which, socialists argue, is the case with the free market. As Leszek Balcerowicz (1991:69) explains, "The core of the socialist economy is the overall economic planning, which substitutes for the market, and private ownership is condemned *because* it makes such planning impossible by giving rise to the spontaneous, anarchic interactions in the economy." It should also be noted that cooperatives, in which profits are returned to the membership, do not qualify as public ownership within socialist theory. Andrew Levine (1988:6) points out, "*Public* ownership means ownership by the public; not by some constituent part of it." Therefore, both the large producer cooperatives that played such an important role in the agrarian settlement of the Canadian West, and contemporary consumer cooperatives, should best be seen as a modification of free market principles rather than as the extension of socialist principles into the North American scene.

Socialists note two additional flaws with capitalism. The first is that its benefits are uneven; some individuals achieve great wealth, whereas others earn just enough to get by, if that. This creates sharply defined and interdependent social classes. Those who own the means of production, referred to as the capitalists (or the bourgeoisie), are dependent upon the workers (or proletariat) for labour, and the workers are dependent upon the owners for wages. However, capital carries more clout than labour, unless the latter is well organized. A cycle of negativity therefore emerges, with the owners exploiting the workers. In this system, socialists argue, all are dehumanized and alienated from their social, compassionate side. Public ownership, in contrast, would enable the state to create a "classless society" and thereby eliminate major social divisions. The second flaw is that capitalist economies run in "boom or bust" cycles: periods of prosperity are followed by periods of recession and sometimes devastating depression. Socialists believe that the economy can be planned to eliminate these cycles, allowing for greater economic stability. However, it should be stressed that the primary argument against capitalism is based upon its negative effects on human nature. A "perfect" capitalist system, free from fluctuations, would still be flawed in the eyes of the socialist, for it would continue to generate and perpetuate inequalities in wealth and social status.

Socialist thought incorporates a complex body of economic principles, political theories and assumptions about human nature. While it overlaps at times with liberalism and conservatism, socialist thought constitutes a distinctive, and in most respects unique, ideological constellation. Its basic tenets can be summarized as follows:

- socialists have an optimistic view of human nature, one that often blends into utopian visions;

- socialists believe that human nature is malleable, and that social and economic institutions can be engineered so as to enable people to live cooperative and community-oriented lives;

- socialists believe that private property should be restricted, if not eliminated; at the very least, the principal means of production should be publicly, rather than privately, owned;

- socialists posit an organic view of society, and reject the unbridled individualism of liberalism in favour of greater order and social responsibility; this supports, in turn, a belief in the virtues of a planned economy;

- socialists place great emphasis on political and economic equality, and argue that the former is contingent upon some reasonable measure of the latter; and

- socialists believe in positive liberty, or the freedom to act; this entails both state intervention and the assumption that true liberty can only be realized within a community context.

As you can see, it would be a mistake to identify socialism solely as support for state ownership and opposition to capitalism. These policies are merely means to a greater end (Qualter 1986:239)—namely, a cooperative society that maximizes humankind's potential. What is important to recognize in socialist thought is its utopian *spirit*. It is this spirit as much as anything else that separates socialism from reform liberalism, and from the benevolent paternalism of classical conservatives.

The basic tenets of socialism are supported by virtually all forms of socialist thought. What, then, explains the radical differences between socialism's two major branches, communism and social democracy? In part, the difference is one of degree. Social democrats, for example, may be satisfied with only a modicum of public ownership, or even with a heavily regulated form of private enterprise, whereas communists are committed to extensive public ownership. The distinction between the two branches also revolves around how socialism should come into effect, and how the socialist state should be structured. It is to disputes on these points that we now turn.

The Ideology of Socialism

- *scope*: Addresses virtually all political issues, although only some forms of socialism embrace private morality. Strong focus on economic issues. Socialism has been brought into play around the world.

- *internal consistency*: Argues that human nature is malleable; a positively constructed socioeconomic system creates a positive human. Restructuring the economy is the key to establishing a positive system.

- *durability*: Socialism has been an important ideology for over 150 years.

- *normative framework*: Humans have the potential to live cooperatively and equally; economic and political systems should be structured to encourage communalism and equality. Society is an organic whole; the exploitation and misery of one undermines the whole.

- *practical guide for political action*: The free market should be replaced (at least partially) by a state-run and centrally planned economy. Private property should be restricted and class divisions reduced or eliminated. Social democrats seek to achieve these ends democratically, whereas communists believe that the existing capitalist system can only be overthrown by force.

- *formal articulation*: Socialist thought has generated an immense volume of written text. Although much of this material finds its intellectual roots in the works of Engels, Lenin and Marx, there have been a host of independent contributors, including Saint-Simon, Charles Fourier, Robert Owen, T. H. Green, G.D.H. Cole and Harold Laski.

BRANCHES OF SOCIALIST THOUGHT

The differences between social democracy and communism are great, and social democratic states bear little resemblance to communist states. Many of the differences stem from beliefs about how socialism should emerge. Social democrats feel that socialism will evolve naturally over time, and they are willing, therefore, to work within the constraints of constitutional democracy. Thus, social democrats form political parties and contest elections. They believe that people will come to recognize the advantages of the social democratic state, and will rationally choose to elect a social democratic government, which will maintain power through democratic elections. This approach has been the dominant form of socialism in western democratic states. It has been expressed in Christian democratic thought, which has bridged the moral and ethical concerns of Christianity with the secular political agenda of socialism, and in the democratic socialism associated with the British Fabian Society at the turn of the twentieth century. It also reflects a strong and optimistic faith in the power of political education.

By contrast, communists feel that socialism will be brought about only by a revolution of the proletariat; there is no confidence that the ruling class will step down voluntarily in the face of electoral defeat. Therefore, the working class must recognize its oppression, rise up and violently overthrow the ruling capitalists—Workers of the world, unite! In this process, a critically important role is played by the

Communist party vanguard which, it is argued, is better able than the proletariat itself to discern the long-term interests of the working class. The vision of the party, unlike the vision of the proletariat, is not blurred by false consciousness. Revolution would be followed by the "dictatorship of the proletariat," during which all opposition and threats to socialism would be removed. Once socialism ceases to be threatened, the dictatorship would wither away, and a stateless, communal society would emerge. As Karl Marx wrote in *Das Kapital* (1867:83), "As soon as the goal of the proletarian movement, the abolition of classes, shall have been reached, the power of the state, whose function is to keep the great majority of producers beneath the yoke of a small minority of exploiters, will disappear and governmental functions will be transformed into simple administrative functions." As we have seen with communist revolutions in China, Cuba, Russia and other countries, the dictatorship of the proletariat has been very slow to wither. In practice, it has become the dictatorship of the Communist party, and thus communism has been associated with the creation of totalitarian states. Such states are as different as they can get from the minimalist, watchdog states associated with classical liberalism.

The evolution-or-revolution distinction reveals fundamental differences between the two branches of socialist thought. Social democrats are willing to "work within the system," and do not seek radical social change. The social democrat does not insist on absolute equality of result, only that results are relatively equalized. She wishes to narrow the gap between the wealthiest and the poorest, but believes that pursuing full equality of result is futile. After a certain point, the law of diminishing returns kicks in—the efforts necessary to produce greater and greater levels of equality are not seen to merit the extra state effort. The goal is to reduce, rather than abolish, class divisions. Social democrats seek a balance between liberty and equality, and are prepared to sacrifice only a modest degree of the former in pursuit of the latter.

The flexibility of social democrats is discernible in their approach to the economy. Social democrats insist, at the most, that all major means of production be nationalized; even relatively extreme social democrats concede that minor means of production may remain in private hands, and private property is accepted. Thus, it is primarily large industries that are to be owned and controlled by the state within a *command economy*. The social democratic mainstream advocates a *mixed economy,* one that allows for a modest degree of competition, while encouraging social cooperation. Social democrats may even avoid public ownership altogether, relying instead on a combination of taxes and economic regulations to redistribute wealth and direct economic growth. Social democrats, therefore, "seek to tame capitalism rather than abolish it" (Heywood 1992:103). The market is not rejected as a system of allocation, but is to be regulated, controlled and supplemented by public enterprise. What is sought is "democratic control of market forces" (Hudelson 1993:162). Or, as Leon Baradat (1994:178) describes the New Deal programs introduced in the early 1930s by American president Franklin D. Roosevelt, they "injected enough socialism into the system to give capitalism a human face." The willingness of social democrats to accept the free market, and to do so under the rhetorical umbrella of socialism, has muddied the conceptual terrain.

If social democrats can be seen as flexible and democratic, communists can be seen as inflexible and, in practice, undemocratic. Communists are less willing to compromise socialist principles; they pursue a stricter level of equality of result, and do not accept a mixed economy. In the communist system, the state controls all property and means of production. For example, the government owned all land in the former Soviet Union. Farmers were allotted land to work, but did not own the property. Admittedly, early theoretical forms of Marxism were emphatically democratic, advocating expanded political rights, universal suffrage, free and frequent elections and the expansion of political equality into the economic realm. In this sense, Marxism sought to extend, rather than curtail, democracy. In the view of Marx and Engels, the dictatorship of the proletariat "was a dictatorship only in the sense that in it the majority class, the proletariat, had the power to pass and enforce laws in its own interests" (Hudelson 1993:151). The democratic aspects of Marxist thought, however, were soon lost from view when communist states emerged.

The undemocratic side of communism that came to the fore can be explained in part by the belief that dictatorship is a necessary but temporary measure, although in practice it has yet to be replaced by community-oriented anarchy. From a communist perspective, competing political parties and conventional democratic elections would make sense only if there were competing class interests. In a classless society, however, there would be no need for party competition; a single party—the Communist party—would be able to represent all interests within society. Communists believe that until a classless society has been achieved, elections are little more than a sham competition between factions of the ruling class, a smoke

FIGURE 4.1: Socialism on the Ideological Landscape

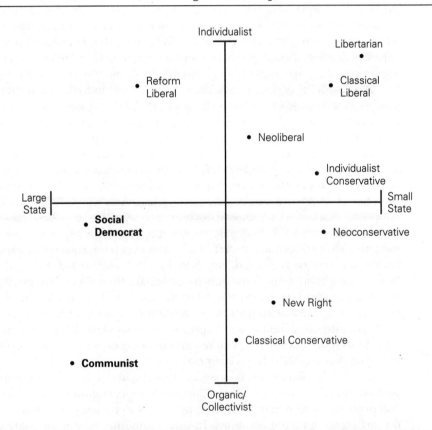

screen for capitalist control. We find, then, that communist parties such as the Communist Party in Canada (note "in," not "of") competed in elections in order to expose the sham rather than to make a serious bid to win office. The small number of votes received by communist candidates was taken as evidence that the system was corrupt, and never as evidence that communism itself was unpopular.

The position of social democracy and communism on the ideological landscape is represented in figure 4.1. The social democrat is both more collectivist and more supportive of the large state than the reform liberal. However, when compared to the communist, the social democrat appears moderate. Communism exhibits high support for both collectivism and the large state, and in both respects constitutes the polar opposite of classical liberalism. Seen in this light, the historical tension between communism and classical liberalism (and the forms of conservatism that incorporate classical liberal thought) is understandable.

EVOLUTION OF SOCIALIST THOUGHT AND PRACTICE

Socialist thought has a long and rich history, dating back over two thousand years, although the term "socialism" was not used until 1827 (Geoghagen, 1984:123). The idea of communal society is first presented in Plato's *The Republic* (circa 380 B.C.), in which he advocated that one class of society, the Guardians, share their property and spouses in common in order to advance social unity. Communal living was also advocated in early Christian thought, particularly in monastic orders. A literary version of socialism was espoused in Thomas More's *Utopia*, published in 1516. More believed that private property divided society into "an idle, extravagant, greedy, unscrupulous minority on one hand, and a poor, wretched and exploited majority on the other" (Geoghagen 1984:123). He recommended, therefore, that money be abolished, and each person have access only to the property needed for survival. Despite such philosophic musings, however, socialism remained primarily a utopian ideal, rather than a practice. Attempts at socialist communities were infrequent and typically short-lived; socialism was nowhere near the fully articulated political ideology we know today. The early religious impulse behind socialism faded, and was not reignited until the early twentieth century when, in North America, Christian reformers played a substantial role in injecting socialist principles into the political system. Then we saw, for example, the Social Gospel movement in Canada, and the heavy involvement of Protestant clergy in radical agrarian reform movements characterized by strong socialist beliefs. More recently, liberation theology in the Third World expresses the fusion of Christian beliefs and socialist principles. Christian concerns with the unfortunate formed a natural bridge to socialist thought; the belief that the meek shall inherit the earth is not far removed from the aspirations of socialists, although meekness is not characteristic of socialist thought and practice.

Ideological life was first breathed into socialism with the industrialization of society. The Industrial Revolution which swept across western Europe in the nineteenth century was characterized by urban poverty, unsafe work conditions, long hours and low wages, and child labour. The social-class differences of feudalism were replaced by the economic-class differences of liberalism. There were three dominant reactions to the inhumane side of capitalism and the worst effects of the Industrial Revolution. The first, noted in Chapter 2, was reform liberalism: the desire to address capitalism's inadequacies and problems within the liberal framework. The second, discussed in Chapter 3, was classical conservatism: the desire to return to the agrarian society of the feudal past, and benevolent paternalism. The third response was socialism: the desire to address "the harsh and often inhuman conditions in which the industrial working class lived and worked" (Heywood 1992:94) by replacing capitalism with a new and better economic system. Private ownership of the means of production, and the inherent inequalities embedded therein, were to be replaced by social ownership and thus greater equality. Like conservatism, socialism did not emerge as an ideological force until the advent of liberalism; it was a reaction to and an indictment of liberalism as an economic doctrine (Lichtheim 1970:29). Both conservatives and socialists objected to the individualism of liberal thought, preferring an organic conception of society. However, whereas conservatives felt that liberals were overly optimistic about human nature and individual potential, socialists held the opposite view.

Recall that the Industrial Revolution occurred in the wake of the Enlightenment and its glorification of science. It is not surprising, therefore, that many eighteenth- and nineteenth-century thinkers who began to articulate socialist theories did so on a "scientific" basis; Richard Hudelson (1993:149) maintains that "the Communist movement grew out of the disparity between the hope of the Enlightenment and the reality of nineteenth-century capitalism." French thinker Saint-Simon, for example, argued that expert planning could create a better economic system than laissez-faire capitalism (Ball and Dagger 1995:126). Positivist Auguste Compte advanced the view that history was progressing according to scientific laws, with an expertly planned socialist state as the end point.

The nineteenth century witnessed the emergence of *utopian socialism*. Two writers, Charles Fourier and Robert Owen, encouraged the creation of hundreds of small socialist settlements in the United States. These communities, derisively described by some as "pocket editions of the New Jerusalem," were to be self-sufficient; all members would hold equal property and share equal responsibilities. The idea was to convert others by showing how successful socialism could be in practice. However, the communes were short-lived and ultimately unsuccessful. The lesson presented was exactly the opposite of what had been intended; socialism, it seemed, failed to provide a practical alternative to capitalism and the free market. The conclusion drawn by the proponents of socialism was that socialism could not be introduced from the bottom up, that more fundamental changes to the *system* were essential.

Socialist thought gained prominent attention with the work of Karl Marx and Friedrich Engels, who based their theories on a progressive, or evolutionary, belief in history. (Marx and Engels published the *Manifesto of the Communist Party* [*The Communist Manifesto*] in 1848; Marx published *Das Kapital* in 1867.) In this sense, Marxist theory drew from science rather than from moral concerns. Like Georg Wilhelm Friedrich Hegel before him, Marx felt that history is a directed rather than random process. For Marx, the evolution from feudalism to capitalism was inevitable, just as the evolution from capitalism to socialism would be inevitable. Although Marxist theory is most strongly associated with communism, it has had a profound impact across the entire spectrum of socialist thought. It is not surprising that, to many people, "socialism," "communism" and "Marxism" are interchangeable terms. However, it is important to remember that while all Marxists are socialists, not all socialists are Marxists (Baradat 1994:174).

Marx introduced a number of key concepts to socialist thought. First, he developed the notion of opposing classes. Previous thinkers had suggested that socialism would emerge from a broad social consensus; Marx asserted that socialism would emerge when the working class wrested power from the capitalists. Second, it is in the writings of Marx that the link between the economic system and human nature is defined. Marx emphasized the class divisions that occur under capitalism, arguing that such conditions cause man to become alienated from his very nature. For Marx, capitalism placed greater value on the accumulation of capital than on human needs. Third, and perhaps most important, Marx argued that capitalism contained within itself the seeds of its destruction. By creating an alienated working class, capitalism brought together the force that would overthrow it.

Marx's reasoning was guided by *dialectical materialism.* Dialectics is a method of reasoning that sees progress emerging from the conflict of two opposing forces; the *thesis* leads to the *antithesis*, conflict between the two produces a *synthesis*, which then becomes the thesis in the next cycle. Hegel used an idealistic dialectical method to argue that consciousness determines history, and that thought creates reality. Marx rejected this idealism, and combined dialectics with materialism, a philosophic school that emphasizes the material world above the metaphysical (consciousness), and relies on science rather than faith. Thus, Marx regarded dialectical materialism as a scientific, rather than idealistic, interpretation of history.

How did dialectical materialism lead Marx to conclude that capitalism would destroy itself? Marx argued that history is defined by the progression and evolution of five modes of production: primitive community, slavery, feudalism, capitalism and socialism. Human society evolves from one mode to another as a result of conflicts, struggles and internal contradictions. For example, the feudal nobility's desire for luxury items allowed a merchant class to emerge; the class undermined the serf-lord relationship and led to the development of capitalism (Baradat 1994:163). Capitalism, in turn, is seen by Marxists as a necessary stage in the progress towards socialism. Marx identified class conflict as the Achilles' heel of capitalism: the working class becomes increasingly unhappy and alienated, and realizes that the capitalist system is the source of their problems. Marx predicted that the working class, led by socialist intellectuals, would overthrow the capitalists; after a brief "dictatorship of the proletariat," the state would "wither away," leaving behind a communal system. The ultimate goal of a stateless society provided an important bridge between Marxism and anarchism. This latter school of utopian thought, which found expression through such writers as Mikhail Bakunin, Jean Grave, Pëtr Kropotkin and Pierre-Joseph Proudhon, was very influential during the late-nineteenth and early-twentieth century. However, the common ground between anarchism and Marxism disappeared when emergent communist states proved to be as far removed from anarchical societies as it is possible to get.

In the Marxist framework, capitalism was a necessary condition for the emergence of socialism. Socialism was considered not so much as an alternative to capitalism as its *successor,* "a different, separate and higher pattern of organisation of human society" (Bus 1991:47). As Andrew Levine (1988:7) explains, "Socialism is post-capitalism: capitalism without private property in means of production." Marx predicted that the natural and inevitable evolution towards socialism would occur internationally over time, with the timing in any particular country being contingent on its stage of capitalist development. In this sense, Marx believed in an *historical materialism* in which economics provided the motive force for human affairs, and morality, religion, art and philosophy provided the ideological superstructure.

Exercise Two: Testing Socialist Views

How disposed are you to the ideological tenets of socialism? Take the following test and note whether you "agree" or "disagree" with each statement. There are no right or wrong answers; the questions are simply designed to identify your preferences. They do so, moreover, in a very rough-and-ready fashion. No claim is made that our scale captures the nuances of socialist thought.

1. Given the opportunity, we all have the potential and desire to act in a cooperative manner.
2. Poverty undermines one's basic humanity.
3. Without a competitive system, no one would have any incentive to work.
4. Our duty to others is limited to ensuring that no one starves.
5. The idea that anyone can succeed if they work hard enough is a myth—the system is structured such that some people can never get ahead.
6. Freedom exists when no one constrains your actions.
7. Society is divided into economic classes; the class into which you are born is usually the class in which you will die.
8. The free market may be imperfect, but a state-run economy would be much worse.
9. Nationalizing industry will reduce social inequalities.
10. Regardless of what we do, we will never achieve full equality; attempts to do so are futile.

Score one point for each "agree" on questions 1, 2, 5, 7 and 9, and one point for every "disagree" on questions 3, 4, 6, 8 and 10. Low total scores reflect little support for socialism; high scores indicate strong socialist leanings.

How would the working class overthrow the capitalists? Marx suggested two ways. First, if the franchise were extended to the working class, the workers could democratically elect socialist parties, which would then begin the evolution to socialism. Such a scenario would be possible, although by no means probable, in states with firmly entrenched democratic systems. The second option was for revolution by the proletariat, a violent civil war that ends with the military entrenchment of the Socialist party. The first scenario was contemplated by Marx, while the second came to be associated with the strategic writings of Lenin. As Mark Dickerson and Thomas Flanagan (1994:131) explain, the difference between the two approaches was brought to a head by the Russian Revolution:

> The eventual result of the Russian Revolution was an irreparable split in the world socialist movement. Those who approved of Lenin and his methods formed *communist* parties in every country and gathered themselves in the *Third International* or *Comintern* .... Those who opposed Lenin regrouped under the general name of *social democracy*, often merging with Christian and other moderate socialists who had been outside the Marxist consensus of the Second International.

Socialism, in both its main forms, became a significant ideological force by the beginning of the twentieth century. In the social democracy camp, Fabian socialists urged British citizens toward the democratic evolution of socialism. European social-ist parties coalesced in the "Second International" and sought power through the polls, while Russian author Leo Tolstoy urged the peaceful transition to a socialist-anarchist state. The social democratic British Labour Party was established in 1900, and won control of the government in 1924. In line with the British model, labour parties were established in Australia and New Zealand. With the end of the depres-sion and the Second World War, social democrats increased their strength across western Europe. The British Labour Party was elected in 1945, and went on to con-siderable success at the polls, although in recent years it has been unable to unseat Conservative governments led by Margaret Thatcher and John Major. The French Socialist Party and the German Social Democratic Party emerged as major players in European political life. The Swedish Democratic Labour Party has been arguably the most successful western European social democratic power; it has been in office, either alone or as the senior coalition partner, since 1951, with the exception of 1976–82. And, across western states, labour unions organized to work for better work-ing conditions and political influence.

Despite these many advances on the social democratic front, socialism had its most dramatic influence with communism. Marx's frequent co-author, Friedrich Engels, simplified and popularized Marx's theories into Marxism. These ideas were further adapted by the Russian intellectual V. I. Lenin. The resultant theory, Marxism-Leninism, was to find its most important expression in the creation of the Soviet Union. Recall that Marx predicted that socialism would evolve out of capital-ism, and was therefore most likely to emerge within industrialized states. "Industrialized," however, is not an accurate description of late-nineteenth-century Russia, whose semifeudal society was based on an agricultural economy and was con-trolled by an autocratic czar. Russia was essentially a police state within which any opposition to czarist rule was violently suppressed. Clearly, according to Marxist the-ory, Russia should not be the site for a communist revolution.

To understand why the Bolshevik revolution of 1917 occurred, one must con-sider the important alterations Lenin made to Marxist thought. First, whereas Marx argued that communism should be a large, inclusive *movement*, Lenin promoted a small, tight-knit communist *party*. Lenin also rejected Marx's idea of an internation-al communist movement. In his view, western trade union movements were friends of capitalism, not allies and promoters of socialism. With the benefits they received through union membership, the western working class had no incentive to revolt against capitalism. Lenin further asserted that the western countries were imperial-ist exploiters of the developing continents (Africa, Asia, South America), that impe-rialism was the highest form of capitalism and that workers in the western states would rather protect this imperialism than take part in an international workers' movement. Indeed, the First World War led to the breakup of the Second International, as support for an international communist movement gave way to national interests. For these reasons, Lenin argued that communist revolutions would necessarily happen on a state-by-state basis, beginning in the countries with the most misery, such as China and Russia.

A second significant alteration to Marx's theory was Lenin's rejection of the lim-ited role for intellectuals. Marx wrote that class consciousness would arise sponta-neously within the working class; the role of intellectuals was merely to help guide the political response of the working class. Lenin, in contrast, felt that the party elite ("the vanguard party") should cultivate class consciousness rather than wait for it to emerge on its own.

Public outrage about Russia's unsuccessful involvement in the First World War culminated in the overthrow of the czar in early 1917. For a few months, Russia was a constitutional democracy, but this brief period ended in October 1917, when Lenin's Bolsheviks orchestrated a military coup. Lenin's government restructured Russian society, seizing the means of production and establishing a new communist state, the Soviet Union. Soviet communism was never associated with democracy; the Bolsheviks succeeded originally by revolution, and secured their position by outlawing all political opposition and establishing a secret police force to detect subversive behaviour. Military rule increased under Lenin's successor, Joseph Stalin, whose reign (1924–1953) was defined by terror. These transformations of Marxist theory into Soviet practice had a profound impact on non-Soviet perceptions of communism, and of socialism more broadly conceived. Just as the practice of capitalism in the nineteenth century provided socialists with one of their strongest weapons, so the practice of communism in the twentieth century provided a powerful weapon for the liberal and conservative opponents of socialism. As Andrew Levine (1988:3) observes, "Existing socialism is capitalism's most effective argument." While socialism in principle can be seen as a way to expand freedom, communist rule appeared to have the opposite effect. Thus, "socialism in practice does not look nearly as appealing as socialism in theory" (Levine 1988: 222).

A second major communist revolution occurred in China in 1948–49. Under the leadership of Mao Tse-tung, and in the aftermath of Japan's Second World War invasion, the Chinese Communist party defeated the Nationalists and drove them into exile in Taiwan. Mao's communist influences were Leninist rather than Marxist. The Chinese revolution was based on the support of the rural peasants, rather than the urban proletariat. Lenin's notions of imperialism strongly influenced Mao, who felt that the Nationalists were bowing to the imperialist forces of the western states. Thus, the capitalism the Chinese communists fought was not within their country; it was an external enemy embodied by *international* capitalism. As Ball and Dagger (1995:166) explain, Mao recast Marxist theory in terms of nationalism; the oppressed proletariat became the oppressed proletarian *nation*, of which China was a prime example, and the oppressive bourgeoisie became the bourgeois nations of the West. The proletarian revolution became the war of national liberation. Mao's reformulation of Marxism had great appeal in the Third World, and there is no question that the success of communism in China, the world's most populous country, solidified socialism's position as the main ideological alternative to liberalism.

The unification of Germany, the collapse of the Eastern bloc, the emergence of noncommunist parties across eastern Europe and the disintegration of the Soviet Union all suggest that communism is now a spent force. China is slowly giving market forces more play in its economy, as are North Korea and Vietnam. Although it may be a little early to eulogize communism, it clearly has become a less significant ideological player in the face of international democratization and the ascendancy of the free market. This leaves social democracy to compete with conservatism as the primary ideological alternative to liberalism in North America and abroad. It is to this competition in Canada and the United States that we now turn.

SOCIALISM IN THE NORTH AMERICAN CONTEXT

The roots of socialist thought are to be found in western Europe's experience with industrialization, and in the interplay of conservative and liberal ideologies in the European political arena. But what happened when socialist ideologies washed ashore in North America? What was their reception in the new world, as opposed to the old?

The simple answer to this very complex question is that socialists found Canada and the United States, and particularly the latter, to be an unfavourable, and even hostile, ideological terrain. As Gad Horowitz (1966:159–60) explains, socialism was less "foreign" in Canada than it was in the United States:

> In Canada, socialism is British, non-Marxist and worldly; in the United States it is German, Marxist and other-worldly .... The socialism of the United States ... is predominantly Marxist and doctrinaire, because it is European. The socialism of English Canada ... is predominantly Protestant, labourist and Fabian, because it is British.

In this context, Louis Hartz (1955; 1964) maintains that socialism found a more receptive environment in Canada. As discussed in the preceding chapter, the "tory fragment" that came north to Canada in the form of United Empire Loyalists fleeing the American Revolution gave the country's political culture a collectivist orientation that the American political culture, liberal to the core and without a tory fragment, lacked. It was easier, therefore, for American ideological opponents to define socialism as foreign and "un-American" than it was for their Canadian counterparts to define socialism as "un-Canadian," a difference that was strengthened by the much greater role played by the United States in the military aspects of the cold war. Yet the fact remains that socialist ideas encountered a resistant ideological climate in both countries; the national differences were relatively nuanced.

The role of nativism[4] in the American rejection of socialist ideas is illustrated by the history of the Socialist party, which enjoyed substantial popular support in the early part of the twentieth century. The party drew heavily from immigrant members of the working class, and was thus vulnerable to nativist attacks. These came to a head when the Socialist party opposed American entry into the First World War. On April 8, 1917, the day after the United States declared war on Germany, a convention of the party in St. Louis, Missouri, passed the following resolution: "We brand the declaration of war by our government as a crime against the people of the United States and against the nations of the world" (Fried 1970:507). Political reaction was swift and harsh, as Richard Hudelson (1993:100) explains:

> Many English-language intellectuals, who had supported the party in the past, now abandoned it. Socialist newspapers were banned from the mail under the espionage act of 1917. Mobs of patriotic citizens attacked Socialist speakers and Socialist offices. Much of the national leadership was arrested and many Socialists were sent to prison. For his courageous speech against the war ... Eugene Debs, the great standard-bearer for the Socialists in presidential elections, was sentenced to ten years in prison.

This reaction blended into opposition to the American Communist party, formed in 1919. It found expression in the 1947 Taft-Hartley Act, which required that all union leaders take an oath that they were not communists, and in the communist witch-hunts of Senator Joseph McCarthy and the House Committee on UnAmerican Activities. In most of these cases, there were no real Canadian equivalents, although public sentiment in Canada was not far removed from the American mood. The basic similarity in public sentiment was illustrated by the 1962 Cuban missile crisis, when Canadians shared the American fear of impending nuclear war and sent naval units to assist the American blocade of Cuba.

A Distant Vision

Although there is no question that cold war competition with the Soviet Union provided a very effective club for opponents of socialism to use on its North American proponents, the Soviet Union was also a source of inspiration and hope for the small Canadian band of communist activists. As Ivan Avakumovic points out in his study of the Communist Party in Canada (CPC), party members "did not consider themselves as merely members of a small party fighting an uphill battle, but as part and parcel of a world-wide movement that had many victories to its credit" (1975:274). Thus, losses on the Canadian front could be shrugged off, or at least accepted as minor setbacks in a much larger crusade. The CPC "could bask in the glory of the Soviet Union whenever the U.S.S.R. presented an attractive face to the western world. It could point out that its own proposals were not utopian because they had already been tried out and proved to work in the 'socialist sixth of the world'" (1975:279–80).

This meant that Soviet exploits in space, or in hockey, could be used to sustain the small communist movement in Canada, to shield its supporters from scorn and derision. However, it also meant that the movement was exposed to any negative press emanating from the Soviet Union or other socialist states. When things went badly abroad, and they often did, the Canadian movement was hurt in the process. The collapse of the Soviet Union would have been a crushing blow, had there been a significant communist movement left by the late 1980s.

Of more importance than the national differences were a number of factors which made the political cultures of both Canada and the United States generally unreceptive to ideological inroads by socialism. The Industrial Revolution had a less traumatic impact on Canada and the United States than it had on Europe; therefore, the two countries were spared the massive urban slums and grim working conditions that characterized the industrial landscape in western Europe. When Marx and Engels were writing about the impact of industrialization on western Europe, Canada and the United States were predominantly agrarian communities with vast expanses of open land. There was no aristocracy or feudal remnant, and although there was certainly a good deal of concentrated wealth, there was still little *inherited* wealth. The prosperity of the new countries was an effective counter to socialist arguments; "American socialism was wrecked on the reefs of roast beef and apple pie" (Denitch 1990:126). The dominant creed was unlimited social mobility for those who worked hard, and although reality often failed to match the creed, there was a good enough fit to call any class-based political analysis into question. Even today, when inherited wealth plays a greater role and corporate capital is perhaps more concentrated than ever before, there are still enough rags-to-riches stories to sustain the mythology of unlimited social mobility—the "American Dream".[5] People such as Microsoft's Bill Gates and Wal-Mart's Sam Walton, film stars such as Jim Carrey, Arnold Schwarzenegger and Sylvester Stallone, and television stars such as "X-Files" actor David Duchovny, Roseanne and Oprah Winfrey serve as icons within a popular and *political* culture that accepts mobility as a foundational value. Admittedly, many may fall along the wayside because they are one microchip shy of Bill Gates or are not quite as cinematic as the leading actors of the day, but they are of little significance in defining the culture within which we live.

Social Mobility and Political Leadership

Recent American presidents and Canadian prime ministers provide powerful examples of social mobility. Although it has not been unknown for political leaders to be drawn from social and economic elites—George Bush, John F. Kennedy, Franklin Delano Roosevelt and Pierre Elliot Trudeau are all examples—the norm has been very different.

Jimmy Carter, Bill Clinton, Lyndon Johnson, Richard Nixon and Ronald Reagan all came from undistinguished, even humble, backgrounds. None came from families of exceptional wealth or social standing, and in some cases their families were broken and dysfunctional. The five have all been self-made men, rising from modest roots to the most powerful political office in the world. All epitomize, therefore, the American belief in social mobility; their careers *prove* that the system works.

The Canadian situation is very similar. Kim Campbell, Jean Chrétien and Brian Mulroney all have modest family backgrounds. Chrétien, for example, was the eighteenth of nineteen children; his father was a machinist in a Shawinigan paper mill. Joe Clark and John Diefenbaker also had modest backgrounds; Clark's father edited a weekly newspaper in a small Alberta community, and Diefenbaker left his own farming background to run a one-man Saskatchewan law office. The point to stress is that political elites in Canada and the United States are generally not drawn from social or economic elites, and are therefore unlikely to serve as lightning rods for class conflict.

While opposition to socialism by the business communities in Canada and the United States was only to be expected, and differed little from the European case, opposition by organized labour was less predictable and diverged sharply from the European experience. In Europe, organized labour provided, and to a degree still provides, the political and electoral muscle for socialism. In North America, however, the dominant creed of organized labour was the "business unionism" advocated by Samuel Gompers, whose opposition to socialism was emphatic:

> Socialism holds nothing but unhappiness for the human race. It destroys personal initiative, wipes out national pride … and plays into the hands of the autocrats .... Socialism is the end of fanatics, the sophistry of so-called intelligentsia, and it has no place in the hearts of those who would secure and fight for freedom and preserve democracy (Gompers 1925).

The major unions in Canada and the United States largely confined their activities to job-related benefits and objectives; they did not try to organize the social or political lives of their members. Although many Canadian unions, and the Canadian Federation of Labour, have been affiliated with the New Democratic Party, and many American unions have been informally affiliated with the Democratic party, union membership has not been transformed into mass-based, left-of-centre political parties or movements.

Although socialists seek in the long run to eliminate class distinctions, socialist analysis in the short run hinges on a class-based construction of society and the political world. In this critically important respect, socialist theories fail to fit the social and political environments in Canada and the United States. An analysis built on class concepts and the centrality of the class struggle is of limited use in a society where class consciousness is very low, where class divisions are fluid and difficult to define and where social mobility is assumed to render class divisions temporary or self-imposed, and in any event, largely irrelevant. Empirical research shows that some of the likely components of social class—income, education, occupation, union membership—are often linked to voting behaviour, but the effects are neither powerful nor consistent. Although political parties have sometimes trolled for votes by using platforms designed to appeal to particular segments of the electorate, class-based appeals have been the exception rather than the rule. Thus, even if people wanted to vote along class lines, they would generally have trouble deciding which, if any, of the competing parties best reflected their class interests. It would not be clear, for example, whether a working-class voter in Canada today would best be served by a Conservative, Liberal, New Democratic or Reform government. Certainly all of these parties would attempt to appeal to the working-class vote, as they would to the middle-class vote. It should also be noted in this context that the first-past-the-post, single-member electoral systems used in Canada and the United States have inhibited the formation of the types of socialist parties that have thrived in the proportional representation systems more typical of western Europe.

Exercise Three: Measuring Social Class

Part of the empirical problem in determining the connection between social class and political behaviour such as voting arises from difficulties in measuring the social class of survey respondents. To understand the extent of these difficulties, imagine that you are able to construct a questionnaire to measure the social class of respondents, and that you could ask respondents up to five questions. Which of the following questions would you use (and why)?:

- respondent's personal income
- respondent's family income
- respondent's level of formal education
- respondent's occupation
- respondent spouse's occupation
- respondent parents' occupations
- respondent's subjective social class ("Do you think of yourself as working class, lower-middle class, middle class, etc.")
- home ownership (does respondent rent or own)
- estimated property value of the respondent's home or apartment
- respondent's union membership
- respondent's membership in private clubs or associations.

Now, imagine that you could ask only three questions in order to establish the respondent's social class. Which three would you ask? If you could only ask one question, what would it be? In any case, would you also have to know the respondent's age? Gender? Race? Number of dependents? Place of residence? A single person, aged twenty-five, living in a small town and making $50,000 a year, is in a different "class" from a married couple, aged forty-five, living with five dependents in a major urban centre and also making $50,000 a year.

Class-based politics usually emerge when class is rolled into more politically salient divisions in the electorate. For example, there was a strong class dimension to nationalist politics in Quebec during the 1960s, but that was because all francophones within the province were portrayed as a "class." Material differences among francophones, which were pronounced, were ignored as francophones in their entirety were identified as a class subordinate to anglophones within the province. (Substantial differences in income and wealth among Quebec anglophones were also ignored.) Class politics in western Canada during the heydays of the Co-operative Commonwealth Federation (CCF) acquired their force from the overlapping cleavage of regionalism; the western agrarian producers became a "class" placed in opposition to central Canada. In the United States, the politics of race can be wed to a class-based analysis of American political life, although not without some distortion. (To subsume racial conflict under the rubric of class conflict may be more misleading than helpful.) For the most part, however, cleavages other than class have dominated domestic politics in Canada and the United States: race, language, region and even religion have been more potent forces in terms of electoral mobilization and party competition. Class conflict occasionally attaches itself to these more fundamental cleavages, but it has not supplanted them. Thus, whereas socialism assumes that class cleavages are *the* most significant divisions in the political community, this has not been the case in North America.

Yet despite this hostile environment, socialism has not been without influence in Canada and the United States. Given that socialism is such a powerful current in the international environment, an environment to which both countries have been very open, it would be surprising indeed to find that socialism had left no imprint. Immigration alone has played a significant role in injecting socialist ideas in the political culture. Small socialist parties have always existed in both countries; as noted above, the Socialist party had a notable presence in the United States during the first two decades of the twentieth century, and the CCF was a significant player in Canadian federal elections between 1935 and 1957. In Saskatchewan, the CCF formed the provincial government from 1944 to 1960. The CCF's successor, the New Democratic Party, watered down its social democracy with reform liberalism, and succeeded in forming provincial governments in British Columbia, Saskatchewan, Manitoba and Ontario, and in being an influential national force from 1962 to its virtual demise in the 1993 general election. As you will see in Chapter 8, socialist thought was also reflected in the populist movements that arose in the American and Canadian Wests at the turn of the century, and played a salient role in the New Left radical politics of the 1960s and early 1970s. The New Left was a large, democratically oriented coalition that included civil rights activists, feminists, anarchists, social democrats, Marxists and pacifists opposed to American involvement in the Vietnam War. This large spread of interests, which fragmented into its component parts by the mid-1970s, spanned ideological elements ranging from socialism and reform liberalism to early forms of neoconservatism.

The Communist Party in Canada (CPC) has run candidates in virtually every federal election since the early 1920s. Communist candidates have not made much of an impact in terms of the popular vote, but they were of considerable annoyance to social democratic parties such as the CCF. During the 1940s, the CCF expended a good deal of energy trying to ward off the Communist party whose embrace was perceived, quite correctly, as the potential kiss of death for the CCF. Communists, in an attempt to show that the middle road of social democracy was impractical, tried to weaken the CCF in whatever manner they could. It should be stressed, however, that the CPC was not particularly revolutionary in style or tone. It was little more than an outrider on a much larger international movement, and recognized itself as such. Nonetheless, it did survive, and was able to maintain a more public and legitimate presence than the Communist party in the United States was able to do (Denitch 1990:187 ff.).

If class-based analyses often provided limited purchase on domestic politics, they offered somewhat greater purchase on the international scene. Thus, for example, left-of-centre political economists have been major players in explaining the economic relationship between Canada and the United States, and between the United States and the world economy. The conceptual language of political economy is heavily imbued with Marxist and neo-Marxist terminology, and scholars in the field have been more heavily influenced by that conceptual terminology than have students of electoral behaviour in either country.[6] The vast and influential Canadian literature on economic nationalism, for instance, draws substantially and successfully from socialist thought. This line of analysis follows a well-established tradition whereby class struggles have been folded into anticolonialism, and socialism and nationalism have been fused (Heywood 1992:94).

The Regina Manifesto

At its first national convention, held in July 1933, the Co-operative Commonwealth Federation (Farmer, Labour, Socialist) set forth an unabashedly socialist platform in the Regina Manifesto. The manifesto began with a ringing condemnation of the status quo:

> We aim to replace the present capitalist system, with its inherent injustice and inhumanity, by a social order from which the domination and exploitation of one class by another will be eliminated, in which economic planning will supersede unregulated private enterprise and competition, and in which genuine democratic self-government, based upon economic equality, will be possible. The present order is marked by glaring inequities of wealth and opportunity, by chaotic waste and instability; and in an age of plenty it condemns the great mass of people to poverty and insecurity. Power has become more and more concentrated into the hands of a small irresponsible minority of financiers and industrialists and to their predatory interests the majority are habitually sacrificed .... We believe that these evils can be removed only in a planned and socialized economy in which our natural resources and the principal means of production and distribution are owned, controlled and operated by the people.

The manifesto closed with equal fire and visionary appeal:

> No CCF Government will rest content until it has eradicated capitalism and put into operation the full program of socialized planning which will lead to the establishment in Canada of the Co-operative Commonwealth.

The CCF's successor was decidedly less visionary, and less wedded to socialist principles. The 1974 NDP campaign slogan was "People Matter More," a slogan with somewhat less revolutionary appeal than the Regina Manifesto, or for that matter, "Workers of the world, unite; you have nothing to lose but your chains."

However, the major impact of socialist thought in both Canada and the United States came on the liberal left. Liberalism was so dominant as an ideological framework, and was so closely attuned to the economic and social environments, that socialist thought was almost inevitably absorbed by the liberal left. Indeed, liberalism's success in absorbing the less contentious elements of the socialist creed left socialists little to contribute to ideological debate on the continent; socialism may have pulled liberalism to the left, but it did not replace liberalism as the dominant ideological creed, or even seriously challenge its preeminence. In Canada, the pull to the left was significantly stronger than it was in the United States, and thus we find publicly funded universal medicare, regional equalization and an extensive infrastructure of Crown corporations and public utilities, one which has only recently come under assault from the combined forces of deficit reduction and conservative ideologies.

In the final analysis, there is no question that the North American legacy of socialism is an expanded form of reform liberalism and its institutional edifice, the modern welfare state. Once social democrats had come to accept the market, the distinction between social democracy and reform liberalism became more difficult to establish or maintain. As Chapter 3 suggests, in the post–cold war environment, the former opponents of socialism have now trained their sights on reform liberalism. The resultant ideological debate spans a variety of issues that have come to be associated with "the liberal left," loosely defined. We find that any form of central economic planning has come under strong ideological attack from the proponents of free trade in the international realm and free enterprise in the domestic realm. "Big government" in all its manifestations is being pared down by assaults on deficit spending, public sector salaries and government regulations of any form. Concerns about public debts and deficits have been used as a club on the universality of social programs. Attempts by the left to promote greater equality through such measures as employment equity programs are meeting increased ideological and public opposition; in the United States, recent court decisions and popular legislative initiatives have sought to roll back employment equity programs. Even the progressive income tax has been challenged by the proponents of the flat tax (whereby all taxpayers would pay the same percentage tax), proponents who appear to be receiving substantial and growing public support. Therefore, the absorption—and dilution—of socialist principles by the liberal left has not shielded those principles from ideological attack, for the entire edifice of the liberal welfare state has become contested ideological terrain.

As social democracy has come under greater attack, its meaning has become less clear. Andrew Heywood (1992:128) explains that social democracy has "come to stand for a broad range of views, extending from a Left-wing commitment to extending equality and expanding the collective ownership of wealth, to a Right-wing belief in market efficiency that may become indistinguishable from modern liberalism and can even overlap with paternal conservatism." This ambiguity complicates any speculations that might be advanced for the future of socialism as we approach the turn of the century.

Exercise Four: Rolling Back the Welfare State

The modern welfare state encompasses a wide range of social programs that touch virtually every aspect of people's lives. If, in the face of public debt and ideological attack, the welfare state is to be rolled back, the question arises as to which programs are going to be cut, or whose ox is to be gored. Consider, then, the following list of programs or program areas:

- publicly funded preschool education
- old age pensions
- elementary and secondary education
- postsecondary education
- medicare
- social welfare (or social assistance)
- environmental protection
- unemployment insurance.

If you were in charge of pruning the welfare state, where would you begin? What would be the first program area you would cut, and why? Where would you cut last, and why?

THE FUTURE OF SOCIALISM

To say that contemporary socialism is in disarray is an understatement. The collapse of the Soviet Union, the enthusiastic embrace of the free market by central and eastern European countries, and, more generally, the end of the cold war and the ideological "victory" of the West have all provoked a great deal of confusion and debate on the left of the ideological spectrum. For critics of socialism (Hayek 1989; Popper 1963), the Soviet Union's command economy, and its underlying assumption that governments are better at predicting future needs than the market, were a favourite object of attack. Many socialists, to be sure, have always seen the Soviet Union as a "grotesque distortion" of Marxism (Hudelson 1993:149) rather than as a model to emulate. Michael Harrington, for example, writes (1989:60) that "the rise of Communist states—dictatorships with centrally planned, nationalized economies— did more to distort and confuse the meaning of socialism than any other event in history." Harrington, therefore, sees the collapse of the Soviet Union as an *opportunity* for socialists, not a setback. However, the more general effect of its collapse has been a widespread rejection of socialism in the Anglo-American democracies. Within Canada and the United States, the growing popularity of conservative thought and the retreat of reform liberalism pose an acute challenge for those on the left, no matter how moderate their beliefs might be. It may also be the case that general patterns of social change are eroding the appeal of socialism. Anthony Giddens (1993:18) argues that "we can speak today of the existence of a citizenry of *clever people*." This poses a problem for socialism, for such people do not function well in the top-down, hierarchical situations associated with central planning:

> Socialism was always based on the idea of subjecting the lower levels of the economy to "intelligent" central direction. But this doesn't work well with systems that have

become highly complex and reflexive—as has happened to modern economies and social conditions (Giddens 1993:19).

In short, the times are tough indeed for the proponents of socialism as the free market and its ideological supporters garner growing support.

There is no question, then, that the optimism of socialists has been shaken. Note the following comment by Colette Audry (1985:37): "If there is one lesson to be learned from the hecatombs of the two world wars, from genocide, from the use of torture as a method of government, from the rise of totalitarian states ... it is that the road to socialism is longer, less direct and infinitely more difficult than our predecessors thought it would be." At the same time, predictions as to the demise of socialism are undoubtedly premature (Geoghagen 1984:147). As Andrew Heywood (1992:95–6) points out:

> [T]he breadth and flexibility of socialist ideology has also been its strength. It is difficult, for example, to predict the end of an ideology that has demonstrated such a remarkable capacity to redefine itself and its goals in the light of changing historical circumstances. Moreover, underlying socialist ideology is a vision of human beings living together in harmony and peace, a vision that has existed as long as human history itself and which is unlikely ever to become irrelevant to political thought.

There are also significant aspects of the contemporary ideological scene that may present opportunities for the revitalization of socialism. The "defeat" of communism and the retreat of socialism do not mean that the flaws of capitalism have disappeared. It is quite likely, for example, that globalization will increase income disparities among and within nation states. Globalization, moreover, poses a serious challenge to many existing political communities, a point pursued at greater length in Chapters 7 and 11. In these respects, it cannot be assumed that liberal or conservative political thought will provide perfect solutions. As Michael Harrington, himself a socialist, caustically notes (1989:278) about conservatism, "It provides eighteenth-century rationales for twenty-first-century authoritarianism, myths of the invisible hand that justify the elitist maneuvers of the visible hand, idylls of the organic community that facilitate the growth of mass society and create both a new poverty and a vacuous hedonism." Given the collectivist or community-centred inclinations of socialism, and a possible political reaction to widening disparities in income and wealth, socialists may find that globalization provides them with a new platform. Certainly in the past, socialism and nationalism have often produced a powerful ideological brew. Finally, it should also be noted that neoconservatism, and for that matter, classical liberalism, are likely to foster growing disparities in income and wealth. To the extent that socialism appeals to those who are disadvantaged in unbridled free market competition, there may be a ready market for socialist alternatives.

But this does not mean that socialist bromides from the past can simply be recycled. The challenge will be to find new ideological perspectives which reflect socialist principles, but are sufficiently attuned to contemporary political and social realities. Nationalized industries and centralized economic planning, for example, are solutions whose time has passed. If the collapse of the Soviet Union proved nothing else, it proved the failure of a centrally planned economy. Socialist thought will therefore need to be reworked, and not simply repackaged, if it is to strike a responsive ideological chord in the next century. The reluctance of traditional socialism to acknowledge, much less embrace, social diversity will have to be overcome if parties on the left are to capture the support of racial and sexual minorities, environmentalists and the plethora of social-interest groups. The complexity of this challenge, and the uncertainty of the socialist response, is nicely illustrated by a comment from Roy Romanow, NDP premier of Saskatchewan, and one of the continent's most successful social democrats:

> We are thinking about our social programs, our health programs, our taxation policies in the light of the 1990s and 21st century politics, which is the politics of globalism, public debt, international competition and modern-day technology. And I don't know if we can successfully tailor the suit to have core NDP social democratic values at its basis—but, by golly, we're going to try (Roberts 1995:A9).

Whether trying will be enough in the face of a strong ideological challenge from the right remains an open question. And yet, optimism remains within an ideological camp always marked by a utopian spirit. As Goran Therborn (1985:250) concludes:

> The winds of history are hardly likely to blow socialists off their feet in the next decade, or decades. But having one's face to the wind also has its attractions, for it offers a freshness which may serve to clarify one's thinking and inspire one with new energy for the struggles to come.

NOTES

1. Liberals and socialists both believe in the capacity for human improvement, although the liberal belief would not extend to perfectability. They differ, however, in the point of departure. Liberals believe we are all born *tabula rasa*, blank slates upon which institutions and experience leave their mark. Socialists believe we are naturally cooperative and compassionate.

2. "Utopian" in this context should not be interpreted as unrealistic or impractical; "visionary" is a more appropriate description.

3. Postmodern socialists are more receptive to subjective, even anti-economistic, lines of thought.

4. For a discussion, see Chapter 8.

5. Walter Young (1969) argues persuasively that the Canadian culture is based on the values and assumption of upward mobility, and therefore poses a considerable obstacle to parties based on more fixed concepts of class.

6. For an excellent snapshot of Canadian political economy scholarship, see Wallace Clement and Glen Williams (1989).

CHAPTER FIVE

Feminism: Diversity Within Unity

For women of my generation, feminism is our birthright. While sexism may still permeate society, we know what it is to live without excessive confinement. We are the first generation to grow up expecting equality of opportunity and equal education, as well as the freedom to express our sexuality. We are the first to assume what feminists had to force society to accept against its deeply ingrained prejudice: that we are the equals of any man.

RENE DENFELD

As an educated, married monogamous, feminist, Christian African American mother, I suffer from an acute case of multiplicity.

SONJA D. CURRY-JOHNSON

Feminism. It is one of those words that everyone uses freely, but few truly understand its meaning. In fact, feminism has different meanings for different people. If two people both claim to be feminists, can we assume that they support the same issues and hold the same beliefs? Not necessarily. Can a person be called a feminist even if she does not adopt the label of feminism? Maybe. Can men be feminists? Probably. Is feminism a belief system, a political movement or an approach to life? Well, it depends. To each of these questions, there are many answers. Some argue that all women are feminists, by virtue of gender. Others assert that feminism is a belief system adopted by some women and some men. Still others feel that feminism is best understood as "waves" of social movement that crest at certain points in time.

Like many words in our vocabulary today, "feminism" has become ambiguous, often dependent upon context for its meaning. But what really is at the core of feminism? Why does feminism draw such impassioned responses from people, either positive or negative? And how does feminism fit into the political and social landscape of the 1990s? To answer these questions, we will place feminism within an ideological framework. This chapter seeks to identify the central themes of feminist thought and to explore how similar beliefs lead to different conclusions, and thus different strands of feminism. The political and social development of feminism will also be explored. Finally, how feminism fits into the broader ideological terrain of western democratic states and how it influences personal identities will be examined. It will be argued that feminism is not only a social movement but also a political ideology that has been developing in strength for well over 150 years. Feminism is arguably the strongest *social* innovator in existence as we approach the twenty-first century, and may be second in *ideological* importance only to the ongoing left-right debates which ripple through liberal and conservative thought. In fact, feminism is a key contributor to those debates.

Why do we classify feminism as an ideology? Although it may not be obvious to the reader, feminism exhibits all the characteristics of a political ideology. As discussed in Chapter 1, a political ideology is a socially constructed and socially transmitted system of political beliefs, rather than an individual belief system; historically, feminism has relied heavily on social involvement, be it in the form of political movements, rape crisis centers or consciousness raising groups. Ideologies provide guides for political action designed to attain normative goals; feminism articulates a number of strategies to reach the goal of an equalized, more balanced society. A political ideology affects an individual's personal identity; feminism clearly does this in contemporary society. Finally, ideologies possess durability; they have withstood the test of time to prove themselves to be more than fads. Feminism has done so. Indeed, it has been a social force for almost two centuries.

The Ideology of Feminism

- *scope*: Varies between branches; Liberal feminism focuses on the public sphere; other feminisms extend their focus to the private sphere, as well; Radical feminism considers all social and political institutions.

- *internal consistency*: Feminism holds that women are oppressed on the basis of their sex; that women can realize this oppression by considering their own experiences; and that overcoming women's oppression requires changes in social norms and attitudes. Liberal feminists do not feel that political and economic institutions must be substantially altered. Radical and Marxist feminists argue that the institutional status quo must change.

- *durability*: Liberal feminism began in the late 1700s/early 1800s. Radical and Marxist feminist movements emerged in the 1960s. Since then, a variety of other branches of feminism have emerged.

- *normative framework*: Men and women are treated differently in society, with women receiving fewer social and economic benefits. This differential treatment leads to the oppression of women. Women have qualities that are valuable to society, and both men and women can benefit from the integration of women into the public realm. Political and social efforts should be made to end oppression. Sexual equality and social betterment are among the goals of feminism.

- *practical guide for political action*: Issues are seen as they affect sexual equality. Some theorists argue that state power should be used to achieve feminist goals; others disagree. In society, individuals should work to end sexism and negative stereotyping.

- *formal articulation*: Large number of writers, including Simone de Beauvoir, *The Second Sex*; Shulamith Firestone, *The Dialectic of Sex*; Betty Friedan, *The Feminine Mystique*; Kate Millett, *Sexual Politics*; Adrienne Rich, *Of Woman Born*; Christina Hoff Sommers, *Who Stole Feminism?*; Naomi Wolf, *The Beauty Myth*; *Ms* magazine; *Signs*.

This chapter begins with an outline of the main tenets of feminist thought, followed by a brief historical overview of the women's movements in Canada and the United States. We will show how the theoretical and political aspects of feminism combine to create a distinct political ideology. We will then introduce three major theoretical branches of feminist thought—liberal, Marxist and radical feminism—emphasizing the tensions between them. Finally, we will consider the political context within which feminism now operates—specifically, who supports and opposes feminism. Although generalizations have been made throughout in order to make the large body of feminist thought understandable to the reader, it must be understood that great diversity exists within each branch of feminism.

Exercise One: Preconceptions About Feminism

Write down your own conception of feminism. What are the core beliefs and values of feminism? What views do you think feminists hold on the following issues: welfare programs; abortion; the free market; religion; the media; gay and lesbian rights; affirmative action? Do you consider yourself a feminist? What do feminists look like, act like? What are the goals of the feminist movement? What social changes can be credited to feminism? Do you believe your life would be better, worse or the same if feminism had never existed?

BASIC TENETS OF FEMINIST THOUGHT

Like liberalism, conservatism and socialism before it, feminism can be seen as having a single base, a core body of thought from which all branches of feminist thought draw.[1] This base is a worldview, or a means of perceiving life and society. Just as the liberal sees the world through the lens of individualism and competition, and the conservative through the lens of hierarchy and morality, the feminist sees the world through the lens of sex and gender.[2] Feminists are aware of the different roles played by men and women in the home, in society and in politics, and question whether such roles are appropriate. The importance placed upon these different roles varies between the branches of feminism. To continue the metaphor, some branches of feminism have stronger lenses than others, and thus see social and political sex differences in greater depth, or in greater number. However, all branches of feminism agree that sex is an important variable in politics and society; sex, in effect, acts as a significant class division.

The term "class" suggests a communality, and an identification with others within the class. This notion of collectivity is often referred to as "sisterhood," or "universal womanhood" (Grant 1993). It is the *politicization* of this sex-class identity that leads to feminism. As Rosalind Delmar (1986:10) notes:

> [T]he unity of the movement was assumed to derive from a potential identity between women. This concept of identity rested on the idea that women share the same experiences: an external situation in which they find themselves—economic oppression, commercial exploitation, legal discrimination are examples; and an internal response—a shared feeling of inadequacy, a sense of narrow horizons. A shared response to shared experience was put forward as the basis for a communality of feeling between women.

Of course, women are a huge social group, comprising more than fifty percent of the world population, and some would argue, therefore, that the potential for fragmentation is unavoidably greater than the potential for unity. Nonetheless, the quest for unity in the face of diversity is central to an understanding of contemporary feminism.

What is it about women that allows them to be so similar that they form a universal social class, despite differences in racial, cultural and economic backgrounds? Feminist writers posit two answers to this question. The first, most obvious answer is the female body (Grant 1993:24). The female reproductive cycle affects the lives of women in many ways: menses creates uncomfortable physical conditions in some women, including mood changes, fatigue and severe abdominal cramping; intercourse can lead to pregnancy and child-rearing; menopause creates further physical discomfort. Men do not experience such biological restrictions. Since women bear children, and traditionally have been responsible for raising them, the "side effects" of sexual activity for men have generally been economic and emotional, whereas the "side effects" for women involve significant physical and lifestyle changes. Thus, it is not surprising that the nineteenth- and early-twentieth-century–feminist movements often focused on issues of contraception and women's health (Rowbotham 1973: 75), while later feminist groups sought the legalization of abortion. As well as the reproductive differences between men and women, there are other physical differences. Women, on average, are smaller than men, less muscular and live longer lives. Size and strength differences between the sexes have been (and continue to be) used to justify the exclusion of women from many occupations.

The second factor argued to unite women as women is "female nature" (Grant 1993:23). This female nature is often juxtaposed with the "opposing male nature"— much like the Chinese concept of *yin* (feminine) and *yang* (masculine). Many feminist theorists do not dispute the stereotypes of women (for example, women are emotional, intuitive, passive, "bitchy"), but instead seek "to explain how these 'female' traits are rational reactions to oppression" (Grant 1993:21). Robin Morgan (1977: 99) writes:

> Stereotypes are powerful things .... *The oppressor may, in fact, never really believe in the stereotype at all—what is important is that the oppressed do.* Women have internalized the image of themselves as weak, incompetent, emotional, unintellectual, dependent.

In addition to accepting stereotypes, many feminists argue that some of these traits, traditionally seen as weaknesses, are actually strengths. After all, the male-dominated systems have resulted in a history of war, tension and environmental destruction (Grant 1993:23). Perhaps a balanced or a female-dominated system would be more beneficial to society; it certainly could not be worse, they espouse. "Thus, value judgements about female nature were attacked while the categories themselves remained intact" (Grant 1993:24).

Where do the differences between male and female nature come from? Some feminists, like Simone de Beauvoir, assert that gender is a social construct, that differences between the sexes are the result of the different socialization received by males and females. Others, such as Shulamith Firestone, maintain that differences are innate, and use examples of behavioural differences in the animal kingdom to support their case. Still others feel that both socialization and biology play a role. However, Judith Grant (1993:24) believes that these divergent opinions on the *source* of female nature do not undermine the importance of the concept to the feminist theory: "Radical feminists disputed judgements made about female behavior, and some disputed the source(s) of female behavior, but all agreed, at least by their written word, that it existed, and that accepting it constituted a fundamental part of feminist politics."

Are shared biology and female nature sufficient to create a universal social class of women? The idea of universal sisterhood emerges not from the similarities themselves, but rather from the *consequences* of these similarities: namely, that women, despite race or economic class, are oppressed because of their sex. Women are oppressed *as women,* on top of and separate from oppression based on race or class (Grant 1993:20). Thus, a black woman is more oppressed than a black man, even if all blacks can be considered socially oppressed. It is this universal oppression that leads to a collectivity based on sex. Since all women are universally oppressed, they can (or should be able to) identify with one another on the basis of that oppression, regardless of race and class differences.

This leads to important and difficult questions. What exactly is oppression? Who is doing the oppressing: All men? Some men? Can women oppress other women? Are social and political institutions responsible? Is this oppression deliberate, or is it a systemic result of our social systems and upbringings? What would nonoppression look like? How can it be achieved? How important is this oppression compared to race and class oppression? One of the foundations of the idea of universal womanhood is that all women are oppressed, but this assertion confronts a problem. Women exist in every economic class, in every race. Although she does not have the advantages of a white middle-class male, can a contemporary white middle-class female really be considered oppressed? Critics of feminism argue that such women fail to meet objective standards of oppression. As Grant (1993:30) explains, feminist theorists have used "experience" to get around this criticism:

> To argue persuasively that oppression was common to all women, feminists had to define oppression differently .... The solution that prevailed was to define 'oppression' subjectively. Oppression included anything that women *experienced* as oppression.

For example, a woman could view living in fear of assault, the division of labour in the home and traditional assumptions about child-rearing as oppression. In addition, individual experiences with sexism in the home, society and the workplace might be viewed as oppression. By defining oppression subjectively, rather than objectively, feminism again inverts the values attached to masculine and feminine. Subjectivity is often seen as a feminine trait, whereas objectivity is seen as masculine (Grant 1993:31). Feminism, unlike prior ideologies, places value on the subjective, and distrusts "objective" standards as being male-biased (Grant 1993:33).[3]

Thus, "experience" became important to feminist theory. The individual experiences of women are seen as sources of knowledge to be drawn upon. A problem for early feminist theory was that most of the feminist writers were white and middle-class (Grant 1993:31), and generalizations made from the collective experiences of white, middle-class writers did not necessarily reflect the experiences of women in other racial and economic groups. For example, a number of early feminist writers focused on the problems facing housewives and women entering the work force, without considering the problems facing working-class and minority women already in the work force. Therefore, many women did not see themselves and their experiences reflected in feminist theories. Alison Jaggar and Paula Rothenberg (1984: 89) note that "[women of color] have correctly identified the issues of the early phase of this movement as issues of concern primarily to white, middle-class or professional women."

A second problem with the concept of "experience" is that its very nature makes it difficult, if not impossible, to discount individual views (Grant 1993:32). What, then, does one do with women who claim to experience no oppression? Feminism parallels Marxist thought in its solution to this problem. As noted in Chapter 4, Marx argues that society is divided into two classes: the oppressed proletariat (the working class), and the oppressing bourgeoisie (the property-controlling class). The proletariat is much larger than the bourgeoisie and could overthrow its oppressors, yet does not do so. Why not? Marx states that the proletariat suffers from "false consciousness," which blinds it from its own oppression. Similarly, some feminists argue that women who do not feel oppressed are suffering from false consciousness due to "male identification." Judith Grant (1993:32) explains, "Early radical feminists concluded that some women were 'male identified' as they were unable to subjectively differentiate their interests as women from those of men."

Seeing the world in terms of sex differences leads some feminists to look beyond questions of politics, and to consider society as a whole. *Any* institution that involves power relations might be examined for differential treatment of men and women. Social-gender roles, the division of labour, education, marriage, motherhood and heterosexuality are but a few examples of the many topics subject to feminist analysis. This broad extension of feminism is captured in the phrase "The personal is the political." Every aspect of life may be subject to critique—a fact that makes feminism a threatening ideology to defenders of tradition. As you shall see later in this chapter, however, not all branches of feminism have a broad scope. Specifically, liberal feminists tend to focus narrowly on political and employment issues. Note also that a broad ideological view is not unique to feminism, but is characteristic of many ideologies. For example, Chapter 3 illustrates that the conservative moral lens examines not only politics, but also "private" issues such as religion, the family and sexuality.

In summary, all branches of feminism support the following tenets:

- women can be considered a social class due to shared biology and nature;

- all women are oppressed in society due to their sex;

- this common oppression enables women to regard themselves as a social class, and binds them together in "sisterhood";

- not all women recognize their oppression; and

- sexual oppression can be found in many power relations in society.

The branches of feminist thought differ in the degree to which they emphasize each tenet, and in their solutions to the problem of oppression. Moreover, the tenets are not always clearly articulated. As Grant (1993:6) explains, "The concepts are often implicit rather than explicit. That is, a thinker can rely on them without really being aware she is doing so."

The tenets themselves may lead to problems for the ideology. Grant (1993:156) notes that the idea of universality creates a "not me" problem; namely, that some women, including women of colour, do not see feminism reflecting their experiences. Elizabeth Hood (1986:201) writes, "The unwillingness of white women to identify with the special problems of black women ... set up barriers between the two groups." Working-class, right-wing and physically handicapped women also argue that feminism fails to address their circumstances and beliefs. As discussed earlier, the subjectivity of experience leads to the problem of women denying oppression. This puts feminism in the uncomfortable position of advocating the interests of women who do not want to be represented by feminism. Finally, politicizing the personal, while valuable to the advancement of women, is in some ways a limited concept: "Things are politicized in contexts. It probably also makes sense to say that things are political because we choose to see them as such" (Grant 1993:182). For example, the choice to patronize certain establishments, or to purchase certain consumer products, or to watch particular television programming, may or may not be political in nature.

These caveats to feminism's basic tenets by no means render feminism insignificant and illegitimate. First, as Grant points out, these concepts can be revised to create a sounder basis for feminist theory. Second, the different branches of feminism rely on and use these tenets to differing degrees; thus, the effects of the problems discussed above may be more significant to one branch than to another. And, most important, feminism can best be seen as a broad-gauge ideology rather than as a tightly coherent theory. This ideology encompasses a long-standing social movement, and is woven into individual identities and perspectives. As such, it can weather problems of inconsistency and contradiction. In fact, feminism may even thrive on diversity of outlook and belief. Given the diverse experiences of over three billion women worldwide, there is no option for the feminist ideology but to accept, indeed embrace, diversity.

We will now turn to a discussion of the women's movement. The reader should note that the division of feminism into distinct and separate branches did not occur until the 1960s, when radical feminism emerged from the New Left movement and liberal feminism gained strength within the political mainstream.

"HERSTORY": THE DEVELOPMENT OF THE WOMEN'S MOVEMENT

The women's movement is commonly referred to as having at least two "waves." The first wave was devoted to seeking the vote for women. Universal suffrage was achieved in American federal elections in 1920, and in Canadian federal elections in 1921. The second wave emerged in the 1960s, and focused on the more general condition of women in society. The second wave is believed by many feminist theorists to continue to the present, although others argue that a third wave of feminism is emerging. This discussion will trace the development of the women's movement in Canada and the United States, highlighting important individuals, groups and events. Keep in mind, though, that the women's movement, like all other social movements, was, and continues to be, mass-based; the identification of specific leaders and events thus serves primarily to illustrate much broader social and political dynamics. The ability of the movement to find and maintain support from both men and women has been the most significant factor in its success.

Although the idea of women's rights was discussed prior to the 1800s,[4] an organized women's rights movement did not form until the nineteenth century. What was life like for a nineteenth-century woman? The conditions varied greatly depending upon social and economic class. A working-class woman often held the double responsibility of family and a factory- or domestic-related job (Rowbotham 1973:33). Women, like children and working-class men, were low-paid employees who endured difficult and demanding work conditions. Middle- and upper-class women had easier lives; however, they were dependent upon their husbands or fathers for economic security. The physical mobility of middle- and upper-class women was limited by the fashions of the time, including the wearing of uncomfortable corsets and heavy full dresses. Moreover, women had limited access to education, particularly at the college level. The legal rights of all women were minimal. It was not until 1882 in the United States that married women were legally allowed to possess property, including their own earnings (Rowbotham 1973:50). Conditions were not as bleak in Canada; Jane Errington notes that "some women found themselves managing property, opening a tavern, and, if widowed, running a family business" (1993:65). In addition to economic dependence, women were socially dependent upon men: "The women were part of the man's belongings, their leisure the sign of his conspicuous consumption" (Rowbotham 1973:47). Children and wives were considered property of men; thus, a woman was "owned" by her father until she married, when ownership was transferred to her husband. Unmarried women were referred to as "old maids" and pitied. Due to the stigma of divorce, married women typically remained married, irrespective of the conditions of that marriage. Information about birth control was limited, and the large resultant families increased female dependence on men.[5]

Interestingly, both the first- and second-wave women's movements were linked to civil rights issues in the United States. The movement to abolish slavery, which gained strength in the 1830s, included a number of women leaders, such as Susan B. Anthony and Elizabeth Cady Stanton. The argument was made that all people, regardless of race or sex, had a right to equality, which extended to voting and political representation (Rowbotham 1992:45–6):

> The first organized movement for women's rights thus came from the movement to abolish slavery. Both movements were inspired by the Universalist case for equal human rights. Both included moral and Christian strands, legitimizing radical action by Biblical quotations … abolition and women's rights organizers broke down many conventional barriers to the public participation of black people and women Rowbotham (1992:52).

The slavery issue was ultimately resolved by the American Civil War in the early 1860s, although many emancipated slaves and their ancestors were prevented from voting by creative lawmaking in the Southern states until the civil rights movement of the 1960s. However, even the *formal* enfranchisement of women was to emerge more slowly. In 1866, British member of Parliament and philosopher John Stuart Mill petitioned the Parliament of the United Kingdom to grant suffrage to women. This bill was defeated. In 1869, Mill published his famous essay, *On the Subjection of Women*, which argues that women should be granted the vote. At this point, the suffrage movement was beginning to take on international strength. American suffragist Susan B. Anthony went to Europe to campaign for women's rights (Millett 1970:81), and women's suffrage groups began to organize in Canada and England. Suffragists such as Canada's Nellie McClung argued that the women's vote "was essential for general social improvement" (Bashevkin 1985:7), that women's more sensitive nature (taken as a given) would make politics more caring and humanitarian.

The pursuit of the franchise was the central issue of the first-wave women's movement, although it was by no means the only issue. Women's groups began to organize, pressing not only for suffrage, but also for legal rights, birth control, access to education and temperance (prohibition of alcohol). Kate Millett (1970:83–4) writes:

> One must recognize the central significance of the franchise in that it aroused the greatest opposition and mobilized the greatest consciousness and effort. Yet in many ways it was the red herring of the revolution—a wasteful drain on the energy of seventy years. Because the opposition was so monolithic and unrelenting, the struggle so long and bitter, the vote took on a disproportionate importance. And when the ballot was won, the feminist movement collapsed in what can only be described as exhaustion.

Women across the United States and Canada had received both the federal and state/provincial franchise by 1922, with the exception of Quebec, where women were denied the provincial franchise until 1940.[6] Although "enfranchisement was granted more as a recognition of and reward for women's wartime contributions than as part of a broad social consensus regarding female rights to legal equality" (Bashevkin 1985:123), it was nevertheless a great victory for the women's movement. Feminists soon learned, however, that the vote alone could not solve women's grievances. Large-scale women's political parties failed to emerge, and the vote distribution between existing parties remained constant, since women tended to vote along class and regional lines, as did men. Policies were not created to attract female voters and, with an absence of women in elected offices, the predicted effect of the "female nature" on politics was not seen.

Women's conditions did begin to improve, more the result of social change than the women's movement per se. In the 1920s, younger women experienced greater sexual liberation than the previous generation. Birth control information became more readily available, although abortion remained restricted (Davis 1988:10). Family size dropped from an average of six children to an average of two (Rowbotham 1973:216). Educational opportunities for women were expanded, and a small number of women entered the professions. Still, women remained dependent upon men. Even with greater educational and employment opportunities, women were financially disadvantaged: in addition to lower wages, women were shut out of many jobs simply by virtue of their sex. Social norms continued to press women towards a domestic life of marriage and motherhood.

The suffragist movement lost a great deal of its energy after the vote was won. In the United States, feminists realized that legislative reforms were needed to create the social changes they sought, and the nonpartisan National League of Women Voters was created in 1920. Among its concerns were child labour and welfare, education and labour laws (Millett 1973:83). At this time in Canada, significant feminist organizations did not exist outside of British Columbia (Bashevkin 1985:14). Few women in Canada and the United States contested public office, but some did meet with success. For example, Canada's first woman member of Parliament, Agnes Macphail, was elected in 1921. Canadian women's groups made a political reappearance in 1927 with the "Person's Case." The Canadian Constitution stated that Senate appointments were limited to "qualified persons." In 1927, women's groups argued before the Supreme Court of Canada that women were eligible for Senate appointments. After the Supreme Court ruled that women did not qualify as persons, the case was presented to the Judicial Committee of the Privy Council (JCPC) (then the highest court of appeal for Canadian law). In 1929, the JCPC reversed the Supreme Court decision and found that women were persons, and thus eligible for Senate appointment. Many feminists saw this as the capstone to their gaining full political rights in Canada (Bashevkin 1985:19). In the United States, campaigns for an Equal Rights Amendment (ERA) to the Constitution began in 1923, and informal campaigns continue to this day.

The Great Depression of the 1930s reduced women's employment. Jobs were scarce, and those that existed were generally given to men. Women returned to the home, but it was a different home. Female education and employment were not only accepted, but encouraged, and "labour-saving" devices such as sewing machines and electric irons altered women's work (Bashevkin 1985:20–1). Newly educated women had less work at home, and diverted their energies towards volunteer associations. These organizations were not necessarily feminist in nature, but they kept women socially involved and presented them with leadership opportunities.

The Second World War demanded significant military forces from Canada and the United States. To keep the economies functioning, women were drawn upon as a reserve labour force. Companies set up day-care services to enable women to meet family demands while working outside the home. However, when the war was over and the men returned, women generally returned to the home. The "baby boom" that followed was combined with a renewed social emphasis on the virtues of domesticity and motherhood. Middle-class women continued to pursue higher levels of education, but many gave up their careers upon marrying. Working-class women continued to be paid less than men and had fewer opportunities in the work force.

The late 1950s and early 60s witnessed the emergence of a dynamic and broadly based civil rights movement. In the United States, mounting racial tensions had put America on the brink of disaster, and student resistance to involvement in the Vietnam War added to this tension. Again, women were highly involved in the civil rights movement, and in the accompanying New Left movement. In each case, however, women experienced considerable sexism. As Alice Echols (1989:25–6) explains:

> Both the new left and the civil rights movement were dominated by men who were, at best, uninterested in challenging sexual inequality. Unlike the old left which acknowledged the existence of male chauvinism and gave token support to women's issues, the new left initially lacked any critical consciousness of gender relations.

Women contributed significantly to the civil rights movement, but were not acknowledged as being important. This fact is dramatized in Stokely Carmichael's notorious statement that "the position of women in the [Student Nonviolent Coordinating Committee] is prone" (Echols 1989:31). Women's groups thus began to break away from the New Left, initially intending to be separate but attached to the movement, but eventually becoming a distinct movement with its own goals and agenda. This radical feminism movement flourished between 1968 and 1973.

The 1960s also saw the powerful emergence of liberal feminism. Betty Friedan's *The Feminine Mystique* (1963), outlining the dissatisfaction that housewives felt, shattered the "happy-housewife" myth. The American Civil Rights Act, passed in 1964, ensured that labour laws applied to women as well as men. Ironically, sex was added to the Civil Rights Act in an attempt to ensure its failure, a conservative strategy that resulted instead in substantial gains for both racial minorities and women. In the United States, the liberal feminist National Organization of Women (NOW) was established in 1964; Canada saw the emergence of the grass-roots, antinuclear-weapons movement, Voice of Women (VOW), in 1960. Pressure from a variety of Canadian women's groups also led to the establishment of the Royal Commission on the Status of Women (RCSW), in 1967, which gave its final report in 1970. The National Action Committee on the Status of Women (NAC) was established in 1973 to lobby for legislative action on the Royal Commission's recommendations. NAC soon grew to be the most prominent voice of the women's movement in Canada.

The significant effects of the second-wave women's movement upon society were visible during the 1970s and 1980s. Women entered universities and the work force in increasing numbers. *Ms.* magazine became an identifiable voice of feminism. The availability of the birth control pill granted women a further degree of liberation, and as a result many sexual norms were relaxed or altered. Young women put off marriage and childbearing, while older women left dissatisfying or abusive marriages in greater numbers. Women slowly began to increase their presence in electoral politics and the professions. In 1973, the activist American Supreme Court found that prohibition of abortion violated women's privacy rights, and decriminalized abortion. American women sought constitutional gender-equality rights through the ERA, but failed when by 1983 the ERA fell three states short of ratification.[7] In contrast, Canadian women were successful in lobbying for gender-equality rights in the 1982 Charter of Rights and Freedoms.[8] In 1988, the Canadian Supreme Court found that existing abortion laws were unconstitutional under the charter, leaving Canada without national abortion legislation and legally permitting abortion on demand.

Within the women's movement itself, more and more fractures were evident. Marxist feminism distinguished itself from radical feminism, as did cultural and socialist feminisms. (These branches are discussed in the following section). To a degree, liberal feminism was absorbed by the political mainstream. Debate on such divisive issues as lesbianism, pornography, prostitution, housewifery and child care took their toll on unity within the movement. In addition to these internal divisions, feminism was attacked from the outside. The religion-based New Right movement targeted feminism as the source of society's ills. The Reverend Jerry Faldwell argued that a "global feminist conspiracy" existed, and that feminism was associated with Satan (Faludi 1991:232, 234). Moreover, the New Right blamed increasing crime rates and "social degeneration" on the women's movement. Susan Faludi (1991:232–3) writes:

> That the New Right fastened on feminism, not communism or race, was in itself a testament to the strength and standing of the women's movement in the last decade. As scholar Rosalind Pollack Petchesky observed, "The women's liberation movement in the 1970s had become the most dynamic force for social change in the country, the one most directly threatening not only to conservative values and interest, but also to significant groups whose 'way of life' is challenged by ideas of sexual liberation." Significantly, the critical New Right groups all got underway within two years after the two biggest victories for women's rights—Congress's approval of the ERA in 1972 and the U.S. Supreme Court's legalization of abortion in 1973.

A "war of words" began between feminists and the New Right, the former advocating "choice" and "equality," the latter advocating "life" and "family values." Right-wing women's groups, such as Canada's REAL (Realistic, Equal, Active for Life) Women and anti-ERA groups in the United States (for example, Concerned Women of America) illustrate that New Right opposition to feminism is not limited to men. The New Right–feminism polarity is more sharply defined in the United States than in Canada, where the classical liberal-dominated political right focuses its fire on economics and multiculturalism rather than on "moral" issues.

By the late 1980s and early 1990s, a significant portion of liberal feminism's agenda appeared to have been realized. As liberal feminism becomes less controversial, the term "feminism" is increasingly associated with radical feminism, rather than with the women's movement as a whole. Many young women take university education and careers for granted while denying feminist affiliations—in effect, living off the avails of feminism while denying its importance to their lives.[9] The increased number of women in the professions and the universities lead many young men and women to believe that the women's movement has succeeded in achieving gender equality. Yet despite this perception of equality, women remain significantly underrepresented in national legislatures, overrepresented in poverty and continue to bear most of the burden of child-rearing and housekeeping. Consider these 1993 Canadian statistics: women comprised eighteen percent of the 1993 federal legislature; only twelve percent of children with working mothers were in *regulated* child care; young women (20–24) earned 84.2 cents to every dollar a young man (20–24) made, with older women (55–64) earning only 53.8 percent of the earnings of older males (55–64); 61.9 percent of single mothers and 47.4 percent of single older women live below the poverty line; and twenty-five percent of all women were estimated to experience sexual assault in their lives (Khosla 1993).

Kate Millett (1970:64) writes: "Changes as drastic and fundamental as those of a sexual revolution are not easily arrived at. Nor should it be surprising that such change might take place in stages that are capable of interruption and temporary regression." It is commonly argued that the first stage of the women's movement ended with the attainment of the vote, and that the second stage began in the 1960s, but where is feminism now? Is feminism still in the second stage? If so, is it at a plateau, in a regression or entering a third stage? We would maintain that, regardless of the actual stage it is in, feminism, or at least its goals, are currently being popularized to appeal to a wider number of women and men. The sentiment of this "popularized feminism" is humanitarian in nature: it seeks overall equality, self-empowerment and the betterment of society. Women's rights are being defined as *human* rights. This popularization of feminism is witnessed in the editorials of such women's fashion magazines as *Glamour* and *Chatelaine*, as well as in the writing of such feminists as Gloria Steinem (*Revolution from Within*) and Naomi Wolf (*The Beauty Myth*, and *Fire With Fire*). The message is pro-women rather than anti-men, and is based on the assumption that bettering the position of fifty percent of society's members will better society as a whole. This popularization of feminism does not necessarily represent a new wave of feminism; it may be a revitalization of liberal feminism within the continuing second wave, or a defense against antifeminist forces.

Exercise Two: Contemporary Need For Feminism?

Alison Jaggar and Paula Rothenberg (1986: 4) write: "Many women entering college today believe that sexism has little to do with them …. They treat women's oppression as a problem of historical rather than contemporary interest …. [these students] seem convinced that unlimited possibilities for career advancement and personal fulfillment await them, possibilities that will not be limited either by gender or race. Does this change in attitude and expectation reflect the gains that the women's movement have made in restructuring our society or does it reflect the power of the media and other institutions to shape our consciousness in a way that distorts our perceptions of reality?"

What do you think? Write down your thoughts and debate them with your classmates.

THE PLURALITY OF FEMINISMS

It should now be clear that feminism is not a coherent, unified body of thought. Feminists differ in their policy agendas, the means thought necessary to achieve ends and the ends to be sought by sexual politics. Rosalind Delmar (1986:9) writes: "The fragmentation of contemporary feminism bears ample witness to the impossibility of constructing modern feminism as a simple unity in the present or of arriving at a shared feminist definition of feminism ... it now makes more sense to speak of a plurality of feminisms than of one." Rosemary Tong (1989:1) agrees: "Feminist theory is not one, but many, theories or perspectives ... each feminist theory or perspective attempts to describe women's oppression, to explain its cause and consequences, and to prescribe strategies for women's liberation."

But how does one divide feminism into separate theoretical domains? Authors vary in the number of feminisms they describe, and consensus on labels and classification systems is rare. This section will emphasize three variants of feminism: liberal, radical and Marxist. These three branches were chosen for the significant roles they play in feminist thought, and for the diversity in their approaches. Other feminisms, including cultural, psychoanalytic, socialist and postmodern feminism, will be defined but not explored in detail. Before we attempt to differentiate among feminist theories, however, a number of important caveats must be made.

First, although emphasis is placed on the differences among the theories, keep in mind that all support the basic tenets of feminism to some degree. Second, the purpose of this section, and of this chapter as a whole, is not to critique or argue in favour of a particular feminist theory, but rather to acquaint the reader with the different theories. It is hoped that the information will provide readers with the ability to identify the different feminisms they encounter in reading and everyday life. In addition, this section emphasizes that feminism is not a single theory but a collection of divergent theories that share a single base. Finally, labeling any social movement is a difficult task. For example, one may hold values representative of liberal feminism without considering oneself a liberal feminist. This issue concerns the importance of individual identification with ideological movements. A person may hold views without considering these views to be political or ideological in nature. Conversely, one may consider oneself a radical feminist without feeling that one's views are adequately reflected in this chapter's definition of radical feminism. This problem exists due to the diversity within feminist theories. Feminism is an extremely dynamic theory buttressed by prolific scholarship, and engaging a large number of supporters and critics.

A tree metaphor will perhaps best explain the situation. We define the basic tenets of feminism as the roots and trunk of the tree, and the different feminist theories as the branches. Each branch on a tree, of course, has smaller branches that shoot off it, and so on. This chapter attempts to explain only the larger branches. Space limitations impel the choice of parsimony over detail, and the feminist theories will necessarily be simplified and generalized. Apologies are extended to any readers who feel their views are not fully explained.

Concepts and Terms

To understand feminist theories, it is important to be acquainted with the concept of public and private spheres. "Distinctions between public and private have been and remain fundamental, not incidental or tangential, ordering principles in all known societies, save, perhaps, the most simple" (Elshtain 1981:6). The public sphere is concerned with politics and the economy—affairs that occur on the "macro" level. The private sphere is concerned with all "micro" affairs: the home and the family predominate in this sphere. Historically, there has been a sexual division of labour, with men tending to the public sphere and women to the private. Thus, men have controlled economic and political affairs, while women have managed homes and raised children. First-wave feminism attempted to gain women access to the public sphere through the right to vote. Second-wave feminism works to further the integration of women into the public sphere by increasing the number and roles of women in the work force and in politics, and by encouraging men to take a more active role in the private sphere. Feminist theories differ in their valuation of and approach to the separate spheres.

A second important concept, introduced in Chapter 2, is systemic discrimination. Systemic discrimination is defined as the unintentional discrimination against a group throughout society or a set of institutions. This differs from direct discrimination, which occurs when an individual or agency deliberately rejects or disadvantages certain social groups. An example of systemic discrimination is seen in Canada's electoral nomination process. Party nominations are not regulated by electoral law, and nomination campaigns can be quite costly, particularly in urban areas. Since women, on average, are paid less than men, are less successful in attaining bank loans and have less access to monied networks, the nomination system works to the disadvantage of women, and systemic discrimination is the result.[10] An example of direct discrimination is witnessed in the policy that women could not be nominated by virtue of sex alone—now a policy of the past. Some cases of discrimination fall in a grey area between these two extremes. Is, for example, a requirement that all fire fighters be over six feet tall and one hundred and eighty pounds direct or systemic discrimination against women and certain visible-minority men?

Exercise Three: Men and Women In Society

List a number of ways men and women differ in society. Are there fields and occupations that one sex tends to dominate? How do the life circumstances between men and women differ? Are men and women treated the same in society, in the work force, in the media? Are the causes of these differences between men and women purposeful (direct discrimination) or unintentional (systemic)? What can be done to address the causes of differential results?

Finally, we need to differentiate between "sex" and "gender." Sex refers to a biological condition: one is either male or female. Gender, on the other hand, is a sociologically created condition. As Judith Lorber (1994:1) writes:

> [G]ender [is] a social structure that has its origins in the development of human culture, not in biology or procreation. Like any social institution, gender exhibits both universal features and chronological and cross-cultural variations that affect individual lives and social interaction in major ways .

This difference between sex and gender leads to questions about differences between men and women. Are masculine and feminine qualities innate, or do they result from socialization? Does the relegation of women to the private sphere lead women to be more nurturing than men, or have women naturally gravitated to the private sphere over time because of an innate nurturing quality? This is a classic "nature or nurture" question, and one's answer to this question influences how one feels towards the different branches of feminism.

Exercise Four: Gender Constructs

Make a list of qualities considered to be "male" and "female." Feel free to draw upon stereotypes (for example, "boys are better at math") as well as your own experiences with male and female friends, instructors and co-workers. After examining this list, do you recognize some qualities that you feel are innate to men or to women? Or do you believe they are all social constructs? Would you argue that such differences between men and women are: i) socially constructed; ii) innate; or iii) a mixture of innate and socially constructed qualities?

Keeping these definitions and the core concepts of feminism in mind, we will now turn to a more detailed discussion of the branches of feminist thought.

FIGURE 5.1: Three Branches of Feminism

Feminism	Nature/Nurture	Source of Oppression	Prescription
Liberal Feminism	Nurture. Emphasis on similarities between men and women	Unequal rights and opportunities, education, sex discrimination	Some favour affirmative action; others feel that equal access to education and the public realm is sufficient
Marxist Feminism	Nurture	Capitalism	Replace capitalism with socialism; valuation of domestic work
Radical Feminism	Nature. Some argue nature and nurture work together. Emphasis on the differences between men and women.	Patriarchy	Varies. Proposed solutions include androgyny, matriarchy and separatism. Celebration of the female.

Liberal Feminism

Due to the popular hegemony of liberalism in North America, liberal feminism is the least controversial of the feminisms. As its name suggests, liberal feminism is associated with liberalism and the principles underlying that ideology: individualism, liberty, equality and meritocracy. Liberal feminists accept existing institutions and structures. They do not, for example, wish to jettison the free market or radically transform representative democracy. What they do seek is women's full integration into those structures. The liberal feminist's behest is "Let us in."

Why should women be integrated into the public sphere? Liberal feminists maintain that men and women are basically the same—that women hold the skills and aptitudes necessary to be efficient and valued workers in the public sphere. In addition, liberal feminists argue that women as individuals benefit from education and employment. "Liberation" for a liberal feminist is acceptance into the public sphere. The differences between men and women, according to liberal feminism, are largely a result of gender socialization and sex-role stereotyping (Elshtain 1981:240). The liberal feminist does not feel "biology is destiny." For example, Joyce Trebilcot (1984:114) argued in the early 1970s that "whether there are natural psychological differences between females and males has little bearing on the issue of whether society should reserve certain roles for females and others for males." For liberal feminists, the question is not "Why should women be included?" but "Why shouldn't they be?"

The liberal feminist's goal is equality. However, as Chapter 2 illustrates, equality does not always mean equal opportunities. The issue of equality has proven divisive for the liberal ideology: classical liberals support equality of right, while reform liberals support equality of opportunity. These are very different goals, and require different policy initiatives. Similarly, liberal feminists diverge on what measures should be taken to ensure women's equality. Some feel that equal rights are enough; with time and education, women will achieve equality in politics, in the sciences, in academia. Others argue that the integration of women into the public sphere will continue to be hindered by systemic discrimination. To overcome systemic barriers, and to speed up the rate of integration, they support affirmative action (or "reverse discrimination"). Affirmative action is the preferential hiring of disadvantaged groups when all other factors (for example, education, experience) are equal. Such action, it is is argued, is necessary to increase the opportunities for women in the public sphere.

Thus, there is a range of views even within liberal feminism. Whether a liberal feminist favours equality of right or equality of opportunity depends on her individual beliefs. Jill Vickers et al. (1993:325) argue that liberal feminism varies on this point between countries:

> [L]iberal feminism has taken a number of quite different forms in different political contexts .... In the United States, liberal feminists have been committed to the absolute equality of opportunity represented by the Equal Rights Amendment .... There has been less emphasis in Canada on legal equality and more on the achievement of economic security than there has been in the agenda of U.S. liberal feminism.

Regardless of the means preferred, liberal feminists all support the same end: equality between the sexes within a liberal democratic state.

Liberal feminists have focused on single-issue campaigns (for example, labour legislation) rather than on large-scale social and sexual revolution (Bouchier 1983:81). Addressing single issues incrementally through legislation and public policy has allowed liberal feminism to have a profound impact on society. Many of the advances women have made in employment and education can be credited to liberal feminism's willingness to "work within the system." Of course, women still have a long way to go before reaching the equality sought by liberal feminists. Moreover, the gains made by liberal feminists are by no means secure—the emergence of women into the public sphere in the last few decades was preceded by centuries in which women were largely excluded from public life. In the big historical picture, the full participation of women in the public sphere is still a new and fragile development.

Exercise Five: Gender Equality

Do you believe that many or most of women's concerns can be dealt with within the context of liberal democracy and its institutional structures? Or do you feel that changes must be made to the "system" before significant changes can be experienced in sexual politics? What exactly do you see as the barriers to full gender equality? How would you define full gender equality? Should special measures (for example, affirmative action and pay equity programs) be used to achieve this equality, or should we wait for this equality to occur naturally, over time? What, in your mind, is a reasonable length of time to wait for gender equality? A decade? Fifty years? A century?

Marxist Feminism

A discussion of Marxist feminism may seem unnecessary at first, since Marxist feminism has not been a dominant force in the Canadian and American women's movements. However, many feminist writers, particularly radical and socialist feminists, have been influenced by the ideas of Marxist feminism. As a revolutionary doctrine, Marxist feminism has made a significant impact on feminist political thought, and thus it is important for students of feminism to be acquainted with its content. It should be noted that although Marx did not systematically address the exploitation of women, the issue is addressed by his colleague, Friedrich Engels, in *The Origin of the Family, Private Property, and the State.* Contemporary Marxist feminism focuses on the oppression of women *within* the capitalist system. Class is considered the greatest source of women's oppression, but women are more oppressed than their male counterparts, since women are subordinate not only to higher classes but also to men. In addition, women are further removed from the means of production than proletariat men, as "women's work" (such as housekeeping, cooking and raising children) is work done to support men rather than to produce materials (Tong 1989:40). The role of this domestic labour is often trivialized and discredited, rather than socially valued (Rose 1986:165). When employed outside the home, women are given "pink-collar" jobs, such as secretarial and nursing positions. For all of these reasons, Marxist feminists argue that a woman's alienation is greater than a man's.

Marxist feminists focus on the economic dependence of women (Jaggar and Rothenberg 1984:85). Their proposals have included calls for socialized domestic work and child care (for example, communal living), wages for housework and "equal pay for work of equal value." Such measures would ensure that women were not financially dependent upon men, thus alleviating some of women's oppression. But for all oppression to be overthrown, Marxist feminists maintain, the capitalist system needs to be discarded, and replaced by communism. Evelyn Reed (1984:135–6) writes:

> The underlying source of women's oppression, which is capitalism, cannot be abolished by women alone, nor by a coalition of women drawn from all classes. It will require a worldwide struggle for socialism by the working masses, male and female alike, together with every other section of the oppressed ....

Thus, Marxist feminists see possible coalitions with working-class men, visible minorities and other oppressed groups.

Exercise Six: Women and Capitalism

Do you feel women are oppressed or exploited by the capitalist system? If so, what is it about capitalism or the free market that leads to this oppression? Consider employment issues, wage differences, advertising, "the beauty myth" and the media's portrayal of women. Are these problems of capitalism, or of society in general? Can these problems be addressed within the capitalist system? What measures would you recommend to make capitalism more accommodating to women?

Radical Feminism

Radical feminism is perhaps the least unified branch of feminism. Substantial creative thought has emerged, and continues to emerge, from radical feminist theory, which focuses on issues of sexuality, gender, reproduction and motherhood (Tong 1989:72). Radical feminists seek to reclaim the feminine, and to celebrate it.

Patriarchy is the central concept of radical feminism. Patriarchy is defined as the overall system of male domination, "a set of social relations between men ... which ... establish or create interdependence and solidarity among men that enable them to dominate women" (Hartmann 1984:177). Radical feminists see the oppression of women under patriarchy as widespread and historical, existing before capitalism and in all cultures (Elshtain 1981:212–3). Radical feminists embrace a very broad social and political critique, as Rosemarie Tong (1989:2–3) explains:

> They argue that it is the patriarchal system that oppresses women, a system characterized by power, dominance, hierarchy, and competition, a system that cannot be reformed but only ripped out root and branch. It is not just patriarchy's legal and political structures that must be overturned; its social and cultural institutions (especially the family, the church, and the academy) must also go.

Issues of sexuality and the body are important to radical feminism. Considerable attention has been given to male control of female bodies, including issues of violence against women, pornography, rape, sexual harassment and the criminalization of abortion. Radical feminists seek to end men's control of women's bodies, and to redefine female sexuality to suit women's needs, rather than men's (Tong 1989:72). Sexual orientation is therefore another issue that radical feminists challenge to varying degrees. For example, Charlotte Bunch (1986:145) writes that "Lesbians must become feminists and fight against woman's oppression, just as feminists must become Lesbians if they hope to end male supremacy." Others, however, are more accepting of heterosexual feminists. Although there is a strong link between lesbianism and radical feminism due to their shared valuation of the female over the male, not all radical feminists are lesbians, and not all lesbians see themselves as radical feminists (Tong 1989:123).

Despite its celebration of the female, radical feminism is defined in part by masculinity. This occurs because femininity is often defined as the polar opposite of masculinity. Jean Bethke Elshtain (1981:205) writes: "Radical feminists sketch a vision of the male that is unrelenting and unforgiving in its harshness .... The problem historically has been that the male, an aggressive and evil being, has dominated, oppressed, exploited and victimized the female, a being of a very different sort."[11] Unlike the liberal feminists, who rely strongly on the nurture argument, radical feminists favour the nature position: male and female differences are largely innate. For example, Shulamith Firestone (1986:139) argues that "biology itself—procreation—is at the origin of the dualism. The immediate assumption of the layman that the unequal division of the sexes is 'natural' may be well-founded." The aim is not to deny difference, but to recognize femininity as a legitimate and, for some radical feminists, *preferred* basis for society.

For the radical feminist, the personal *is* the political. Although all feminisms attempt to politicize the private sphere to a degree, radical feminism takes this position further. *All* acts, no matter how private, are political in nature. Love, sexual orientation, physical appearance, birthing techniques—all are open to political definition and interpretation (Elshtain 1981:217). Note, however, that "political" does not mean "open to state action." Many radical feminists see the state as the ultimate patriarchal institution—hierarchically based, exerting power over the meek, confrontational and imposing. "Political" in this context means "participating in a power system."

What is the solution to patriarchy? Answers to this question range from the creation of a more androgynous society to the creation of a matriarchal society (Tong 1989:95), from Charlotte Bunch's extreme lesbian separatism to the more moderate goal of restructuring economic and private relations within a predominantly heterosexual society.[12] Of course, a new society is doomed to the same problems unless male domination is ended. To establish a gender-neutral, woman-friendly heterosexual society, radical feminists argue, many of the existing institutions would need to be altered to remove male bias and allow for female qualities such as compassion and consensus. For example, majority rule and representative democracy might be replaced by a more consensual form of government.

Radical feminists differ in their willingness to work within existing power systems, and in the means they are willing to use to seek their ends. Some radical feminists, such as Catherine MacKinnon, advocate state censorship of pornography to limit the male exploitation of the female body. Others oppose state censorship since it gives a large patriarchal institution the power to decide which materials are acceptable. In Canada, recent antipornography legislation has resulted in an increase in the amount of gay and lesbian pornography that is stopped at the Canada-U.S. border, but has had little effect on the heterosexual, male-oriented pornography targeted by radical feminists.

Exercise Seven: Feminist Policies

Make a list of at least ten recent political, employment and social issues relating to women. After completing the list, identify which issues are liberal, Marxist and radical feminist in nature. Do some issues fall between two branches of feminism? Rank-order the issues according to their importance to society. Which issue is the most pressing, in your opinion? Which is the least important? Is there a pattern to your responses? Do you tend to prefer issues related to a particular branch of feminism?

Criticisms of the Three Branches

Each branch of feminism has its share of critics, with much of the criticism coming from the other branches. Liberal feminism is attacked by its critics for its willingness to "work within the system." Marxist feminists in particular feel that liberal feminists buy into a flawed social system. Liberal feminism is also charged with not going far enough. For instance, liberal feminism's "tendency to valorize a gender-neutral humanism over a gender-specific feminism" has been attacked by non–liberal feminists (Tong 1989:31). Liberal feminism's perceived failure to oppose patriarchy is seen by some as implicit support for the structures of patriarchy and "male-oriented" norms. Although women are integrated into the public sphere, men have yet to be equally integrated into the private sphere, leaving child-rearing and housekeeping in the female realm. Therefore, separate spheres still exist: one for men and women, another for women only. Jean Bethke Elshtain (1981:243) argues that liberal feminism's desire to maintain the public-private divide leads to the devaluation of the private sphere, and this is a problem that liberal feminists are now addressing. Finally, some non–liberal feminists question liberal feminism's outright acceptance of nurture over nature (Tong 1989:32).

Criticisms of Marxist feminism come from a number of directions. First, Marxist feminists are criticized for placing too great an emphasis on work, when other factors also serve to oppress women (such as reproductive concerns and physical abuse). Socialist feminists (who have modified Marxist feminism substantially) maintain that "our conception of the mode of production must be enlarged so that it ... includes the way in which people have organized to produce and distribute the means of satisfying their needs for sexuality, nurturance, and babies" (Jaggar and Rothenberg 1984:88). A second, and related, criticism deals with the conclusion that women's oppression would cease under a communist system. This is perceived as simplistic and overly optimistic, particularly in light of the communist experiences in Eastern Europe and the former Soviet Union, where women failed to achieve true social equality with men. Yet, despite these criticisms, Marxist feminists have made significant contributions to feminist thought:

> [T]hey have helped us understand, among other things, how the institution of the family is related to capitalism; how women's domestic work is trivialized as not *real* work; and, finally, how women are generally given the most boring and low-paying jobs (Tong 1989:51).

Not surprisingly, radical feminism also has its share of critics; any movement that so challenges existing social institutions and norms is bound to meet with resistance and opposition. The man-bad–woman-good dualism is problematic for many. Others question radical feminism's reliance on biology as the definition of female nature (Tong 1989:127). The varied prescriptions for patriarchy (for example, matriarchy and separatism) are also subject to criticism. Yet, despite these criticisms, it is important to recognize the contribution radical feminism has made to feminist thought in general, and to mainstream political thought. Radical feminism has expanded the boundaries of political debate, bringing formerly "private" issues such as wife-battering, incest, sexual harassment and rape into the public sphere and consciousness. This illustrates that what was radical twenty years ago is considered mainstream today. Although society may continue to disagree on the correct way to approach these problems, their legitimacy as *social* problems is rarely questioned. Radical feminism has also increased appreciation of female qualities, history and culture. Universities now offer classes on gender roles and academic degrees in women's studies. As Rosemarie Tong (1989:138) writes: "All movements need radicals, and the women's movement is no exception." The radical feminists have helped to empower women and to politicize the personal.

Backlash Within?

Feminism is increasingly experiencing an internal fracturing, with various writers critiquing particular positions and approaches to feminism. Such criticisms differ from external critiques in that they represent attempts to strengthen feminism by addressing unpopular or inconsistent positions. Much of the criticism is focused on feminisms that emphasize the wrongs of men. Two important feminist critics are Naomi Wolf and Christina Hoff Sommers:

> "[V]ictim feminism," as I define it ... casts women as sexually pure and mystically nurturing, and stresses the evil done to these "good" women as a way to petition for their rights .... While we can sympathize with those who need this approach when times are bad, we must also realize that it proves dangerous when times change .... victim feminism is obsolete ... (Wolf 1993:xvii).

> American feminism is currently dominated by a group of women who seek to persuade the public that American women are not the free creatures we think we are .... The feminists who hold this divisive view of our social and political reality believe we are in a gender war .... The large majority of women, including the majority of college women, are distancing themselves from this anger and resentfulness. Unfortunately, they associate these attitudes with feminism, and so conclude that they are not really feminists (Sommers 1994:16, 18).

Part of the problem, Christina Hoff Sommers (1994:18) suggests, is that such feminists cut off the possibility of internal dialogue:

> [M]ale critics must be "sexist" and "reactionary," and female critics "traitors," "collaborators," or "backlashers." This kind of reaction has had a powerful inhibiting effect. It has alienated and silenced women and men alike.

The solution, she argues, is for other feminists to speak out.

Other Branches of Feminism: A Quick Description

Socialist feminism attempts to restructure Marxist feminism so as to address problems of gender-related oppression. For the socialist feminist, sexual oppression is equal in importance to class oppression, and the extinction of the latter will not be sufficient to end the oppression of women. Many socialist feminists regard "capitalism and patriarchy as mutually interdependent and reinforcing systems" (Jaggar and Rothenberg 1986:89); others see capitalism and patriarchy as forces working to oppress women (Tong 1989:175). Regardless of the relationship between capitalism and patriarchy, socialist feminists feel that both must be addressed to end female oppression. One well-known socialist feminist is Alison Jagger.

Cultural feminism, an offshoot of radical feminism, seeks to replace male-centered institutions and values with female-centered institutions and values (Vickers 1993:327). Cultural feminists emphasize the differences between male and female, and celebrate the feminine. Alice Echols (1989:6) defines cultural feminism as a "countercultural movement aimed at reversing the cultural valuation of the male and devaluation of the female." Cultural feminists find class analysis to be "irrelevant to women" since it is male in nature (Echols 1989:7). Essentially, cultural feminism is the vein or strand of radical feminism which suggests that patriarchy be replaced by matriarchy. One well-known cultural feminist is Josephine Donovan.

Psychoanalytical feminism attempts to "[develop] the Freudian corpus in feminist directions" (Tong 1989:143). Sigmund Freud's theories on infanthood, child-parent relations (the Oedipus complex), female morality and biological determinism are reworked and reinterpreted in this vein of feminism. Although many feminist theorists, including Kate Millett and Shulamith Firestone, have attacked Freud as being antiwoman, psychoanalytical feminists maintain that Freud was misunderstood, and that he has continuing relevance for an understanding of feminist issues. One well-known theorist in this field is Carol Gilligan, who attempts to explain male/female differences in concepts of morality in her book, *In a Different Voice.*[13] Psychoanalytic feminists argue that a woman must look within (that is, into the psyche) as well as to outside sources to find the roots of her oppression.

Postmodern feminism is drawn from postmodern theory—"a philosophical stance that challenges generally accepted beliefs about reality, knowledge, truth, and transcendence" (Grant 1993:129). Gender is seen as a social construction, but gender differences are not necessarily negative. Women's distinctness, or "Otherness," as Simone de Beauvoir would say, is viewed as "a way of being, thinking, and speaking that allows for openness, plurality, diversity, and difference" (Tong 1989: 219). Two well-known postmodern feminists are Simone de Beauvoir and Hélène Cixous.

Women of colour have also made unique and important contributions to feminist thought. Writers such as bell hooks explore the additional oppression experienced by visible-minority women. Jaggar and Rothenberg (1984:89) write: "Although women of color do not utilize any single theoretical framework, their writings invariably reflect a concern that the complexities of race and gender (and often class as well) be explored simultaneously." Women of colour challenge the existing branches of feminism to consider the concerns of *all* women, rather than make generalizations from a white, middle-class perspective. As Jee Yeun Lee (1995: 210) asserts, "Women of colour do not struggle in feminist movements simply to add cultural diversity."

Summary

This brief overview of feminist thought has stressed that there is no *one* feminism. Despite the basic tenets they share, feminists of different branches do not share common agendas, perspectives or solutions. Generalizations made about "feminists" are often unfair; by attempting to lump together such diversity, an injustice is done to all branches of feminism. It should also be clear at this point that the branches of feminism overlap and diverge at many points. A person may identify herself as a socialist feminist on some issues, a radical feminist on others and as holding a position between liberal and radical feminism on remaining issues. Another person may consider himself to be a liberal feminist on all issues. Such flexibility allows feminism to be attractive to a wide range of people. At the same time, it can lead to a confused political debate when the same terms are used in very different ways.

FEMINIST THOUGHT AND THE LEFT-RIGHT SPECTRUM

Positioning the feminist branches along the left-right spectrum described in Chapter 1 is problematic for two reasons: first, the left-right spectrum measures attitudes towards state involvement in the *economy*, whereas many feminist issues concern state involvement in *society*; second, there is diversity in the approaches towards the state *within* the branches. Radical feminism, for example, incorporates those feminists who want differences between men and women accommodated by means of legal structures (for example, the prohibition on pornography) and those who want the state to be dismantled (anarchists). Liberal feminists range from those who feel legal and political equality for women is sufficient, to those who feel measures should be taken to ensure equality of opportunity. For these reasons, it is difficult to think of feminism, or its individual branches, as holding clearly defined positions on the left-right spectrum.

In popular discourse, the entanglement of feminism with left and right comes when we begin to identify the political supporters and opponents of feminism. If the discussion of the range of feminist thought has given the impression that feminism has no significant opponents, this impression should be corrected. Antifeminism is a force that becomes more politically active as feminism becomes a greater source of social innovation. Susan Faludi calls this antifeminist movement a "backlash" against feminism, one of a series of backlash movements in the twentieth century. She (1991:232) writes:

> Every backlash movement has had its preferred scapegoat: for the American Protective Association, Catholics filled the bill. For Father Coughlin's "social justice" movement, Jews. For the Ku Klux Klan, of course, blacks. And for the New Right, the enemy would be feminist women.

Backlash movements are reactions against loss of power and changing social norms. Such negativity does not occur if a group or movement is not considered a threat. In this sense, then, the backlash shows the success that feminism has had, to date, in transforming the social and political order.

But what does feminism threaten? At the least, it threatens the traditional division of labour. As women enter the public sphere, they often ask their husbands or partners to accept greater responsibility in the private sphere. At the most, feminism threatens everything. Ideas of marriage, democracy, the free market, parenting, religion and spirituality, culture, sexuality—all are questioned. No topic is taboo, particularly for radical feminists who question every institution that involves power relations. This can be seen as threatening or even dangerous by those who wish to

---

Why Is Feminism So Controversial?

Feminism has been subject to a number of critiques. Some of its opponents dislike the entry of women into the public realm. Others are threatened by feminism's association with the political left. And many people feel content with the status quo, and oppose any movement that threatens its existence. The range of criticism extends from the misogynist to the philosophically based. Just as knowing someone is a feminist leaves a great number of questions unanswered (for example, "What kind of feminism?"), knowing someone is opposed to feminism does not necessarily give much perspective into their overall political views.

Some opposition to feminism may be attributed to misconceptions of the women's movement. Like the civil rights movement, feminism has experimented with a number of ideas: equality (seeking sex- and colour-blindness); affirmative action; integration; and separatism. The diversity of feminist proposals creates an often confused public debate, with people using the same terms to refer to different subjects. For example, Bob may say that he is against feminism, because he feels feminism will lead to an expanded state. Joan may strongly oppose women's employment, arguing that a woman's place is in the home. Are both equal opponents of feminism?

---

protect and preserve the existing order, or, as in the case of the New Right, a social order of the past. The New Right is "not so much defending a prevailing order as resurrecting an outmoded or imagined one" (Faludi 1991:231). The idea of removing or restricting women in the public sphere may seem outlandish to young people today, but this is what the reactionary extremes of the family-values movement desire. "Family values" implies the re-creation of the 1950s-style family: two heterosexual parents, "breadwinning" father and stay-at-home mother. Thus, the New Right, which seeks to reintroduce the patriarchal family, might be seen as the polar opposite of radical feminism.[14]

It should be noted that not all members of the New Right are men, just as not all feminists are women. As noted earlier, antifeminist women's organizations do exist in Canada and the United States. Clearly, feminism (whichever branch) and antifeminism are belief systems that can be adopted by anyone to any degree. Political identities are adopted—one's attitudes towards feminism are not determined by one's sex. Thus, although it may appear counterintuitive at first, there are women who are strong supporters of the New Right, and men who are radical feminists. (There are also many men and women who support the New Right for reasons unrelated to feminism, pro or con.) What is important in determining beliefs is not sex, but the desired social outcome. Political measures, be it affirmative action or banning women from combat, must be seen as means to that desired social end.

The association of the New Right with opposition to feminism suggests that individuals and political parties who locate themselves on the left of the ideological spectrum will be relatively supportive of feminist movements, interests and objectives. To date, this has largely been the case. Feminists have relied heavily on government intervention to overcome the effects of discrimination, systemic or direct, and it has been those to the left who have most supported government intervention in the economic and social orders. Since women are overrepresented in poverty, women have also been disproportionate beneficiaries of the programs associated with the modern welfare state. It is worth speculating, therefore, what might happen if the ideological center of gravity in western democratic states continues to slide to the right. Will feminists become increasingly isolated in the shrinking left-of-center pole of the electorate, or will there be a rapprochement between feminism and the political right? Will feminism be powerful enough, either by itself or in coalition with other social movements such as racial-equality movements, to arrest any further ideological slippage to the right?

THE FUTURE OF FEMINISM

Has feminism reached its desirable limits? Women are attending university in equal rates to men. Women are expected and accepted in the work force. Wife-battering is no longer considered an acceptable part of marriage. Men are interested in parenting, and claim to be taking on a more active role in the household. Young girls grow up expecting to be doctors and astronauts as well as mommies and nurses. Women and men have greater access to and information about birth control. Reproductive technologies have advanced to the point where postmenopausal women have borne children.

Perhaps the most significant effect of the feminist movement has been a change in social norms and attitudes. The result is a *perception* of greater equality between men and women. However, social realities do not fully or even adequately reflect this perception. In the working class, single mothers have little access to education and employment. Within the middle class, there is a much greater degree of equality, but to say equality of opportunity exists may be pushing the mark. Many social norms need to be altered before genuine equality exists. For example, girls need to be encouraged to develop their leadership skills. Engineering, mathematics and the "hard" sciences, as well as the trades, must be seen as viable and attractive career options for young women. Boys should be encouraged to develop their nurturing skills; "caring" professions such as nursing, child care and full-time parenting must be respected as options for men.

But what would an equal society look like? Men and women would be encouraged to share both the public and private spheres, and the distribution of labour within the spheres would be similar between the sexes. Thus, men would be more active in child-rearing and housekeeping; fatherhood would involve more than paying the bills and administering discipline. Steps have been made in this direction already: many fathers are actively involved in their children's lives and care, even in divorced families. But issues of "deadbeat dads" (fathers who refuse to pay child support) and emotionally absent fathers remain.[15] For society as a whole to advance and improve, parenthood needs to be taken seriously by both parents. This does not mean that one parent must remain at home, or that parents must remain together, or that a 1950s-style family unit must be re-created. What it means is that responsibility for children should be shared; the form that this takes may vary from situation to situation.

By this point, it should be apparent that feminism goes beyond these issues of separate spheres. In fact, feminism continues to evolve at a rate that makes the term large and unwieldy. Many political programs and agendas, many perspectives and attitudes, are combined under the catchall term "feminism." This is both a virtue and a hindrance. The virtue is that variation within feminism illustrates an acceptance and encouragement of diversity in thought. The single label encourages the branches to form coalitions when politically relevant, thus enabling the emergence of unity and cooperation. The hindrance comes when opponents of feminism use the term to signify only those elements which are perceived as extreme; in effect, classifying all of feminism by its most radical and least popular thinkers. It is possible that feminism needs to redefine itself—before its opponents do. This may require clarifying common positions, and emphasizing the branches of feminism when relevant, in order to prevent opponents from making sweeping statements about it designed to mislead the public.

So what is the future of feminism in Canada and the United States? Arguably, feminism is becoming more popularized through the combination of many aspects of liberal feminism with some of the less extreme positions of radical feminism. Differences between men and women are neither denied nor emphasized; neither sex is seen as more virtuous or socially important. This sentiment is less controversial than many previously invoked by radical feminism; it invites both women and men to work towards a common purpose—a society that allows each individual to develop fully, regardless of sex. Women are encouraged to empower themselves and men are encouraged to develop their nurturing sides in order for each to further personal development. A continuation of this sentiment will lead to significant social and political change. Barriers based on sex will be considered intolerable and violence of any form will be deemed an attack on all of society. Economic models and accounts will be modified to ensure that "women's work" is fully acknowledged (Waring 1988).

Within this movement there will be differences. For example, some people will accept the idea of shared-sex responsibility for both spheres, but will oppose legislation that encourages women into the public sphere and men into the private sphere. Others will not find such legislation problematic. Some will argue that the free market will create this shared division of labour over time; others will argue that legislative measures will be required to aid the process. And of course, the backlash movement seeking to return to separate spheres will continue to exist.

Naomi Wolf (1993:132) writes that "a feminism worthy of its name will fit every woman, and every man who cares about women, comfortably." In the near future, feminism will attempt to meet this criterion, but will remain opposed by the political right. Distinctions between the branches of feminism may persist and deepen, or they may reduce in importance. The future, as always, remains largely uncertain. However, it is safe to assume that feminism will continue to be an important political, social and *ideological* force as we enter the twenty-first century.

NOTES

1. For an in-depth, articulate discussion of the core concepts of feminism, see Judith Grant (1993). Grant identifies three core concepts: universal womanhood, experience and personal politics. This chapter concurs with, and draws heavily upon, this basic framework. It should be noted that Nancy Cott also writes that there are three core components to the feminist ideology. These components are similar, but not identical, to the concepts noted by Grant. Cott (1987:3) identifies: 1) gender-group identification (similar to Grant's universal womanhood); 2) opposition to sexual hierarchy (Grant's personal politics); and 3) the presupposition that women's condition is socially constructed.
2. The distinction between these two terms will be explored more fully later in this chapter.
3. This distrust of objectivity is by no means absolute; feminists often use statistical data to strengthen their demands for policy change.
4. See, for example, Mary Wollstonecraft, *A Vindication of the Rights of Women*. Cambridge: Cambridge Univ. Press, 1792.
5. Birth control and abortion were not outlawed in the United States until the 1870s. However, at that time, birth control methods were unreliable (for example, the "rhythm method") and abortion was a physically risky undertaking (Davis 1988:8).
6. Women in Newfoundland were granted the vote in 1925; Newfoundland was not a Canadian province at the time.
7. The American Constitution requires that a proposed amendment be passed by a two-thirds vote in both Houses of Congress, and then be ratified by three-quarters of the states. Congress passed the Equal Rights Amendment Bill in 1973, but it failed to secure ratification by three-quarters of the states within the ten-year time limit. Despite its failure, the ERA campaign was successful in bringing gender-equality issues to public attention.
8. Section 15 of the Charter reads: "(1) Every individual is equal before and under the law and has the right to equal protection and equal benefit of the law without discrimination and, in particular, without discrimination based on race, national or ethnic origin, colour, religion, sex, age, or mental or physical disability. (2) Subsection (1) does not preclude any law, program or activity that has as its object the amelioration of conditions of disadvantaged individuals or groups including those that are disadvantaged because of race, national or ethnic origin, colour, religion, sex, age, or mental or physical disability." Section 28 reads: "Notwithstanding anything within this Charter, the rights and freedoms referred to in it are guaranteed equally to male and female persons."
9. For a discussion of this, and a critique of radical feminism, see Rene Denfeld, *The New Victorians* (1995).
10. Women experience similar problems attaining nominations in the American context.
11. Rene Denfeld (1995) refers to this vision as "the antiphallic campaign."
12. A number of small feminist economic institutions were created in the 1970s to attempt this (Jaggar and Rothenberg 1986:219).
13. Gilligan's work has not been without its share of criticism from social scientists.
14. The New Right is not defined solely by its attitudes towards feminism. See Chapter 3 for further discussion.
15. This is by no means meant to imply that all mothers are perfect caretakers of their children.

CHAPTER SIX

Environmentalism: Expanding the Boundaries of Ideological Thought

WITH RONALD HALLMAN AND MICHELLE HONKANEN

*When we try to pick out anything by itself, we find it
hitched to everything else in the universe.*

JOHN MUIR

*Environmentalism, in the deepest sense, is not about environment. It is not about
things but relationships, not about beings but Being, not about world but the
inseparability of self and circumstance.*

NEIL EVERNDEN, *The Natural Alien*

*After some ten millennia of a very ambitious social evolution, we must reenter nat-
ural evolution again .... I do not mean that we must return to the primitive life
ways of our early ancestors, or surrender activity and techne to a pastoral image of
passivity and bucolic acquiescence. We slander the natural world when we deny its
activity, striving, creativity, and development as well as its subjectivity. Nature is
never drugged. Our reentry into natural evolution is no less a humanization of
nature than a naturalization of humanity.*

MURRAY BOOKCHIN, *The Ecology of Freedom*

One has only to read the daily newspaper or tune in to the evening news to get a
sense of the wide range of environmental issues confronting contemporary
societies. Debates continue about the quality of urban air and water supplies. We
are told that over-fishing, marine pollution and the destruction of coral reefs threat-
en not only our economic livelihood but the oceans themselves. Logging firms battle environmentalists over the fate of old-growth forests in North America, and rain

forests around the world face the inexorable pressures of economic development. Acid rain has been linked to stunted growth or "forest death" in trees, embryo evaporation in birds' eggs and human health problems such as bronchitis (Switzer 1994:259).

How should we deal with this onslaught of information and concern? In coming to grips with this challenge, it may be useful to consider a framework within which to think about environmental issues in general. Environmentalism suggests just such a framework. It provides a worldview that weaves together ethical principles with a broad set of recommendations for the behaviour of individuals, firms, neighbourhoods, nation-states and the global community. In all of these regards, environmentalism is an *ideological perspective* designed to shape political values, behaviours and institutions. Indeed, environmentalism is one of the more important ideological currents at play as western democratic states move into the twenty-first century. Its most forceful proponents envision a radically transformed economic, political and social order, while even its more moderate proponents envision substantial alterations to personal beliefs and public policies.

This chapter will explore the ideology of environmentalism. We begin by outlining its branches and core values, then discuss the rise of contemporary environmentalism. We then place environmentalism within the parameters of ideological thought, and explore the extent to which it is an ideology like other ideologies. This will enable us to locate environmentalism within the broader ideological context of western democratic states. The chapter concludes with an examination of some of the major challenges facing environmentalism, and a brief consideration of its future on the ideological landscape of the twenty-first century.

Exercise One: Defining Environmentalism

Write down your own definition of environmentalism. What are the principal beliefs, values or objectives that are brought into play by such a definition? What groups and/or individuals do you associate with environmentalism? Is it more difficult to define environmentalism than you imagined?

Often, we collapse a myriad of complex theories, values and objectives into a single, innocuous term. While this simplification can be useful, the diverse array of conceptualizations which individuals bring to environmental debates cannot be ignored even though they further complicate an already complex issue.

At its core, environmentalism refers to a concern for the protection and preservation of the natural environment, including its physical features, flora and fauna. In contemporary usage, however, that core has been expanded to include a concern for the artificial or humanly constructed environment. Thus, urban problems relating to water, air, architecture and noise pollution are very much part of the environmentalist agenda, along with deforestation and the protection of wildlife, ocean mammals and biodiversity. So, too, are a number of less visible issues, including chemicals in the food we eat, the thinning of the ozone layer, global warming and air quality within the sealed buildings in which most of us study and work—the "sick building" syndrome. Environmentalism also extends to a complex set of scientific and technological issues, and to an equally complex set of social and political issues, including nuclear nonproliferation and international disparities in the distribution of resources, population and industrial development. Indeed, the scope of environmentalism is extremely broad. It stretches from the hard sciences of biology and chemistry to human ethics, from concerns with simple biological organisms to concerns with the economic and political structures that play a major role in shaping society, and society's impact upon the natural world. To understand this phenomenon, a fair measure of compression and simplification will be necessary. As the chapter evolves, a more nuanced picture of environmentalism will emerge, but until then we will paint with a rather broad conceptual brush.

BRANCHES OF ENVIRONMENTALISM

Environmentalism is a complex social and political phenomenon that includes a wide range of values, behaviours, groups and theoretical perspectives. In order to provide some conceptual grounding for this phenomenon, it is useful to distinguish between *reform environmentalism* and *ecologism*. The distinction between the two is akin to the distinction between "light green" and "dark green," or, alternatively, between "shallow" and "deep" ecology.[1] In other words, each represents a "pole" on opposing ends of the green spectrum. Although they are related to each other and must ultimately be seen as parts of a larger whole, it is helpful to begin by viewing them individually.

Much of what we normally associate with environmentalism falls within the bounds of reform environmentalism. Reformism offers a "managerial" strategy for dealing with environmental problems, maintaining that these can be resolved without fundamental changes to our current political or economic systems, or to the values which undergird these systems (Dobson 1990:13). Reformists, then, advocate "fine-tuning" our mode of existence through, for example, programs of pollution abatement or the recycling of wastes. Also within the reformist camp is the contention that a "technological fix" will eventually resolve the burden of our environmental problems.

Two broad groups of environmentalists find themselves within the reformist camp. Forming a majority of the environmental movement, *personal environmentalists* advocate green consumerism, composting, recycling, bringing one's own bags to the supermarket, drinking coffee from reusable containers rather than Styrofoam cups and minimizing one's impact on hiking trails and beaches. The slogan "Rethink, Reduce, Reuse and Recycle" captures the basic creed. Personal environmentalism finds itself decidedly on the reformist end of the green spectrum because it is rarely linked to any underlying analysis of the political or economic system. Few perceive a connection between their recycling box and the need to dismantle capitalist modes of production, or to abandon living in large metropolitan communities in favour of much smaller, self-supporting communities. Rather, many individuals simply identify with the principles of environmentalism, and their behaviour, and in some cases even their personal identities, are then coloured by those principles. Personal environmentalism is people acting *as individuals* in an environmentally conscious way; it is neither political nor ideological in character.

The *environmental movement* politicizes action and thereby provides a link between personal environmentalism and the public-policy process. This second branch of contemporary environmentalism encompasses a wide range of groups and organizations devoted to the pursuit of environmental objectives. Some have a very narrow focus and membership base, while others pursue global objectives and recruit members by the thousands, even the tens of thousands. (Greenpeace, which originated in Vancouver, British Columbia, as a protest movement concerned with American nuclear tests in the Aleutian Islands, is now estimated to have a worldwide membership of close to 4,000,000.) Although not all environmental organizations have a political mandate, all are engaged to some extent in the political process in reaching local, national or even international objectives. This definitive entanglement with politics distinguishes the environmental movement from personal environmentalism. Politicization establishes it as "deeper" than personal environmentalism, further along the green spectrum, but the environmental movement is still reformist in nature. As Andrew Dobson notes, "[T]his is because, while many of the members might individually subscribe to the necessity for the radical changes in our political and social life ... the organizations do not explicitly do so" (1990:14). Neither personal nor politicized environmentalism, then, carries or promotes an ideological agenda.

The perhaps less well known, second "pole" of the green spectrum is an extensive body of political and philosophical literature grouped under the heading *ecologism*. This ideological branch of environmentalism spans a number of theoretical perspectives along the "deep" side of the green spectrum, including bioregionalism, ecofeminism, social ecology and the more radical deep ecology. Ecologism distinguishes itself from reformism in its insistence that environmental problems can be abated only through fundamental and radical changes to our existing relationship with nature, and consequently, to the social, political and economic institutions which are founded upon this relationship (Dobson 1990:13). It is argued that the current "human-centred," or *anthropocentric* model of man's relationship with nature is the primary cause of environmental degradation. Ecologists maintain an *ecocentric* position, arguing that the moral standing of the nonhuman world merits human consideration, and that nature should be preserved for its own sake. From this premise, it is concluded that humans should exercise both caution and humility in their "interventions" with the nonhuman world (Eckersley 1992:28). This ethic, ecologists argue, should be reflected in renewed political, social and economic institutions. It is in this sense that ecologism casts environmentalism into an ideological mould.

Bioregionalism is the most comprehensive branch of ecologism, one that provides an exhaustive synthesis of "the lessons of nature" within a model of the human community. Bioregionalism tries to kindle a sense of awe and veneration for the natural world in order to ensure that its patterns will be emulated within the human community. To this end, the proponents of bioregionalism submit that humans become "dwellers in the land, to relearn the laws of Gaea, to come to know the earth fully and honestly" (Sale 1991:42). Bioregionalism is informed by two ecological laws:

> The first law is that the face of the earth is organized not into artificial states but natural regions, and those regions, while varying greatly in size, are mostly much more limited than those defined by national boundaries ... [The second is that] all biotic life is divided into communities, differing in size, complexity, development, and stability, but existing everywhere, throughout every econiche (Sale 1991: 55–62).

FIGURE 6.1: Aspects of Environmentalism

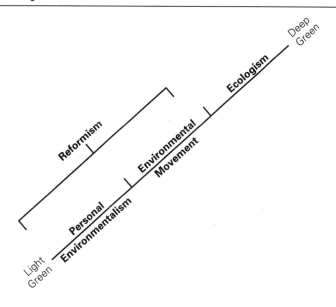

Bioregionalism attempts to replicate these natural laws within a model of the human community, a model wherein humans live in appropriately scaled, self-sufficient and self-regulatory communities which are defined by their bioregion. As Anna Bramwell points out (1994:90), one of the more interesting features of such bioregional communities, and in this sense, the environmental state, is the assumption of stability or stasis. The assumption is often made that nature itself works towards "a balanced, harmonious, integrative state of maturity which, once reached, is maintained for prolonged periods" (Sale 1984:229). This stability is in direct contrast to the dynamic and evolutionary character that is commonly attributed to western democratic states.

BASIC TENETS OF ECOLOGISM

Of course, all environmentalists have "a concern with maintaining a long-term sustainable relationship between man and his environment on this Earth" (Macdonald 1989:19). However, the agenda of contemporary environmentalism has broadened considerably from this narrow base. The fact that a good deal of environmentalism is not even primarily concerned with the natural environment (Bramwell 1989:221–2) distinguishes the environmental movement from other single-issue interest groups, and is the key factor propelling it onto the ideological stage. But, whether or not these variegated interests carry across the entire movement is a matter for debate. Environmentalism is an *evolving* ideology which thus far has been "truncated" by the narrow focus associated with reformism (Paehlke 1989:3), a focus that ecologists are trying to expand. Robert Goodin's argument (1992:86–87) that a "clarity of moral vision" underlies environmentalism points to the possibility that this fledgling ideology may someday find itself in the "ring" of contemporary ideological politics. To explore this possibility, we have to examine the tenets of ecologism in some depth.

The moral vision described by Goodin finds its roots in the science of ecology, hence the labelling of ideological environmentalism as "ecologism." Ecology suggests a way of looking at the world which is fundamentally different from that which is offered by the dominant scientific paradigm and its emphasis on objectivity, technology and material progress. Within ecological thought, "the world is an intrinsically dynamic, interconnected web of relations..." (Eckersley 1992:49). Ecology is inherently holistic; it demands a *breadth* of focus which is able to examine the "whole picture" and not simply its respective parts. The well-known "global" perspective of green theory stems from this worldview. Moreover, ecology calls for a *lengthened* focus, a "flow-based" or "continuous" style of thought which is able to envision the long-term consequences of behaviours.

Ecologism provides a mechanism through which complex problems within the human community can be understood and solved. Particularly with respect to environmental problems, ecologism advocates a multifaceted approach, drawing from both reformist and radical perspectives alike. Furthermore, ecologism embraces the notion of coalition-building between environmentalism and other reform movements. Most important, the ecological approach is able to trace the interconnections between many different, and not intuitively connected, problems within modern society, ranging from pollution to social injustice and the alienation of individuals from society (Eckersley 1988:55). In a similar vein, the ecological worldview draws linkages between the personal and political spheres, and between the local and global spheres. Hence, personal, local environmental actions, such as recycling, are recognized for their macrocosmic implications.

The ecological worldview requires humans to embrace a holistically based ethical system in their relationships with the rest of nature. Primary within this ethical system is a deep respect for the laws of nature. According to these laws, humans are "organisms-in-environment" (Eckersley 1988:56), a part of, rather than separate from or above, the rest of nature. A corollary to this view is the recognition of the intrinsic value of all life-forms. In the extreme, this recognition can be translated as a desire to minimize and even, as we will see in Chapter 10, to eliminate the line between the human and nonhuman world. Deep ecologists, for example, seek to cultivate an "ecological consciousness ... a state of being that sustains the widest possible identification with other life forms" (Eckersley 1988:57). Moreover, a sense of respect for nature generally adds a note of humility to the human relationship with the rest of the natural world, a humility often captured in the spirituality associated with aboriginal peoples.

Ecological environmentalists oppose the "arrogance" of western thought, which sanctions an attitude of conquest towards nature and reduces her to an agglomeration of exploitable resources. For example, in the ecological worldview, the modern imperative for unlimited economic growth is unrealistic within a finite ecological system. Ecologists, then, favour economic activity which is sustainable within the contexts of both ecological stability and longevity. Thus, renewable resources, energy- and materials-efficient production processes and the production of useful and durable products is preferred. In a related argument, ecologists are critical of the imperative towards unlimited consumption that accompanies the mandate for continuous economic growth. Maintaining that recycling alone is insufficient, ecologists call for an ethic of "voluntary simplicity" wherein vulgar consumption is rejected.

Ecologists assert that the perceived reduction in the standard of living following as a result of this new ethic will be compensated by an improved quality of life. The focus, then, is upon nonmaterial satisfactions (Dobson 1990:89–90).

The proponents of ecologism reject the view that environmental problems are soluble through technological advances, or through political or economic adjustments (Paehlke 1989:150). To ecologists, this view is an example of human arrogance vis-à-vis nature, as it assumes that human capacities are superior to those of natural processes. Ecologism, therefore, calls for "appropriate technology," a term popularized through E. F. Schumacher's highly influential *Small is Beautiful.* Appropriate, or "soft" technology is environmentally benign, alleviates monotonous work and is more open to democratic control than is "hard" technology (Capra and Spretnak 1983:94–5).

Ecological theorists also advocate the adoption of an ecological worldview with respect to relations within the human community. Robyn Eckersley (1992:54–55), for example, argues that human relationships arc intrinsically interdependent, and should embrace an "ecological notion of self." Murray Bookchin's (1991) influential concept of *social ecology* [2] posits that human society would benefit from adopting the example of nature, whose nonhierarchical model of unity-in-diversity, interdependence and cooperativeness is the primary source of its strength. Accordingly, ecologism supports an interdependent and cooperative human community which remains true to the concept of unity-in-diversity. To this end, three models are drawn from nature. First, the science of ecology shows that diversity within a biological community promotes stability and sustainability. Ecological theory emulates this model in its celebration of *diversity* within the human community. Second, the ecological principle of interdependence implies the *equality* of all members of the biotic community. This principle is generalized to the human community in ecologism's strong stand on egalitarianism, seen, for example, in policies of social justice which call for the redistribution of wealth and equality of opportunity. Third, ecologism attempts to replicate the model provided by natural environment, wherein, it is argued, individuals are *autonomous*, self-governing entities. The community, in the ecological view, should provide a setting which enables the full expression of individuality; it should be a "vehicle for personal liberation" (Tokar 1992:156–7).

Taken together, these principles make a strong case for the radically participatory and democratic society envisioned by ecological theorists (Dobson 1990:24–27). Politically, Robert Goodin (1992: 124) argues, this implies "the full, free, active participation by everyone in democratically shaping their personal and social circumstances." Moreover, effective democratization requires the contraction of decision-making units to a size that makes issues comprehensible and relevant (Goodin 1992:130). To this end, environmentalists in general (Goldsmith 1972; Roszak 1978), and deep ecologists in particular support decentralized forms of governance, support that is reflected in the credo "Small is beautiful" and the more general emphasis of new social movements on greater democratization.

Within ecologism, then, nature is upheld to be the supreme value; the ecological worldview and ethical system are inspired by nature's processes. This worldview presents a radical challenge to the credo underlying contemporary political, economic, religious and cultural institutions. As Fritjof Capra (1982:16) maintains, ecologism offers an alternative to the dominant paradigm: to the thoughts, perceptions and values that form our conventional vision of reality. The extent of this challenge becomes even clearer when we turn to the philosophical foundations of ecologism.

A common theme within environmental thought is the "fall" of the western world from an organic, cooperative ethic in close harmony with the patterns of the natural world to our present condition of environmental degradation and industrial malaise. Anthropologists suggest that traditional, preliterate peoples lived in harmony with nature, with the seasons and other natural cycles. They saw no distinction between humans and the rest of nature, and there was no hierarchy in this view of nature (Devall and Sessions 1985:96–7). Moreover, the earth was worshipped as a goddess, whose fertile and abundant spirit permeated everything (Tokar 1992:9). Admittedly, portraits of prehistory must be taken with a large grain of salt, but there is little question that the lifestyles of our early ancestors were sustainable within the context of the natural world. And, to this day, tribal peoples around the globe maintain an intimacy with nature which seemingly pervades every aspect of their lives. However, this worldview has come, and continues to come, under attack from alternative philosophical orientations.

The western worldview, and in particular the predominant view of man's relationship with nature, is characterized by *anthropocentrism*, "the belief that there is a clear and morally relevant dividing line between humankind and the rest of nature, that humankind is the only or principal source of value and meaning in the world, and that nonhuman nature is there for no other purpose but to serve humankind" (Eckersley 1992:51). In part, this orientation finds its roots in the Judeo-Christian tradition. The account of creation in Genesis, for example, situates man in a position of dominion over the remainder of nature. As Peter Marshall (1992:97–98) observes, Christians "have traditionally interpreted the divine command of Genesis to mean that man should conquer, enslave and exploit nature for his own ends." Moreover, the Christian dualism between the body and the spirit situated man alone among God's creations in his possession of a "living soul."[3] Man's duty was to suppress the "beast" within himself and to elevate his soul (Marshall 1992:108). When this perspective was extended to the natural world, nature was denied its previous sanctity and its manipulation was divinely sanctioned.

The Scientific Revolution of the sixteenth and seventeenth centuries[4] advanced the Judeo-Christian project. Several modern notions were popularized during this era, but none more so than the mechanistic view of nature wherein the universe was likened to a machine whose workings could be understood through mathematical laws. Cultural constraints which had prevented the manipulation of nature were effectively dissolved with this mechanistic conception. Carolyn Merchant (1980:3) explains that "as long as the earth was considered to be alive and sensitive, it could be considered a breach of human ethical behavior to carry out destructive acts against it." Such ethical constraints fell as the Scientific Revolution took hold. Adding to this, René Descartes confirmed the philosophical dualism that had previously been posited. He argued that there is a "fundamental division between two independent and separate realms; that of the mind, or *res cogitans* ... and that of matter, or *res extensa*" (Capra 1982:60). In other words, the breach between man and nature that had been suggested by Plato and advanced by Christianity was fortified during the Scientific Revolution. However, it was now man's *reason* that separated and elevated him above nature (Pepper 1986:65).

The ethic that undergirded scientism was decidedly optimistic. Isaac Newton, having achieved a "grand synthesis" in his mathematically formulated "world-machine," believed that the mystery of the universe had been solved. Scientists such as Francis Bacon argued that this understanding of the "laws of nature" would enable those laws to be used for the benefit of the human condition. The power to manipulate the environment, in other words, became equated with "social progress" (Pepper 1986:55). This further control of the physical environment was buttressed by the Industrial Revolution, and was normatively supported by the capitalist imperative for unlimited economic growth and technological advancement (Pepper 1986:65). Thus, the scientific project, and consequently the technological project, became the dominant paradigm for the next 250 years, and the paradigm the environmentalists would eventually confront.

In summary, the basic tenets of environmentalism, ones that receive particular amplification within ecologism, are as follows:

- a deep respect for the laws of nature;
- a recognition of the intrinsic value of all life-forms;
- an enthusiastic embrace of both biodiversity and social diversity;
- support for an organic conception of society that acknowledges interdependence, and that minimizes hierarchy and the separation between the human and nonhuman worlds;
- a holistically based ethical system that draws inspiration from the natural world;
- a preference for participatory democracy and political decentralization; and
- support for a sustainable economy, reduced consumption, more equitable distribution and voluntary simplification of consumption and lifestyles.

THE HISTORY OF ENVIRONMENTALISM

Environmentalism evolved in three major phases, and elements of each remain today. Although the progression of environmentalism can be understood as a linear pattern, by no means did the introduction of a new phase render the previous phase insignificant. The roots of environmentalism extend well back to the nineteenth century, to early attempts to protect the natural environment and landscape from the transformational impact of industrialization and urbanization. The primary themes at that time were conservation and preservation. Conservationists sought to protect resources in order to ensure future development, and this perspective of "enlightened self-interest" led to a focus on "resource management" (Eckersley 1992:35–6). (The notion of sustainable development also falls into the conservationist camp.) Preservationism sought to preserve wilderness for its aesthetic or spiritual value. John Muir, founder of the Sierra Club in 1892, and Henry David Thoreau are two well-known preservationists from the era. Preservationists looked at the wilderness as "a subject of reverence, enlightenment, and a locus of threatened values" (Eckersley 1992:39). Conservationists and preservationists have an anthropocentric value system; they seek to preserve wilderness in order to satisfy specifically human needs.

Environmentalists of the first phase looked to state ownership to protect wilderness areas from encroachment (Bramwell 1994:35–6). To this end, the founding of Yellowstone National Park in 1872 was a major event in the evolution of environmentalism in the United States. This early stage of environmentalism was also marked by the emergence of national conservation societies. In the United States, these included the National Audubon Society, founded in 1905, and the Wilderness Society, founded in 1935. In Canada, early environmental advocacy groups include the Federation of Ontario Naturalists (1931) and the Ontario Parks Federation (1936). Until the early 1960s, these organizations and environmental interests had not coalesced around "the unifying ideas and symbols of political movements" (Macdonald 1989:16). There were many organizations devoted to environmental concerns, but the larger banner of "environmentalism" had not yet been unfurled.

In its second phase, environmentalism was catapulted onto the public stage with the publication of Rachel Carson's landmark study, *The Silent Spring*, in 1962. Carson's work, and the scientific community's growing involvement in ecological studies, drew public attention to hazards greater than the local environmental problems of air pollution, waste disposal and urban blight to the newly identified global problems of acid rain, ocean pollution, atmospherical change, ozone thinning, deforestation and species extinction. Thus, while many environmentalists continued to "act locally," there was a growing imperative to "think globally." Environmentalism became associated with a global consciousness which made a nice fit with ecological visions of an interdependent world,[5] and attention came to be focused on problems that could not be addressed by local authorities, or even by national governments.

The environmental scene became more complex with the publication of two additional landmark works during the ensuing decade, the Club of Rome's *The Limits to Growth* (1972), and *Blueprint for Survival* (1972) from the editors of *The Ecologist*. These studies highlighted the crisis that would occur as a result of unlimited resource consumption coupled with exponential population growth. As Eckersley (1992:11–13) notes, they "posed a considerable challenge to the sanguine belief that we could all continue with business and politics as usual." The studies also supported the assertion that the goal of constant economic growth flies in the face of the earth's long-run requirements for survival. Generally, the second phase of environmentalism was apocalyptic in tone. The "survivalist school" of this era fostered a sense of urgency which gave rise to notably authoritarian solutions to environmental problems; conventional democratic politics, including competition among interest groups over the direction of public policy, were dismissed as too slow and uncertain. Theorists such as Garrett Hardin, viewing the choice as between "leviathan or oblivion," called for "mutual coercion, mutually agreed upon..." (Eckersley 1992:14–15).

Ecologism, and environmental thought more broadly defined, falls within the third phase of environmentalism. This phase is marked by its philosophical bent, as environmentalists began to reexamine the foundation of industrial-capitalist society and its contribution to the environmental crisis. Hence, the notions of "limits to growth" and "sustainability" were introduced. Ecologists ventured into the wants/needs debate, arguing that many of our purported "needs" are actually manufactured desires (Dobson 1990:17–18). The ecological critique disputed not only the worldview of the Scientific Revolution, but thousands of years of western thought. As Robert Paehlke (1989:36) observes:

> At stake was not merely the wise use of resources or the setting aside of ecological reserves. The new environmentalism claimed that problems lie at the very heart of the modern political economy, even in our basic philosophical and cultural outlook.

Everything fits together—the physical, chemical, biological, social, political, economic and philosophical worlds—and must be understood as a whole. The symptoms of environmental problems may be measured biologically, but the disease itself lies in our socioeconomic organizations, and the solutions are ultimately political.

Ecologism challenged the relationship of humans to the nonhuman world, arguing, for example, that nonhuman beings should have rights and legal standing.[6] Moreover, as Robyn Eckersley (1992:18) notes, ecologism began to articulate the opportunities for cultural renewal, the "emancipatory potential," latent within this critique. Energies were directed towards the renewal of the human community, the human relationship with nature and the revival of civil society itself.

Given its long and complex history, it is not surprising that contemporary environmentalism finds organizational expression in many forms. Robust environmental organizations are characteristic of most contemporary western democratic states. The 1991 *Green List*, published by the Canadian Environmental Network, listed more than 2,500 environmental organizations, ranging from national organizations such as the Canadian Wilderness Association, to the localized, community-based NIMBY[7] groups such as the Williams Lake Fly Ash Committee. Environmental organizations are active in a number of countries; the Sierra Club, for example, has branches across both Canada and the United States, even though it began its life in the western United States. In addition, there are transnational organizations like Greenpeace and the World Rainforest Movement which do not have a national focus or home, but instead address environmental concerns that spill across national boundaries and political jurisdictions.

Contemporary environmentalism, moreover, comprise agencies and departments of national, state and local governments. Highly visible initiatives have been taken at the national level. For example, Canada's *Green Plan* (1990) sketches in a political framework for the pursuit of environmental objectives, and the United States' Clean Air Act (1984) legislated a political strategy for environmental action with respect to oil pollution, ozone layer depletion, climate change, federal facility cleanup, reforestation, ecosystem restoration and education (Crane 1992:81). Contemporary environmentalism also goes well beyond national governmental structures to include intergovernmental, transnational and international institutions (for example, the United Nations). This internationalization of environmentalism is reflected in a number of international agreements and initiatives, including the 1987 report of the World Commission on Environment and Development, *Our Common Future*, which advocated sustainable development as a primary objective for all governments to pursue.[8] Similarly, the 1988 World Conference on the Changing Atmosphere, the 1992 *World Development Report* published by the World Bank, and the United Nations Rio Conference on Environment and Development (Earth Summit) in 1993 are recent attempts to deal with the political and substantive issues of global environmental action.

Ecologism itself is most often manifested in smaller-scale alternative projects of community-building. These projects reflect the Gandhian creed that dramatic political change must be preceded by a change in the consciousness of society at large. Hence, the burden of the ecologists' work is in consciousness raising through the practical development of ecological principles. Moreover, these community projects speak to the possibility and practicality of the sustainable society. The LETSystem, developed in Courtenay, British Columbia, is a variation on the barter system which encourages local economic development (Dobson 1990:150–1). Cooperatives, and co-op networks such as Co-op America, provide alternatives to prevailing economic patterns; they allow for cooperative and accountable business practices while developing a "socially responsible marketplace" (McLaughlin and Davidson 1994:377–78).

Exercise Two: Die Grünen

Green ideology had its moment of political glory in March 1983, when members of the German Green Party were elected to twenty-seven seats of the West German national Parliament. The Greens were a decidedly alternative party, whose elected members distinguished themselves by their colourful attire, the diversity of their occupational backgrounds and a surprisingly equal gender distribution. They have been able to offer what is, to date, the most comprehensive example of ecologism in practice. Based upon their "four pillars" of *ecology, social responsibility, grass-roots democracy* and *nonviolence*, the Greens declare that they offer a new vision of politics which is able to "transcend the linear span of left-to-right" (Capra and Spretnak 1983:3).

The Green platform is based upon the worldview provided by ecologism. Its first principle, ecology, delineates the Green commitment to model their policies according to the interrelationship between humans and the natural world. The Greens adopt from social ecology a belief in the linkage among the social, economic and ecological realms. The Green commitment to social justice, for example, is couched in a discussion about realigning the imperative for never-ending economic growth. The Greens promote a "radical stand for human rights," calling for an end to discrimination on the basis of gender, race, social group, religion or sexual preference. They also support decentralization and grass-roots democracy. All "leadership" positions within the party are frequently rotated, and are designed to function as conduit between grass-roots organizations and legislative bodies (Capra and Spretnak 1983:38–9). The final pillar of the Green platform calls for an end to both personal and state-sanctioned violence; the Greens seek to redress the exploitive violence they believe is inherent within competitive and hierarchical economic relationships.

Despite the initial success of the German Greens, their achievements since 1983 have been sketchy.[9] Their central problem has been the difficulty in bridging the gap between theory and practice. Specifically, the Greens' attempt to pursue an ideological agenda through conventional political channels has rendered them successful at neither. Because their platform is value-centred, they have been unwilling, and perhaps unable, to make the compromises and build the coalitions necessary for success in the political world. Moreover, the "salvageable" elements of their program have been co-opted by the major parties, leaving the broader ideological message behind.

Given the current political system, is it inevitable that ideological parties will fail? What, then, is the best way to effect ideological change? What strategy would you recommend to the Greens? In formulating your answers, consider the historical development of now-established ideologies, such as liberalism and socialism.

Several experimental communities have been established to demonstrate the possibility of consensual, cooperative and participatory forms of government, including the Findhorn community in Scotland and Sirius in Massachusetts (McLaughlin and Davidson 1994:123–4). Diverse research and educational institutions have been established to investigate the possibility of the sustainable community. The Rocky

Mountain Institute in Colorado, for example, researches alternative technologies in resource and energy conservation. Bioregional think tanks, such as Turtle Island in Vancouver, British Columbia, explore the possibility of the decentralized society, and the Center for Living Democracy in Vermont works to educate citizens in democratic methods of decision-making.

The environmental agenda, then, has found expression in diverse and seemingly unrelated forums. But as Anna Bramwell (1994:27) points out, even the basic beliefs in reducing pollution, preserving animals, and recycling "have not been adopted in isolation from [a] justifying ideology." All of this suggests that environmentalism should be seen as a broad, ideological current with the potential to transform not only personal beliefs and values, but also political practice, institutional structures and patterns of public policy.

ENVIRONMENTALISM AS AN IDEOLOGY

Up to now, we have referred obliquely to environmentalism as an *ideology*. Is this a reasonable description? If we apply the definitional characteristics outlined in Chapter 1, there is little doubt that environmentalism qualifies as an ideology.

Environmentalism is a *social construction* in that individuals do not construct their own particular brands of environmentalism. Rather, they buy into preexisting packages of environmental thought, values and behavioural prescriptions. This shared nature of environmental belief systems allows us to speak of environmentalism as an ideology. It should be stressed, however, that different belief systems are available to the "ideological consumer"; whether one ascribes to the tenets of deep ecology or to those of reformism will depend upon individual values and beliefs. The choice of package and the degree to which one buys into it will be coloured by personal experience.

There is little question that environmentalism is *political*, that it offers a guide to political action and a lens through which the political world can be viewed. As Douglas Macdonald (1991:31) notes, the politicization of environmentalism has spawned the realization that environmental protection is inextricably linked to various other social issues. It has led to the creation of government departments and agencies charged with managing and regulating environmental concerns. Environmentalism has also found political expression within a multitude of interest groups, social movements and political parties which, to a greater or lesser degree, have picked up the green banner of environmentalism. At a more basic level, ecologism challenges our foundational assumptions about representative democracy and the institutional structure of the contemporary state.

Environmentalism displays considerable *scope*. Given that issues of conservation, preservation and pollution can affect people's lives in many ways, environmentalism *as an ideology* has the potential to touch people directly throughout the day: as we contemplate the food we eat, decide whether to walk or drive, or whether to spend a bit more for "green" products. The potential scope expands even more when linkages to other social, economic and political issues are identified. Indeed, it is difficult to imagine a day in which one is not affected by some form of environmental concern or issue. While we can isolate environmentalism analytically as a field of study, it is important to remember that it is broadly embedded within the context of "real life."

Exercise Three: A Day In the Life of Joe Q. Student

0545: Joe's electric alarm clock rings. He turns on the lights, brews a pot of coffee and goes for a jog in the nicely maintained park (he can't believe the city is thinking of rezoning it for condominium development). Later, he enjoys a long shower.

0630: After blow-drying his hair, he sits down to read the morning paper. He is struck by the volume of advertising and inserts in the printed media. He reads a story about how the government is curtailing jobs by imposing stricter emission limits on polluting industries. There is also an article citing a famous naturalist's calculation that 27,000 species of plants and animals disappear annually (three per hour). In quoting Edward O. Wilson, it says that "some ten to twenty percent of the species alive today will be gone due to habitat loss in the next thirty years" (*Globe and Mail*, December 15, 1994: A22).

0725: Joe turns on the half-full dishwasher before embarking on his thirty-five-minute drive to university. As he negotiates his way through rush-hour traffic, he "cranks up" the stereo to enjoy his favourite song. Joe often considers taking the bus to school, but the cost of a bus pass is almost equal to that of parking.

0800: Joe is studying the sciences. His classes are large and, despite poor ventilation, the rooms are well heated. He often wonders if the bright fluorescent lights are the cause of his frequent headaches.

1200: Joe buys his lunch in the campus cafeteria. After eating, he ensures that his milk carton, candy-bar wrapper, Styrofoam lunch plate and unused paper napkins are deposited in the garbage can. The pop can is set aside for recycling.

1730: Joe cleans up his laboratory work area with the prescribed chemicals and ensures that they are thoroughly disposed of down the sink. He is careful to wear gloves so as not to irritate his skin.

1800: On the drive home, Joe is struck by the view of downtown—the lights in the office towers are very eye-catching at night. Arriving home, he microwaves something for supper and pours himself a cold soda over ice. While eating dinner, he reads in the *Atlantic Monthly* (February 25, 1995: 22) that for every species that the U.S. Fish and Wildlife Service has removed from the Endangered Species List over the past two decades, it has added more than a *hundred* others.

2300: Before bed, Joe watches the late-night news on television. The newscaster is wrapping up a story about an ocean oil spill that resulted from a freighter running aground. Apparently, local politicians are considering new legislation to deal with such accidents. Joe wishes that politicians and the media would address issues that have more relevance to the lives of "average" citizens.

In reading about Joe's day, did you identify the social, economic, health and political issues that were implied? Take a moment to think about the many activities and issues in your life that are related to the environment.

As an ideology, environmentalism demonstrates reasonable *internal consistency*. While one environmentalist may focus on species protection and another on the emission of greenhouse gases, the basic tenets are supported across the range of environmentalist thought. Furthermore, Andrew Jamison et al. (1991:3) suggest that consistency is enhanced by the "knowledge interests" which are so critical to new social movements such as environmentalism:

> [A] social movement exists when a distinct set of knowledge interests is present in the consciousness of activists and reflected in organisation, when these knowledge

interests form the basis not only for the collective identity, but also for coordination and cooperation between those organisations which identify themselves on their basis.

As C.A. Rootes explains (1992:465), the degree to which new social movements will be able to mobilize the type of political discontent expressed by such groups as environmentalists will depend upon "the interplay of other knowledge interests, the political strategies of activists and their opponents, and the cultural and institutional milieu within which the interaction takes place."

The *normative guideposts* of environmentalism are perhaps rather obvious: all environmentalists are concerned with protecting the natural environment from harm. Beyond this general commitment, there is a healthy diversity of thought, a diversity which permits individuals to choose among quite different packages of environmental beliefs. Hence, citizens need not be "bean-eating homeopaths constantly chanting mantras" (Goodin 1992:18) in order to identify with environmentalism; they may select those personal behaviours and public policies that fit their lifestyles. Radical greens may find this ideological diversity troubling, but by being too dogmatic themselves they run the risk of losing the political support of more moderate environmentalists. As Sara Parkin (1988:176) suggests, a divided, heterogeneous approach to environmentalism may even afford strategic advantages to greens: "There is no way in which one division of the green movement can carry out the whole range of offensive actions that will be required to survive …. The green movement will only succeed if the specialist divisions share out the jobs according to the abilities of their foot-soldiers and the sort of territory over which they operate best."

Environmentalism is more than a bundle of special concerns and loosely defined social attitudes; it also finds *formal articulation* in written texts. A substantial body of material exists that traces the roots, evolution and current state of environmentalism in different societies. Contemporary carriers of the creed, including Murray Bookchin, Andrew Dobson, Robyn Eckersley, Robert Goodin and Robert Paehlke, continue to rethink and recast the ethos and messages captured earlier in the works of such writers as Rachel Carson, Garrett Hardin and E. F. Schumacher. This also reinforces environmentalism's *durability*. As noted above, the roots of environmentalism go well back into the nineteenth century, and its formal articulation as an "ism" goes back at least forty years. And, when we look ahead, it is clear that environmentalism is not about to slip from the political agenda of western democratic states, although its prominence on that agenda is by no means guaranteed.

ENVIRONMENTALISM, ECONOMICS AND THE LEFT-RIGHT SPECTRUM

As previous chapters have shown, a great deal of contemporary ideological debate ranges across the left-right spectrum and addresses the appropriate relationship between the state and the economy, the conditions under which business activity should be subjected to public regulation and the extent to which the state should redistribute the monetary gains which accrue to individuals from their participation in the economy. Given that environmentalism challenges some of the basic assumptions and values of the contemporary economy, it is inevitable that environmentalists should become entangled with this broader ideological debate. What we find, however, is that potential support for environmentalism is to be found across the left-right spectrum (Paehlke 1989:194).

Environmentalism as an Ideology

- *scope*: Evidence of environmental thought and action is prevalent in many aspects of social, economic and political life; touches many, if not most, aspects of our personal lives.
- *internal consistency*: Even across competing and complementary branches, environmentalism demonstrates core values that remain largely immutable.
- *durability*: Even as environmentalism expands and evolves over time, it continues to gain salience and legitimacy as it becomes more firmly entrenched in social, economic and political debates.
- *normative framework:* Provides a framework within which to think about the "good society" and to evaluate the role of both man and nature.
- *social construction*: Individuals buy into preexisting packages of environmentalism rather than constructing their own particular brands.
- *practical guide for political action*: It has a recognizable "place" on the political agenda; it provides a guide to political action, and a lens through which to interpret the political world.
- *carriers of the creed*: High-profile proponents of each branch of environmentalism can be identified.
- *formal articulation*: Written expression of the tenets of environmentalism move it beyond the idiosyncratic beliefs of individuals and the realm of folklore.

It is not difficult to find similarities between environmentalism and the various perspectives along the conventional ideological spectrum. Environmentalism carries an affinity with conservatism, for example, in its romanticization of nature, and in adherents looking for a return to preindustrial society. There is also a conservative element in the environmentalists' "prudent" concern for planetary health and for the interests of future generations, as well as in the view that humans should play a stewardship role with respect to the environment. Moreover, environmentalists extend the liberal notion of "rights" to include nonhuman entities and future generations (Paehlke 1989:191–2). Further, there are many linkages between environmentalism and socialism. Notably, environmentalists share the socialist desire to intervene in the marketplace on behalf of the disenfranchised. Andrew Dobson (1990:172) ventures to say that environmentalism poses a challenge to the "hegemony" of socialism at the left end of the spectrum. Ecologism, he argues, has co-opted the socialist principles of equality and community, while having rejected the most contentious elements of the socialist program: excessive bureaucracy, centralization and high levels of government spending.

Environmentalism's affinity with the political left shows up in a shared concern for *collective* interests. Note, for example, that many environmental challenges such as global warming, species extinction and ocean pollution reflect the "tragedy of the commons," a phrase introduced to environmental literature by Garrett Hardin (1968:1243–48). He postulated that in the absence of effective pricing mechanisms, individuals will maximize their use of the "commons," deriving short-term individual benefits while deferring the long-term costs of overuse to society as a whole. Environmentalists assert that this destructive phenomenon persists even today, more than a quarter of a century after Hardin's warning. As Porter and Brown (1991:21–30) explain:

Environmental Protection Under the Free Market

In its early stages, environmentalism was strongly associated with the political left. Environmental protection was assumed to be contingent upon an interventionist state; if the free market was allowed to run unchecked, the environment would suffer as firms placed profits and growth ahead of environmental protection. However, since the collapse of the Soviet Union and the growing awareness of the catastrophic damage inflicted on the environment by socialist states, there has been a growing emphasis on finding free-market mechanisms through which to advance environmental protection.

Free-market efforts to deal with environmental trade-offs include instruments such as tradeable emission permits and deposit-refund systems. In each case, an effort is made to account for all the costs associated with production and consumption—even those that accrue to the public as a whole through environmental degradation. The key, in each case, is to encourage producers and consumers to "clean up their acts" by forcing them to internalize the costs associated with environmentally degrading activities.

The main difficulty in persuading individuals to act responsibly with respect to environmental protection is the absence of property rights. Nobody "owns" our waterways, our air or our scenic landscapes. Hence, traditional capitalism has failed to impose costs upon those who "use or abuse" these resources. *Tradeable permits* effectively assign air or water "property rights" to those producers who receive them, while placing an upward limit on pollution levels (since the number of permits is fixed). While "cleaner" producers may be able to sell their permits to their less efficient counterparts, those who pollute will pay for dirtying the air or water. On balance, then, industry is presented with an economic incentive to clean up its act in order to avoid the high costs of obtaining pollution permits.

Deposit-refund systems work in the opposite manner, as far as payments are concerned. In the case of bottles and cans, for example, an additional cost (the deposit) is charged to consumers at the point of purchase. If consumers return the used container to a central collection site, they are rewarded for their effort—the deposit is refunded. If they choose not to do so, the deposit is forfeited, effectively forcing individuals to internalize the environmental costs of their decision. Although the cleaning and returning of containers to centralized collection sites may be inconvenient to individuals, deposit-refund systems are intended to provide an economic incentive for responsible environmental behaviour.

Economic actors have maximized their own interests by disposing of their toxic wastes in the oceans and other dangerous chemicals in the atmosphere because it was the cheapest way to do it. They have logged tropical forests and taken as many fish from the oceans as they could because it was profitable. The environmental costs of a polluted atmosphere or depleted fish stocks have been passed on to human society as a while, whereas benefits of cheap waste disposal and exploitation of natural resources accrue to specific groups.

Insofar as market systems fail to reflect the real costs to society of resource exploitation, they encourage overconsumption of resources and thereby promote environmental degradation. Because some economic actors are able to benefit at the expense of the environment, and indeed, are encouraged by market incentives to do so, environmentalists argue that free market systems are unable to generate maximum social welfare where environmental matters are concerned.

Exercise Four: Is Environmentalism a Luxury?

Many debates surrounding environmental trade-offs revolve around notions of prosperity. Some suggest that environmentalism is a "rich man's luxury" and that only during periods of relative prosperity is it reasonable to focus on environmental protection; when people are unemployed and hungry, job creation and economic growth must take priority over environmental concerns. Explain why you agree or disagree with this line of thought. Are your views consistent with those of your classmates? Is it inevitable that we will sacrifice environmental protection when times get tough? And is it inevitable that developing countries will attach greater priority to economic growth than to environmental protection?

The entanglement of environmentalism with more conventional ideological debates is by no means restricted to the management of the environmental commons. Central to the politics of environmentalism are the distributive effects of alternative policies and the degree to which governments should regulate the economic and social orders, issues that are typically captured by the left-right spectrum. (Environmentalists tend to support government intervention and regulation in the pursuit of environmental protection, and thus fall towards the left end of the spectrum.) At times, though, ideological debate within environmentalism is not carried out along the left-right spectrum, but instead rejects the validity of that spectrum altogether. Ecologists, for example, maintain that they are "neither left nor right, but out in front." This categorical rejection of the left-right spectrum derives from the contention that environmentalism's left and right wings are built upon the "super-ideology" of industrialism. Industrialism, it is argued, is based upon false assumptions of unlimited economic growth, continual expansion of the means of production (technological "fixes"), continual availability of exploitable resources and an unlimited capacity of the earth to absorb wastes. Ecologists contend that since industrialism, whether driven by the left or the right, inevitably leads to the exploitation of the natural environment, they must work beyond the ideological spectrum (Porritt 1984:43–4). They suggest, furthermore, that a paradigm shift in the values underlying the ideological spectrum is required, one that may well be under way across western industrial states (Inglehart 1977; 1990). It is precisely to this shift that the ideological focus of environmentalism is directed.

If we move beyond the confines of the left-right debate, we find that environmentalism is also entangled with a large number of other ideological currents in western states, although the nature of that entanglement is often far from straightforward. The term "ecofeminism," for example, suggests a substantial overlap between feminism and environmental theory, one that is at times based on shared and negative perceptions of "man" as an aggressive and destructive force within the human and nonhuman environments. If we extend our reach further beyond conventional western European styles of political thought, additional ideological linkages with environmentalism can be found. There are clear links, for instance, between aboriginal religions and the more spiritual side of environmentalism, particularly with respect to deep ecology. There are important points of contact and overlap between ecologism and broader currents of spirituality that include such things as "Earth-bonding rituals," hiking and walking within nature, t'ai chi and activities celebrating the changing seasons (Devall and Sessions 1985:24–8). These exercises are designed not only to reduce the individual's dependence upon the material culture, but to promote an ecological consciousness. Note should also be taken of the linkages between environmental thought and the philosophy promoted by Mohandas (Mahatma) Gandhi.[10]

Ecofeminism

The blending of feminism and environmentalism (Caldicott and Leland 1983; Collard 1988; Diamond and Orenstein 1990; Griffin 1978; King 1989; Lenz and Myerhoff 1985; Plant 1989) has been called ecofeminism, a belief system that "sees women and nature as sharing both a common oppression and common qualities of nurturing and life-giving" (Mellor 1992a:236). As a consequence, "women have a unique standing from which to address the ecological crisis." Andrew Dobson writes (1990:28) that "ecology claims feminism as a guiding star," and Andree Collard (1988:102) asserts that women have an affinity with nature that stems from their biological role as mothers. As Jacqueline Vaughn Switzer points out (1994:369), ecofeminism is "a very broad term encompassing issues beyond those of the mainstream environmental movement, including women's power as consumers, reproductive rights, international debt and trade, and women and militarism."

Luanne Armstrong's analysis (1993:6) of the tools and methods that facilitate the oppression of both women and the environment is instructive for an understanding of ecofeminism. She speaks to the colonial attitude of early Europeans, an attitude which saw animals, natural resources and people (slaves) as a means to the accumulation of wealth. According to Armstrong (1993: 6), "This attitude did not allow for the idea that people, animals, and natural resources might have intrinsic interest, value, and worth." She identifies the many hierarchies that oppression seems to presume: males are more important than females, adults are more important than children, the wealthy are more important than the poor, whites are more important than people of colour and people are more important than animals. These entrenched hierarchies are patriarchal and economically based; she argues that they foster not only the exploitation of natural resources, but also the ongoing domination and subversion of other peoples, cultures and the natural world. Feminism and environmentalism unite in a rejection of such patriarchal structures.

However, the linkage between feminism and environmentalism may be weaker than is generally assumed. Mary Mellor (1992a:234–30) maintains that feminism does not lie at the core of the environmental movement: "Women's input into green thinking is becoming ghettoised into ecofeminism, it is not the core of green thinking, it is just one voice among many others." She warns that "women must be careful that in uniting ecology with feminism the balance of the partnership is not tipped towards saving the planet at the expense of the politics of women's liberation" (1992a:244–5).

Exercise Five: Generational Change

Some writers suggest that we have witnessed a sea change with respect to environmental values, and that such values are more pervasive and more deeply entrenched today than they were a generation ago.

What do you think? Is your outlook toward the environment markedly different from the outlook of your parents? Of your grandparents? If there has been a change, how would you describe it? Will the change persist? Will the outlook of your children to the environment be similar to your own, or do you expect further change? Has there also been a generational change in *behaviour* relating to environmental protection and stress? Does your behaviour pose more or less strain on the environment than that of people like you a generation or two ago? Do you consume more? Recyle more? Travel more? Use more or less energy?

POLITICAL DIMENSIONS OF ENVIRONMENTALISM

Environmentalism makes a substantial contribution to ideological debate in western democratic states. In this section, we explore several manifestations of this contribution: economic growth and the notion of sustainable development; the tension between centralization and decentralizaton; the challenge to political boundaries posed by bioregionalism; and institutional adaptation in the face of environmental challenges and change.

Economic Growth and Sustainable Development

One of the most central concepts in contemporary environmentalism is that of "sustainable development." The report of the Brundtland Commission (1987:43) defined sustainable development as "development that meets the needs of the present without compromising the ability of future generations to meet their own needs." The stress is on pollution abatement, conservation and protecting the inheritance of future generations, *combined with* real per capita growth in the gross domestic product.

One of the interesting things about this concept is the underlying assumption that development can be compatible with environmental protection; the debate shifts from whether development should occur to the appropriate kind and extent of development. This, in turn, leads to some tension within environmental thought. As Anna Bramwell explains (1994:142):

> Sustainable development implies that sustainable growth is possible, whereas to the deep Greens growth will always lead to environmental damage. In this most Green of concepts, therefore, lay the operational destruction of deep Green ideals, by "normalizing" the growth ethic, by accepting the goal of maximizing human welfare.

Sustainable development opens the door for economic growth in developing countries and thus provides an answer to the accusation that the environmental goals of the developed world are being pursued at the expense of the less-developed world. It does so, however, by also assuming that "global equity should be a factor in balancing human welfare against maintenance of a stable ecosystem" (Bramwell 1994:146). This means that growth in developing countries will have to be balanced with zero or negative growth in the developed countries. To the extent that this trade-off is required, it may not be one that most North American environmentalists have come to realize, much less accept.

The Tension Between Centralization and Decentralization

There is an uneasy tension within environmental thought between decentralization and centralization. First, there is considerable emphasis on the need for greater *decentralization*, for dismantling centralized decision-making institutions and creating a better fit between governance and ecosystems. As was suggested earlier, decentralization can be identified as the core environmental political principle. Robert Goodin, for example, concludes (1992:15) that greens "are decidedly of the view that decentralized, egalitarian political mechanisms are to be preferred to centralized, hierarchical ones."[11] But, second, there is considerable emphasis within environmental thought on the need for new *global standards and practices*, and thus for new global institutions charged with the protection of the environmental commons. Over the past few decades, environmentalism has drawn attention to a set of global environmental concerns upon which decentralized political decision-making would appear to provide little leverage, and which at least in the short term call for political action at the transnational and international level. Barry Commoner argues (1990:236) that action at the level of the nation-state is not enough: "What the United States—or indeed any one country—does will not in itself end the war against nature. It is a global war and only global action will end it." The dilemma is now to act globally while promoting political decentralization.

Both ecologists and reformists support decentralization, but the latter are more likely to acknowledge that there are pressing problems of large scope which cannot be addressed through a radical decentralization of political decision-making. As Stephen Young explains (1992:39), the tension between centralization and decentralization might be resolved in the short term by a strong state. Then, after a new environmental ethic is in place, and in a scenario reminiscent of early Marxist theory, the strong state could wither away, to be replaced by new decentralized structures more coterminous with bioregions. Robert Goodin makes essentially the same point with reference to how environmentalists see political parties (1992:146): "In the ideal world to which greens aspire, a world of decentralized communities governed by direct democracy, the role of parties—green or otherwise—would largely fade away."

There is, incidentally, a related tension between the decentralist impulses of environmentalism and its concomitant stress on the emergence of what Judith Plant (1989a:253) refers to as a "planetary community." The tension is minimal if such a community is based only on shared values. However, if we begin to articulate a political skeleton for such a community, it becomes increasingly difficult to reconcile planetary forms of government with decentralized decision-making. Perhaps federalism on a global scale provides the necessary balance, but, to date, this is not a case that has been made by environmentalists.

The proponents of decentralization often fail to recognize that the price of decentralization may be a loss of community *power*, despite greater local *control*.

Robert Goodin (1992:152) observes that "people are being given more and more power over less and less. Or, more precisely, more and more of what really matters will now ordinarily cut across communities and therefore lies in the hands of those who are to be responsible for negotiations with other communities." The price of decentralization is jurisdictional fragmentation, and the price of fragmentation is a loss of political control to the specialists and elites of intergovernmental relations. Goodin (1992:153) also notes that it is often assumed that a harmonious relationship among decentralized communities will emerge in a way analogous to the natural order:

> There is, after all, no central organization imposing order on nature. Rather, the plants and animals of each area simply adapt to their own locality, while at the same time incidentally feeding into the larger scheme of things. Ecologically, the global order emerges out of these local adaptations and interactions among them.

Yet to assume that a sound ecological order will emerge smoothly, if at all, from a multitude of decentralized political communities is to turn a blind eye to human history. For those who recognize that decentralization must be orchestrated, at least in the short run, there is often reference to such ambiguous schemes as "federations of communities" and "self-sufficient collaboration" (Goodin, 1992:151). But none of these takes us very far in describing a viable relationship among decentralized communities through which global problems could be addressed.[12]

Political Boundaries and Bioregionalism

An important component of environmental political thought is found in environmentalism's commitment to bioregionalism. Anna Bramwell (1994:87) explains two ideas that are embedded within the notion of bioregionalism:

> The first [idea] is that the earth is divided up into natural eco-regions, which can be broken down into smaller and smaller units, but which are all naturally self-contained geographical and biological units .... The second idea is that human societies would be happier, more self-sufficient, more diverse, the risk of conflict between peoples more contained, if they lived in a self-reliant way within these boundaries, and, if possible, within smaller units.

At least implicitly, bioregionalism calls for a fundamental redrawing of political maps, altering boundaries both within and among countries to make them more congruent with natural regions. Jeremy Rifkin (1991:286) suggests that biospheric politics "will need to create a new, competing spatial map whose governing configuration more clearly follows the geographical lines of regional ecosystems on the local level, while encompassing the entire biosphere on an international level" (1991:286). New political maps will also require new political institutions, both local and international.

Rifkin's appeal for the realignment of political boundaries illustrates the magnitude of the task many environmentalists have set for themselves. While political boundaries among and within nation-states are not immutable, we know how resistant they can be and how destabilizing boundary change can be; civil war is more commonly associated with boundary change than are peaceful adjustments to the social and economic order. If boundary change is a precondition for success in meeting the environmental challenges to come, we may be in for a very difficult time.

However, it is interesting to note the conclusion drawn by Mebs Kanji and Neil Nevitte (1995) in their analysis of the 1990 World Values Survey. They argue that the survey evidence strongly supports Lynton K. Caldwell's belief (1985) that high levels of public concern for the environment lead to increased levels of support for "doing away with political borders." Indeed, they conclude that a clear majority of Americans, Canadians and Mexicans support the idea of continental integration *if* it would promote the more effective management of environmental issues.

Institutional Adaptation and Change

We face two closely related questions in addressing the potential linkage between environmentalism and institutional change. First, does environmentalism *as an ideology* pose a significant transformational challenge to existing political institutions? In other words, does it suggest alternative institutional structures and architectural principles? And second, can the *objectives* of environmentalism be met within existing institutional arrangements, assuming there is the political will to do so? Given the institutional inertia that is characteristic of western democratic states, this second question is of particular importance.

Alexander Cockburn and James Ridgeway (1979:377) maintain that if, in the future, environmental conditions remotely approach the predictions of environmentalists, environmentalism will likely "become a force of the first order in domestic politics and one that can no longer be ignored." However, whether this force will necessitate institutional change is another matter. Many environmental objectives can be realized within and through existing institutional frameworks. For example, a NIMBY organization may oppose a proposed landfill site, but if sufficient political pressure can be mobilized to shift the site into some other community, then the organization has met its objective and there is no need to pursue broader political change. On a different front, air pollution can be reduced through regulatory regimes and financial incentives which do not require institutional change to be successful. Indeed, it is hard to avoid the conclusion that most western industrialized states have made significant strides in addressing environmental problems without indulging in significant institutional change. Nor, for that matter, is there any clear evidence that environmental interests have been advanced by major changes in the institutional environment, such as those induced by Canada's 1982 Constitution Act; for example, the creation of a constitutionally entrenched Charter of Rights and Freedoms has not increased the political leverage of environmentalists, nor has it sparked any sustained interest in an environmental charter.

Moreover, there are significant collective action constraints on the environmental movement's ability to mobilize its membership base for the promotion of diffuse environmental interests, thus further preventing a cogent environmentalist challenge to the status quo (Vogel 1993:237). These constraints may be so great in the case of such issues as the protection of biodiversity and the ozone layer that the movement may have little option but to rely on other means of policy influence, including the courts and conventional lobbying, that do not require mass mobilization. The localized and NIMBY-based issues around which mobilization is the easiest are also the ones most remote from broader debates on institutional or constitutional reform. Certainly recent Canadian experience has shown that the capacity of the environmental movement to mobilize its constituency, and for that matter to coalesce around a single spokesperson or organization, may be quite limited. Environmental groups and issues were not on the agenda during the constitutional debates of 1981–82 and 1987–90, and played, at best, a marginal role in the debates surrounding the Charlottetown Accord and the 1992 constitutional referendum.

All this is not to suggest, incidentally, that political institutions are irrelevant for the pursuit of environmental objectives. Just the opposite conclusion holds true. Note, for example, David Vogel's discussion (1993:271) of the differential impact of parliamentary and separation-of-powers systems on the representation of diffuse environmental interests in the policy-making process:

> [O]n balance a separation-of-powers system is likely to be more responsive to orga-nizations representing diffuse interests than parliamentary systems …. [B]ecause the U.S. system provides multiple points of access, a highly motivated minority of citizens has a greater opportunity to be heard.

The fusion of legislative and executive powers within the Canadian parliamentary system, and the resultant strict party discipline, provide a tougher legislative setting for environmental lobbies than does the American system. The argument, then, is not that institutions are irrelevant to environmentalism. Rather, it is that existing institutions may provide ready forms of access for environmental interests, and that policy instruments currently in place may take us a considerable distance in addressing environmental problems. Yet, in some cases, and particularly those involving transboundary problems such as acid rain, existing regulatory regimes and institutional structures may not be up to the task of effective environmental management.

It should also be noted in the context of institutional adaptation and change that environmentalists may be driven as much by strategic considerations as by more basic principles. The critical question is what set of institutional arrangements works best under given circumstances. For example, American environmentalism in the 1970s supported a more activist role by the federal government, and favoured shifting power from what were seen to be recalcitrant state governments. Then, when Presidents Reagan and Bush dominated the national stage and dismissed much of the environmentalist creed, the states emerged as an important line of defense for environmentalists, and the impetus for policy innovation shifted emphatically to state governments. With the 1992 election of the Clinton–Gore team to the White House, strengthening the role and powers of the federal government again had strategic appeal. Thus, it would be a mistake to assume that environmentalism can be characterized by a fixed strategic plan. The pattern of friends and foes among levels of governments in federal states may change dramatically with the shifting fortunes of political parties, and with the ebb and flow of ideological tides through both parties and governments.

The basic question is whether institutional change is necessary for the public policy objectives of environmentalism to be met. Certainly there is no doubt that political structures broadly considered are an important factor in the attainment of environmental objectives. As Courtney Brown (1994:301) notes: "[P]olitics is at the root of all attempts at environmental management." There is also consensus extending into the empirical political science literature (Brown 1994:302) that a substantial change in political consciousness may be essential if environmental protection, and perhaps even survival, is to be assured. But is institutional reform an appropriate or even necessary means for achieving this change in consciousness? Individuals will continue to address environmental issues through their own personal behaviour, and may find attempts to embed those behaviours within broader ideological visions to be nothing more than intellectual mind games. It may be, then, for many environmentalists, although *not* for ecologists, the solutions to environmental problems can be found within the conventional fabric of public policy.

ENVIRONMENTALISM AND ITS CRITICS

It has become increasingly difficult to identify opponents of environmentalism, or at least opponents of its more moderate elements. (Opponents of deep ecology are not difficult to find.) As Bramwell observes (1994:180), "few, faced by an opinion poll, would declare themselves to be anti-planet, or pro-planetary destruction, just as few would declare themselves as being in favour of nuclear war." The reader may have the impression that environmentalism is an inexorable force bound to transform our economic, political and social institutions. It is therefore important to stress that environmentalism is not without serious internal debates and external critiques, both of which cast some doubt upon its transformative potential.

Given the breadth and complexity of contemporary environmentalism, it is not surprising that points of tension exist within environmental thought. It would be unrealistic to expect consensus, particularly among those who celebrate and champion the diversity of life. Environmentalists, after all, range from those whose environmentalism is confined to the private realm of individual behaviour, to those who are actively involved in the political process, and from those whose personal values are informed only at the edges by ecologism, to those who are passionately committed to biocentric values. Thus, some degree of fragmentation within the environmental movement is inevitable.

Consider again, for example, the distinction between "light green" and "deep green" environmentalists. The distinction is nicely captured by Bill McKibben (1989:209), who notes that "environmentally sound is not the same as natural." Light green environmentalists may be satisfied with the environmentally sound, while deep green environmentalists seek to protect nature for its own sake. For the latter, "the value of nature is no longer regarded as wholly reducible to its value to God or to humanity" (Goodin 1992:8); the protection of nature is seen as an end in itself. Light green environmentalists, who seek to protect the *human* interests compromised by environmental degradation (Goodin 1992:6), are more likely to be reformers prepared to work within the status quo, to improve and build upon existing institutions. The changes they seek do not threaten the core values of the economic, political or social orders. However, as reformers, or *realos* in the European context, they are attacked by deep ecologists for trying to repair a system that should best be left to collapse (Young 1990:149). This situation, incidentally, is reminiscent of the tension within democratic states between social democrats, who wanted to reform the system to make it more compatible with socialist principles, and hard-line communists who believed that reform would only postpone the inevitable collapse of capitalism.

In addition to this internal debate, several external critiques of environmentalism can be identified. Critics quarrel with the mounting body of scientific evidence used by environmentalists to support their case. They argue, for instance, that it is by no means certain that changes in world climatic conditions are precursors of environmental apocalypse. Rather, they suggest that the scientific evidence presented today may represent only a snapshot of a narrow time period, a picture that would be better understood in the context of average conditions measured over many centuries. Note, for example, a 1995 editorial in the influential *Economist* magazine, entitled "Global Warming and Cooling Enthusiasm":

> Greens will no doubt continue to paint their scary pictures of the future. What, they will ask, if climate change were to entail a sudden lurch that led to half the world starving to death in 50 years time? The best answer is that anything can happen in half a century: even an invasion by aliens, say. On present evidence, though, any huge catastrophe looks highly improbable. There is still time to bask in the sun.[13]

Critics argue that changes associated with global warming may simply reflect natural fluctuations in world conditions—fluctuations that would have been occurring regardless of humankind's actions. The difficulty is that we do not have all the answers; only time can prove whether the environmentalists' interpretation of the scientific evidence is correct. The question that environmentalists ask is whether we can risk adopting a wait-and-see attitude.

Those who question the seriousness of environmental problems may also point to the unbridled promise of technology. In the same manner that modern science allows us to repair or reverse many of the effects of illness and adverse lifestyle habits, so, too, does the technological potential exist for us to repair the ozone layer, clean up the Great Lakes and purify the air we breathe. Just as critics of environmentalism argue for the acceptability of depleting resources today in view of future "substitutes," they appear willing to accept continued environmental degradation today with the expectation that we will devise methods to clean up our mess at a later date. Environmentalists, needless to say, lack this optimism. At the very least, they would argue, we need to hedge our technological bets by changing our behaviour *now*.

A second group of critics suggest that low-level exposure to carcinogens and the loss of species are the inevitable cost of progress on other fronts. This line of thought questions the primacy of environmental problems; its proponents may place economic development and issues such as poverty ahead of the survival of a particular species of owl or butterfly. Such critics attach primacy to human beings and their welfare. As the reader can well imagine, conflicts over the relative value to attach to competing environmental interests are not easily resolved. In 1990, a contingent-valuation survey was conducted in the United States to estimate the value of designating certain forested areas in the Pacific Northwest as "habitat conservation areas." One thousand respondents were surveyed by mail, and so began the issue of the northern spotted owl, significant because of its dual role as an endangered species and as an indicator of the overall health of the old-growth forest. Depending upon the assumptions economists employed in the study, the calculated non-use value of the forests varied from three times to forty-three times the value indicated by logging. Yet, despite widespread agreement that the forest was a resource to be valued and protected, there was intense pressure on decision-makers to allow logging in the area. The tension arose largely from a conflict over whether the needs of human beings, or ecosystems in general, should be granted primacy.

Critics of environmentalism sometimes object to the use of the "spaceship earth" metaphor, in which we are all portrayed as passengers within a sealed ecosysem hurtling through space. This metaphor, critics argue, promotes a "false conscious-ness" (Cockburn and Ridgeway 1979:385). The assertion that we are "all in the same boat" says little about our relative positions in that boat; while western industrialized nations may rest in the luxury of the staterooms, developing nations are frequently relegated to what some would refer to as the filthy bilges below the floorboards. Critics may therefore argue that insofar as nations in the "pampered" West have achieved economic prosperity in a climate of technological advance, it is well and good for them to turn their attention to environmental challenges. For the less devel-oped nations, however, this option may not exist since the relative costs of stopping or reversing the effects of environmental degradation are much higher than in west-ern states.

This line of criticism underscores that it is by no means certain that a common set of green values exists around the world. Consequently, the pursuit of environ-mental values can sometimes be seen as "environmental imperialism" or even "envi-ronmental racism." As Jacqueline Vaughn Switzer (1994:362) notes: "This resentment can be seen in the attitudes of the Japanese public, indignant over what is perceived as American hypocrisy over whaling. The United States continues to defend the rights of its native groups to hunt whales for 'cultural' reasons, but is critical of the Japanese, who consider whale meat a delicacy for similar 'cultural' reasons." The assertion of "neutrality" within environmentalism is therefore called into question by its critics. Consider, for example, the redistributive issues that would arise if world energy consumption were to be stabilized at a particular level. As Giorgio Nebbia (1972) writes in his preface to *La Morte Ecologico*: "The developing countries would have to have three times as much energy at their disposal as they do today; the social-ist countries could by and large maintain their present level of consumption; but the highly industrialized countries of Europe and the USA would have to reduce their consumption enormously and enter upon a period of *contraction*." To even contem-plate such a redistribution is to embark upon intense ideological debate over redis-tributive justice, a debate that has been central to western democratic states for generations.

It is also worth noting that some concern has been raised about the depth of ecologists' attachment to democratic values. At one level, all environmentalists dis-play a strong commitment to democratic values and, in particular, to the application of those values within small, decentralized communities. Their emphasis is on direct democracy and more immediate citizen participation in community decision-mak-ing. At the same time, there is a strong theocratic element to ecologism that cannot be easily reconciled with democratic principles, or at least with the conventional expression of those principles in representative institutions. In a hypothetical state based on a constitutional foundation provided by green values, the general direc-tion of public policy would be set, and would be considered beyond the pale of nor-mal democratic discourse. Ecophilosophers with the authority to interpret the state's founding values would enjoy a political eminence uncharacteristic of intellectuals in more conventional democratic states. Anna Bramwell (1994:163–4) observes:

> Nature itself provides the values, but these are transmitted according to the deep
> ecologists' perception of them. Despite the apparent humility of the ecologists'
> stance before Nature, they are people who have access to special knowledge, who
> become part of the elite: who are saved.

Thus the ecophilosphers would be the keepers of the faith, and the keepers of the communal flame. Whether they would also be keepers of the democratic faith is by no means assured.

Finally, we should point out the "passive" critics of environmentalism, individuals who are indifferent rather than actively opposed to environmental action. This indifference, combined with the dead weight of inertia within the political system, need not imply any criticism of environmentalism, but it may have the same practical impact on the evolution of public policy. Passivity will slow initiatives aimed at repairing previous damage and preventing future degradation; it may also prevent environmentalism from assuming a commanding position on the political agendas of western democratic states.

THE FUTURE OF ENVIRONMENTALISM

On the eve of the twenty-first century, it seems unlikely that the pressing nature of environmental challenges will diminish in the near future. Indeed, environmentalists argue that the opposite is true, that emergent issues will give increased significance to environmentalism. On the domestic front, environmental concerns relating to population growth, economic development, technological and climatic change, food production, fisheries, forestry, water, energy and non-fuel minerals will combine to challenge the way that nations make decisions. The cumulative effects of global environmental degradation will continue to generate pressure for international action and the formation of new international institutions.

Just as it is unlikely that environmental challenges will disappear or even diminish in the decades to come, it is equally unlikely that environmentalism itself will disappear. Environmentalism is deeply embedded in the institutional structures of contemporary states, in a complex web of public policies, in the political and even corporate culture and in the personal lives of citizens. Over the past decade, "green businesses" have provided one of the few areas of growth in an otherwise flat North American economy. However, all of this is not to say that environmentalism will continue to be a prominent feature on the *ideological landscape*. It is only one of a number of currents working to refashion the ideological landscape, and there is no guarantee that environmentalism will necessarily fare well in the competition with other ideological currents. As Edward Bell (1993:140) points out:

> In any historical era, a large number of social movements come into being and attempt to change society. Some compete with other movements for public support and political power, while others are more or less on their own, too powerless to be noticed by the larger public and too weak to elicit a response even from those whose interests they oppose .... Most never gain a substantial following, much less embark on a large-scale mobilization.

Insofar as environmentalism exists within a competitive ideological arena, its future success within that arena is by no means assured. It may be, for example, that competing ideological currents associated with global economic change or religious fundamentalism will be stronger than those associated with environmentalism. While we do not suggest that environmentalism is "too powerless to be noticed by the larger public," the success of the movement may well depend upon environmentalists' ability to fashion, and indeed their interest in fashioning, effective coalitions with other proponents of political and social change.

This chapter has presented environmentalism as more than a collection of "green" theories and policy objectives. Indeed, we have suggested that it is reasonable to think of environmentalism as a distinct ideology. While it is true that significant divisions exist within the environmental movement, a set of core values remains common to the movement and to the ideology as a whole. Given that threats to the environment will continue to pose challenges to future generations on several fronts, environmentalists will continue to take up the torch, to challenge the economic-growth paradigm that dominates society and to encourage value change on a global scale. As an ideology, however, environmentalism will benefit from remaining sensitive to the social conditions in which it is operating. Murray Bookchin (1989:24) writes, almost "all ecological problems are social problems...." and Cockburn and Ridgeway (1979:395) argue that:

> [A] political ecology that does not regard as central the fact of structural unemployment must be rightly perceived as marginal or frivolous: a political ecology that does not integrate such central economic issues into its analysis and programs has failed before it begins—a victim of the same tunnel vision that has been the crippling limitation of the middle-class reform movement for the last few decades.

Ideological intersections such as ecofeminism, or those between environmentalists and the proponents of social justice, may be valuable *if* environmentalists are prepared to wade into the political and social debates associated with other, complementary ideological currents.[14] But while reform environmentalists can likely imagine collaborating with other movements in tinkering with existing institutions in the name of environmental protection, deep ecologists are likely to dismiss attempts at reform as little more than exercises in rearranging the deck chairs on the Titanic as the world moves ever closer to environmental disaster. This suspicion of reform is grounded in the deep ecologist's conviction of the need to supplant, rather than reform, the dominant, economic paradigm and its emphasis on growth, increased productivity and technological innovation. Yet, despite these divergent approaches, all branches of environmentalism adhere to a basic principle: the need for humankind to maintain a long-term sustainable relationship with the global environment.

So where does this discussion of environmentalism leave us? Robert Paehlke (1989:3) reminds us that environmentalism "provides a very useful base from which to make individual life choices, from which to take collective political action, and from which to decide a surprisingly broad range of public policy issues." In short, environmentalism is a political ideology, and one that is likely to endure as we pursue a better understanding of humanity's ongoing role in the natural world.

NOTES

1. The first to formulate the foundation of deep ecology was Arne Naess.
2. Murray Bookchin's acclaimed *The Ecology of Freedom* is known as his magnum opus to this end.
3. This idea can be traced to the broader Platonic notion of dualism within human beings; for example, between the mind and body, or between reason and the passions.
4. The "Scientific Revolution" refers to the collective work of Nicolaus Copernicus (1473–1543), Johannes Kepler (1571–1630), Galileo Galilei (1564–1642), Francis Bacon (1561–1626), René Descartes (1596–1650) and Isaac Newton (1642–1727).
5. The ultimate extension of this line of thought is the notion of "Gaia," in which Earth is seen as a single, albeit extraordinarily complex, organism.
6. An excellent example of this movement is found in Christopher Stone, *Should Trees Have Standing?* (Los Altos: Kaufmann, 1974).
7. NIMBY is the acronym for Not In My Back Yard. In the environmental context, it refers to locally based opposition to such things as nuclear reactors and waste disposal facilities. Another frequently encountered acronym is NOTE—Not Over There Either!
8. The commission, headed by Norway's Prime Minister Gro Harlem Brundtland, is also referred to as the Brundtland Commission.
9. Although green parties have enjoyed modest success in several countries, they have been a negligible factor in North America. For example, in the 1993 Canadian general election, the Green Party fielded seventy-nine candidates but captured only 0.2 percent of the national popular vote. Their failure may have more to do with Canada's single-member, first-past-the-post electoral system than with the inherent strength (or weakness) of environmentalism within the country.
10. For a discussion of this linkage, see Roger Gibbins and Michelle Honkanen, "Environmentalism and the Politics of Mega-Constitutional Change," in Brian Galligan and Peter Russell (Eds.), *Redesigning the State: The Politics of Constitutional Change* (Sydney: The Federation Press, forthcoming 1996).
11. It is interesting to note that decentralization and egalitarianism are commonly collapsed into a single political characteristic in the environmental literature. It is by no means clear, however, that decentralized decision-making processes are necessarily egalitarian.
12. The German Greens have advocated the use of direct democracy, including national referendums, as a means to coordinate decentralized communities (Goodin 1992:155).
13. Reprinted in the *Globe and Mail*, April 3, 1995, p. A17.
14. A somewhat different intersection is that between environmentalism and the proponents of a free market economy, an intersection occupied by those who have been trying to create effective market mechanisms for environmental protection. If the proponents of the free market are in fact riding the ideological wave of the day, then this intersection could be critically important to the achievement of environmental objectives.

CHAPTER SEVEN

Nationalism and the Decline of Territoriality

There can be no fifty-fifty Americanism in this country.
There is room here for only hundred per cent Americanism.

THEODORE ROOSEVELT

Nationalism is an infantile disease.
It is the measles of mankind.

ALBERT EINSTEIN

Our country! In her intercourse with foreign nations may she
always be in the right; but our country, right or wrong.

STEPHEN DECATUR

Nationalism is a phenomenon of great historical importance and contemporary relevance. As Peter Alter (1989:4) observes, it is "a political force which has been more important in shaping the history of Europe and the world over the last two centuries than the ideas of freedom and parliamentary democracy or of communism." Nationalism taps some of our most basic political attachments to the land and to our primary communities. This almost primordial core of nationalism[1] is nicely captured by the independence manifesto (1968:14) of Quebec nationalist and former premier René Lévesque:

> We are Québécois. What that means first and foremost—and if need be, all that it means—is that we are attached to this one corner of the earth where we can be completely ourselves: this Quebec, the only place where we have the unmistakable feeling that "here we can really be at home."

In different settings, nationalism has brought out the best and worst of the human condition; it has both enriched our cultural life and unleashed the dogs of war. What is unclear, however, is the degree to which nationalism is a political *ideology*. The purpose of this chapter is to probe the ideological aspects of nationalism, and then to position nationalism on the broader ideological landscape of western democratic states. This will enable us to address the future of nationalism within a rapidly changing ideological environment characterized by increasing globalization and erosion of the territorial foundations of political life.[2]

The impact of nationalism on patterns of political thought and behaviour is likely reduced by some ideological currents, and potentially enhanced by others. As Chapter 11 suggests, new social movements such as environmentalism and feminism challenge the territorial preoccupations that are central to nationalism, whereas populism and some forms of conservative thought may strengthen those preoccupations. Therefore, predicting the future of nationalism within the global village of the twenty-first century is a very chancy undertaking. Yet, while the future of nationalism is open to debate, there is no question as to its profound impact in the past (Smith 1979:1):

> Of all the visions and faiths that compete for men's loyalties in the modern world, the most widespread and persistent is the national ideal. Other faiths have achieved more spectacular temporary success or a more permanent footing in one country. Other visions have roused men to more terrible and heroic acts. But none has been so successful in penetrating to every part of the globe ... No other vision has set its stamp so thoroughly on the map of the world, and on our sense of identity.

Clearly, it would be foolish to dismiss the potential of nationalism to shape the ideological contours of western democratic states in years to come.

THE MEANING OF NATIONALISM

Nationalism, unlike many other political ideologies, does not have a clear intellectual point of origin. As Anthony Birch (1989:13) points out, "There is no nationalist equivalent of liberalism's John Locke, conservatism's Edmund Burke, or communism's Karl Marx."[3] It is possible, however, to mark the time at which nationalist ideologies began to emerge. They first appeared in the late 1700s and early 1800s as a reaction to universalistic assumptions of the day, assumptions rooted in the union of the Roman Empire and Christianity. "Against the universalism of the past," Hans Kohn (1965:15) writes, "the new nationalism glorified the peculiar and the parochial, national differences and national individualities." While the assumptions of universality had found expression in the individualism and liberalism spawned by the Enlightenment, the emergent nationalist theories were "based on the belief that man is a social animal, deriving his character and aspirations from communities that share a common culture" (Birch 1989:14). Thus, nationalism was, to a significant degree, a reaction to liberalism, much like socialism and conservatism. Although, as Richard Jay (1984:187) notes, "the roots of nationalism lie in the eighteenth-century liberal idea that the authority of government derives from the governed," liberal individualism was not so much embraced by early nationalist thinkers as it was expanded and transformed. Benjamin Akzin (1964:46) explains:

> Where liberal democracy demands a political structure in which the individual, together with his peers, determines the regime under which he is to live and expects such regime to grant him the utmost opportunities for self-expression consistent with other established community goals, nationalism adds the demand that the sum total of individuals constituting an ethnic group be given collectively a similar right, again with the expectation that the resulting regime will offer maximum opportunities of

self-expression and growth to those values which the members of the group hold in common, i.e., to national values.

The growth of nationalism was facilitated by the development of powerful state institutions in the nineteenth century. The blending of nationalist ideas and such institutions gave nationalism its particular character and force, and set it apart from earlier patriotic attachments. For this reason, nationalism has been generally considered a modern phenomenon. The French Revolution is widely accepted as its opening act (Symmons-Symonolewicz 1968:30–1),[4] and the Napoleonic wars as the vehicle for its spread across western Europe. In his classic study of nationalism, Boyd Shafer (1955:5) asserts that "any use of the word nationalism to describe historical happenings before the eighteenth century is probably anachronistic."[5] Further, he argues (1955:167–8) that by the twentieth century, the nation had become "the supreme community and nationalism the supreme sentiment."

Early nationalist thought drew from various intellectual streams that rejected liberal individualism, and proposed instead that people were inextricably embedded in their communities. The work of French philosopher Jean-Jacques Rousseau in the late 1700s made a significant contribution, as did Hegel's *Philosophy of Right* (1821), which portrayed the state as the highest expression of human effort. Rousseau's disciple, German historian Johann Gottfried Herder, "deeply resented the increasing adoption by Germany's social élite of the French language, Parisian fashions, and, as he saw it, the shallow rationalism and materialism of French Enlightenment" (Jay 1984:193). Hans Kohn (1965:31) maintains that Herder was:

> [T]he first to insist that human civilization lives not in its universal but in its national and peculiar manifestations. The creative forces of the universal individualized themselves primarily not in the single human being but in the collective personalities of human communities. Men were above all members of their national communities; only as such could they be really creative, through the medium of their folk language and their folk traditions.

Herder argued that "humanity had its roots in and derived its values from a number of national cultures, each of which had its own virtues and no one of which could rightly lay claim to universality" (Birch 1989:17). He used the term "*Volk*" to refer to such cultures and maintained that each *Volk* offered a distinctive contribution to civilization (Jay 1984:193). Consequenctly, each warranted protection by its own national government. Every language, Herder believed, is unique, and not "simply a particular way of expressing universal values" (Breuilly 1994:57). Significantly, however, Herder was not a modern nationalist in that he did not demand the creation of nation-states: "To him nationality was not a political or biological but a spiritual and moral concept" (Kohn 1965:31). Indeed, Herder and others like him "distrusted the state as something external, mechanical, not emerging spontaneously from the life of the people" (Kamenka 1993:83).

Another German theorist of the time, Johann Gottlieb Fichte, expanded the conceptual domain of nationalism to include "elements of national pride, verbal aggression and messianic political vision" (Birch 1989:19). Fichte drew particular attention to the special qualities of German culture and language, and has thereby become associated with the more extreme manifestations of German nationalism. While he maintained that language provided the general foundation for nationality—"It is true beyond doubt that, wherever a separate language is formed, there a separate nation exists, which has the right to take independent charge of its affairs and to govern itself" (Birch 1989:19)—he placed particular value on the German language. Fichte argued that languages such as English, French, Italian and Spanish are derivative or bastardized, and therefore less capable of providing a firm foundation for nationality. German, on the other hand, was a pure and natural language (Birch 1989:19), and the special character of the German language and people meant that Germans had an obligation to impose the virtues of their culture on the world. Through Fichte's work, which has been described as chauvinist, racist and anti-Semitic (Kamenka 1993:85), German nationalism became linked to an expansive imperialism that was to bear its most bitter fruit in Hitler's Third Reich.

Writers like Fichte helped establish a close link between nationalism and culture, thereby putting into place many of the conventions by which "nations" are identified and defined. They also provided an important nationalism conduit for the nineteenth-century Romantic reaction to eighteenth-century rationalism, and to its fellow traveller, liberalism. As Richard Jay (1984:193) notes, nationalism was able to harness the Romantic spirit: "In the freedom and life of the nation could be found a repository of moral values and emotional commitment, filling the gap vacated by traditional religious faith."

Nationalism has been a long-standing object of scholarly inquiry, which has generated a rich literature covering several centuries of nationalist thought and movements worldwide. The attempt to fit a single term to such a diverse political history, and to do so in a scholarly tradition that has placed great value on the uniqueness of various national experiences, has not produced a conceptual consensus. Boyd Shafer observes (1955:7) that "nationalism is what the nationalists have made it; it is not a neat, fixed concept but a varying combination of beliefs and traditions." In essence, however, nationalism can be tied to some basic, even simple, concepts. At its core is the desire for congruence between nation and state,[6] a desire often expressed as a quest for national self-determination, political sovereignty or home rule (Kellas 1991:3). Nationalists assert that the "nation" should exercise autonomous political control over a given piece of territory, with the result being the "nation-state." This territory may be possessed already or only coveted (Shafer 1955:7), but in either case, discussions of nationalism focus on two issues: first, the congruence of nation and state, or extent to which the nation and state coincide; and second, the degree of political control exercised by national governments.

The Congruence of Nation and State

If nationalism is the desire for congruence between an identified nation, on the one hand, and the state apparatus of a specific territorial domain, on the other, we can readily find examples for which the correspondence between nation and state has been less than perfect, and where the lack of fit has sparked nationalist movements. Nationalism in Quebec, for example, is associated with the quest by the Québécois for greater political control over the territory of Quebec, control which for many would mean the creation of an independent state. Scottish nationalists seek greater political autonomy for Scotland, as do Basque separatists for their region of Spain, and Tamil nationalists for their territorial claims in Sri Lanka.[7] It is precisely where there is a lack of congruence between the nation and state institutions that we would expect nationalism to emerge as an ideological conviction and political movement.

The Meaning of "Nation"

Nationalism presumes a world divided into nations, and provides a "theory of political legitimacy" for this division (Jay 1984:185); Nationalists assume, moreover, that nationality should be the primary political division, coming before more secondary divisions that might follow from class, occupation, gender or religion. But what are the "nations" which provide the building blocks for nationalism? Nations are generally thought to have objective features that create bonds among their citizens and distinguish them from those of other nations. Indeed, one of the reasons the national division is seen as primary is that the nation is assumed to encompass many of the other factors that might otherwise divide a political community. Thus, nations are often based on a distinctive ethnicity, race, language or religion, or on some combination of these. The nation *as a political community* gives expression to this unique cluster of characteristics.

It is not always the case, however, that nationalism depends on idiosyncratic characteristics. The United States, for example, shares the English language with many other countries, does not have an "established" religion and is increasingly complex with respect to race and ethnicity. The American "nation" is therefore less distinct than the Hungarian or Portuguese nations, but this has not resulted in a diminished sense of nationhood. In fact, nationalism as a political doctrine may be more essential in countries that are neither homogeneous nor unique in their demographic composition. In such cases, the "common features" that bind the nation together are likely to be state institutions and shared political ideals rather than demographic characteristics. Thus, the state and nation blend into one.

This leads to the point, stressed throughout the extensive body of nationalism literature, that the nation is more than an amalgam of objective characteristics. As James Kellas (1991:2) explains, nations have both objective and subjective characteristics. In one of the earliest and still surprisingly relevant studies of nationalism, Carlton Hayes (1926:12) writes that nationality cannot be reduced to racial heredity or physical environment: it is "an attribute of human culture and civilisation, and the factors of zoology and botany are not applicable to it." Hans Kohn (1965:10) makes a similar point: "Although objective factors are of great importance for the formation of nationalities, the most essential element is a living and active corporate will. It is this will we call nationalism, a state of mind inspiring the large majority of a people and claiming to inspire all its members." Peter Alter (1989:10) concludes that "the nation is a politically mobilized people," and Hugh Seton-Watson (1977:5) maintains that a nation exists if "a significant number of people in a community consider themselves to form a nation, or behave as if they formed one."

Given that nationalism is first and foremost the desire to achieve congruence between the boundaries of the nation and state, there are a number of different means nationalists may use to improve the degree of fit, and a number of situations where the lack of fit has promoted a nationalist response. Probably the most common form of nationalism arises when an identifiable "nation" attempts to create or seize a territory over which it can exercise a sufficient degree of autonomous political control. The early history of most western democratic states show examples of this first form of nationalism. Contemporary examples include the nationalist movement in Quebec where, as noted above, Québécois nationalists seek to transform a Canadian province into an independent state; the Zionist movement which led to the establishment of the state of Israel in 1948; the Palestinian movement which, since 1948, has sought an independent Palestinian state in the Middle East; and the determination of aboriginal peoples in North America to establish autonomous, self-governing communities. In such cases, the nation would be less clearly defined than where political boundaries have already been established and citizenship criteria are in place, although the definition of who constitutes the nation is open for perpetual debate even within well-established nation-states. The transformation of nations to nation-states, which is the form that nationalism has taken historically, provides the most commonly understood definition of nationalism, one strongly associated with the anticolonialism that swept through Africa and parts of Asia in the decades following the Second World War.

Nationalism is associated not only with creating states within which preexisting nations can exercise political control, but also with efforts to sustain and even create the nation itself. It is a mistake to assume that the nation always precedes the nation-state, for in some cases the nation is a creation or product of the state. E. J. Hobsbawn (1990:10) explains: "For the purposes of analysis nationalism comes before nations. Nations do not make states and nationalisms but the other way around."[8] Ernest Gellner (1983:4) goes even further when he suggests that "the existence of politically centralized units, and of a moral-political climate in which such centralized units are taken for granted and treated as normative, is a necessary though by no means a sufficient condition of nationalism."

Anthony Smith (1983:175) pursues this theme when he notes that "where nationalism arises without a pre-existent nation, the 'nation' for which it strives is only an embryo, a project, a 'nation of intent.'" Here, the American experience *following* the successful War of Independence (1775–83) with Britain provides a useful example. In the late 1700s and early 1800s, the American state was in place even though its institutional articulation was not yet complete and military conflict with Britain was to erupt again in the War of 1812. However, it was not clear whether a national community in fact existed, whether a diverse immigrant population and the former colonies had coalesced into a recognizable and durable nation. (As the Civil War demonstrated, it took almost 100 years to answer this question definitively.) Therefore, much of the early energy of American nationalism was directed towards creating a cohesive national community that would coincide with the territorial boundaries of the United States (Kohn 1962:14–15), boundaries which at the same time were being pushed steadily to the west and south. This early nationalism included the efforts by Daniel Webster to formally define American usage of the English language, and thereby to create a linguistic vehicle for the expression of a distinctive American culture.

The effort to nurture, indeed to create the American nation, and to provide that nation with full opportunity for cultural expression, was echoed in Canadian nationalism of the 1950s and 1960s. This latter nationalism was associated with various steps taken by governments of the day to protect and promote the national culture and identity: the creation of a new flag, the founding of cultural bodies such as the Canada Council and the National Film Board (NFB), the aggressive use of state agencies like the Canadian Broadcasting Corporation (CBC), the introduction of Canadian-content regulations for radio and television broadcasting and restrictions on American investment. Such nationalism is common even within long-established nation-states, for it cannot be assumed that nation-states, once established, will perpetually endure. In this context, ongoing efforts by the government of France to purify the popular usage of the French language can be seen as an attempt to shore up the cultural distinctiveness and vitality of the French "nation" in the face of the challenges posed by European integration and the broader forces of globalization.[9] It should be noted, however, that nationalist attempts to preserve traditional values and cultures may entail a form of false consciousness. Ernest Gellner (1983:124) explains that the nationalist ideology inverts reality: "It claims to defend folk culture while in fact it is forging a high culture; it claims to protect an old folk society while in fact helping to build up an anonymous mass society."[10] Certainly in the Canadian case, the culture fostered by state-sponsored nationalism has been a form of high culture which, like a thin veneer, covers a mass popular culture that is largely American in origin and content.

A third way in which the congruence between a nation and a given political territory can be improved is to redefine the people to fit the territory. A good example is provided by the francophone minority within Canada. Francophones have traditionally constituted close to thirty percent of the total population, although that proportion has dropped to just under twenty-five percent in recent years. However, the francophone population has been overwhelmingly concentrated in one province, Quebec, where approximately eighty percent of the population is francophone. In eight of the other nine provinces, francophones form a relatively small and steadily declining proportion of the population. (New Brunswick, whose linguistic composition is similar to that of the country at large, is the exception.) Over time, then, the focus of nationalist sentiment among francophone Canadians has shifted from French Canada to Quebec, and the associated "nation" has changed from French Canadians to the Québécois.[11] Therefore, nationalist ideologies which, in the past, were directed towards the position of French Canadians in Canada are now directed towards the creation of an independent Quebec, and francophones outside Quebec are no longer regarded as members of the "nation." This redefinition of the national community has also entailed the controversial expansion of that community to *all* residents of Quebec, including those whose mother tongue is English.

A fourth means of improving the fit between nation and state—and a means associated with the most troublesome aspects of nationalism—is to expel "impure" individuals and groups who are not "of the people." Such expulsion takes many forms. It has frequently entailed denying full political rights to those deemed by their race, religion or ideology to be "foreigners." This nativist impulse[12] was associated with the denial of the electoral franchise to Chinese Canadians in British Columbia until the 1950s, and possibly with the internment of West Coast Japanese Americans and Japanese Canadians during the Second World War. In the United States, the nativist impulse characterized McCarthyism and the House Committee on UnAmerican Activities which, during the 1950s, tried to identify the ideologically impure, particularly communists and sympathetic fellow travellers, and to drive them from positions of influence in cultural and political life. The expulsion of white Europeans following successful decolonization in some African countries provides another example. An extreme and horrific form, although one that reflected more than mere nationalism, was the Holocaust—the savage effort by Nazi Germany to exterminate Jews and others deemed to fall outside the Aryan nation.[13] More recent examples of "ethnic cleansing" are provided by the civil wars in Burundi, Rwanda and the former Yugoslavia.

Ethnic and Territorial Nationalisms

Anthony Smith (1983:216–7) draws a useful distinction between *ethnic* and *territorial* nationalisms. *Ethnic* nationalisms "start from a pre-existent homogeneous entity, a recognisable cultural unit; all that is necessary is to protect and nurture it. The primary concern, therefore, of 'ethnic' nationalists is to ensure the survival of the group's *cultural* identity. That entails ensuring the *political* survival of the group and the physical protection of its members." *Territorial* nationalisms "start from an imposed political identity, and possess no common and distinctive cultural identity to protect." The task for territorial nationalists is to create, rather than protect, a national culture.

James Kellas (1991:51–2) draws a similar distinction between *ethnic* and *official* nationalisms. The former is associated with "ethnic groups such as the Kurds, Latvians, and Tamils, who define their nation in exclusive terms, mainly on the basis of common descent." As Kellas points out: "In this type of nationalism, no one can 'become' a Kurd, Latvian, or Tamil through adopting Kurdish etc, ways." *Official* nationalism, for which the United States provides a prime example, encompasses "all those legally entitled to be citizens, irrespective of their ethnicity, national identity and culture." One can "become" an American in a way that one cannot "become" a Kurd.

The milder and more innocuous manifestations of this last form of nationalist congruence bring into play an important distinction between *ethnic* and *civic* nationalism.[14] Ethnic nationalism defines the political community in narrow, ethnic terms. Thus, for example, full political rights might be granted to those of Estonian ethnic descent living in Estonia, or even abroad, but not to the residents of Estonia whose ethnic background is Russian, Polish or German. The "nation" does not include all those living within the territorial boundaries of the nation-state. In civic nationalism, this is precisely the definition of the nation, which is regarded as coterminous with the territorial boundaries of the state. A civic conception of Québécois nationalism, for example, would include all residents of Quebec as part of the Québécois, regardless of their ethnic origin or mother tongue; an ethnic conceptualization would restrict the Québécois to those with roots in the original French Catholic community that settled the province in the seventeenth and eighteenth centuries. Ethnic nationalism, including its most innocuous forms, is most clearly identified with the nation-state, whereas civic nationalism is more appropriately identified with a territorial state.

There are, then, many ways by which nationalist movements may seek to create better congruence between nation and state. The Québécois seeking an independent Quebec, the Irish at the turn of the century who sought, and eventually won, an independent Ireland, and Indian nationalists in the 1940s who finally brought to an end British imperial rule on the subcontinent, are all examples of nationalist movements. However, nationalism may arise even when the formal fit between nation and state is not a matter of debate.

The Degree of Political Control Exercised by National Governments

Nationalist movements can be sparked by the conviction that the state or, more specifically, the nation acting through state institutions, is unable to exercise sufficient political control over its territory. Nationalism can come into play within well-established nation-states if there is a widespread perception that the state's political autonomy has been compromised, that state institutions are too constrained by external actors or that non-nationals are receiving too big a slice of the social and economic pies. In other words, nationalism can be a response to an inadequate degree of political control, or at least to the perception of inadequacy; it is closely related to the promotion and defence of political sovereignty. This second dimension of nationalism is of particular interest in the contemporary context in which globalization poses a growing challenge to the sovereignty of even the strongest nation-states.

Definitions of Nationalism

- "What is nationalism? It is simply the manifestations of the natural and spontaneous solidarity that exists among members of a human group sharing a historical and cultural tradition from which the group derives its distinctive identity." Michel Brunet, "The French Canadians' Search for a Fatherland." In Peter Russell (Ed.) *Nationalism in Canada* (Toronto: McGraw-Hill Ryerson, 1966), 47.

- Nationalism is "that sentiment unifying a group of people who have a real or imagined common historical experience and a common aspiration to live together as a separate group in the future. This unifying sentiment expresses itself in loyalty to the nation-state." Boyd Shafer, *Nationalism: Myth and Reality* (New York: Harcourt Brace, 1955), 10.

- "Nationalism is a state of mind, in which the supreme loyalty of the individual is felt to be due the nation-state." Hans Kohn, *Nationalism: Its Meaning and History*, rev. ed. (Princeton, N.J.: D. Van Nostrand, 1965), 9.

- Nationalism is "both an ideology and a political movement which holds the nation and the sovereign nation-state to be crucial indwelling values, and which manages to mobilize the political will of a people or a large section of a population …. nationalism exists whenever individuals feel they belong primarily to the nation, and whenever affective attachment and loyalty to that nation override all other attachments and loyalties." Peter Alter, *Nationalism* (London: Edward Arnold, 1989), 8–9.

- Nationalism is "an ideological movement, for the attainment and maintenance of self-government and independence on behalf of a group, some of whose members conceive it to constitute an actual or potential 'nation' like others." Anthony D. Smith, *Theories of Nationalism* (London: Duckworth, 1983), 171.

- "[N]ationalism is just one particular form of politics. Like all forms of politics it is entangled in a world of material interests, of corruption, and self-seeking rhetoric …. Like all forms of politics it derives much of its power from the half-truths it embodies. People do yearn for communal membership, do have a strong sense of us and them, of territories as homelands, of belonging to culturally defined and bounded worlds which give their lives meaning." John Breuilly, *Nationalism and the State* (Chicago: Univ. of Chicago Press, 1994), 401.

A good example of this dimension of nationalism is again provided by the Canadian experience during the 1960s and 1970s. At that time, there was growing concern that the economy was dominated by American firms and investment, that Canadian culture was being overwhelmed by American cultural industries and artifacts and that Canada was unable to exercise significant autonomy on the international stage. While the physical existence of Canada was not at risk, there was acute concern that its distinctive cultural values were, that Canadians were not benefitting sufficiently from their economy and that the country's natural resources were passing into foreign control. The nationalist response was to demand that American ownership be rolled back, that cultural interests and artisans be protected from American competition and that the government exercise greater independence in its foreign policy. This demand enjoyed broad popular and partisan support; all the major political parties included nationalist planks in their campaign platforms. It eventually achieved expression in a wide array of legislative initiatives (for example, the creation of the Foreign Investment Review Agency, Canadian-content regulations for television and radio broadcasts, establishment of Petro Canada) designed to strengthen Canadian control of the national economy, and to ward off cultural intrusions from the United States.

Also within the Canadian experience, the quest for aboriginal self-government provides an additional example of nationalism as the pursuit of greater political control within an already established territorial community. For most First Nations, a reasonably secure land base has been in place since the establishment of Indian reserves in the late nineteenth century.[15] Until recently, however, aboriginal peoples have not been able to exercise significant autonomous control over their land base; they have been constrained on all sides by the Indian Act (1876) and the Department of Indian Affairs, by federal and provincial legislation and even by international treaties and conventions dealing with such matters as hunting restrictions on migratory birds on North American flyways. The search for self-government, therefore, is an attempt by aboriginal peoples to attain greater political control over their own land and communities, a search analogous to other forms of nationalism which seek to protect and enhance the political autonomy of "national" governments.

At times, the nationalist quest for greater political autonomy and control can be directed towards internal or domestic targets. For example, the nationalism associated with anticolonialism in Africa was directed not only at the imperial power but at the local elites who governed on behalf of the imperial power, and thereby enjoyed privileged access to social status and economic spoils. As Ernest Gellner (1983:1) also notes, nationalism is a theory of political legitimacy which requires that "ethnic boundaries within a given state … not separate the power-holders from the rest." Populist movements can therefore harness nationalism by placing economic and political elites "outside the people," making them targets for nationalist attacks. If, for example, business elites are portrayed as members of a religious minority, and therefore not "true" Americans or Canadians, then a populist challenge to those elites can be strengthened and legitimated by nationalism. In western democratic states, Jews have been a particularly vulnerable target in this respect (Lipset and Raab 1970). Particularly relevant here is Peter Alter's chilling description (1989:38) of what he terms *integral* nationalism, where the nation takes on absolute virtue:

> Integral nationalism casts off all ethical ballast, obligating and totally subordinating the individual to one value alone, the nation. '*La France d'abord*', 'My country, right or wrong', 'You are nothing, your people everything', are the kinds of moral commands to which integral nationalism binds the faithful and with which it legitimizes the use of physical violence against the heretic and minorities.

Finally, nationalism often arises when greater political control is sought beyond the boundaries of the nation-state. For example, nationalism is often brought into play when states attempt to exercise political or economic influence outside their borders.[16] In the extreme, nationalism may be the cause of war, where it is then accentuated by and mobilized for military conflict. In a less extreme form, nationalism can be associated with the assertion of extraterritoriality, the claim that one's citizens and economic interests should not be bound by the laws of other states. This may also take the form of asserting that one's own laws should apply in other states. During the early 1970s, for example, a major source of nationalist tension between Canada and the United States came from American insistence that American firms operating in Canada be bound by American trade law.[17] A Canadian-based but multinational firm was prohibited from selling locomotives to Cuba because such a sale would violate American trading-with-the-enemy legislation. Nationalism, therefore, is connected with the desire to protect one's citizens and national interests in the international domain.

Similarly, nationalism can result in the attempt to project one's own national values onto other countries and the world. By the end of the nineteenth century, nationalism became fused with imperialism. Richard Jay (1984:197) explains:

> The nation-state itself began to seem too small a stage on which to fulfill national purposes. Writers and politicians began to proclaim the 'civilizing mission' they had to bring the light of their national values into dark corners of the world; a mission, according to Rudyard Kipling, which was the 'white man's burden.'

Thus, "Englishmen dreamed fondly of bringing Anglo-Saxon institutions to the world, Frenchmen of the civilizing mission of France, Russians of Slavic unity or international communism, Germans of the supremacy of their *Kultur*, and Americans of their manifest destiny" (Shafer 1955:179). Patriots in these countries, Boyd Shafer (1955:180) suggests, equated love of nation—*their* nation—with the welfare of all humankind.

Observations on Nationalism and Patriotism

- John Dryden: "Never was patriot yet, but was a fool."
- Samuel Johnson: "Patriotism is the last refuge of a scoundrel."
- Edith Cavell, speaking to her chaplain shortly before her execution by a firing squad in 1915: "Standing, as I do, in the view of God and eternity I realize that patriotism is not enough. I must have no hatred or bitterness towards anyone."
- President Thomas Jefferson: "The tree of liberty must be refreshed from time to time with the blood of patriots and tyrants. It is its natural manure."
- Guy de Maupassant: "Patriotism is the egg from which wars are hatched."
- Kin Hubbard: "It seems like the less a statesman amounts to, the more he loves the flag."
- Charles de Gaulle: "Patriotism is when love of your own country comes first; nationalism is when hate for people other than your own comes first."

To this point, we have defined nationalism by the quest for congruence between nation and state, and the exercise of autonomous political control by the nation-state over its own territory and, at times, beyond. However, these two dimensions do not exhaust nationalism's conceptual domain. Many scholars (Bellah and Hammond 1980; Hayes 1960;

Shafer 1955:178; Shafer 1972:131–5), have drawn important conceptual linkages between nationalism and religion; some have even described nationalism as a form of secular religion. Note, for example, this observation by Carlton Hayes (1960:10):

> There are degrees of nationalism, as of any emotion. Our loyalty to nationality and the national state may be conditioned by other loyalties—to family, to church, to humanity, to internationalism—and hence restricted in corresponding degree. On the other hand, nationalism may be a paramount, a supreme loyalty, commanding all others. This usually occurs when national emotion is fused with religious emotion, and nationalism itself becomes a religion or a substitute for religion.

One dimension of nationalism that we have saved to the last is the normative dimension. There is no question that nationalism is often seen, and perhaps is generally seen, in negative, even pejorative, terms. In large part, this perception springs from the central role that nationalism played in military conflicts over the last two centuries, and particularly from the role it played in the First and Second World Wars (Kohn 1965:79–80). For many, including the architects of the postwar European community, the excesses of Nazi Germany came to symbolize nationalism and all for which it stands. Peter Alter (1989:27) observes:

> After the Second World War, the vast majority of Europeans equated nationalism with bellicose aggression, the unbridled urge for expansion, and racism. They regarded it as the expression of a blinkered mentality which had brought immeasurable calamity down upon Europe.

Even before the atrocities inflicted by the Third Reich, Carlton Hayes (1926:246) attributed the following aspects to nationalism:

> An intolerant attitude and behavior towards one's fellows; a belief in the imperial mission of one's own nationality at the expense of other, particularly at the expense of backward, peoples; a habit of carrying a chip on one's national shoulder and defying another nationality to knock it off; a fond dwelling on past wars and a feverish preparing for future wars, to the neglect of present civil problems; a willingness to be led and guided by self-styled patriots; a diffidence, almost a panic, about thinking or acting differently from one's fellows; a spirit of exclusiveness and narrowness which feeds on gross ignorance of others and on inordinate pride in one's self and one's nationality.

Nationalism is frequently lumped together with jingoism, imperialism, chauvinism, racism and even fascism; it has also been associated with the worst aspects of social Darwinism and the presumed competition among nations in the survival of the fittest (Kohn 1965:73).

Although the negative aspects of nationalism cannot be denied, it is important to recognize the positive values which are associated with nationalism. It has promoted freedom for nations, if not necessarily individuals, by being "the most powerful dissolvent of empires the world has ever known" (Ward 1959:33). Nation-states and the nationalism they inspire provide a vehicle through which people can pursue collective goals (Ward 1959:30) and nurture a cultural community. Nationalism can provide a community identification at a time when other forms of social attachment are weakening. Here Anthony Smith (1983:193) states, with limited enthusiasm, that to the nationalist, "men are not 'realized', humanity is 'unfulfilled' and hence 'underdeveloped', until the world is constituted into nation-states, which give political recognition to the aspirations to nationhood latent in every individual, whether he recognises it or not." The assessment by James Kellas (1991:1) is more positive:

> Nationalism has been considered essential to the establishment of a modern industrial society. It gives legitimacy to the state, and inspires its citizens to feel an emotional attachment towards it. It can be a source of creativity in the arts, and enterprise in the economy. Its power to mobilize political activity is unsurpassed, especially in the vital activity of 'nation-building'.

It is worth noting that sacrificing one's life for one's country is often portrayed as the noblest act; Nathan Hale's last words before being hanged by the British in 1776—"I only regret that I have but one life to lose for my country"—perfectly capture the nationalist creed. In this context, Benedict Anderson's comment (1991:9–10) on the tomb of the Unknown Soldier is particularly interesting:

> No more arresting emblems of the modern culture of nationalism exists than cenotaphs and tombs of Unknown Soldiers .... Void as these tombs are of identifiable mortal remains or immortal souls, they are nonetheless saturated with ghostly *national* imaginings .... The cultural significance of such monuments becomes even clearer if one tries to imagine, say, a Tomb of the Unknown Marxist or a cenotaph for fallen Liberals.

What is at issue, then, is partly a matter of perspective; where you stand on nationalism depends on where you sit. We are inclined to see our own nationalism as a positive virtue, and the nationalism of others as a threat.

In summary, nationalism embraces a number of central tenets and themes:

- it asserts the desirability of congruence between nations, variously defined, and the political apparatus of the state;

- it defends the nation's need for autonomous political control over its territory;

- it assumes that the nation is the primary object of political allegiance; and

- it promotes freedom of action for nation-states on the international stage.

Whether these coalesce into a coherent ideological package is an issue to which we now turn.

Exercise One: Normative Assessment of Nationalism

What is your own normative assessment of nationalism? If pushed to make the choice, would you judge nationalism to be a positive or negative phenomenon? When do you think nationalism is most likely to be a positive force in human affairs? When, or under what conditions, is it most likely to be a negative force?

How would you assess the nationalism of your own country? Is it more or less benign than other forms of nationalism with which you are familiar? What makes it so? In what respect is it attractive? Unattractive?

When are you most likely to consider yourself to be a nationalist, and when are you most likely to reject the label? Can you identify nationalist figures whom you admire and respect? Whom you view with some suspicion or distaste?

IS NATIONALISM AN IDEOLOGY?

Thus far, the discussion has dodged an important question—the extent to which nationalism should be seen as a political ideology. Or, perhaps more usefully, when and under what conditions might nationalism assume an ideological form? To answer these questions, we must first note that nationalism is broadly recognized as a political doctrine (Alter 1984; Birch 1989; Breuilly 1994; Jay 1984; Kellas 1991; Smith 1983). Indeed, it is the politicized nature of nationalism that distinguishes it from patriotism.[18] Nevertheless, while the heavy political content of nationalism supports an ideological conception, we can provide a more nuanced answer to the above questions by bringing into play the conceptual framework developed in Chapter 1. What happens when we apply this template to nationalism?

- There is no question that nationalism is *socially constructed*. Nationalism entails a sense of identification with a *community* that reaches well beyond the individual in time and space. Its symbols and cultural expression are collective products. Robinson Crusoe could not be a nationalist until he met Friday.

- For many of the same reasons, there is no question that nationalism is *socially transmitted*. The means through which nationalism is commonly expressed— national holidays, civic rituals, anthems, war memorials, military campaigns— are all social in character. While we could conceivably sing the national anthem alone in the shower, and fly the flag where it is unlikely to be seen, most expressive acts of nationalism require an audience; they are community, rather than solitary, events. In most countries, furthermore, the social transmission of nationalist sentiment is a conscious act that takes place through school curriculums, citizenship ceremonies, holidays and pledges of allegiance.[19]

- When compared to other ideologies, nationalism does not encompass a very comprehensive *system of political beliefs*. It may address the appropriate relationship between one's own country and that of others, and in cases where there are significant non-national domestic players, it may address domestic-group relations. However, nationalism seldom touches upon the issues that dominate ideological discourse in most western democratic states. For example, to know that an American is a "nationalist" provides little insight into how she might position herself with respect to environmental protection, gun control, young offenders, abortion, employment equity or economic deregulation.

- In some cases, nationalism receives little *formal articulation*. Nationalist beliefs and sentiments may pervade the political culture yet seldom find their way into accessible printed texts. In a typical American bookstore, for example, it would be easy to find whole sections dealing with feminism, environmentalism and contemporary debates between liberals and conservatives, but a request for books on "American nationalism" may well confuse even the most helpful clerk. In other cases, nationalism receives extensive articulation. Canadian nationalists have written at great length about the Canadian-American relationship, the threat to national culture and values and the challenges posed to the Canadian economy. It would therefore be relatively easy to walk into a Canadian bookstore and come out laden with nationalist tracts, just as it is relatively easy to identify those individuals who are *carriers of the creed*.

- It is not easy to assess whether nationalism embodies a *significant measure of scope, internal consistency and durability*. As noted above, nationalism often embraces a limited political agenda that has little relevance for most issues of domestic politics. At the same time, nationalist ideologies can be very durable, and are often firmly anchored in historical events and mythologies. As such, they are consistent, telling a story that has been polished and embellished over the years by a subtle recasting of historical events to make them fit the pattern prescribed by nationalist beliefs.

- Nationalism clearly provides a *normative framework*. It places a high value on national sovereignty and the state's political autonomy. It assigns moral credit to those who serve the state and national community, attaching the highest possible honour to those who give their lives in defence of their country and the greatest dishonour to those who betray their country. In most legal systems, treason is a more heinous crime than murder.

- In most domestic situations, nationalism fails to provide a clear *guide for political action*. Rarely can citizens rank the major parties by their degree of loyalty to the state, and then vote accordingly; parties which eschew patriotism are seldom serious contenders for public office. It is unlikely, therefore, that a nationalist will have as useful a road map for political action in domestic politics as a feminist, liberal or environmentalist will have. (When nationalism fails to provide a practical guide for political action, it blends into patriotism, or a simple love of one's country and national community.) Yet nationalism may provide a clearer road map than any of the above for individuals trying to position themselves on the international landscape. And, on occasion, nationalism may provide a guide for domestic politics. This was the case in the 1988 Canadian election debate over the proposed Free Trade Agreement, and in the American and Canadian debates over the North American Free Trade Agreement (NAFTA). The difficulty was that both proponents and opponents of the agreements attached nationalist arguments to their case. And it has certainly been the case with the Bloc Québécois and the Parti Québécois, both of which have provided Quebec voters with detailed guides to political action.

Exercise Two: Nationalism and Voting

To what extent does nationalism provide you with a *guide to political action*? To answer this question, think ahead to the next parliamentary or presidential election. Is nationalism likely to play a role in party platforms? Will parties—all parties? specific parties?—attempt to mobilize nationalist sentiment? Is nationalism likely to be a factor when you make up your mind how to vote? If so, what is the weight of that factor compared to others which you might consider?

Given the above assessment, we can draw a number of conclusions about the ideological aspects of nationalism. Although nationalism assumes many different forms across time and space, all are generally ideological in character. As a predisposition, nationalism allows individuals to locate themselves upon the broad canvas of international politics. It provides an important sense of identification with one of the most powerful of all political communities, the nation-state. And, at times, it enables individuals to position themselves with respect to domestic political issues. Nationalism, therefore, belongs in the ideological pantheon of western democratic states. What remains to be determined is its relationship with other occupants of the pantheon.

The Ideology of Nationalism

- *scope:* Fairly limited in most cases, encompassing relations between one's own country and foreign interests. However, can become entangled in domestic intergroup relations and, in virulent forms can even affect such matters as consumer behaviour, interpersonal relations and intermarriage.
- *internal consistency:* Nationalist ideologies are often interwoven with a variety of other ideological perspectives. Canadian nationalists, for example, could well be liberals, conservatives, feminists, environmentalists or socialists. As a consequence, nationalism appears to lack the internal consistency associated with other ideologies.
- *durability:* Nationalism both predates and is a product of the modern nation-state, and has been an influential force in human affairs for more than two centuries. The contemporary vitality of ethnic nationalism in many countries suggests that nationalism will persist as an important ideological current well into the next century.
- *normative framework:* The nation-state is an important object of citizen loyalty and identification. Threats to the autonomy and integrity of the nation-state should be resisted. If necessary, there are no limits to the sacrifices individuals should be prepared to make for the state.
- *practical guide for political action:* Primarily a means by which individuals orient themselves to the international environment: most areas of domestic politics are untouched by nationalist ideologies. In some cases, however, nationalism will shape the choice among political parties and perceptions of intergroup conflict within the nation-state.
- *formal articulation:* Nation-states have a plethora of nationalist symbols, writers and texts. Often, the most powerful expressions of nationalism come from outside the political community, through novelists, poets, singers and painters. It is in times of national and international crisis that political leaders come to the fore as carriers of the creed.

NATIONALISM ON THE IDEOLOGICAL LANDSCAPE

As discussed earlier, the ideological landscape of contemporary western democratic states is fluid and complex. How, then, do we locate nationalism on this landscape? Are there complementary ideological currents and trends that might strengthen the impact of nationalism in the years ahead? Are there currents that might reduce its strength? To answer these questions, we turn to a discussion of the specific fit of nationalism with the primary ideological currents of the times. However, it will not be possible to locate nationalism on the basic left-right spectrum, although it can be located on the individualism-collectivism continuum. As Richard Jay (1984:192) points out, nationalism is "politically indiscriminate between the Left, the Centre, and the Right." Thus, with respect to the most widely used convention of ideological discourse, nationalism is truly androgynous.

Complementary Ideological Currents

At its core, nationalism embraces a strong emotional and public policy commitment to the preservation and promotion of the national political community. It has, then, a strong collectivist streak. Boyd Shafer (1955:6) explains that nationalism often entails "a mystical devotion to a vague, sometimes even supernatural, social organism which, known as the nation or *Volk*, is more than the sum of its parts." Even if we reject the mystical aspects of nationalism, nationalist ideologies give primacy to community interests and values; the phrase, after all, is "I only regret that I have but one life to lose for my country," and not the other way around. We would expect, therefore, that nationalism would be most compatible with ideological perspectives which also have a community or collective orientation. For example, classical conservatism and domestic manifestations of socialism both give significant weight to the political community, and are potentially compatible with nationalist ideologies focused on the preservation and promotion of that community. Conservatism was particularly compatible with nationalism in the past as few traditional conservative ideologies were transnational in character; most were rooted in the history and tradition of unique societies, as was nationalism. It is not surprising that nationalist symbols figured prominently in conservative thought and rhetoric.

By contrast, socialism has often been transnational in character. Marx called upon the workers of world to unite, arguing that they had nothing to lose but their chains. To the extent that socialism promotes class identifications which cross national boundaries, it is incompatible with the essence of nationalism. In practice, however, social-democratic parties and movements have generally worked comfortably within the constraints of national boundaries. In addition, trade unions have seldom been enthusiastic supporters of free trade, fearing that unconstrained international competition could lead to the loss of union jobs at home. Thus, while in theory socialism and nationalism may appear to be at odds, in reality this has seldom been the case. Communist regimes have certainly not been incompatible with nationalism; no one would argue that the former Soviet Union, China or Cuba have been indifferent to the appeal and orchestration of nationalism. As Eric Hobsbawn (1977:13) argues, Marxist regimes following the end of the Second World War became increasingly national and nationalist in form and substance. In this context, Louis Snyder (1968:33) goes so far as to state that the association "of nationalism with socialism was one of the most significant trends of the twentieth century."

The interplay of populism and nationalism is perhaps the most mutually reinforcing ideological nexus.[20] At some level, and as discussed in greater detail in the next chapter, populism entails an appeal to "the people," reminiscent of the *Volk* in early nationalist thought. Anthony Smith (1983:264) explains: "If [populism] means the elevation of the uneducated, whose will to rule directly (in their own persons) as against the established order is the nub of the matter, then populism is a logical extension of one element of the nationalist doctrine, the supremacy of the nation." The devices of direct democracy, embraced by contemporary North American populism, are designed to provide the people with a direct voice in democratic governance. These devices not only provide a means by which the "national will" can be articulated, they also venerate the national will and thereby provide nationalists with greater ideological leverage on domestic politics.

In summary, if contemporary ideological currents are carrying us towards more populist and conservative political regimes, these currents may enhance the impact of nationalism. The retreat of socialism also opens up greater ideological space for the play of nationalism, particularly in central and eastern Europe. However, these are not the only ideological currents at play in western democratic states. And, as Konstantin Symmons-Symonolewicz (1970:41) notes, "Nationalism has had to struggle for the control of human minds against competing ideologies" for the past 200 years.

Competing Ideological Currents

As a political doctrine, nationalism gives primacy to *national* interests, identities and loyalties. Hence the ideological currents that are most likely to challenge nationalism are those which give political primacy to other forms of interests, identities and loyalties. In a general sense, the most challenging ideologies are those which assign minor importance to the *territorial* organization of political life. Here a number of ideological candidates come immediately to mind.

Feminism, for example, gives political primacy to interests, identities and loyalties based on sex and gender rather than on territoriality. This is not to say that feminists explicitly oppose the nation-state, or that feminist organizations are "anti-American" or "anti-Canadian," for neither is true. However, feminists do not concede primacy to the national political community. Instead, they advance gender-based interests and identities that sweep across conventional political boundaries, including those which divide nation-states. This, after all, is what is entailed in the definition of women's rights as human rights. Feminists also draw attention to sex-based differences *within* national communities, and thereby implicitly challenge the assumptions of homogeneity upon which nationalist doctrines often rest. The point is not that one must choose between being a Canadian (or American, or whatever) or a feminist, for one can obviously be both.[21] Rather, feminism is likely to blunt the intensity of nationalist sentiment and national attachments; the feminist is always aware of a community of women that reaches beyond the nation-state, just as she is aware that many of her national compatriots do not share her commitment to feminist values and principles. To a significant degree, then, feminism and nationalism compete for space on the ideological terrain of western democratic states.

Much the same conclusion can be reached with respect to environmentalism. Once again, the point is not that environmentalists are anti-American or anti-Canadian, for they are not. However, they are committed to a set of environmental values and interests which do not stop at the boundaries of the nation-state. Their interests, like those of feminists, are transnational, and while those interests may find partial expression within national political systems, they cannot find full expression. Environmentalists recognize that at times, although by no means always, environmental and national interests may clash; environmental organizations frequently find themselves contesting the "national interest" of states, as witnessed when Greenpeace and others protested France's 1995 nuclear tests in the South Pacific. When that happens, at least ardent environmentalists will be inclined to support the former over the latter, and to this degree their nationalism is tempered. Environmental theorists also recognize that global environmental interests may be difficult to protect within a world divided into nation-states; as discussed in the last chapter, the protection of the "global commons" may get lost in a world that sanctifies the political sovereignty of nation-states. Environmentalists, therefore, are inclined to look for new forms of political organization to strengthen the international protection of the environment with respect to such concerns as species extinction, depletion of the ozone layer, ocean pollution and global warming.

It is important, of course, not to overstate the degree to which environmentalism and nationalism collide. Many environmentalists are concerned primarily with environmental interests that fit easily within the jurisdiction of single nation-states; the protection of a specific natural habitat, for example, may not raise questions of national sovereignty. At times, nationalist pride may draw from environmental values perceived to be vested in one's country. In addition, many environmentalists are characterized by a set of personal behaviours—recycling, waste reduction, organic gardening, limiting their individual impact on the environment—which have minimal political content and are unlikely to conflict with the "national interest." Still, at some level, environmentalism, like feminism, does compete with nationalism for space on the ideological terrain; the "environmental nationalist" is likely to be more constrained in her commitment to nationalism than the individual with no sense of personal engagement in or identification with environmentalism.

Finally, does liberalism also constitute an ideological current that competes with nationalism on the ideological terrain? Intuitively, it is difficult to square liberalism with nationalism. The two share a commitment to popular sovereignty, but the level of that commitment is very different. The liberal's commitment is first to the individual, whereas for nationalists, individual interests are subordinate to those of the nation. The individualism that is so central to liberal thought fits uncomfortably within nationalist ideologies which suggest that the individual derives meaning from a larger whole (Kedourie 1960:39; Trudeau 1968). Liberalism is also associated with a universal conceptualization of human rights that sweeps across political boundaries. Thus, for a liberal, the assertion of national sovereignty is not seen as a legitimate defence for the violation of human rights, and in this respect the liberal's approach to nationalism is similar to that of feminists and environmentalists. The most problematic tension between liberalism and nationalism, however, comes from the former's stress on the primacy of the individual, and on that individual's rights, and the latter's stress on the primacy of collective interests. Within the context of nationalism, the sacrifice of the individual, or the individual's rights, to the larger national interest makes sense. Thus, we find the tensions that emerged in the United States during the 1950s, when the House Committee on UnAmerican Activities was prepared to sacrifice the rights of individuals for its conception of the larger national interest, and where civil liberties groups found themselves strongly opposed to the nationalist agenda of the committee. A similar tension emerged in Canada in 1970 when the federal government imposed the War Measures Act, and its constraints on civil liberties, in response to a terrorist threat from a small group of Quebec separatists, the Front de Libération du Québec (FLQ).[22]

In some important respects, therefore, liberalism cuts across the grain of nationalism, and constitutes an ideological competitor. Yet, in most circumstances, the conflict has not been serious. Liberal democratic states have been nationalist states, and the circle has been squared through the assertion that the defence of the liberal democratic state is essential if liberal democratic principles are to be protected. Thus, the American liberal can also be an American nationalist on the international stage if she is convinced that the United States not only epitomizes liberal-democratic values, but also provides the instrument through which such values are protected and promoted in less fortunate parts of the world.

THE FUTURE OF NATIONALISM

Nationalism has been such a strong political force over the past two centuries, it is easy to see it as an inevitable part of the ideological landscape of western democratic states, a fixed pole about which other ideological currents swirl. Certainly Ernest Gellner (1983:112) supports the case for inevitability:

> As the tidal wave of modernization sweeps the world, it makes sure that almost everyone, at some time or another, has cause to feel unjustly treated, and that he can identify the culprits as being of another 'nation'. If he can also identify enough of the victims as being of the same 'nation' as himself, a nationalism is born.

Yet, as Boyd Shafer (1955:56) points out, nothing is inevitable: "Nations, nationalities, nationalisms exist, not because of any inevitable, inexorable historical laws or metaphysical historical phenomena but because of the total culture of modern times and that historical series of events and ideas which happened to produce them in this culture." In short, nationalism is open to ideological challenge. As an ideological perspective, or even as a simple emotional orientation, nationalism has been subjected to strong and perhaps even growing normative criticism over the years. We have also identified a number of ideological developments, including feminism and environmentalism, which constitute a significant challenge to the territorial base upon which nationalist identities and ideologies rest. Thus, the assault on nationalism is more than normative; it draws from the broader erosion of the territorial dimensions of political life. As stressed throughout, nationalism emphasizes the territorial features of political life. It assumes that where we live is important to how we see and interpret the political world, and that we share a basic emotional and political bond with those who live within the same political (that is, territorial) boundaries. This, in turn, means that developments like environmentalism and feminism, which challenge the centrality of territory, also challenge the primacy of nationalism. Although that challenge is still not acute, there is no denying its presence as a transformative force on the ideological landscape.

Nationalism and Internet

Internet and other forms of global electronic communication have spurred the emergence of "virtual" communities which, in many ways, are the polar opposite of the territorial communities upon which nationalist ideologies are based. The virtual communities of Internet have no territorial foundation at all; the physical location of members is irrelevant, as indeed are such other individual characteristics as race, ethnicity, age and gender. On the World Wide Web, home pages rather than a geographic or national location are used to describe the virtual neighbourhood in which one lives (Robert Everett-Green 1995). In this sense, virtual communities challenge the primacy of territorial communities, including but by no means restricted to those encompassed by nation-states.

A further challenge to nationalism comes from globalization. As befits such an expansive concept, globalization can be seen from a number of perspectives, all of which have significant implications for nationalism and nation-states. First, the term "globalization" acknowledges the degree to which national barriers to the movement of trade, investment, people and ideas have been lowered in recent decades, and the likelihood that they will be lowered even more in years to come. This has meant, in turn, that the effective sovereignty of nation-states has been reduced: "The formation of common markets, political unions, regional associations and the increasing authority of supranational laws, agreements and institutions have severely limited even the internal sovereignty of the nation-state" (Kamenka 1993:78). In short, modern capitalism is a powerful corrosive force as far as nationalism is concerned, and globalization is erasing the "lines on maps" that have been so important to the territorial underpinnings of nationalism. Put somewhat differently, "The particular ways in which most aspects of our lives have been bundled or packaged in containers called nation-states have been subtly eroded" (Elkins 1994:1). The implication is that nation-states will become less important players in the global environment, and as a consequence will also become less important in the lives of their citizens.

Second, the term "globalization" is often used not only to describe that barriers are going down, but also to convey the normative message that they *should* be going down. While nationalism has tended to emphasize the particular aspects of national communities, globalization draws our attention to values shared across those communities. In many respects, therefore, "globalism" is emerging as an ideological perspective in its own right (Rieff 1993–94; Robertson 1992), one that forms the polar opposite to nationalism. Marjorie Ferguson (1992:87) refers in this context to "the resurgent economic determinism at the heart of the globalization rhetoric emanating from postmodernists, media imperialists and corporate publicists alike." Although the nationalism-globalism continuum is not yet a serious contender to the traditionally dominant ideological continuums of left and right, or liberalism and conservatism, it is coming into play more and more as we move towards the twenty-first century. Nationalism, therefore, is being challenged on both utilitarian and normative grounds.

Finally, globalization can be seen as the telescoping of social and political life so that the distinction between local and global is greatly reduced, although not eliminated. Globalization, Roland Robertson (1992:8) suggests, "refers both to the compression of the world and the intensification of consciousness of the world as a whole." Anthony Giddens (1993:18) captures the effect globalization has in "altering the relationship between the local and the global" in this way:

> Globalisation expresses the increasing role of 'action at a distance' in human social affairs. In other words, to an increasing degree, our lives are influenced by activities and happenings that occur at a great distance from us ....The opposite is also true; the actions we take as individuals today are globally consequential—a decision to purchase a certain item of clothing, for example, has implications not only for the global economy but for the world's ecosystems.

Giddens (1990:64) also defines globalization as "the intensification of worldwide social relations which link distinct localities in such a way that local happenings are shaped by events occurring miles away and vice versa." What is unclear, however, is the impact of this altered relationship on nationalism. As the global and the local begin to merge, what happens to the intervening nation-state? Does that state become less relevant as a mediator or screen between the individual and the global environment? And if it does, as is surely the case, does it also become less relevant for the manner in which we organize our economic, political and social lives?

However, the assumption that globalization will have a corrosive effect on nationalism should not be accepted without question. As noted above, there are ideological currents that reinforce the territorial dimensions of political life, and therefore nationalism. Moreover, there is considerable evidence (Hobsbawn 1990; Robertson 1992:5) that nationalism is not on the wane across the board. Michael Ignatieff's examination (1993) of the "new nationalism" in Croatia, Serbia, Germany, Ukraine, Quebec, Kurdistan and Northern Ireland should give serious pause to anyone contemplating the disappearance of nationalism. It may be, then, that *both* nationalism and globalization are increasing. There are also likely to be domestic political reactions to globalization as employment is threatened, and as globalization imposes new, postindustrial class cleavages. Globalization may thus cause nationalists to come to the defence of the nation, and to articulate more forceful nationalist ideologies. Richard Jay (1984:212–3) explains:

> Nationalism stands out against greater cultural homogeneity in the world. It is …
> partly *because* of the 'internationalization' of human life that nationalism retains its
> hold. When greater cultural homogeneity means, in practice, the proliferation of
> American soap operas, there are likely to be people demanding political action to
> preserve the beauties of medieval Welsh poetry. When political unification entails a
> mass of petty regulations emanating from Brussels, it is unlikely that the beast of
> 'national sovereignty' will lie down.

As Barbara Ward (1959:30) noted long before our contemporary infatuation with globalization, the "standardizing tendency in our modern industrial system makes one all the more eager to cling to any sense of separate personality, culture, or tradition. National differences offer the best hope for variety and difference and in this measure foster taste and creativeness in the midst of our industrial uniformities." We are brought, then, full circle to Johann Gottfried Herder's nineteenth-century concern about the negative impact of France on Germany's cultural traditions and communities. Now, as in the past, internationalization is bound to prompt a nationalist response.

This response may be intensified by a populist reaction to the loss of political control that is part of globalization (Harrison 1995:259):

> What we are witnessing, in effect, is a redefinition of political boundaries, with the
> resultant removal, in real time and space, of democratic control and responsibility
> from people affected by corporate decisions. Put another way, globalization, in the
> form that is currently being carried out, does not separate politics from economics;
> it simply renders Adam Smith's "invisible hand" more invisible than ever.

In the past, populism sought to use political power to break up concentrated economic power, and if globalization represents the enfeeblement of government and the growth of concentrated corporate power, it may well evoke a similar response. If, as former Liberal cabinet minister Eric Kierans suggests (Newman 1995), the new borderless world is one emptied of every value and principle except accumulation, then this too may trigger both a nationalist and populist response. It has already done so from the Islamic movement, which opposes "the conception of the world as a series of culturally equal, relativized, entities or ways of life" (Robertson, 1992:102).

Blood & Belonging

"The key narrative of the new world order is the disintegration of nation states into ethnic civil war; the key architects of that order are warlords; and the key language of our age is ethnic nationalism. With blithe lightness of mind, we assumed that the world was moving irrevocably beyond nationalism, beyond tribalism, beyond the provincial confines of the identities inscribed in our passports, towards a global market culture which was to be our new home. In retrospect, we were whistling in the dark. The repressed has returned, and its name is nationalism."

Michael Ignatieff, *Blood & Belonging: Journeys into the New Nationalism* (Toronto: Viking, 1993), 2.

Globalization is too easily associated with the spread of democracy. But when political power shifts to the global arena, it enters a forum where there are no democratic institutions, and no reasonable prospect of democratic institutions. Therefore, globalization, unlike nationalism, fails to provide a useful context for democratic citizenship. As discussed in greater detail in Chapter 11, while we encounter increasing reference to the "global citizen," global citizenship has little in common with more conventional forms of citizenship. The global citizen exercises no political control over a global government, nor is he responsible to such a government. There is neither representation nor taxation. The global citizen is at best a global consumer, purchasing products and ideas from markets around the world, but this is not citizenship in a political sense. The global citizen may exist within a global media environment, but that environment stops well short of a political community in any meaningful sense of the term. The global citizen is a pale reflection of the national citizen we have come to associate with the nation-state. On this issue, James Kellas (1991) talks about the human need for belonging, a need that has been addressed by nationalism and is certainly not addressed by globalization. One can be a citizen of the world in only the most abstract sense. Thus, it would be a mistake to write off nationalism too quickly.

At the same time, the important territorial communities of the future may not be the large, pluralistic and abstract communities we have come to associate with the contemporary nation-state. More than fifty years ago, Hans Kohn (1944:9) stressed the artificial nature of the national community: "Nationalism—our identification with the life and aspirations of uncounted millions whom we shall never know, with a territory which we shall never visit in its entirety—is qualitatively different from the love of family or of home surroundings." This point has been picked up more recently by Benedict Anderson (1991:6), who draws our attention to the "imagined political community" we call the nation: "It is imagined because the members of even the smallest nation will never know most of their fellow-members, meet them, or even hear of them, yet in the minds of each lives the image of their communion." The counterweight to globalization may be a more localized community, perhaps the city-state rather than the nation-state. It may be within local communities, and only within local communities, that we can be political citizens and preserve some measure of cultural distinctiveness. Therefore, nationalism may not disappear so much as achieve a different, more localized focus. Territoriality will not disappear as a means by which people assign importance in political life, and the need for group affiliation which nationalism has addressed in the past (Kedourie 1960:101) is also unlikely to disappear. There is no reason, however, that territorial identifications need to be lodged primarily in the conventional nation-state.

NOTES

1. In an early study, Hans Kohn (1944:4–5) writes that nationalism used in its growth "some of the oldest and most primitive feelings of man." There is a natural tendency in man, he maintains, "to love his birthplace or the place of his childhood sojourn, its surroundings, its climate, the contours of hills and valleys, of rivers and trees."

2. For a wide-ranging discussion of these latter themes, see David Elkins (1995).

3. Benedict Anderson (1991:5) makes a similar point: "Unlike most other isms, nationalism has never produced its own grand thinkers: no Hobbeses, Tocquevilles, Marxes, or Webers."

4. Richard Jay (1984:188) describes the French Revolution as the "launching pad" for nationalism.

5. There is no consensus on this point. Anthony Smith (1976) concurs, but Frederick Hertz traces much deeper intellectual roots for nationalist thought. See *Nationality in History and Politics* (London: Kegan Paul, Trench, Trubner & Co., 1944) Chap. VIII.

6. This definitional core is found throughout the literature on nationalism. For examples, see John Breuilly (1994:1), Ernest Gellner (1983:1) and Eric Hobsbawm (1990:9).

7. For a discussion of the Tamil case, see Eric Hobsbawm (1990:6–7).

8. A similar line of argument is advanced by Ernest Gellner (1983:48–9).

9. Johann Gottlieb Fichte expressed a similar concern about the purity of the German language. As John Breuilly (1994:60) explains, "For him language mirrored the national soul, and to purge the language of alien impurities was to defend the national soul against subversion by foreign values."

10. Ernest Gellner (1983:124) illustrates this point by noting that "pre-nationalist Germany was made up of a multiplicity of genuine communities, many of them rural. Post-nationalist united Germany was mainly industrial and a mass society."

11. It should also be noted, of course, that many francophone Canadians retain a primary national allegiance to Canada rather than to Quebec.

12. Trevor Harrison (1995:7) defines nativism as "A belief system forged out of the conjunction of nationalism with ethno-cultural, religious, and/or racial prejudice."

13. For a discussion of national socialism as a nationalist phenomenon, see Peter Alter (1989:50–54) and Anthony Smith (1979:55–62).

14. For a very useful discussion of this distinction, see Michael Ignatieff (1993:2–6).

15. A substantial part of the status Indian population of Canada, however, does not live in Indian communities, and therefore lacks a land base. Moreover, only a small fraction of the total Métis population, the fraction living on Métis settlements in Alberta, has any form of recognized land base.

16. When one country tries to take over another on the basis of some shared ethnic, cultural or racial characteristic, it is known as *irredentism*.

17. This conflict reemerged in 1995 as the American government tried to tighten hemispheric embargoes on trade with Cuba.

18. Nationalism also has a more collective orientation than does patriotism, which can be very individualistic.

19. Even in countries such as Canada, where citizens sometimes pride themselves on a relatively weak sense of nationalism, considerable public resources are committed to the inculcation and social transmission of nationalist beliefs and values. This extends to advertising spots on television which highlight the country's past and the creation of ministries such as Heritage Canada, charged with the mandate to fan the embers of nationalist sentiment.

20. Louis Snyder (1968:31–34) treats the association of nationalism with both populism and socialism as a single phenomenon.

21. Quebec feminists, for example, reject any tension between feminism and Québécois nationalism.

22. For a somewhat biased discussion, see Denis Smith, *Bleeding Hearts....Bleeding Country: Canada and the Quebec Crisis* (Edmonton: M.G. Hurtig, 1971). For a broader discussion of the theoretical dilemmas terrorism poses for liberal states, see Paul Wilkinson, *Terrorism and the Liberal State* (London: Macmillan, 1977).

CHAPTER EIGHT

Populism: Ideology or Methodology?

WITH T. H. KAMENA

Equal rights for all, special privileges for more.
JACKSONIAN CAMPAIGN SLOGAN, 1836; revived by Populists, 1896

*We have witnessed for more than a quarter of a century the struggles of the two
great political parties for power and plunder, while grievous wrongs have been
inflicted upon the suffering people. We charge that the controlling influences
dominating both these parties have permitted the existing dreadful conditions to
develop with no serious effort to prevent or restrain them....They propose...to destroy
the multitude in order to secure corruption funds from the millionaires.*
POPULIST PARTY PLATFORM, 1892

Wealth belongs to him who creates it.
POPULIST PARTY SLOGAN, 1892

*J*ohn Steward is a farmer. Janet Barnes is a suburban worker with a steady job, but an
income and lifestyle that would place her in the lower-middle class. They are different in
many ways, but both live in the areas where their own parents grew up, and both have similar
complaints about politics.

*John and Janet feel that the political system is run on their backs for the benefit of people
above and below them in society. Politicians habitually favour their rich friends, and when a
decision is made on behalf of someone else, it is for the special interests of the unemployed, the
"disadvantaged," ethnic groups or immigrants. John and Janet think the entire system works
against their interests, even though they see themselves as typical, everyday people.*

*Then a voice calls out, echoing the concerns of John and Janet, and they begin to listen.
Around the voice a movement arises. The voice says, "Enough of elites, enough of special interests, it's time the people, the* real *people, took charge of their country."*

This story, fictional though it may be, is typical of the birth of a populist movement. Such movements have emerged more than once in North America; they
rocked the American political system in the 1890s, the Canadian system in the 1920s

and 1930s and now constitute a significant ideological challenge to both. At its best, populism strives to make democracy more accountable to the electorate, to give people a larger voice in political decision-making. At its worst, it can be nativist, exclusionary and divisive.

This chapter examines the ideological call to give more "power to the people." We begin by identifying the central themes of populism, and determining to what extent populism can be seen as an ideology, and to what extent it is more appropriately seen as a political methodology associated with the techniques of direct democracy. The discussion then locates populism on the ideological landscape of North America, and explores its fit with other ideological perspectives. Next, the analysis turns to some of the direct-democracy strategies that populists have advocated to increase the leverage of "the people" on the political process. Finally, the chapter examines criticisms that have been raised about populism, and discusses the future of populism within the North American setting.

BASIC TENETS OF POPULISM

Although populism is not steeped in philosophical texts to the same extent as liberalism or socialism, it is not devoid of philosophical foundations. Some of the principles upon which populism is based are traceable to the eighteenth-century French philosopher Jean-Jacques Rousseau, and while it would be stretching the point to call Rousseau a populist, his *Discourse on the Origin of Inequality* (1755) articulates themes which are broadly reflected in contemporary populist thought. Rousseau argued for a more egalitarian society, suggesting that "man is best when he is closest to nature in societies that are simple, unrefined and egalitarian," and that people in those societies "were also wiser than the sophisticated individuals who despised them" (Canovan 1981:241). This idealization of the common people is central to populist thought. Populism was addressed more explicitly in the works of Friedrich Engels, V. I. Lenin and Karl Marx (Harrison 1995:7–8), although they portrayed it as a reactionary movement of the petty bourgeoisie, lacking any positive content. Populists were accused of trying to "roll back the wheel of history" (Harrison 1995:8), a charge frequently leveled at contemporary populists by non-Marxist critics.

From a North American perspective, there is no question that the most important roots of populist thought are lodged in the American founding. As George McKenna (1973:xii) observes, populism "is the perennial American 'ism,' with its roots extended at least as far back as the American Revolution and a development which, while directed toward different objects at different times, has never obliterated the essential qualities which stamp it as a uniquely American movement." Populists in the 1890s saw themselves "retrieving the basic ideals of the American founding, as opposed to projecting a utopia whose fulfillment could occur only in the distant future" (Schwartz 1980:16). Richard Hofstadter (1955:62), one of populism's harshest critics, reaches a similar conclusion about the Populist revolt of the 1890s: "The Populists looked backward with longing to the lost agrarian Eden, to the republican America of the early years of the nineteenth century in which there were few millionaires and, as they saw it, no beggars, when the laborer had excellent prospects and the farmer had abundance, when statesmen still responded to the mood of the people and there was no such thing as money power." Some writers (Bellah 1985:30) link the emergence of populism to the individualism that was so important to the revolutionary creed. Andrew Jackson, who called planters, farmers and labourers the nation's "bone and sinew," and bankers "the fat," is generally identified as the "founding father" of American populism (Will 1988), although George McKenna (1973:xiv) gives that credit to Thomas Jefferson.

Of course, populism today is certainly not unique to the United States. It has also assumed a prominent position on the Canadian political landscape. Indeed, populism has held that position since the early 1920s. It has a particularly long tradition in the West, where virtually all of the Canadian populist movements first took hold (Gibbins and Arrison 1995). However, the American roots of populist thought must be kept in mind, especially since they played a direct and immediate role in the evolution of Canadian populist thought.[1]

Exercise One: The Meaning of Populism

The populist label is thrown around with considerable abandon in popular discourse. It is applied not only to outsiders challenging the status quo, but also to individuals at the very centre of political and cultural life. For example, former president Ronald Reagan, who described the government as "a large barnacle which has to be scraped off the backs of the people" (Bell 1985:46), has been labelled a populist, and the *New York Times* called Bruce Springsteen the "populist musician" of our age.

Who comes to your mind when you think of the term "populist"? Can you draw up a list of ten or twelve people who you would describe as populists? How many of those are political figures?

When you describe someone as a populist, does this description suggest negative or positive connotations? What are the specific connotations that you attach to the term? In your view, is it a good or bad thing to be described as a populist?

What themes, then, are carried forward from the American revolutionary tradition into more contemporary populist thought in Canada and the United States? First, populists believe that virtue lies with the common people (Brugger and Jaensch 1985:8). This theme is perhaps best reflected in the first principle put forward in the Reform Party of Canada's 1993 election manifesto: "We believe in the common sense of the common people ... their right to be consulted on public policy matters before major decisions are made, their right to choose and recall their own representatives and to govern themselves through truly representative and responsible institutions, and their right to directly initiate legislation for which substantial public support is demonstrated."[2] Edward Shils, who, like Richard Hofstadter, was a critic of populism, argued that populists believe that the people are not only the equal of their rulers, they are, in fact, better (Allcock 1971).

A second common feature of populism is the view of "the people" as a relatively undifferentiated whole, not associated with just one class or group, even though populist movements have often emerged from particular classes. In this respect, Bill Brugger and Dean Jaensch (1985:8) point out that "the people" are rarely seen in class terms, and George McKenna (1973:xvi) discusses the class "unconsciousness" of populists. It is relatively easy, therefore, for populists to speak of a "national will" which, once identified, can then make political dissent appear illegitimate. This feature, more than anything else, provides the ideological bridge between populism and nationalism. It should also be noted that "the people" is often a very contested concept among populists, and cannot be assumed to include all of those resident within a given territory (Harrison 1995:14). Some of the racist and nativist elements associated with populism arise because "the people" are defined in such a way as to exclude foreigners, including those who are "foreign" by virtue of their ethnicity or religion rather than by virtue of their formal nationality. In this fashion, critics and opponents can be cast beyond the pale of *legitimate* national politics; socialists, for example, become agents of an international communist conspiracy.

The third common feature is populism's emphasis on the equality of individuals. The early slogan of American populist movements—"Equal rights to all and special privileges to none"—resonates with contemporary populists who tend to oppose affirmative action or multiculturalism policies that single out particular groups, including women and racial minorities, for special treatment. Those who gain special status because of wealth or who claim it because of "disadvantage" are typically denigrated by populists. Note, for example, Jeffrey Simpson's comment (1994: 121) on the Reform Party of Canada: "The middle class resentments that simmer in the Reform Party are directed against elites, to be sure, but also against welfare cheaters, uppity social activists, feminist rhetoricians and other minoritarian pleaders, who by dint of access to the media and the politicians' desire to curry favor, twist public priorities to assist themselves, leaving excessive burdens of taxation and burgeoning regulations to restrict the freedoms of the hard-pressed, overtaxed and underappreciated majority." The equality supported by contemporary populists is equality of right, and perhaps of opportunity, but not equality of result.

From this egalitarianism, it follows that populism reflects and nurtures anti-elitism. Tension between elites and the "grass roots" is common to all forms of populism. J. B. Allcock (1971), for example, concludes that populism emerges when a section of society is only partly integrated into its structures, and when people within that section see themselves as being kept outside an elite-driven system that works against them. In the 1950s, Senator Joe McCarthy attacked the Harvard intelligentsia, effete snobs and communists, all of whom were rolled into the "lace handkerchief crowd" (McKenna 1973:xviii). Political "elites" in the populist worldview often include elected representatives, leading to the populist's fundamental critique of representative democracy, and his support for a variety of direct-democracy techniques designed to bypass or override representative institutions.

The anti-elitism of populism is associated with a belief in simple solutions to complex problems. Note, for example, George McKenna's observation (1973:xiii):

> The populist believes that the 'plain people' of America, which for him includes almost everyone, are in basic agreement with one another about what is right and wrong, fair and foul, legitimate and crooked. Fancy dialectics are unnecessary to discover these kinds of truths: we need only search our hearts.

There is, as Alan Crawford (1980:4) explains, "an alarming impatience with the complex and cumbersome processes of government, an anti-institutionalism that often manifests itself in a frivolous disregard for established channels, a desire ... to 'end-run' the bureaucracy, the courts, and even the Congress and state legislatures." In this context, populism blends into anti-intellectualism, which McKenna (1973: xxii) identifies as the feature of populism that most clearly distinguishes it from liberalism, and from the intellectually driven neoconservative movement. This feature has been reciprocated by antipopulist sentiment among intellectuals, including many scholars of populism such as Daniel Bell and Richard Hofstadter. Intellectuals and populists recognize one another as the enemy, and there is little love lost.

The populist distrust of elites can take extreme forms. At times, populists believe that elites "maintain their position by conspiratorial means" (Brugger and Jaensch 1985:8). The juxtaposition of elites and "the people," the assumption that the interests of the two are fundamentally opposed, makes conspiracy theories attractive. They are brought into play to explain why the minority interests of elites prevail in a supposedly democratic political system based on majority rule.

A sixth feature of populism is the tendency to be profoundly, even passionately, opposed to political parties and partisanship. This sentiment, which still runs deep within North American populism, was neatly expressed in the 1890s by William Jennings Bryan, a U.S. populist and presidential candidate who warned against "the tyranny of political partisanship" which is "fundamental, all pervasive and permissive of all other political evils." Bryan, who remained a Democrat throughout his life, concluded that "as long as men regard the political instrumentality through which a principle is to be obtained as of more moment than the principle itself, just so long we will have corrupt politics" (Argersinger, 1974:304). The Non-Partisan League, which enjoyed considerable popularity in the American Midwest and Canadian West around the turn of the century, was an important populist vehicle.

Populism and the Fear of Bigness

Fear of bigness has been a long-standing element of populist thought, but the targets of that fear have changed in interesting ways. In the late nineteenth century, populists campaigned against big business, and in particular against the banks, trusts, railroads and "plutocrats," broadly defined. Big government, which was not really very big by today's standards, was seen as an essential counterweight to concentrated economic power; it was part of the solution, not part of the problem.

More recently, the target of populist anger and fear has shifted from big business to big labour and, particularly, to big government. Hence Ronald Reagan's comment about scraping the barnacle of government off the backs of the people. This shift has led to an alliance between populists and the business community, and to an ideological convergence with conservatism. Here Jeffrey Simpson's analysis is particularly insightful:

> The mantra of corporate plutocrats has always been, even at the turn of the century when government was small, that government was too big, intrusive and expensive. In the decades when populism wanted to use government against the corporate elite, that elite feared populism. Now the two are joined together in an ideological crusade against government, fuelled by the genuine excesses of government that produced the high taxes against which plutocrats and populists rage together.
>
> In theory, however, populism and plutocracy are enemies, because populism is profoundly democratic whereas plutocracy is elitist. Populism decries hierarchy; plutocracy demands it. Populism seeks redistribution of income and opportunity; plutocracy, especially when based on inherited wealth and corporate gigantism, defies both, while offering homilies about Horatio Alger .... Out there lurking at a time of declining real incomes is populism's democratic, anti-elitist instincts, which can and should be turned against the privilege, power, self-satisfaction and huge salaries of plutocracy.

Jeffrey Simpson, "The temporary marriage of populism and corporate plutocracy," *The Globe and Mail*, June 29, 1995: p. A16.

Finally, populism may be associated with the belief that "a new order of society might be brought about by a single act of redemption" (Brugger and Jaensch 1985). This act need not be revolutionary, and may even take place through existing political structures. Examples of populist movements which have pointed to an "act of redemption" include the proposal by the Alberta Social Credit Party in the 1930s to dramatically increase the money supply through the monthly payment of "social credit," and the People's Party support in the 1890s in the United States for the coinage of "Free Silver" as the solution to a host of economic problems. Current populist calls for more direct democracy may also be seen in such a light.

In summary, a number of themes are common to most forms of populism. Populists are those who believe that:

- virtue lies with the "common people";
- the "people" are not to be identified with any specific class or region;
- there should be equal rights for all, and special privileges for none;
- there are simple answers to complex problems;
- there is a fundamental tension between the interests of elites, including partisan politicians, and the interests of common people;
- elites, which often maintain their position by conspiratorial means, are not to be trusted; and
- a new social order might be brought about by a single act of redemption.

These tenets provide the foundation for populism. But, in the same way that the foundation of a house provides only a suggestion as to what the house might look like and how its rooms should be organized, the tenets outlined above set only general guidelines as to how populist movements build their "houses." As we will see shortly, populist houses of quite varying design have been constructed in North America, houses located across the right-left spectrum.

Given these recurrent themes in populist thought, it should be relatively easy to define populism. It is, in fact, by no means an easy task. Indeed, entire conferences have been devoted to the task; the London School of Economics sponsored the To Define Populism conference in 1967, and failed to come up with a definition! Even the search for broad characteristics has produced similar, yet distinct, strains of the phenomenon. Margaret Canovan (1981:13), for example, rejected defining populism as a singular phenomenon, and instead, has developed a typology of seven types of populism (farmers radicalism; peasant movements; intellectual agrarian socialism; populist dictatorship; populist democracy; reactionary populism; politicians' populism) divided into two groups—"agrarian" and "political." Nonetheless, a core definition can be extracted from the diversity of populisms that have manifested themselves in North America. Populism emphasizes conflict between elites and the common people, with the "just" side being the common people. More specifically: Populism is an anti-elitist, anti-class strand of political thought and action which gives legitimacy to disaffected segments of society seeking to gain greater political and economic power, which sees those disaffected groups as the "common" people, and which sees society's virtue and goodness as centered in such people.

Our definition is close to Canovan's political definition of populism, but does not reject the agrarian side.

Definitions of Populism

- "[P]opulism constitutes an attempt to create a mass political movement, mobilized around symbols and traditions congruent with the popular culture, which expresses a group's sense of threat, arising from presumably powerful 'outside' elements and directed at its perceived 'peoplehood.'" Trevor Harrison, *Of Passionate Intensity: Right-Wing Populism and the Reform Party of Canada* (Toronto: Univ. of Toronto Press, 1995), 5.

- "The point [of populism] is not to build a new ship of state but to make the old one work again by scrubbing off all the barnacles of accumulated privilege." George McKenna, *American Populism* (New York: Putnam, 1973), xxi.

- "Populism places primacy on the vaguely formulated concept of *the people* and stresses their importance in social and political life. It extols the virtues of *ordinary people*, their beliefs and institutions .... Populism invariably opposes the establishment and claims to champion the interests of *the people*, fulfill their aspirations, and represent the *popular will.*" James Midgley, "Ideological Roots of Social Development Strategies," *Social Development Issues*, 15:1 (1993), 8.

- "The underlying current permeating every realm of Populist thought is man's quest for a just social order. By this, Populists mean a social order which not only eliminates poverty but develops and controls technology for the general well-being; one which not only insures widespread suffrage and a fair count but makes participation in the political process meaningful ...." Norman Pollack, *The Populist Mind* (Indianapolis: Bobbs-Merrill, 1967), xix.

- "[Populism] refers to grass-roots political movements that call for popular control over a network of concentrated political and/or economic institutions allegedly wielding unwarranted power .... Such movements depend for their success on the mass participation of ordinary citizens rather than the finances and organizational power of small elites." Alvin Finkel, "Populism and Gender: The UFA and Social Credit Experiences," *Journal of Canadian Studies*, 27:4 (Winter 1992–93), 76–7.

The definition of populism on the preceding page does not imply any specific *policy direction*; this is appropriate because populism does not offer a single policy prescription that can be applied across the board. A useful example is provided by debates over free trade. Populism can at times be nativist, favouring isolationism and rejecting close ties, including trade ties, to foreign countries. The anti-NAFTA forces in the United States opposed the trade agreement for all of these reasons, although one might see this nativist, isolationist element as being a more important factor in the opposition from the right wing. But left-wing populism may also be nativist, seeking to keep immigrants out so that job opportunities are maintained for the current populace. At the same time, agrarian populists have typically sought freer trade in order to open up international markets for their products. Populist movements in the United States at the turn of the century took such a view, as did many populist movements in western Canada. The Reform party has generally been a supporter of free trade, even though many agrarian producers in western Canada are now increasingly wary of free trade.

Turn-of-the-Century Populism

They came and went in little more than a generation, but the Populist movement in the United States at the turn of the century and the Progressive movement that followed left a lasting impact on American politics. Much of the impetus for direct democracy in American states today was provided by the Populists and the Progressives.

In 1892, the People's Party, often called the Populist Party, was formed. As Louis Koenig writes (1971: 83): "Seemingly every grievance-bearing son of humanity ... entered the party." Farmers merged with trade unionists, supporters of "easy" money, even Prohibitionists, and the party's platform reflected this amalgamation. It called for public ownership of the railroads and communications, the implementation of a graduated income tax and a massive increase in the money supply. The Populists also sought to change the political system through institutional reform, and called for the introduction of the referendum and initiative, the direct election of U.S. senators (who at that time were selected by state legislatures) and a one-term limit on the president. The best way to effect policy change, they argued, was to change the tools of policy-making. In 1892, the Populist candidate for president won twenty-two electoral college votes and received more than one million popular votes.

By the early 1900s, the Populist Party was in decline, but its institutional-reform agenda was picked up by the Progressive movement. The Progressive movement, built around Protestant, middle-class Republicans (Schwantes 1989:277), shared with Populists a dislike of the status quo, and a belief that institutional change was an avenue for societal change. And institutional change did begin to occur. States, particularly in the West, began to adopt the referendum and initiative (see definitions later in chapter). Starting with South Dakota in 1898, nineteen states had adopted the referendum and initiative by 1918, and three others added the referendum alone (Cronin 1989:51). Many states also introduced primaries for the nomination of candidates. In 1912 and 1913, constitutional amendments were ratified to provide for the introduction of a national income tax and the direct election of senators.

Although the Populists and Progressives were quite different groups in many ways, one figure spanned both movements. William Jennings Bryan was a lifelong Democrat, first elected to the U.S. House of Representatives from Nebraska in 1890, but his causes were those of the Populists and later the Progressives. Early on, Bryan's primary issue was silver. At the time, the United States was on the gold standard and had not accepted silver for coinage since 1873. The coinage of silver would increase the money supply, a policy favoured by farmers and other hinterland producers who saw it as a way to increase the prices of their commodities. For obvious reasons, it was also supported by silver miners in the West.

In 1896 and 1900, Bryan, as leader of the silver wing of the Democratic Party, won the Democratic nomination for president. He received the 1896 nomination after winning over the convention through a famous speech which he concluded by saying, "You shall not crucify mankind on a cross of gold" (Koenig 1971:197).

Bryan's campaigns, however, were unsuccessful, and when the silver issue faded as new gold reserves increased the money supply, he gave more emphasis to other populist issues. In 1908, now as leader of the progressive wing of the Democratic Party, Bryan ran a third unsuccessful campaign for president. As secretary of state in the Wilson administration, Bryan signed the proclamation of ratification for the constitutional amendment which provided for the direct election of U.S. senators. Bryan, a pacifist, resigned in 1915 to campaign for neutrality in World War I, even calling for a referendum on the 1917 declaration of war.

Despite having the Populist Party's support, Bryan was never a "Populist" with a capital P; in fact, he may have harmed the party by taking many of its ideas to the Democrats (Koenig 1971:394), and by overemphasizing silver in 1896. There can be little doubt, however, that Bryan was a populist in attitude; his nickname was "The Great Commoner" (Koenig 1971:456). The last event of Bryan's political career, concluded just days before his death, was the 1925 Skopes "Monkey Trial" in which a Tennessee teacher was on trial for teaching evolution. Bryan defended the belief of the "common man" in creationism against the more intellectually driven theory of evolution. In Bryan's political universe, "the common man was suffering, meritorious, and heroic."

Before leaving this definitional discussion, it is useful to return briefly to Margaret Canovan's distinction between *agrarian* and *political* populism. The former is a type of "rural radicalism" that arises from conditions in which peasants or farmers have been hit hard by economic changes and seek relief (Canovan 1981:8–9). The People's Party in the United States, the Progressives of the early twentieth century in both Canada and the United States, and Social Credit and the Cooperative Commonwealth Federation (CCF) in Canada during the 1930s are good examples of agrarian populism. In his analysis of the Saskatchewan CCF, Seymour Martin Lipset (1950:17) describes the conditions that led to "agrarian radicalism." Settlers went into debt in an effort to get their farms started, then found themselves held hostage to monopolies in purchasing basic agricultural supplies, and in selling and transporting their product. Because of this, farmers sought to break free of "big-business domination" by advocating public ownership of various sectors of the economy, including banking, transportation and utilities. In neighbouring Alberta, agrarian populism took a different form, although the primary target of discontent was still the financial sector. The populist unrest mobilized by Alberta's Social Credit movement targeted the banks, financiers (the "50 bigshots") and national monetary policy as primary concerns, and sought a fundamental restructuring of Canada's financial system along with an expansion of the money supply through the issuance of "social credit." In this last respect, Social Credit bore a striking resemblance to earlier populist demands in the United States for the introduction of a silver standard.

The most dramatic Canadian success story for agrarian populism came in the 1921 general election when the newly formed Progressive Party of Canada captured sixty-four seats in the House of Commons, second only to the 116 seats won by the Liberals. At the time of the 1917 election, the established parties had been divided by a bitter national debate over military conscription, and Progressive candidates were able to pick up the votes of many disaffected Liberals and Conservatives. The Progressives were also able to ride a wave of agrarian discontent in the prairie provinces and rural Ontario, a wave accentuated by more general social discontent in the postwar period.

The Progressives' populist credentials were evident. Progressive members of Parliament were unwilling to organize as a party in the House of Commons, and therefore declined the opportunity to form the official opposition, a strategic resource that was then picked up by the smaller Conservative caucus. The Progressives resisted formal leadership, rejected party discipline and committed themselves to supporting the government of the day when it was right, and opposing it when it was wrong. Unfortunately, the Progressives' abandonment of the conventional attributes and behaviours of political parties left them ill-equipped for the intensely partisan environment of the House. Their loosely-knit caucus soon fell prey to the personal and policy inducements of the Liberal government and its leader, Mackenzie King. In the 1925 general election, the number of Progressive MPs fell to twenty-four; all but two were elected on the prairies. Twenty Progressive MPs were elected in 1926, and only twelve in 1930, at which point the Progressive remnants were absorbed by new protest parties emerging in western Canada.

Canovan (1981:8–9) describes her second form of populism, political populism, in the following terms:

> [T]he emphasis here is much less upon any particular socioeconomic base or setting, and much more upon political characteristics. When the term is applied to devices of direct democracy like the referendum, to mobilization of mass passions,

to idealizations of the man in the street, or to politicians' attempts to hold together shaky coalitions in the name of 'the people,' what those who talk of 'populism' have in mind is a particular kind of political phenomenon where the tensions between the elite and the grass roots loom large.

This brand of populism is currently exemplified in Canada by the Reform party and, perhaps to a lesser extent, in the United States by Ross Perot's United We Stand America. In New South Wales, the Australian Labor Party, led by Jack Lang during the 1930s, provides a less contemporary example.

Most agrarian populist movements in North America thrived from the 1890s to the 1930s. When many people worked the land, it made sense to see the farmer as the representative of the "common people." With urbanization and then suburbanization, however, the "common people" changed to people living in the suburbs holding nine-to-five jobs. Farmers have become the exception, rather than the rule, and even though the independent farmer might still have some common cause with populism, such a farmer is increasingly rare in an agricultural environment characterized more by massive "agribusinesses" than by the independent yeomen of yore. In short, the demographic base for agrarian populism has been sharply and irrevocably eroded by the passage of time. Yet, if social change has undercut the base of agrarian populism, it has done nothing to decrease the potential base of political populism. Indeed, it could be argued that the latter's appeal has been enhanced by rapid technological change which has made direct democracy more practical. Moreover, contemporary populist movements still draw disproportionate support from rural areas and small towns, where the population remains more homogeneous than in the cities, and where the traditional themes of the virtue of the common people and suspicion of elites retain significant support. A good example comes from Australia. During the lengthy premiership (1968–87) of Sir Joh Bjelke-Peterson in Queensland, the Liberal/National coalition maintained power through its populist appeal to rural and semirural areas, and by gerrymandering the electoral boundaries to strengthen its support in those areas. Similarly, Reform's recent success in Canada is partly attributable to its strong support among rural and small-town voters, although the party has enjoyed substantial suburban and urban appeal.

IS POPULISM AN IDEOLOGY?

Is it appropriate to conceptualize populism as an *ideology*? Some might argue that populism is more an emotional predisposition than a coherent pattern of political thought. Certainly populism does not prescribe a singular set of outcomes it wishes society to achieve. It is not clear, for example, what a *populist policy* would be with respect to unemployment, environmental protection, Medicare, deficit reduction or military defence. As J. F. Conway (1984:140) suggests, at best it may be a *general* ideology "embodying the highest principles of political and economic morality which all classes ought to embrace." Various populist movements have had little communication with one another—there is no Populist International in the way that there has been a Socialist International—and only a handful of populist groups have actually identified themselves by the term "populist" (Worsley 1969:218); the idea of a formally articulated populist theory may seem elitist to a populist, who would rather see politics brought down to a more "practical" level. Nor, for that matter, have populist leaders been noted for their written articulation of populist thought. Indeed, devotion to the written word could be the kiss of death for many populist leaders.[3] Consequently, some of the best sources of populist thought are compendiums of speeches (McKenna 1973; Pollack 1967) rather than detailed, theoretical expositions. Despite this, populism is not devoid of philosophical foundations and identifiable tenets, and displays reasonable coherence across its various manifestations.

Populism meets the ideological criteria presented in Chapter 1, although not without some qualifications:

- *"A socially constructed and transmitted system of political beliefs"* Populism fits this condition well. It arises within society, specifically within elements of society which see themselves as being left out of political decision-making by elites. Populism captures a sense of alienation, but more than individual alienation; populists believe that the majority of people, people *like themselves*, are denied an effective voice in the political system.

- *"Some significant measure of formal articulation, scope, internal consistency and durability"* The populist critique consistently argues against elite behaviour that is seen as harmful to the interests of the common people. The scope of this argument is broad enough to embrace political institutions, the structure of the economy and social policies. Populism has been articulated by political parties and movements in North America for more than a century. The internal consistency of populism is most apparent in its assessment of underlying political problems and the appropriate forms of institutional reform; it is less apparent with respect to the specifics of public policy. It is more coherent as a critique than as a solution. As Alvin Finkel (1992–93:77) notes: "The ideology of populists is fairly unsophisticated and fluid relative to that of Marxist socialists or of conservatives."

- *"Provides both a normative framework for understanding the political world and a practical guide for political action"* A populist sees the political world as a struggle between elites and special interests on one side, and the common people on the other. Populism seeks to give the common people a more direct role in governance in the belief that this would be more democratic, and not coincidentally, more congruent with their interests.

It is debatable, however, to what extent populism provides *"a practical guide to political action."* As noted above, populism is seldom associated with a specific public-policy position or positions. To label someone a populist provides little prescriptive insight into that person's stance on the major policy debates of the day; the focus of populism is more on the political *process* than on *outcomes*. For this reason, Canada's preeminent contemporary populist, Reform leader Preston Manning, refuses to describe his populism as an ideology. As Tom Flanagan explains (1995:2–3), for Manning, populism is "not an ideology but a methodology, not a doctrine or a set of positions but a process for discovering the will of the people and thereby overcoming superficial divisions among the people." However, despite its lack of policy specificity, populism still represents a comprehensive ideological outlook on the political world. It may be a less fully developed ideology than others, but it is an ideology nonetheless.

The Ideology of Populism

- *scope*: Focuses on societal relationships between elites and the masses. Contains political, economic and sociological elements.

- *internal consistency*: Weak, at least in comparison to other ideologies. More coherent as a critique than a solution. There is always a call for power to the common people, but what that entails and what it should produce with respect to public policy varies from movement to movement.

- *durability*: Emerged under a wide variety of conditions over the last 150 years.

- *normative framework*: A belief in the "common sense of the common people." Virtue in society lies with the common people, who are being held back by the conspiratorial and self-interested actions of elites.

- *practical guide for political action*: Calls for a restructuring of the political system, and sometimes the economic system, to take power away from elites and give it back to the common people. This often includes expansion of direct-democracy devices.

- *formal articulation*: William Jennings Bryan; Preston Manning; the People's Party in the 1890s; agrarian radicalism in the 1920s and 1930s.

POPULISM IN CONTEMPORARY IDEOLOGICAL SPACE

Populism is not associated with a particular set of public-policy predispositions; it rarely stands on its own, but instead draws policy guidance from other ideological currents (Laycock 1990:15–19). This alone complicates the location of populism on the left-right spectrum, but the matter is further complicated by the fact that scholarly interpretations of populism have themselves been highly ideological. Scholars have seldom approached their subject with anything close to impartiality, and therefore the description of populism as left-wing or right-wing has had as much to do with the ideological predispositions of the scholar as with the nature of the phenomenon.

Early scholars (Hicks 1931; Lipset 1950; Morton 1950) stressed the progressive elements of populism, and thus located populism on the left of the political spectrum. Then, two major works by Daniel Bell and Richard Hofstadter in 1955 identified right-wing populism with authoritarian and anti-Semitic currents in American political life. It was associated with anti-intellectualism and the search for conformity, and was linked to the virulent anticommunism and scaremongering of Senator Joe McCarthy; the descendants of populism in the Midwest and South were portrayed as the "shock troops" of McCarthyism (Schwartz 1980:14). In the late 1960s and early 1970s, populism was rediscovered by scholars writing from a more left-wing perspective. Thus, Norman Pollack, for example, tried to expunge anti-Semitism from interpretations of American populism, and challenged Hofstadter's characterization of populism as retrogressive (1967:xvi):

> [Populism] did not seek to restore a lost world of yeoman farmers and village artisans; still less did it wallow in the self-pity of an agrarian mystique …. to say they borrowed from the past is not the same as saying they were imprisoned by the past.

Others linked populism favourably with the student radicalism and antiwar movements of the times. Populist beliefs were seen to express long-standing American preferences for decentralized government and community control, and in this respect populism blended into the empowerment themes that appealed to women, gays and lesbians, environmentalists and community activists of all stripes (Dubiel 1986). Note, for instance, S. M. Miller's discussion (1985:3) of *neo-populism*:

> One of the advantages of neo-populism is that it is a locally oriented, democratic *alternative* to centralized socialism. It departs from socialist notions of increased statism and nationalization of industry that leaves power in the hands of bureaucrats and politicians. In moving toward this alternative to nineteenth-century visions of socialism, neo-populism *Americanizes* radicalism by connecting radical efforts to the American past, to American values.

In the 1980s and early 1990s, scholarly interpretations swung back to the right as Ross Perot, Ronald Reagan, George Wallace and the New Right in the United States (Crawford 1980), and the Reform party in Canada (Dobbin 1991; Harrison 1995) were portrayed as manifestations of right-wing and often reactionary populism.

Clearly, then, populism cannot be neatly captured by the left-right spectrum. As Alvin Finkel (1992–93:77) concludes, "Populist movements can be seen as existing on a continuum between left and right; the place of individual movements on this continuum shifts over time." But if a left-right location is difficult to determine, what about populism's fit with more specific ideological perspectives? Unfortunately, there is not a great deal more clarity when the focus is sharpened. Take the example of feminism. There is little question that early populist movements in Canada and the United States were part of the vanguard promoting greater equality and opportunity for women (Youngdale 1975:118). They were an important component of the broader suffragist and temperance movements, and women played an important leadership role within populist organizations (Finkel 1992–93:78). However, contemporary populism is generally seen as an ideological current that runs counter to feminism. The populist stress on equality for all and special treatment for none stands in opposition to employment equity programs and political perspectives which give value to group identifications that fragment "the people." Variants of feminism which emphasize the value of difference and diversity get a rough ride in populist forums driving home the basic political equality of all citizens regardless of gender, colour or race.

The relationship between populism and liberalism is similarly complex. The populist focus on equality of rights fits within classical conceptions of liberalism, and there is no question that early populists were seen as "liberals" challenging the established social and economic order. However, contemporary populism challenges many of the programs and values associated with the modern liberal-democratic state. Populists today reject the "big government" that became so integral to the postwar reform liberal agenda, and populism is linked, at least in the popular mind, to ideological currents of conservatism and the New Right. Note, for example, Daniel Bell's discussion (1985:57) of Ronald Reagan's political populism:

> The populist conservative seeks to instill public tutelage in private moral conduct and to remove all public restraint on private economic conduct. Mr. Reagan wants a strong government (undergirded by a strong military) in foreign affairs, and a weak government (with little social responsibility for the general welfare) in domestic affairs.

Perhaps nationalism provides the only unambiguous fit with a complementary ideological perspective. As George McKenna (1973:xvii) explains, the avowed aim of populism

> is to speak not for any class or group but for the entire nation. From its inception populism has been integrally related to patriotism, and this is another factor that distinguishes it from some, although not all, kinds of social democracy. It would not unite "workers of the world" but "workers—and farmers, and small businessmen, firemen and policemen, barbers and beauticians, secretaries and schoolteachers and just about everyone else except the idle rich—of America.

Given populism's emphasis on "the people," and the general identification of the people with a specific territorial community, it is not surprising that populism often blends into nationalism and even jingoism (Hofstadter 1955:85). The community-centred focus of much populist thought also provides an ideological bridge to socialism, a bridge crossed by such groups as the CCF in the past, but shunned by North American populists today.

The political content of populist movements in western Canada has often been infused with regional alienation. As Preston Manning (1992:119) writes, "Whenever populism has become a force to be reckoned with in western Canadian politics, it has been energized by 'western alienation'—a conviction shared by generations of western Canadians that their region and interests have not achieved equality with the constitutional and economic interests of Quebec and Ontario, and that systemic change is necessary to achieve such equality." The linkage between populism and western alienation has become so strong that populist values are often given short shrift outside the region by those who are not convinced of the merits of western Canadian grievances.

As mentioned earlier, populists believe elites often maintain their position by conspiratorial means. However, there is not necessarily agreement amongst populists on who comprises the elites, and the perception of the conspirators' identities influences the ideological path a populist movement takes. Those who see the conspirators as wealthy economic elites, and who sympathize with those at the low end of the socioeconomic spectrum, will support populism with a left-wing-policy agenda. Those who are suspicious of individuals below them on the socioeconomic ladder tend to support forms of populism with a right-wing agenda. Populism's resultant ideological diversity is illustrated by figure 8.1, which combines the left-right spectrum with Margaret Canovan's distinction between agrarian and political populism. The horizontal axis indicates the location of specific populist movements on the conventional left-right spectrum, while the vertical axis indicates whether the movement is agrarian or political.

The confusion that often arises in trying to locate populism on the conventional ideological landscape was well illustrated by George McKenna's work in the early 1970s (1973:xxiv):

> Unlike socialists, [populists] tend to blur class distinctions, lumping all, or nearly all, together into the category of "plain people." Unlike other economic nationalists, they are chary of state ownership or supervision. Unlike liberals—with whom they agree in their reluctance to accept nationalization—they prefer plain people to experts, familiar beliefs to unconventional opinions, the heart (or "soul") to head, the inspirational to the syllogistic.

Agrarian Populism in Western Canada

It can be argued that despite getting a later start than the populist movements in the United States, populists in Canada have had more success—at least at the polls. While American populists and the Progressives that followed them eventually won battles for institutional reform and policy change, the Canadian groups had more success in winning power. Two of the most successful were the CCF/NDP in Saskatchewan, and Social Credit in Alberta.

CCF/NDP

In 1933, the Cooperative Commonwealth Federation (CCF) held its first national convention in the depths of the depression, and produced the Regina Manifesto, one of the finest examples of well-articulated left-wing populism. Although some of its agenda was class-based, the CCF also called for the "common people" to overcome the elites. As the Regina Manifesto stated: "Power has become more and more concentrated into the hands of a small irresponsible minority of financiers and industrialists, and to their predatory interests the majority are habitually sacrificed."

With time, some of the CCF's more radical proposals were toned down, but the new party long remained a repository of left-wing protest in the West. In 1944 the CCF won power in Saskatchewan, becoming the first "socialist" party in North America to control a state or provincial government. The CCF had reasonable success on the federal scene, electing 112 MPs in the seven elections held between 1935 and 1958 inclusive. However, sixty-three percent of those MPs came from the prairies, and forty-six percent came from Saskatchewan alone. In 1961, the CCF dissolved and, with the Canadian Labour Congress, created the New Democratic Party. Despite its links to organized labour and middle-class urban intellectuals, the NDP retained a flavour of populism. As late as 1984, the NDP federal election campaign (Gibbins 1985:47) made much of appealing to the "average Canadian," and tried to place an elitist label on the Liberal and Progressive Conservative leaders by calling them the "Bobbsie Twins of Bay Street." At least some of the NDP's support came from populist protest against the two established parties, a base of support that may have been lost when a new protest party, the Reform party, emerged with such force in the 1993 election.

SOCIAL CREDIT

While the CCF made headway in Saskatchewan, another western protest party, Social Credit, was swept to power in Alberta in 1935 and remained in office until 1971. Social Credit governments also dominated British Columbia politics from the early 1950s to the late 1980s. Like the CCF, the Alberta Social Credit arose in the depths of the depression, but there were some differences. First, Social Credit replaced an existing populist movement, the United Farmers of Alberta, which had governed the province since 1921. Second, Social Credit did not seek the redistribution of wealth or public ownership, as the CCF did, but rather a change in monetary policy that would create more wealth through the distribution of "social credit." In the 1935 election campaign, at a time when the average rent was $9 a month, Social Credit promised to give each household $25 a month.

Much of Social Credit's monetary policy was introduced as provincial legislation between 1937 and 1939, but was struck down by the courts as falling outside the jurisdiction of the Alberta legislature. By the 1940s, Social Credit had abandoned its "funny money" policies and became a more traditional conservative party. The Social Credit parties that governed Alberta and British Columbia in the post–World War II era were not all that close to the party that swept Alberta in 1935. Particularly in British Columbia, the party's main platform became guarding free enterprise from the "socialist hoards" of the CCF/NDP. Social Credit elected eighty-four MPs in the seven elections held between 1935 and 1958, with eighty-six percent of those coming from Alberta. John Diefenbaker's Conservative sweep in 1958 spelled the end of the federal party in western Canada, although a Quebec offshoot, the Ralliement Créditistes, enjoyed considerable success through 1979. Provincially, Social Credit was moribund in Alberta by the early 1980s, and on its deathbed in British Columbia by the early 1990s. But at least a piece of its legacy lives on. The leader of the Reform party, Preston Manning, is the son of Ernest Manning, the Social Credit premier of Alberta from 1943 to 1970.

FIGURE 8.1: Spatial Representation of Populism

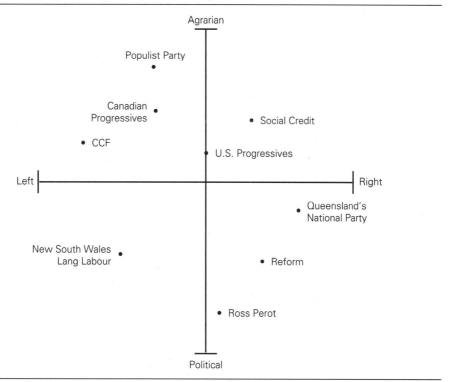

However, this confusion does not negate the conclusion that populism has been and remains an important ideological current in North America, one that has helped shape the more concrete evolution of political practice across the continent.

POPULIST POLITICS

Populism constitutes the rejection of both political parties and elites. How, then, do populists achieve some purchase on political systems which are driven by parties and elites? As S. M. Miller (1985:4) explains, populist empowerment

> does not unfold a magical process by which everyone feels better. There has to be a political process that makes empowerment a positive and democratic experience in the community. Such a positive experience requires a [political structure.]

Miller argues that populism must be more than a political outlook; if it is to be effective, it must be wedded to national administrative and institutional structures. However, this need is easier to recognize than to address. It is difficult to contain populism within the narrowly structured format of interest-group politics, for how can an ideology that speaks for the "people," broadly defined, be expressed through interest-group politics? Populists, therefore, are thrust back on three options: the formation of "non-party" populist parties; charismatic leadership; or the tools of direct democracy. While the last option offers the best intuitive fit with the ideological tenets of populism, the first two have been surprisingly important in the mobilization and expression of populist discontent.

Populist Parties

Hostility towards the partisan organization of political life has been a recurrent theme in populist thought. In an 1898 speech, American populist Percy Daniels (Argersinger 1974:308) condemned parties in language that would still find a receptive audience today:

> Parties as they exist today are bellowing imposters and organized frauds, sowing little but deception and garnering little but spoils and corruption .... They are either reliable machines of plutocracy and the corporations, or they are the handy tools of hypocrites and harlequins ....

Yet, such sentiment notwithstanding, populism in North America has spawned a large number of parties, some of which have enjoyed considerable success. While parties may be shunned in *theory*, this has not been the case in *practice*.

At the same time, the transition from populist movement to party politics has been a treacherous passage that many, and perhaps most, populist movements have failed to navigate, or have failed to do so while keeping their populist principles intact. Note, for example, Peter Argersinger's comment (1974) on the People's Party:

> What was significant about original Populism, after all, was that it developed outside the political system—and precisely because the system had proved incapable of responding to real needs. Yet in the transformation of Populism from a mass movement into the People's party, much of its democratic and directly responsive nature was lost. Populism became incorporated within the same system and the People's party became subject to the same influences that guided the other parties.

Thus, early-American populism, which began as a rejection of party politics, was eventually drawn into and destroyed by party politics. Whether the same fate awaits more contemporary movements, including the Reform Party of Canada, remains an open question. There is no question, however, that constructing a bridge between populist principles and the rejection of partisanship, on the one hand, and the effective exercise of political power, on the other, is a difficult task. Populists may be antiparty, but to seize power, a party vehicle is needed. As the Canadian Progressives demonstrated, the avoidance of party politics is not the solution. The trick is to keep populist parties from becoming like other parties. To be fair, though, it should also be recognized that *all* parties face problems in reconciling their "true believers" with the tactical compromises necessary for electoral success.

Charismatic Leadership

In some respects, the concept of "populist leadership" may seem like an oxymoron. Yet, despite the identification of the common people as the most virtuous segment of society, populist movements tend to be led not by the grass-roots collectively, but by a single charismatic leader at the front of the movement. Jean-Jacques Rousseau even advocated this, calling for a "lawgiver" who would preside over society (Canovan, 1981: 243). One Canadian commentator, writing about the Reform party, suggested that the apparent contradiction of grass-roots identification and strong leadership is perfectly understandable because the goal of popular participation means few strong competing power centers rise up to challenge the leadership of the party (Simpson 1994). Without this competition, those who are upset with the party's direction must appeal to the grass roots. The grass roots, however, are likely to maintain loyalty to the leader, who often is the "voice" around which a movement arises.

The prominence of strong, charismatic leadership in populist movements may be linked to the belief in a common or national will. If populists believe in such a will, then the individual who can give it voice is in a powerful position indeed; this person can speak "for the people" in a way that pluralistic leaders cannot (Riker 1982:238). Thus, for example, populism may strengthen the role of the presidency in American politics: "Caesarism" may be the fulfillment of democracy "if democracy is understood in terms of a monolithic doctrine of the general will" (James Burnham, cited in Crawford 1980:8). The president, Alan Crawford (1980:8) argues, "is viewed by New Rightists as a position from which opinions are broadcast, deriving its force less from party or executive responsibility than from the broad moral authority the office commands as the only truly national and plebiscitary spokesperson." Given, however, that populism also constitutes a rejection of established political elites, the populist leader in the plebiscitary mould is likely to be cast as an outsider running against, rather than within, the system. It is not uncommon, therefore, for American presidential contenders to describe themselves as outsiders, running against Washington, a strategy used successfully by Jimmy Carter, Ronald Reagan and Bill Clinton. Canadian columnist Robert Fulford (1994) once stated, "Populist suspicion of Washington has always been a powerful influence on American thought." In Canada, many of the most successful populist leaders have run from a base of moral authority lodged in the church.

The list of charismatic populist leaders is extensive, and would certainly include William Aberhart and Preston Manning in Canada, William Jennings Bryan and Ross Perot in the United States, and Jack Lang and Joh Bjelke-Peterson in Australia. W.A.C. "Wacky" Bennett, Social Credit premier of British Columbia for most of the 1950s and 1960s, is another example of a charismatic populist leader; Bennett used to run on the slogan "Progress, Not Politics." Others, like Huey Long in the United States and Juan Perón in Argentina, have ventured outside democratic norms to extend their power. Bill Brugger and Dean Jaensch (1985) described even Bjelke-Peterson's Queensland administration as autocratic populism. This label may seem contradictory, but it is not. Bjelke-Peterson ran a very personalized, premier-centered government, all the while doing so in the name of the common bloke. A populist leadership style is not at odds with many notions of democratic government, for it is difficult to condemn a leader for being in touch with, empathetic towards and responsive to the "average voter." Most democratic politicians would be happy to wear the populist brand.

One of the more intriguing recent examples of a populist leadership style was the 1992 presidential candidacy of billionaire Texas businessman Ross Perot, who ran outside the party system entirely and used his personal wealth to communicate directly with voters, often through infomercials replete with extensive charts. The Perot campaign began, appropriately enough, with a February appearance on CNN's "Larry King Show." Perot's support grew quickly following this appearance, even going past twenty percent in some polls. By July, Perot had enough petition signatures to be on the ballot in twenty-four states, but was sliding in the polls and receiving increasing media scrutiny. On July 16, 1992, during the Democratic Party convention, Perot pulled out of the race, although the signature drive continued. In early October, and now on the ballot in all fifty states, Perot returned to active campaigning. He concentrated on a short list of specific issues—cutting the deficit through sharply reduced spending and increased taxes on gas, tobacco and social security and opposition to free trade—and a more general promise that roughly said, "Put me in charge and I'll get it done." There was also talk of populist-style institutional change, of going around Congress and directly to the country via "electronic town halls." His supporters were largely homogeneous, coming from white, suburban, middle-class backgrounds, more likely to be male than female and slightly older than the electorate as a whole (*Economist*, May 16, 1992:32). Part of Perot's appeal to this "Middle America" constituency was that, unlike leaders from the established parties, Perot owed nothing to special interests; even his campaign was self-financed. In the election, he garnered nineteen percent of the popular vote, and finished second in one state (Utah).

Perot's campaign was, without doubt, populist in tone and character, even though his personal wealth made him a very unlikely representative of the average American. In a postindustrial society such as the United States, the common people reside in suburbia, and it was to this group that Perot appealed most strongly. In his campaign, Perot asked the people to encourage him to run; he spoke directly to the people, avoiding the "elites" of the mainstream media. Perot's authoritarian streak, the "just give me the power to do the job" attitude that seemed to ignore constitutional restraints, can also be seen as populist, although in a narrower way. We have seen populism's propensity for building movements that fall in line behind charismatic leaders, although one must wonder how Perot, balding, with big ears and a squeaky voice, can be seen as projecting charisma. References to "Juan Perot" and slogans like "Ross for Boss" may have had a light-hearted air to them, but they also carried an element of accuracy. The boundary between charismatic and authoritarian leadership is easily transgressed. To conclude, although populism plays to democratic themes and principles, it cannot be assumed that populist leaders themselves epitomize the democratic ideal. As we will see in the next chapter, populism and fascism often share significant similarities.

Direct Democracy

The polar opposite of charismatic leadership or plebiscitary democracy, at least in strategic terms, is *direct democracy*—that is, to cut out leadership altogether and place legislative authority directly in the hands of the people. Populists have created a number of such alternatives, premised on individual equality and providing a means to circumvent both political parties and representative institutions. The populist appeal to direct democracy has found a substantial audience in recent years.

Most populist movements seek to reform democratic institutions through the application of one or more direct-democracy devices. An *initiative* is legislation proposed by citizens through petition. If enough petition signatures are obtained, the measure is put to a popular vote and, if backed by a majority, it becomes law without the need for legislative ratification or consent. *Referendum* refers to items sent to the people by the government for popular approval; referendums are not necessarily binding on the legislature and government of the day. (A hybrid of the initiative and referendum is the *direct referendum*, in which petition signatures are obtained to place recently passed legislation before the voters for their acceptance or rejection.) *Recall* is the procedure for removing public officials through a vote generated by petition (Cronin 1989:2). More recently, the range of devices through which to operate more direct democracy has been expanded. The "electronic town hall" concept floated by Ross Perot and American political scientist Benjamin Barber (1984:273–78) is one such expansion. In the United States, where the incumbency rate of congressmen and other legislators has been high, the *term limits* movement has also gained momentum. Term limits, it is thought (Will 1993), would bring legislatures closer to the citizens by eliminating the "career politician" who never had a "real job" and is thus out of touch with the electorate; elected offices would be returned to "citizen legislators." In addition, calls for campaign-financing reform, particularly through the restriction of Political Action Committees, have received attention in the United States. In Canada, populists have also sought changes in parliamentary rules to weaken party discipline and allow more freedom for the individual member of Parliament.

Most democratic states have quite limited experience with direct democracy, particularly at the national level. Membership in or other issues involving the European Union have been the most common topics of referendums in Europe,[4] although constitutional issues have also been raised, most notably in France and Spain. Switzerland has used direct democracy the most extensively, and in this respect is an exception to the European rule. The Swiss vote on national referendums and initiatives every three months, and also have many referendums and initiatives at the cantonal level. It can be argued, however, that direct democracy emerged in Switzerland out of the nature and history of the Swiss Confederation, rather than from a populist urge, although this has not prevented populists from praising the Swiss model. Italy has held eighteen national referendums since 1973 (Kobach 1993:229). In New Zealand, an important referendum in 1993 changed the electoral system from a single-member, first-past-the-post system to a mixed system of single-member districts and proportional representation, like the electoral system in Germany. New Zealand has also adopted the Citizens' Initiated Referendum Act.

Although national referendums have been used only occasionally in Canada, they have had a dramatic impact. The 1992 constitutional referendum on the Charlottetown Accord is the most recent example. Despite strong elite support and an intergovernmental agreement backed by the federal government, all twelve provincial and territorial governments and four national aboriginal organizations, the referendum went down to defeat by a 55–45 margin across the country, with majorities of voters in only four provinces supporting it.[5] Three provincial referendums have also been central to Canadian political history—the two-stage referendum which brought Newfoundland into Confederation in 1949, the unsuccessful sovereignty-association referendum in Quebec in 1980 and the 1995 Quebec sovereignty referendum, where a narrow defeat (50.6% voted NO) rocketed the political system from coast to coast. Direct democracy has been more widely used provincially than nationally. Every province has held at least one referendum on Prohibition, British Columbia now has recall legislation in place and in 1991 Saskatchewan held a referendum on whether abortions should be financed by the provincial medical insurance plan. Manitoba and Alberta have enacted legislation requiring a referendum before taxes can be increased or new taxes instituted, and British Columbia now permits legislative initiatives. It was the commitment of Alberta and British Columbia, and initially Quebec, to hold a provincial referendum on any constitutional amendments that forced the 1992 national referendum on the Charlottetown Accord. Direct-democracy devices have thus become a significant force in Canadian politics even though there is no consensus on what a reasonable national-decision rule might be, and no consensus on how referendums might best be accommodated within the conventions of responsible parliamentary government and federal institutions.

Australia and the United States have provided fertile ground for direct democracy.[6] In Australia, all proposed constitutional amendments are brought before the people in conjunction with federal elections. For approval, these referendums must be passed not only by fifty percent of the voting electorate, but also by a majority in at least four of the six states. From 1906 to 1988, forty constitutional questions were put before the Australian electorate, with only eight being approved. Four others received a majority of the national vote, but did not pass in enough states to gain approval. Although there are no *national* direct-democracy devices in the United States, they are common at the state level. A referendum is required to approve state constitutional amendments in forty-nine of the fifty states—the exception being Delaware. Some twenty-six states, mostly in the West, use the initiative. Many of these states adopted the initiative during the populist surge of influence around the turn of the century (Cronin 1989:51).

Exercise Two: When Should Direct Democracy Be Used?

Referendums and initiatives are means of letting the people have a direct say on public-policy issues of the day. However, not all issues are equally suited to direct democracy, and some might best be decided by elected representatives. Of the following issues, which do you think should best be submitted to the people, and which should best be left in the hands of elected representatives?

- taxation policy
- abortion policy
- expansion of the North American Free Trade Agreement (NAFTA)
- foreign aid
- military intervention in crisis spots such as Bosnia or the Persian Gulf
- gun control
- euthanasia
- law and order issues
- environmental policy
- immigration policy
- legalization of marijuana
- constitutional amendments
- death penalty

The most extensive use of the initiative has been in California, where residents voted on 264 initiatives in the 1980s (Boyer 1991:144). Perhaps the most famous California initiative occurred in 1978, when Proposition 13 slashed property taxes in half and triggered tax-cutting initiatives across the country (Cronin 1989:3). In 1993, voters in the state of Washington rejected an initiative that would have rolled back taxes, but passed another that put a cap on increases in state revenues. Some issues addressed by initiatives are more esoteric. In 1975, for example, a Nevada county initiative legalized brothels (Barber 1981:283–4). Other initiatives have focused on institutional reform: fourteen states passed term-limit initiatives in 1992, another six states did so in 1994 and only in Utah did a term-limit proposal fail.

Initiatives are generated by petition drives. In the American model, the petition, which contains the exact wording of the proposed law, must receive a designated percentage of the total vote in the last election of a state governor if the measure is to be placed on the statewide ballot. That percentage is typically eight percent, although in some states it is five or ten.[7] In Switzerland, a fixed number of signatures (100,000 at the federal level) is needed to bring the measure to ballot in a vote held separately from legislative elections (Canovan 1981:200). Canada has had limited experience with the initiative, although the process has recently gained a toehold in Saskatchewan and British Columbia.[8] The Reform party advocates a national initiative system for Canada, and calls for a low petition requirement of three percent of the electorate or about 800,000 signatures (Manning 1992:325). The party claims that "(w)ith the initiative in place, citizens can get around obstructive politicians and strategically located special interests to ensure that matters relating to the general interest are placed before the people." Reform would also seek a constitutional amendment to make such initiatives binding on Parliament.

The recall of elected representatives prior to the next general election is the most radical of the three basic direct-democracy devices. Whereas the initiative and referendum are a means to bypass elected representatives, the recall is a direct assault on the independence of those representatives. A total of fifteen American states and numerous local jurisdictions have recall provisions. The lowest state threshold for a petition to achieve a recall election is in Montana, where statewide officials can be recalled by ten percent of the voters registered in the most recent election (Cronin 1989:126). Most states have a much higher requirement, typically twenty-five percent, and in some cases, as high as forty percent. If the required signatures are obtained, an election ensues, either as a straight yes or no on the official being recalled, or as a full-fledged election with a list of candidates (Cronin 1989:150).[9] In either case, recalls are rarely successful beyond the local level. Only one state governor has been successfully recalled, in North Dakota in 1921, although a recall drive against Arizona governor Evan Mecham in 1987 would probably have been successful if Mecham had not been impeached and convicted first (Cronin 1989:124–5). Canada's lone experience with recall was short-lived and rather bizarre. In 1936, the newly elected Social Credit government of Alberta passed enabling legislation for recalls. The following year, an attempt was made to recall Premier William Aberhart. The government promptly repealed the legislation *retroactively* (Boyer 1992a:35). The recently enacted and as yet untested recall legislation in British Columbia requires a petition signed by forty percent of registered voters in the previous election, and a recall petition cannot be filed within eighteen months of that election. In all these cases, the stringent requirements that a recall campaign must meet offset to a considerable degree the potentially disruptive impact of the recall on representative democracy.

The populist call for direct democracy arises from criticisms of *representative* democracy, criticisms based on a feeling that "special interests dominate the political process to the detriment of the people" (Canovan 1981:178). In a system of representative democracy, the electorate does not make legislative decisions itself, but chooses representatives to make those decisions. The linkage between the representative and the electorate, or in populist terms, "the people," lies in periodic elections in which the representative seeks another term of office. Populist demands for more direct democracy occur when a significant proportion of the electorate believes the linkage has so weakened that the representative is no longer listening to the electorate, but rather to lobbyists, special interests or party leadership (Cronin 1989:10). For hard-line populists, the term "politician" is almost an epithet. Describing the views of early Canadian populists, David Laycock (1990:75) writes that they believed "politicians were a breed apart from 'the people', intent on sustaining social-political impotence for honest producers."

It is not surprising, then, that populists see marked differences between the elite-driven outcomes of legislatures, on the one hand, and the views and desires of the common people, on the other. This view was particularly strong in western agrarian populist movements during the first half of the twentieth century. Those groups sought greater protection against powerful special interests, but those same interests, namely, railroads, corporations and trusts, were seen as controlling the legislatures (Cronin 1989:44–6). However, the call for more direct democracy has not been limited to agrarian populists. For instance, a change from the politics of "power" to the politics of "participation" was a key call of the student movements of the late 1960s (Canovan 1981:186). Direct democracy is a part of the platform of many "new social movements," such as environmentalism and feminism. The Reform Party of Canada has also argued that the current representative system has allowed for policies that go against what the people want. In Canada, the Goods and Services Tax (GST) instituted by the Progressive Conservative government in 1991 has served as a lightning rod for such discontent.

The drive for direct democracy is not an altruistic, value-neutral idea, for there is an assumption that changing the system will change the outputs to the benefit of those seeking the systematic change. Agrarian populists, for example, felt short-changed by a system they believed was catering to urban-based economic elites. Thomas Cronin (1989:49) quotes an Oregon populist from the turn of the century: "The important thing was to restore the lawmaking power where it belongs—in the hands of the people. Once (you) give us that, we could get anything we wanted."[10] Patrick Boyer's (1992b:3) point that Canadians have been content to see the system as something far from themselves, that Canada has been a "timid democracy," supports this claim. If outputs are satisfactory, there appears to be little discontent with elite leadership. Canadians may feel distant from their government, but if they are happy with the outputs that governments provide, they are unlikely to seek change. It is only when some segment of the population sees itself as unrepresented and disadvantaged that populism's call for direct democracy really takes hold.

> ## Exercise Three: Limits to Direct Democracy
>
> Pause for a moment, and consider what you think of direct democracy. What are its benefits? What are its dangers and limitations? How qualified do you feel to vote on policy issues? How qualified do you feel others are to vote on policy issues?
>
> Perhaps you live in an area where direct-democracy devices are used and have voted in a referendum or initiative. How does this experience shape your opinion about these devices? Having used them, are you (or would you be) more likely or less likely to support their use? How would you respond if they were taken away?

The debate over direct democracy has provided an important bridge between populism and right-wing conservative thought (Crawford 1980). In both cases, there is a suspicion that established institutions, including legislative assemblies and the courts in particular, have lost touch with the people. Direct democracy is therefore seen as a means to sweep aside institutional constraints on the popular will. At issue in this debate are the principles of representative democracy which for generations have provided the institutional cornerstone for western democratic states.

CRITICISMS OF POPULISM

In many respects, populism constitutes an affirmation of basic democratic values; it is a call for government "of the people, by the people, for the people." At the same time, populism has been subjected to a good deal of criticism, much of which stems from the political science community. Certainly political scientists have been strong supporters of representative democracy, believing in the need to filter public opinion through representative institutions and the courts. In this respect, Ian McAllister (1991) maintains that significant differences in values and attitudes between elites and masses remain, even as the education gap between the two narrows. Political scientists argue that because the average citizen does not have the resources for decision-making that elites enjoy, the choice for voters should be limited to selecting which elites will govern. Russell Dalton (1984), however, shows that the average citizen's increased ability to gain information has weakened party linkages; as a result, voters are less likely to follow party cues—which can be seen as elite-driven—and more likely to make their own decisions.

Criticisms of what became populist thinking can be found far back in history. In *The Republic*, Plato described how leaders who have a base of popular support in the masses can easily turn into tyrants. Other criticisms concern "the tyranny of the majority." At the time of his visit to North America in the nineteenth century, Alexis de Tocqueville (1984:114) argued forcefully that majority status should not be construed as license to run roughshod over minorities:

> A majority taken collectively is only an individual, whose opinions, and frequently whose interests, are opposed to those of another individual, who is styled a minority. If it be admitted that a man possessing absolute power may misuse that power by wronging his adversaries, why should not a majority be liable to the same reproach? .... the power to do everything, which I should refuse to one of my equals, I will never grant to any number of them.

James Madison, in Federalist 51, raised similar criticisms of "the tyranny of the majority" in arguing for the separation of powers in the American Constitution. In fact, the American system was originally designed to keep the people from having too great a direct say in government. The House of Representatives was directly elected, but the Senate was chosen by state legislatures and senators were given longer terms (six years) than were members of the House (two years). The president was selected not by the people, but by an electoral college; and the Supreme Court was placed entirely outside the reach of the people.

More recent criticisms have come from "elite" theorists of democracy, who claim that well-educated elites make the best decisions for society. Gabriel Almond and Sidney Verba (1965) argue in the classic work, *The Civic Culture,* that the most stable democracies are those which, despite their participatory elements, retain a degree of deference and apathy. In *Political Man,* Seymour Martin Lipset (1960:115) questions the ability of those of low socioeconomic status to accept democratic norms:

> Acceptance of the norms of democracy requires a high level of sophistication and ego security. The less sophisticated and stable an individual, the more likely he is to favor a simplified view of politics, to fail to understand the rationale underlying tolerance of those with whom he disagrees, and to find difficulty in grasping or tolerating a gradualist image of political change.

If the populist view of the virtue and "common sense of the common people" provides one end of a spectrum, Lipset's view provides the other. Like Plato, Lipset argues that, compared to more educated elites, the working classes are more intolerant and are more predisposed to demagoguery than to democracy. Lipset (1960:167–70), among many others, associated populism with the intolerance of McCarthyism in the United States during the 1950s, and denounced McCarthyism as "populist extremism." Neoconservative writer Daniel Bell (1985:63) carried this criticism through to populist unrest of the 1970s, arguing that the populist "flattering of the multitudes" opened the door to an assault not only on traditional authority, but also on pluralism and political tolerance.

In *Liberalism Against Populism,* William Riker uses social choice theory to argue that populist theories are unworkable. He asserts that populists believe "participation in rule making is necessary for liberty" (1982:12). Thus, "what the people ... want ought to be social policy," and "the people are free when their wishes are law" (1982:238). Riker, however, uses a series of mathematical models and social choice theory to show that we cannot determine what the wishes of the people are. Voting does not determine a "common will," it merely tells us which of the presented alternatives has been chosen. If a different method of voting had been used, it is possible that a different outcome would have emerged from the same set of options. Because populist theory depends on voting to illuminate the will of the people, Riker maintains that populist theory is flawed.[11]

Perhaps the most problematic feature of populism lies with its majoritarian character. A society that places virtue with the common people and which seeks to achieve that group's goals may be an unpleasant place for those who do not meet the definition of "common," whether the differences making them uncommon are ethnic, racial, economic, religious or ideological. Populism is intrinsically hostile to minorities, no matter how those minorities might be constituted, and to both institutional and constitutional protections for minority rights. But then, this majoritarianism is also the source of populism's greatest appeal. Within the context of populism, every individual is equal, and claims for special treatment are denied. It is not surprising that, for many people, this is precisely how democratic government should be defined and made operational.

THE FUTURE OF POPULISM

The prospects of populism in the next ten to fifteen years are far from clear. Although the growing "cognitive mobilization" of the populace and technological change bode well for populism, the increasing diversity of society and the growing use of rights-based arguments in the political life of many industrialized states challenge populist thought and practice.

As mentioned earlier, the work of Russell Dalton indicates that a "cognitive mobilization" is occurring in western societies. Through increasing educational opportunities, expanding sources of mass media and other related factors, the electorates in industrialized societies are becoming more educated, more aware and more able to make their own decisions about important issues. As a consequence, the "common people" are becoming not only less common but also less willing to defer to elites. A more informed, involved populace has a greater desire to be directly involved in political decision-making, and may have a considerable appetite for the use of direct-democracy devices. It is no longer self-evident that the common people are not informed or interested enough to be making policy decisions.

Technological change also allows for the potential expansion of direct democracy. Internet and other electronic forums provide an avenue for freer and faster discussion of almost anything, including politics. Benjamin Barber and Ross Perot have both floated the idea of "electronic town halls," and the Reform Party of Canada has held on-line and cable television shows where the party puts forward a political question and asks viewers to phone in to register their answers (Nasrullah 1995). One such forum asked callers to choose among three listed plans for cutting the budget deficit. It is not inconceivable to envision a day when decisions will be approved, or even made, by citizens voting at home through their computers.

Even as this technological change is occurring, however, other factors work against populism. Most of these factors entail a rejection of the ideology's majoritarian outlook, one that becomes more problematic in a society with significant minorities. The United States and Canada are experiencing growth in the size of ethnic and religious minorities. As the populace becomes more diverse, the possibility of a "tyranny of the majority" becomes more threatening. Because populist thought implies that the common people are fairly homogeneous, with shared values, desires and beliefs, increasing diversity can be a source of tension. It should also be pointed out, however, that increased numerical strength also provides minorities with a greater opportunity to make use of the referendum and initiative.[12]

The more significant challenge to populism comes from the increased use of rights-based arguments and the related use of the courts as a counterweight to majoritarian forms of political decision-making. Rights-based groups work from a very different set of assumptions about society, assumptions so different that one could describe the populist and rights-based groups as polar opposites. Populism, particularly through its support of direct democracy, is unashamedly majoritarian, whereas rights-based groups believe some things are so fundamental that they not only cannot be subjected to majority rule, but they must be protected from that rule. Therefore, rights-based groups look to the courts, which sit outside of the electoral democratic process. One example of the inevitable tension between the two perspectives arose in the 1994 California referendum on the status of illegal immigrants. Initiative 187, which sought to limit the access of illegal immigrants to education and health care, was passed by the California electorate by a substantial majority. Within twenty-four hours of passage, some twenty-seven lawsuits had been filed seeking court injunctions to stop the measure as unconstitutional. To further complicate the matter, some of the lawsuits seeking to block the "majority will" came from organizations such as school boards, themselves elected and publicly funded. The issue will likely be decided in the U.S. Supreme Court, where similar legislation was narrowly struck down in the early 1980s.[13] Initiatives which end up in court battles are not new or unusual. From 1960 to 1980, ten statewide initiatives were passed by California voters. Seven of those initiatives had at least some portion of the original proposition struck down by the courts. Sections of the well-known Proposition 13 of 1978, which slashed property taxes and limited future increases in property-tax rates, were struck down by appellate courts (Magleby 1984:53),[14] although later upheld by the U.S. Supreme Court.

There is a degree of irony in the debate between rights-based and populist groups. While the two may battle each other, they also constitute a two-pronged attack on traditional forms of representative democracy. Both attempt to weaken the power of legislatures. Rights-based groups challenge legislative action through the courts, whereas populist groups seek to take decisions away from legislatures and give them to the broader populace through direct democracy. This legislative erosion is furthest along in the United States, but Canadian conventions of parliamentary government are also being eroded, though more from the rights end of the continuum. Until 1982, Parliament could act as it saw fit in all issues, as long as it did not violate the federal-provincial division of powers set out in the Constitution Act of 1867. The 1982 Constitution Act changed this through the introduction of the Charter of Rights and Freedoms, and acts of the federal or provincial legislatures can now be struck down on the basis of a violation of rights.

The populist push for institutional reform may become more complex in the near future. The traditional tension between representative democracy and direct democracy remains, but must now take into account those political actors who work primarily through the judicial system. The judicialization of politics notwithstanding, it seems that deference to elite leadership is on the wane across the board. A specific illustration is provided by a cable television–rate increase which produced an uproar in many Canadian cities late in 1994. Much of the protest focused on how federal regulators and cable companies had chosen what new channels would be available to the consumer and how these channels would be packaged. As a *Globe and Mail* commentary (January 13, 1995) pointed out, "Canadians are more and more confident of their own judgement and less and less willing to accept the benevolent paternalism of their 'betters.'" The commentary concluded that "the decline of elite governance and the rise of citizen power seems unstoppable."

Exercise Four: Direct Democracy as a Strategic Option

Think of four or five issues that are important to you. Ask yourself what would be the best avenue for seeing your point of view implemented into law or public policy, assuming for the moment that you have all of these avenues available to you. Are the chances for success best through the legislative process? Through direct democracy? Through the courts?

What kinds of issues are likely to have the most success through which avenues? Would a shift to more populist forms of government change the likely winners and losers in political life?

In conclusion, populism can be difficult to categorize as an ideology. It is not really new, having been around in various forms for more than a century, yet it rarely gets mentioned as a "traditional" ideology. Its propensity to blend into other ideologies, and the resulting policy diversity associated with populism, also cause difficulty in definition. Even so, populism can be seen as an ideology, with a core belief system that values and even deifies "the common people," and vilifies elites. In the postindustrial age, the distrust of elites is populism's most visible feature. The institutional reforms advocated by populists may be slow to emerge, but their progress does seem linear—once granted, direct-democracy devices have rarely been rescinded. One may question the extent of populism's impact on contemporary politics in western democratic states, but nowhere on the horizon do there appear to be forces which will eliminate the populist impulse. The tension between representative and direct democracy is likely to be as enduring as democracy itself.

The first great wave of populism broke against the shores of the American political system in the 1890s. As Peter Argersinger (1974:303) concludes, perhaps too harshly, that wave failed because it failed to *transcend* the political system: "[I]t was killed by those very factors of politics that its founders had intended to kill: prejudice, elite manipulation, corruption." Whether the current wave of populism will succeed in transcending the political system is one of the most interesting ideological questions facing us.

NOTES

1. American populist unrest also rippled through Australian politics around the turn of the century.
2. Reform Party of Canada 1993 *Blue Book*.
3. A clear exception is Reform leader Preston Manning, who has written at considerable length about his populist vision.
4. Seven of the fifteen current members of the European Union (EU) (Austria, Britain, Denmark, Finland, Ireland, France and Sweden) have had referendums concerning EU membership or some aspect of EU policy.
5. The 1992 referendum was only the third national referendum in Canadian history; the other two were on the prohibition of alcohol, in 1889, and on military conscription, in 1942. Both passed nationally but were massively rejected in Quebec.
6. Some evidence of this fertile ground can be found in the opening lines of the American and Australian constitutions. The U.S. Constitution begins in a very populist tone with the words, "We the people," even though the Constitution itself attempted to put checks on "popular" rule. The Australian document makes mention of the people, saying, "...the people of (the six states) ... unite in one indissoluble Federal Commonwealth under the Crown..." Contrast this to the Canadian Constitution Act of 1867, which makes no mention of the people, only provinces. Furthermore, an appeals court ruling on a 1916 Initiative and Referendum Act passed by the Manitoba legislature said, "In Canada there is no sovereignty in the people" (Morton 1944:287).
7. In the "legislative initiative," an alternative form used in some states, the petition goes directly to the legislature, which can pass it immediately or send it back to the people.
8. In Saskatchewan, nonbinding initiatives may be brought to the electorate if fifteen percent of the voters sign a petition. In British Columbia, an initiative can be put on the ballot if a petition is signed by at least ten percent of the voters in each and every constituency. To pass, the initiative must be supported by fifty percent of the registered voters (not of those actually voting), and by more than fifty percent of the registered voters in at least two-thirds of the province's constituencies.
9. Some jurisdictions go through the confusing and contradictory procedure of doing both at the same time.
10. William U'Ren, quoted in Thomas Cronin (1989:49). Originally quoted in Scott W. Reed, "W.S. U'Ren and the Oregon System," Senior honors thesis, Princeton Univ., 1950, 18.
11. Riker's argument focuses exclusively on elections, and particularly on elections where there are more than two candidates. He makes only one brief reference to referendums. In a referendum or initiative, the phrasing of a question may make a difference, but the vote itself is nearly always a simple yes or no.
12. The Swiss experience is a good example of this.
13. Proponents of Proposition 187 likely realized it would be challenged in the courts, but hoped that changes in the composition of the Supreme Court might change the outcome this time around.
14. Some initiatives have been ruled unconstitutional and taken off the ballot before a vote. Massachusetts and Oregon, for example, allow for a review of an initiative's constitutionality by state officials even before signatures are gathered (Cronin 1989:220).

CHAPTER NINE

Fascism: The Statist Extreme

WITH FREDERICK S. WALL

*Everybody must know or remember, that when Hitler and Mussolini spoke in public,
they were believed, applauded, admired, adored like gods...We must remember that
these faithful followers, among them the diligent executors of inhuman orders, were
not born torturers, were not (with a few exceptions) monsters: they were ordinary men.*

PRIMO LEVI

*Liberalism denied the State in the interests of the particular individual; Fascism
reaffirms the State as the true reality of the individual.*

BENITO MUSSOLINI

Why study fascism? This question incurs lively debate among contemporary political theorists. Can we glean anything useful from a study of the ideology, or are we merely giving unwarranted exposure to an anachronistic explosion of national and racial hatred? Or, perhaps even worse, are we providing a stage for hate-mongers who continue to pose a serious threat to the social order?

There is no question that a clear understanding of fascism is disturbing to attempt and difficult to achieve. There is also no question that fascism is on the extreme fringe of liberal-dominated political discourse in Canada and the United States, and therefore could be ignored by those trying to grapple with mainstream ideological debate. But, as students of politics, we have an intellectual obligation to examine and understand the ideas that have animated, and continue to animate, extremist movements worldwide, ideas that have shown the ability to emerge with dramatic force on the political landscape. In order to understand and demystify fascism, and to comprehend its outcroppings in North America, we must analyze its doctrines as fully and responsibly as we can. If, as Roger Griffin (1995:11) suggests, we wish to inoculate ourselves and others against the reemergence of fascism, it is essential that we understand its roots, framework and appeal.

Exercise One: Preconceptions About Fascism

From the following list of terms, select those you think are related to fascist ideology. Save your list and assess your perceptions at the end of the chapter.

Individualism	Sovereignty
Organicism	Laissez-Faire
Anti-Semitism	Conflict
Security	Freedom
Duty	Optimism
Militarism	Authoritarianism
Violence	Tolerance
Control	Hatred
Fear	Hope
Pessimism	Elitism
Belonging	Tradition
Socialism	Nationalism
Spirituality	Reactionary
Visionary	Myth
Left	Right

It is important to first clarify our use of some key concepts. Although the term "fascism" is often used interchangeably with "nazism," they are conceptually distinct. Fascism, or *fascismo*, developed in Italy and found its primary and most complete articulation in that country. Nazism, although closely related to fascism, had significantly different influences and emphases, and is best seen as a variant of the larger fascism ideology. The importance of this distinction will become clear as our study of fascism progresses.

THE IDEOLOGICAL BACKGROUND

A proper understanding of fascism requires a exploration of the ideological and historical context into which it emerged. Such an undertaking is necessary not only because fascism is a relatively recent phenomenon, but also because fascist thinkers explicitly position themselves against a particular intellectual backdrop.

The Crisis of Liberalism

A growing dissatisfaction with modern society led to the birth of fascism. At the beginning of the twentieth century, classical liberalism was the dominant ideology. As discussed in Chapter 2, classical liberalism favoured liberty as its central value, and it was unquestionably a liberating force. Not everyone, however, saw liberation as a wholly positive experience. One of the forces freed was modern science, which had undergone extraordinary growth during the eighteenth and nineteenth centuries. But the growth of science had come at the expense of traditional ways of life and established beliefs. This led to what Max Weber (1958:139) called the "rationalization," or "disenchantment" of the world, the belief that:

[O]ne can, in principle, master all things by calculation. This means that the world is disenchanted. One need no longer have recourse to magical means in order to master or implore the spirits .... Technical means and calculations perform the service.

If science is the dominant paradigm, then we are left with a crucial values gap, for science cannot establish that "the existence of the world which these sciences describe is worthwhile, that it has any meaning, or that it makes sense to live in such a world" (Weber 1958:144).

Liberalism uprooted traditional social structures in the name of liberty, and modern science undermined traditional beliefs in the pursuit of truth. In place of these traditional roots, liberalism offered an ethic of individual self-determination and a state which declared itself neutral among individual goals. But such freedom of choice had left many people feeling adrift and uncertain. The resultant dissatisfaction with liberal society was foretold in a scathing remark by Thomas Carlyle (1956:174), a Scottish historian writing in the late nineteenth century:

> Call ye that a Society .... where there is no longer any Social Idea extant; not so much as the Idea of a common Home, but only of a common over-crowded Lodging-house? Where each isolated, regardless of his neighbour, turned against his neighbour, clutches what he can get, and cries 'Mine!'...Where your Priest has no tongue but for plate-licking: and your high Guides and Governors cannot guide; but on all hands hear it passionately proclaimed: *Laissez faire*, leave us alone of *your* guidance, such light is darker than darkness; eat you, your wages and sleep!

As Michael Oakeshott (1991:372) describes it in more contemporary terms:

> [F]or many the invitation to make choices came before the ability to make them and was consequently recognized as a burden ... What some recognized as happiness, appeared to others as discomfort.

Rather than embracing this "disenchanted world," many sought refuge from it. Yet to conclude this is not to explain why fascism was an attractive refuge. Fascism, after all, was not the only possible response to concerns about liberalism. As discussed earlier, for example, socialism was very much a reaction or response to liberalism, as was conservatism. The socialist alternative, however, was experiencing difficulties of its own.

The Crisis of Marxism

Marxism promised that alienation and inequity would be alleviated by the impending revolution. But, early in the twentieth century, a number of practical and theoretical developments were beginning to call the Marxist faith into question.

Robert Michels was a socialist writer whose seminal work, *Political Parties* (1915), examined the activity of political parties in general and socialist parties in particular. He despaired at his conclusion, namely that "leadership is a necessary phenomenon in every form of social life" (Michels 1962:364). It is the permanence of leadership that Michels referred to as the "iron law of oligarchy," the proposition that every organization will develop a dominant elite which will rule in its own interests. The ideological implications of Michels's findings were significant. If the end of alienation would not be attained until we reached the "classless society," then

Marxism could not provide the requisite liberation, for it would necessarily generate a "new class," namely the leaders and apparatus of the revolutionary party. Any attempt to overthrow this new class would require a counter-organization, and "who says organization says oligarchy." Doctrinal developments within Marxism, moreover, supported Michels's argument. The Leninist revision of Marxism, for example, set out the need for an intellectual vanguard to impose from without a revolutionary consciousness on the proletariat, an imposition which in practice led to "democratic centralism." But the Leninist modification, which seemed to affirm Michels's conclusions, was by no means the only vital development.

Definitions of Fascism

Fascism, reduced to its essentials, is the ideology of permanent conflict (Lyttleton 1973:12).

It is possible to define fascism, or identify the "fascist minimum," in terms not of a common ideological component, but of a common mythic core (Griffin 1995:2).

In its essential character, fascist ideology was a rejection of materialism—liberalism, democracy and Marxism being regarded simply as different aspects of the same materialist evil (Sternhell 1994:148).

A hypernationalist, often pan-nationalist, anti-parliamentary, anti-liberal, anti-communist, populist and therefore anti-proletarian, partly anti-capitalist ... with the aim of national social integration through a single party and corporative representation (Linz 1995:300).

Socialism also suffered severely from the failure, at least initially, of the economic predictions of Marx. Not only had class polarization not come to pass, but, if anything, the opposite was true. The late nineteenth and early twentieth centuries had witnessed the expansion of the franchise, increasing democratization and a rise in general prosperity. Pauperization had not occurred and the spontaneous rise of the proletariat seemed more and more unlikely. Furthermore, the growth of trade unionism had provided workers with an effective outlet to seek remedies for their grievances within the liberal framework. As Zeev Sternhell (1994:13) notes, "Marxism had not foreseen a situation in which the proletariat ... would one day come to the conclusion that bourgeois democracy could also serve its own interests."[1] The increase in class integration and mobility reduced the saliency of class as a key identifier and undercut the very notion of class conflict as the driving force of history.

The experience of World War I, and especially the behaviour of the German Social Democratic Party, further undermined the belief in the primary importance of class. As Michels (1962:357) noted at the time:

> The war has shattered this theory at one terrible blow. The German Socialist Party, the strongest, wealthiest, and, best organized section of the working-class international ... suddenly and emphatically declared its entire solidarity with the German Emperor. Throughout the proletarian mass there has not been reported a single instance of moral rebellion against ... German imperialism...

The lesson of the First World War seemed clear: if humanity had one dominant cleavage, it was not between the proletariat and the bourgeoisie, it was between nations.

A further important development for the birth of fascism was the revisionist Marxism of Georges Sorel[2], a thinker upon whom the short-term failure of Marx's economic predictions had a profound impact. The expansion of the franchise and the increasing prosperity of the early twentieth century had, at least temporarily, falsified the predictions of Marxist economics. Nonetheless, although revolutionary socialism could no longer be asserted as an economic and historical "necessity," Sorel nevertheless retained hope for a revolution. His vision, however, was markedly different from that of traditional socialism. He believed that the masses could not, especially in light of the recent economic developments, be counted upon to spontaneously overthrow bourgeois society. According to Sorel, the appeal to historical materialism was a weak one—what really generates action is a "social myth"; in Sorel's view, "Psychology had to compensate for the deficiencies of economics" (Sternhell 1994:25). Sorel argued that the masses must be provided with an energizing myth, one which would motivate them to overthrow bourgeois society. He found this myth in the "general strike," a violent and transformative uprising by the working class: "The general strike ... like the Napoleonic battle, is to completely annihilate a condemned *regime*" (Sorel 1914:297). Sorel compared the myth of the general strike to the force which, he claimed, animated Catholicism:

> Catholics have never been discouraged even in the hardest trials, because they have always pictured the history of the Church as a series of battles between Satan and the hierarchy supported by Christ; every new difficulty which arises is only an episode in a war which must finally end in the victory of Catholicism (1914:22).

Rather than passively wait for the proper economic conditions for a revolution to occur, Sorel's revision of Marxism emphasized activity, and violent activity in particular. Indeed, for Sorel, violence was the key to heroism, and to the new civilization: "It is to violence that Socialism owes those high ethical values by means of which it brings *salvation* to the modern world" (1914:295). Sorel sought freedom from disenchantment through a celebration of heroism and the irrational. As Zeev Sternhell (1994:91) notes:

> A new vision of political ideals thus came into existence, one that sought to mobilize the masses by means of myths. It supported the idea of violence .... It envisaged a moral, intellectual, and political revolution ... with an intense pessimism and a fundamental antirationalism.

Sorel's theory provided hope to those alienated from liberal society, but whose faith in the Marxist solution had waned. The emphasis on violent, mythic politics, combined with the repudiation of bourgeois society, provided fertile intellectual ground for the genesis of fascism.

Although fascism is not simply a revision of socialism, the two doctrines are deeply intertwined. The fascists shared with the Marxists a revulsion at liberal society, but they disagreed fundamentally as to the means and reasons that it should be overthrown. In fact, the fascists detected a distinct kinship between liberalism and socialism, one they felt ignored vital elements of human nature and misunderstood human freedom. The fascists argued that the battle between liberalism and socialism was really a factional squabble, a dispute between materialistic doctrines whose differences lay solely in method. What was needed, therefore, was not a revision of liberalism or socialism but an entirely *new* mode of politics, one which could incorporate the permanence of leadership, the rise of nationalism and the importance of myth.

One of the first thinkers to articulate this new mode of politics was Alfredo Rocco, a former Socialist party activist in Italy. Rocco served as minister of justice in Mussolini's government from 1925 to 1932, and as Adrian Lyttleton (1973:243) notes, "No other minister under Mussolini exercised comparable power for such a long period of time." Rocco is of particular interest here because he was at once a sophisticated thinker and an accomplished jurist, responsible for writing many of the laws of fascist Italy. Thus, we will pay special attention to his *Political Doctrine of Fascism*, written in 1925.

BASIC TENETS OF FASCISM

Human beings, according to the fascist philosophy, are a species which organize into numerous "fractions" known as societies. Since "there is no unique organization of the human species, there is not *one* but there are *several* human societies. Humanity therefore exists solely as a biological concept not as a social one" (Rocco 1972:322). Thus, while human beings share biological characteristics, their inherent sociability leads them to divide into distinct groups, or societies. According to Rocco (1972:322), societies represent the intersection of man's biological and social nature, "each one possessing a peculiar organization ... a life which is really its own." Although human beings share with other species material needs such as food and shelter, what differentiates man is the ability and desire to strive for *spiritual* ends. These spiritual ends, however, cannot be sought in solitude; they can only be sought collectively, as a member of a *people*. A *people* is defined as a fraction of the species which exhibits *spiritual unity*, defined by Rocco as "more or less ... unity of language, of culture, of religion, of tradition, of customs, and in general of feeling and volition ... of territory" (Rocco 1972:322). All human beings are social animals, and no individual can exist outside of society. One is born into and fundamentally defined by the fraction of the species to which one belongs. These fractions are arranged hierarchically, but the arrangement is not static; spiritual ends are something that "every form of society strives to attain as well as its stage of social development allows" (Rocco 1972:322).[3]

Another essential component of fascist ideology is the belief in *organicism*, the belief that the state is a living organism. In this respect, the fascist state represents the absolute extreme of collectivism and the polar opposite of the individualism championed by liberalism. In fascist thought, the state is prior to, constitutive of and wholly superior to the individual. As a consequence, fascist ideology is unapologetically totalitarian in scope, denying all boundaries between the private and the public. Indeed, as Giovanni Gentile argues (Lyttleton 1972:307), such a distinction is spurious: "The state and the individual are one and the same thing, or rather inseparable terms of an essential synthesis." Since any individual action may affect the larger collective, all activity is necessarily the concern of the state. Furthermore, since the organism always trumps the individual, this means that every activity may, perhaps must, be controlled by the state. Mussolini (1972:332) himself stated:

> The Fascist State, the highest and most powerful form of personality, is a force, but a spiritual force, which takes over all the forms of the moral and intellectual life of

man ... It is the form, the inner standard and the discipline of the whole person; it saturates the will as well as the intelligence ... it is the soul of the soul.

The collectivism of fascism requires not only responsibility to the whole but also sacrifice, "even up to the total immolation of individuals, on behalf of society" (Rocco 1972:323). Against the rationalism of the "disenchanted world," fascism offers *duty* in the service of a state which represents the "unity of the indefinite series of generations" (Rocco 1972:323). Earlier chapters have established that the primary value for liberalism was liberty; for conservatism, order; and for socialism, equality. We may now add to that list by recognizing the primacy of *duty* in the fascist doctrine.

The preeminence of duty also illuminates the fascist conception of heroism and leadership. Fascism as a totalitarian doctrine advocates not only a single-party system but an extreme centralization of power. N. Kogan (1968:13) summarizes the process: "The party dominates the state; the apparatus dominates the party; the secretariat dominates the apparatus, and the leader dominates the secretariat and manipulates the system." It would be a mistake, however, to interpret such a system as simply megalomaniacal. Rather, the chain of duty which culminates in one-person rule is an extension of fascism's organic principle. Since the state is an organism which is of primary normative value, and since its value spans and unites generations, it must be protected from being exploited in the interest of any one group of individuals, or even in the interest of a single generation. This protection is required not because injustice will be done to a future group, but because it is a crime against the entity which unites all generations—the state. As this protection is difficult to accomplish, fascism not only bans factions within the state[4] but also "insists that government be entrusted to men capable of rising above their own private interests and of realizing the aspirations of the social collectivity, considered in its unity and in its relation to the past and future" (Rocco 1972:325). Those capable of such leadership are very rare individuals, persons who eschew their own interest and have the capacity to respond to a unique, heroic duty—"the higher demands of society and of history" (Rocco 1972:325). Thus, while the citizen's duty is to obey the state, the leader has an obligation to ensure that the state is governed in the best interests of the past, present and future generations of a specific "people."

Although fascism represents the most extreme form of collectivism, it is vital to understand that the idea of freedom is not abandoned so much as it is radically transformed. As mentioned in Chapter 4, socialism sought to set "people free from the condition of material dependence that has imprisoned them since the beginning of time" (Baradat 1994:180–1). However, as Rocco (1972:322) argues, "Man is not solely matter; and the ends of the human species, far from being the materialistic ones we have in common with other animals, are rather, and predominantly, the spiritual finalities." The appeal to "spiritual finalities" is particularly important if one accepts Weber's proposition about the "disenchanted world." If traditional beliefs were to be undermined, a great many people would be left in spiritual despair and confusion. Without clear spiritual guidance, human beings would find themselves in a struggle for physical survival without spiritual meaning. As Mussolini (1972: 334) suggested, without some external meaning, "men would be only by-products of history, who appear and disappear on the surface of the waves."

The organicist doctrine, in which a special people are linked through time by the state, fills the vacuum of meaning by extolling the value of duty as the road to freedom:

> The man of Fascism is an individual who is nation and fatherland ... suppressing the instinct for a life enclosed within the brief round of pleasure *in order to restore within duty a higher life free from the limits of time and space*: a life in which the individual, through the denial of himself ... through death itself, realizes that completely spiritual existence in which his value as a man lies (Mussolini, 1972:329).

The fascist doctrine argues for a radical extension of the notion of positive liberty discussed in Chapter 2. Since man is not only matter, the state should not become active to remedy only material inequity. Rather, since human beings are fundamentally spiritual creatures, the state should remove spiritual disharmony and malaise. In order to free people from their spiritual "shackles," it is necessary to address the problem of *temporality*, to overcome the despair caused by human mortality in a disenchanted world. Time is given meaning by reference to a transcendent duty to a greater whole, a whole which links past, present and future. According to Mario Palmieri's 1936 work (1972:344), "Fascism ... answers emphatically that life *has* a meaning, that it has a purpose and a goal, and that it has worth and dignity and beauty." Moreover, the transcendent meaning offered by the fascist ideology is available to all members of the state, regardless of class: "No man is an outcast in the social system of Fascism, no man is worthless; no man, that is, who belongs to the Fascist nation and to its life" (Palmieri 1972:347).

The absorption of the self into the fascist state represents the most puzzling and paradoxical development of liberty in the modern world: the desire for freedom *from* self-determination.[5] Even though fascism was explicitly totalitarian from the outset, it nevertheless secured significant popular support. Where freedom to make important choices seemed daunting, or where the consequences of freely taken actions were difficult to bear, the fascist state was there to remove the burden; it rebuilt identities, provided individuals with certainty and security and functioned as "the soul of the soul." Large numbers of people freely willed complete self-domination, demanding and accepting an end to the "burden" of self-determination.[6]

Although fascist ideology rejected the primacy of materialism, it was not without its own economic doctrine. Both capitalist and socialist economics were thought to be wholly inadequate and inconsistent with fascist principles. The primacy of the state in fascist ideology rendered the acceptance of a laissez-faire economy impossible, while practical socialist alternatives had not emerged.[7] Fascist economics sought instead to bring order to the market economy without imposing the inefficiency of complete state ownership. Since the state is constitutive of all individuals and groups, class interests are subsumed under the mediation of the political leadership. As Mussolini (1975:38) describes it, "It is no longer economy aiming at individual profit, but economy concerned with collective interests." Mario Palmieri (1972:355) maintained that *corporatism* is the extension of the organic ethic to the economy "because it is first of all, and above all, a translation of Ethics into Economics, an application of Ethical principles to economic facts." The corporation's main objective is to increase the power and prosperity of the state, and to that end the fascist state would license a corporation to manage each specific industry. Mussolini licensed twenty-two corporations in total, ranging in interest from forestry to viticulture. These corporations were administered by councils which were composed of equal numbers of employers, workers and members of the party. This particular arrangement was designed to include all groups within the state in the operation of the economy, an economy which promised to be more stable than capitalism and more efficient than socialism (Mussolini 1975:114–31).

To summarize, the ideology of fascism rests on a number of basic tenets, among which the following are of particular importance:

- humanity divides naturally into national societies based on a common language, religion, culture or ethnicity and united in the pursuit of spiritual ends;

- the state is an organic entity that is prior to and wholly superior to the individual; as a consequence, there is no legitimate boundary between the private and public worlds;

- generations are linked through the state, and in this way fascism addresses the mortality concerns of individuals;

- duty is the road to freedom, and provides the cornerstone value of the fascist state;

- strong leadership is essential if the state is to rise above the narrow self-interest of individuals and groups; and

- the economy should be organized along corporatist lines which transcend the economic interests of classes, employers and individuals.

In contrast to the common preconception that fascism springs only from the brows of thugs, it should now be clear that it is a sophisticated, if ultimately dangerous, body of thought. Italian fascism was an intellectual as well as a political movement, and its criticisms of liberal society were both harsh and profound. Nevertheless, as an active doctrine it suffered a significant internal defect.[8] Its explanation of evil—

The Ideology of Fascism

- *scope*: Fascism is totalitarian in scope, denying completely the separation between the personal and the political. Although primarily a European phenomenon, pockets of fascism have emerged in most industrial nations.

- *internal consistency*: In fascism, the state is constitutive of the individual; as such, the goals and needs of the state take primacy over those of the individual. In return, the state provides security, order and a purpose for the individual. In nazism, race is the constitutive element.

- *durability*: Fascism and nazism are twentieth-century phenomena, currently relegated to the fringes of most political spectrums. Nevertheless, as the twenty-first century approaches, no industrialized nation is entirely without a fascist movement of some kind.

- *normative framework*: Fascism is an extreme form of organicism which claims that human individuals are components in a unique society which comprises the past, the present and future generations. As such, *duty* is the primary normative value.

- *practical guide for political action*: Since the fascist state is a totalitarian and ethical entity, the economy must be organized according to the needs of the state. The state subsumes and transcends class and individual interests in a corporatist economy.

- *formal articulation*: Fascism takes its bearings from Alfredo Rocco, Georges Sorel, Giovanni Gentile, Mario Palmieri and Benito Mussolini. The tenets of nazism can be found in the writings of Houston Stewart Chamberlain, Adolf Hitler, Alfred Rosenberg and Richard Wagner.

that materialism had led to the degeneration of the national community—was an effective, if complex, rallying cry so long as fascism was an opposition movement. But once Mussolini seized power in Italy in 1922 and began to assume control, it became increasingly difficult to blame the old materialist doctrines for whatever malaise continued to exist. Factions within the state had been banned, the economy had been altered significantly and the state was beginning to assume the promised totalitarian role. What, then, could explain the persistence of evil and continued spiritual unease? The answer was to be found in scapegoats, and it was an answer that was to be taken to a hideous extreme in Germany.[9]

NAZISM: RACIALISM AND THE POLITICS OF HATRED

Fascism, in the Italian form, comprised a number of disturbing elements in its doctrine, not the least of which was its uncritical embrace of totalitarianism. But no doctrine is as perplexing or disturbing as the virulent fascist variant known as national socialism, or nazism. Its intellectual content is both sparse and repellent—words which are far too charitable to describe its results in practice. Nazism shares with fascism a belief in organicism, corporatism and leadership, as well as in the importance of myth. All of these commonalities, however, have different justifications in nazism, and therefore it is important to distinguish between fascism and nazism. Indeed, this is a distinction insisted upon by Joseph Goebbels, the minister for enlightenment and propaganda in Adolph Hitler's government: "[Fascism] is ... nothing like National Socialism. While the latter goes deep down to the roots, Fascism is only a superficial thing ... [Mussolini] is so bound to his own Italian people that he lacks the broad qualities of a worldwide revolutionary and insurrectionist" (Arendt 1968:7). Goebbels's assessment is probably correct; fascist Italy was never truly an imperial force and it did not advocate worldwide revolution. Nazism explained its purpose quite differently.

Nazism replaces the fascist conception of the state with a rigid racialist doctrine. Ernst Huber wrote in 1939 that "race is the natural basis of the people ... As a political people the natural community ... strives to form itself, to develop itself, to defend itself, to realize itself" (1972:370). As Hitler expressed it, race is not only constitutive but a permanent determinant of worth: "Nature [dislikes] the mixing of a higher race with a lower one, as in this case her entire work of higher breeding, which has perhaps taken hundreds of thousands of years, would tumble at one blow" (Hitler 1972:375). For nazism, human nature is racial nature, and duty is thus owed to the race rather than to the state. Or, as Hitler wrote in *Mein Kampf* (1924), "All that is not race in this world is trash" (in Cohen 1972:377).

At the apex of the racial hierarchy, according to nazism, is the Aryan race, which is the dominant creative culture. The Aryan race, the culture-founding race, is contrasted with two other forms, the culture-*bearing* races and the culture-*destroying* races. The former are mere receptacles for the culture of the dominant race, while the latter are inferior races whose only purpose is the alleged destruction of the culture-founding race (Hitler, in Cohen 1972:376–78). If the myth of racial superiority were true, however, all of the setbacks in the recent history of the Aryan race—Germany's defeat in World War I, the inflation crisis of the 1920s, the Great Depression—would be difficult to explain. Hitler, therefore, made use of a grotesque, albeit culturally rooted, fiction to explain evil: he claimed that Jews were engaged in a worldwide conspiracy against the "white race which they hate, to throw it down from its cultural and political height and in turn to rise personally to the position of master" (in Cohen 1972:384). Although Jews were alleged to be racially inferior, what made them dangerous within the Nazis' logic was their international reach and supposedly insidious nature: "[The Jew] systematically tries to lower the racial level by a permanent poisoning of the individual ... in the domain of culture he infects art, literature, theater ... he pulls the people down into the confines of his own swinish nature" (in Cohen 1972:384–5). The alleged omnipresence of a Judaic conspiracy allowed not only for a totalitarian state, it also allowed the Nazis to adopt an aggressive expansionist position in order to preserve racial purity. Since the race is allegedly being threatened by an international menace, the state must react through its foreign policy and, ultimately, through force of arms.

With the expansive demonology of nazism, the implementation of corporatism takes on additional symbolic importance. The corporate state is not only a new economic system which transcends the class differences of capitalism, it further represents the liberation of the state from control by allegedly insidious foreign sources, namely Jews. As Paul Ritter (1995:144) argues, "This awakening means not only the shaking off of the Asiatic-Jewish spirit which enslaved us, but also drawing once again on our own resources which reside in blood and race ...." Nazism's myth of racial purity was therefore given further impetus by the conspiracy theories embedded in the notion of an international Jewish threat.

Nazism as a phenomenon is disturbing in itself, but we should be further troubled by the fact that of those movements that are described as fascist today, virtually all may be described as neo-Nazi, and virtually all of them make reference, in one form or another, to Jewish culture as the source of evil. Why is this? Two reasons suggest themselves immediately. First, nazism is a much simpler doctrine than fascism, with a more fearful and accessible explanation of evil. Hatred is highly accessible and nazism places it in the centre of its theory where it is can serve as a lightning rod for all manner of discontent. The accessibility of a doctrine is a vital issue for any movement that wishes to emerge from the extreme fringe of political discourse. Second, for those who accept the initial premise of an international racial conspiracy, the doctrine is unfalsifiable; any evidence brought against it can be turned around and used as evidence of the conspiracy itself. For example, anyone bringing evidence to debunk *The Protocols of the Elders of Zion*[10] (the most infamous anti-Semitic tract) may be summarily dismissed as simply another conspirator, attempting covertly to attack the Aryan race. Ideological believers, therefore, can invoke a conspiracy theory to insulate their beliefs from any possible challenge or falsification, an insulation which gives nazism a disturbing durability at the fringe of political discourse in western democratic states.

FASCISM IN NORTH AMERICA

At its core, fascism is a collectivist ideology, and for that reason alone it has experienced great difficulty in gaining anything more than a toehold in North American ideological discourse. As Louis Hartz (1955:1964) and Gad Horowitz (1966) illustrate, the political culture of North America is emphatically liberal, and therefore an emphatically illiberal ideological perspective like fascism would have a difficult time finding an audience. It is not surprising, therefore, that fascism and its variants originated in Europe and found their greatest strength there. However, it is important to note that, on a few occasions, there have been significant outcroppings of fascism in North America, particularly in those regions of the continent where collectivism has been a relatively robust component of the political culture. In both these respects, Canada provides a useful illustration of the fact that the North American environment is by no means immune to fascism's appeal.

Any discussion of fascist movements in Canada should begin with Adrien Arcand. Based in Montreal, Quebec, Arcand established the best-organized and most influential fascist movement in Canada. A journalist, Arcand edited and published a number of independent newspapers in the late 1920s and early 1930s. These newspapers became the voice of his extreme nationalist organization, L'Ordre Patriotique des Goglus, a group devoted to the independence and restoration of Quebec society. Nationalist movements are certainly not a novelty in Quebec, but what set Arcand's organization apart was his intense anti-Semitism.

Arcand claimed that the difficulties in Quebec society were attributable to Jewish influence. As Martin Robin (1992:114) describes it: "In the Jewish menace, Arcand and the Goglus discovered a comforting magic key to the mysteries of the world, the one true source of the afflictions of modern society." To overcome these evils, Arcand envisaged a racially pure, corporatist Quebec. While one would expect such views to have confined Arcand to the margins of Canadian politics, he in fact gained a disturbing amount of influence. Carmillien Houde, mayor of Montreal in 1928, was endorsed by Arcand; Houde went on to become leader of the provincial Conservative party (Robin 1992:91). More important, however, Arcand was the director of publicity in Quebec for R. B. Bennett's prime ministerial campaigns in both the 1930 and 1935 elections (Robin 1992:153), a party position for which he was specifically recruited. Thus, although Arcand's beliefs did not reflect those of the Quebec mainstream, he nevertheless wielded considerable mainstream influence for a time.

Arcand died in 1967 and bequeathed an unfortunate legacy—his vast library of hate literature—to a young man, Ernst Zundel, who would later become infamous for spearheading a more contemporary variant of neo-nazism in Canada (Weimann and Winn 1986:13). Zundel has been responsible for, among other things, providing a leadership role for youth recruitment in organizations such as the Heritage Front, which espouse aggressive racialist and anti-Semitic doctrines.[11] Fascism in Canada, however, has not been limited to the neo-nazi variant. When Mussolini came to power, Italian fascism received significant support, particularly in Quebec. Mussolini's alliance with the Catholic church (enshrined in the Lateran Pact of 1929) further enhanced his appeal in predominantly Catholic Quebec. As Lita-Rose Betcherman (1975:32–33) notes, Mussolini's cause was taken up by the francophone cleric and nationalist Abbé Lionel Groulx and his followers, who suggested that "happy peoples ... have found dictators." Acceptance of Mussolini and Italian fascism was a mainstream phenomenon: "Defending the position that Fascism was good for Italy, a team of Knights of Columbus debaters at McGill defeated a visiting Oxford team. A Canadian senator contributed funds to a church in which Mussolini adorned a fresco above the altar" (Robin 1992:212). Open admiration of Mussolini declined at the outset of the war, but the extent of his early appeal in Quebec demonstrates that Canada was by no means isolated from the ideological currents that were so dramatically reshaping European society.

Although small fascist movements have arisen in Canada, they have never made sustained headway. As suggested above, this may be due to the fact that North America is predominantly liberal and individualistic, rendering appeals to radical collectivism foreign to conventional political discourse. The only hope such appeals have of acceptance is if they are cloaked in more familiar terms or emerge in more collectivist regional cultures. Certainly, racist movements have existed, and indeed continue to exist, but they have not taken on the extreme collectivism characteristic of fascism.

Any complacency over the potential appeal of fascism within North America must be treated with some caution, given that there are signs of fascism's revival elsewhere in the world. In the wake of the disintegration of the Soviet bloc, a number of movements have sought to dominate the post-communist political landscape. One particularly malignant competitor is the 70,000-member group, Pamyat ("memory"), established in the former Soviet Union in 1987 with the stated intention of founding a new czarist order to restore the medieval greatness of Russia (Griffin 1991:176). The new order, it is charged, is necessary to rectify the damage caused to Russia by "Zionism":

> Who has blackened our history and culture?... Who has been ruining the economy all this time and destroying [our] agriculture?... Who arranged the disaster at Chernobyl and made a vast region of land unusable?... We, together with the people, demand that all forces be mobilized to explain the danger Zionism represents in our country ... (cited in Griffin 1995:374–5)

Pamyat's ugly message has the potential to find a wide audience in the current turbulence of post-Soviet political culture. Russia is in the midst of tremendous upheaval, and the possibility exists for an opportunistic movement to seize on the existing cultural discontent and provide a focus, not only for its hatred, but also for its hopes: "Raise up the deepest layers of the history and culture of the Motherland! Penetrate with solicitude the people's traditions, folklore, ethos, and all the wisdom accumulated by our people and all the peoples on earth!" (Pamyat 1995:375–6). Given Russia's status as a major nuclear power, it is of particular importance that this movement be monitored with great care.

A second sign comes from recent doctrinal developments in fascist thought, developments designed to broaden and modernize its appeal. Roger Griffin's recent scholarship in the study of fascism[12] draws our attention to three particular developments. In the first, John Tyndall, a British neo-Nazi involved in the music industry, has attempted to regenerate the myth of cultural decline by referring to it as "spiritual AIDS" (1995:368). The organism, in this case the British state, is beset by a terminal disease, a disease which began with the adoption of liberalism. Thus, Tyndall argues, "Our thinking must begin with an utter rejection of liberalism and a dedication to the resurgence of authority" (1995:369). His neo-Nazi mythology suggests that although "we are confronted by a global enemy," a new breed of man is emerging, one prepared to lead the way to the new civilization, a civilization based on "the White European Race ... a cultural and above all *racial* entity" (1995:370).

While Tyndall's revisions amount to little more than a change in rhetoric, Hartwig Huber's 1989 article, "The Immortal Principle" (Griffin 1995:365–66), represents an attempt to capture existing ideological space by adopting mainstream language. Unlike virtually every other fascist or nazi ideologue, Huber is willing to accept the idea of "rights," although he suggests that existing doctrines are lacking:

"The human rights of 1789 were incomplete ... if they are to be complete ... they must include collective human rights, namely the human rights to home and identity!" (Griffin 1995:366). Ironically, Huber sees fascism as a means to *expand* the rights foundation of contemporary states. The important point to stress, however, is Huber's attempt to bring fascism within the rights-based discourse of western democratic states.

Finally, the contributions of British historical revisionist David Irving are worth examining. It would seem that the activities of a historian would be, at worst, an annoyance in the broader dynamics of ideological debate. But the importance of revisionism lies in its attempt to gain a modicum of academic credibility for neo-fascist or neo-nazi thought. It represents an aggressive attempt to crawl in from the margins of ideological space through the use of an academic discipline. Roger Griffin (1991:168) describes the revisionist method as follows: "By using sophistry and bad faith to exploit genuine problems involved in social science methodology as well as empirical gaps in the historical record ...[they] imply the benign or misunderstood nature of the Nazi project." It is important to remember, however, that Irving himself is under no illusion about the nature of the Nazi project: "My own experiences ... have converted me into the most fanatical enemy of Jewry ... what matters is not whether they are to blame, but whether or not we are obliged to put up with the Jewish yoke any longer" (Griffin 1995:338–9). The attempts to engage in historical revision represents the attempt to add more sophisticated ideological content to the neo-nazi movement and, in turn, to gain the sheen of legitimacy. Perhaps the most disturbing element in the emergence of academic neo-nazism is that, in order for it to work, it requires individuals who are willing and capable of conducting parahistorical research; this serves as a sobering reminder that hate is not the exclusive preserve of the unsophisticated.

Exercise Two: "Fascist" as Label

The terms "fascism" or "fascist" are often used as rhetorical weapons in ideological debate and political discourse. Thus we find, for example, that even mainstream and thoroughly democratic parties and individuals are dismissed as "fascists" by their political opponents. Newt Gingrich, Preston Manning and Ronald Reagan have all been tarred with the fascist brush, even though none of the three have the remotest connection with the fascist ideology described in this chapter. This raises the question as to why the fascist label is so readily used, and what it is meant to convey. Can you recall from your own experience individuals, parties or events that have been described as fascist? If so, what do you feel the label was meant to convey? Given your current understanding of the fascist ideology, do you feel the label was appropriately applied? Can you think of groups or individuals within the North American political arena which do in fact fit the label, whether it has been applied yet or not?

INTERPRETATIONS OF FASCISM AND NAZISM

Previous chapters have tried to place a variety of ideological perspectives on the conventional left-right scale. This can also be done in the case of fascism, although in doing so we lose sight of some of its most important characteristics. Figure 9.1 shows that fascism falls to the extreme collectivist end of the individualist-collectivist spectrum, a position that reflects the ideology's belief in an organic state. We have placed fascism to the left of centre along the large state–small state spectrum, although this location is open to debate. The location reflects in part corporatist, and therefore state control of the economy, the rigorous regulation of moral activity by the state and a propensity for lavish military expenditure. However, given that we have not seen fascist *governments* for some time, it is by no means clear how such governments would behave in contemporary circumstances.

FIGURE 9.1: Fascism on the Ideological Landscape

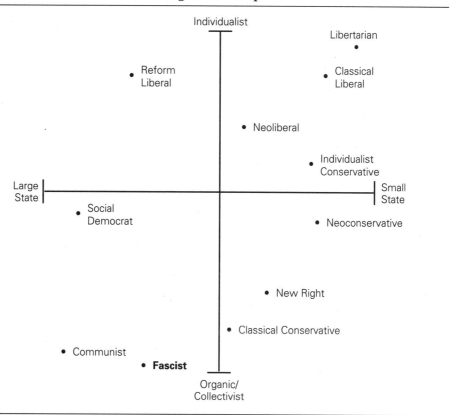

As mentioned at the outset, coming to terms with fascist ideology is both difficult and disturbing. It is not surprising, then, that a number of competing explanations have emerged, all of which seem to capture something of the essence of the movement. One school of thought suggests that fascism can best be understood as a variation of socialist philosophy, an attempt to reach socialist goals through different means. The classic articulation of this position can be found in Friedrich Hayek's *The Road to Serfdom*. Hayek (1944:29) suggests that the intellectual histories of fascism and socialism are not coincidental: "Everyone who has watched the growth of these movements in Italy or Germany has been struck by the number of leading men ... who began as socialists and ended as Fascists or Nazis." But fascism and socialism share more than just personnel. As James Gregor (1968:305) argues, "Classical

Marxism, Leninism and Fascism all share a common normic model of man, a collectivist ... conception of man that conceives the fulfillment of human personality as a function of social interaction."[13] One might ask, however, if socialism and fascism shared so many beliefs, why, in practice, did they constantly struggle against one another? Hayek (1944:29–30) offers one possible explanation:

> They competed for the same type of mind and reserved for each other the hatred of the heretic ... While to the Nazi the communist, and to the communist the Nazi, and to both the socialist, are potential recruits who are made of the right timber ... they both know that there can be no compromise between them and those who really believe in individual freedom.

The key difference between fascism and socialism, in Hayek's interpretation, is tactical rather than intellectual. Fascism and socialism are merely engaged in a factional dispute over the loyalty of the same group of followers, and over the same collectivist ideological space.

The Hayekian interpretation is persuasive in many respects. It links seemingly disparate movements by emphasizing their common antiliberalism, and it seeks to account for the fact that fascism did emerge, in personnel and thought, out of the crisis of Marxism. Indeed, both fascism and socialism share an antiliberal revolutionary spirit, and both claim to have solutions to the economic and social woes of modern life. Nevertheless, the Hayekian account is not complete. Fascism also incorporated theoretical elements which are foreign to socialist thought, even in the revised, Leninist variety: the exultation of conflict, the focus on national traditions and regeneration, and, perhaps most significant, the emphasis on spiritual, rather than economic, liberation. While the last point is still antiliberal, it is fundamentally antisocialist, as well. So, while Hayek's interpretation is sound, it does not present the entire picture.

Not surprisingly, the Marxist interpretation differs significantly from the position advanced by Hayek. The Marxist interpretation suggests that the rise of fascism represents a desperate attempt by the capitalist system to stave off its own demise at the hands of the workers. In this view, fascism is best understood as a revolt of the bourgeoisie, or as Palmiro Togliatti (1976:3) puts it, "the open dictatorship of the bourgeoisie." This dictatorship, Marxists would argue, is a hysterical attempt by the bourgeoisie to maintain power in the face of increasing worker activism, and it deploys visions of nefarious external enemies to distract the working class from their true enemies, the owners of capital. The result of this new dictatorship is mass suffering and repression in the name of capitalism. The organization of fascist societies testifies to their attempt to modify, but maintain, capitalism: "Fascism is the product of capitalist society, and for all its anti-capitalist rhetoric ... it is unwilling and unable to surpass that society" (Kitchen 1976:84).

Although the Marxist interpretation of fascism is important and widely influential, it is ultimately unpersuasive. If it were true, one might have expected to see fascism come to power in many more countries than it did; Italy and Germany were not the only countries with liberal governments and disenfranchised, active workers. More important, however, is that fascism as a phenomenon grew, at least in part, out of the crucial ruptures in Marxism. It is questionable whether, at the time of fascist ascendance, Marxism provided a coherent alternative. The only revolutionary alternative was Leninism, but workers might surely be forgiven if they did not want to replicate the experience of postrevolutionary Russia. One might suggest that the disarray of socialist theory and practice conceded vital ideological space to fascism.

A more promising approach is pursued by G. L. Mosse and Zeev Sternhell, who suggest an interpretation that sees fascism as part of a broad cultural revolt. Mosse exhorts us to remember that fascism "was the only mass movement between the wars which could claim to have a largely cross-class following" (1995: 304). Fascism, therefore, cannot be reduced simply to economic or class-based explanations; rather, it "was everywhere an 'attitude towards life', based upon a national mystique which might vary from nation to nation" (Mosse 1995:303). Specifically, the new "attitude" represented by fascist ideology was a repudiation of the ruling liberal ideology and its attendant rationalism and materialism. As Sternhell (1994:254) notes, fascism is best understood as a celebration of the violent and the irrational against the modern world, the belief that "a culture could exist based ... on the spirit of the group ... this revolt of the feelings and instincts, of energy, of the will, of primal forces, this search for new values could ensure the integrity of the community." The view of fascism as cultural revolt is useful in that it is able to account for a diverse range of influences as well as for the broad appeal of fascist ideology. While exploring this approach, however, it is vital that one does not overstate the manner in which fascism is a repudiation of modernity. Although fascism is committed to the destruction of liberal society, in its transformation of the idea of freedom, fascism is also an internal critique of modernity and an extension of its principles.

Perhaps the most general conclusion this commentary draws is that fascism is of more than historical interest. The debates it sparks have not disappeared even if our traumatic experience with fascist states steadily recedes in our collective memory. This brings us back to the outset of this chapter which noted that there was some controversy over the merits of a study such as this one. If we are correct in identifying a significant critique of liberalism in the fascist doctrine, then as serious students of political ideology, we must at least attempt to come to terms with the arguments made against our societies. And as mentioned earlier, although fascism and its variants have been successfully marginalized, they have not disappeared. Therefore, it would be a mistake not to attempt an understanding of this dark corner of ideological space.

NOTES

1. One might also note, as Sternhell does briefly, that economic critiques such as those of Bohm-Bawerk and Mises were beginning to suggest the difficulty of establishing a socialist economy.

2. The best account of Sorel and his influence on both fascist and socialist thought is found in Zeev Sternhell's *The Birth of Fascist Ideology* (Princeton: Princeton Univ. Press, 1994) 5–91.

3. It is important to note that nothing in Rocco's conception of spiritual unity implies or requires anti-Semitism. In fact, Italian fascism had numerous Jewish supporters.

4. Fascism is a totalitarian doctrine which, by its nature, must demand a monopoly on claims to truth. As such, factions within the state are considered redundant and obsolete.

5. This is not to underplay the enormous role of force used by fascist movements once in power, especially in Nazi Germany. Nevertheless, both Mussolini and Hitler enjoyed substantial electoral popularity.

6. Michael Oakeshott's conception of the *individual manqué* is especially enlightening in terms of the flight from freedom. See "The Masses in Representative Democracy" in *Rationalism in Politics* (Indianapolis: Liberty Press, 1991), especially pp. 380–91.

7. It is important to note that the rise of fascism followed Lenin's disastrous experiments with "War Communism." Indeed, Lenin's adoption of the New Economic Policy was a retreat from socialist economic principles and a move towards the accommodation of minimal market principles. For a good analysis of the failures and revisions of Leninist political economy, see Mary McAuley, *Soviet Politics 1917–1991* (Toronto: Oxford Univ. Press, 1992) 24–49.

8. Fascism, of course, suffers from a number of defects external to the doctrine, as well. The specific point here is to establish the internal difficulty which leads, in other fascist doctrines, to the adoption of anti-Semitism.

9. The relation of the Italian fascist movement to anti-Semitism is complex. In the early writings, there is no trace of it at all, and most of the evidence suggests that it was resisted in most of the fascist circles in Italy. Nevertheless, Mussolini, in a reversal of his position of only two years prior, adopted an anti-Semitic position in 1938, to the chagrin and confusion of many in Italy. See A. J. Gregor, *Contemporary Radical Ideologies: Totalitarian Thought in the Twentieth Century* (New York: Random House, 1968) 150–57.

10. The exact date of the *Protocols* is disputed, but it is generally accepted that it was developed by the czarist police in 1900. The *Protocols* have no specific author; they were supposed to convey the idea of an unnamed cabal who were planning to take over the world. Thus, their "appeal" is transnational because they have no author, but rather provide the guidebook for international chicanery.

11. The best recent discussion of contemporary neo-nazi movements in Canada is found in Warren Kinsella's *Web of Hate* (Toronto: Harper Collins, 1994).

12. See, for example, the compendium *Fascism* (New York: Oxford Univ. Press, 1995) and the treatise, *The Nature of Fascism* (London: Routledge, 1991).

13. As noted in Chapter 3, conservatives also have a collectivist vision.

CHAPTER TEN

The Radicals:
Ideologies at the Edge

WITH JODI COCKERILL

*Ideologies are harmless, uncritical, and arbitrary opinions
only as long as they are not believed in seriously.*

HANNAH ARENDT

Ideologies are fighting creeds.

MICHAEL POLANYI

In order to capture the influence of ideologies on "average North Americans," the preceding chapters have downplayed the more pernicious aspects of ideologies. Certain facts have been neglected thus far. Average North Americans do not spike trees; they do not prepare for "the coming race war" by stockpiling weapons and they do not believe motherhood is an outmoded patriarchal institution. In short, average North Americans do not take ideological convictions to their logical limits. Yet, there are those few who do, capturing both media attention and public disdain. These radicals are the subject of this chapter. They are not numerous enough to show up in public opinion surveys, and indeed may be the least likely to partake in them, but they nonetheless shed light on the ideological edge of western democratic states.

This chapter examines radicalism as a political phenomenon, both in its own right and as it relates to ideologies. The inquiry proceeds in two stages. First, it examines radical *theory*. Two real-world cases that are radical by self-definition—the deep ecology movement and the work of feminist Shulamith Firestone—are studied in this analysis of radical theory. The second stage deals with radical *action*, or radical theory put into practice. In this case, two contemporary movements, the Nation of Islam and white nationalists, are used to explore a distinctively radical style of political action.

Readers are advised to pay careful attention to the mechanisms by which radical movements convince potential adherents. Indeed, to justify extra-legal violence and to convince rational people to renounce natural self-regard in favour of a supremely important "cause" requires ingenuity. In this context, it is important to track the transitions that radicals make from rhetoric to revolution, and the logic by which radical ideologies justify illegal action. It is also important to note the tendency of radical movements towards revolutionary violence, and the strict control that revolutionary movements impose on their members. Finally, the reader is asked to observe the specific complicity of ideologies in justifying both social control and violence, even terror. Kenneth Minogue (1985:222) writes that:

> [I]deology poses an *essentially* unsoluble problem for the West. In pronouncing the rottenness of a civilization, it is actually declaring a hatred of any possible human life. What it proposes is the cosmic equivalent of a suicide pact.

An exposure to ideologies in their extreme incarnations alerts readers to the destructive potential embedded within some ideological systems. And although we may decide not to endorse Minogue's position, we must at least come to understand it.

In this chapter, "radical" refers to any *individual, group* or *theory* endorsing a political program that prescribes *immediate* and *total* social change. Endorsement, moreover, is taken to be active rather than passive. Radical movements draw support not only from an activist core but also from "fellow travellers" or sympathizers with the cause; for the purposes of this discussion, however, it is the active supporters who will be treated as radical. Activists, not fellow travellers, seek to destroy existing institutions, and only activists display the devotion, the fixity of purpose, that is characteristic of radical movements.

We also should be clear on our somewhat unconventional use of the term "movement." Four instances of radicalism will be studied, each will be referred to as a movement, but each is quite different from the other. In the 1950s and 1960s, the Nation of Islam was a single religious organization working towards explicitly articulated goals. By contrast, both white nationalists and deep ecology are much more diffuse movements involving a large number of organizations and individuals unevenly pursuing loosely convergent goals. Shulamith Firestone is not a movement at all, but a radical feminist theorist. Yet, as a representative example of the extremes of radical feminist theory, her work, *The Dialectic of Sex: The Case for Feminist Revolution* (1972), is important. In it, we find solutions that are not only astonishingly broad in scope, but also an extreme articulation of the well-known radical feminist creed, "The personal is political." As the product of an "engaged intellectual," it is a treatise filled with incitements to act, and it is this transition from theory to action that enables us to place Firestone within the broader context of radical movements. Thus, each movement examined in the chapter, whether predominantly theoretical like Firestone's work and deep ecology, or predominantly active like the Nation of Islam and white nationalists, is impelled by its logic to call for action in pursuit of its goals.

Finally, a note on why these four movements were selected as illustrative cases from the many examples of radicalism in the real world. They were chosen for two reasons. First, they are contemporary and North American. Second, each exposes us to a different facet of radicalism. In deep ecology, we see the influence of radical philosophy on the activist group Earth First! In *The Dialectic of Sex*, we see a theoretical argument pushed to the point where it becomes a call for revolutionary action. In the separatist solution of the Nation of Islam, we find evidence of the radical impulse to withdraw from established institutions. Finally, the activist rhetoric of white nationalists illustrates the radical renunciation of existing institutions, and the advocacy of violent intervention to overthrow them. The four cases, therefore, provide snapshots of a much larger, and continually changing, radical terrain. They are not the whole, but they bring aspects of the whole into sharper analytical focus.

RADICAL THEORY

Radical theories may be highly idiosyncratic and even exotic in their perspectives on the political world, but they are far from rare in the experience of western democratic states. The freedom of political expression associated with liberal democracy has created the space for a dazzling array of radical theories. It is therefore necessary to be selective in our choice of examples, although any attempt to select a *representative* sample is doomed to fail; the possible candidates span too wide a range. Our examples have been chosen because they are on the radical edge of much broader, mainstream currents of ideological thought. They are of interest because they have helped shape those broader currents, and also because they illustrate an extreme expression or extension of more conventional ideological discourse. Thus, deep ecology and the radical feminism of Shulamith Firestone bring into sharper focus some of the tenets of the larger environmentalist and feminist movements. More important, they help us understand what might happen should environmentalism or feminism be taken to their extremes.

From Radical Theory to Radical Movement: Deep Ecology

> *Passion and vision are essential, but without action they are empty.*
>
> DAVE FOREMAN

Chapter 6 introduced readers to the history of environmentalism's ideological development, and to the distinction between light green and deep green environmentalists. A brief discussion of *anthropocentrism* and *biocentrism* was also included. Recall, then, that both light and deep green environmentalists point to the earth's various degradations—overpopulation, the extinction of higher species, disappearance of pristine wilderness spaces, overconsumption of fossil fuels, ozone depletion—to justify political action. The Sierra Club, the Audubon Society, the World Wildlife Fund and other reformist environmental organizations insist that substantial improvements are required if the planet is to survive. Less moderate groups, such as Greenpeace, demand immediate action, and use flamboyant media tactics to gain public support. However, radical groups like Earth First! do not press for reform. Instead, they prepare for the imminent downfall of the human species, and seek meanwhile to thwart the "industrial machine." Their disdain for reform parallels the disdain that radical Marxists display towards the attempts by social democrats to repair the market economy; reform, adherents of Earth First! believe, can only *postpone* the system's inevitable collapse.

Therefore, although the different environmental groups all face the same crisis, their responses vary widely. That variation is interesting. Why would Earth First!ers dismiss the possibility not only of reform, but even of humanity's survival? Certainly, part of the explanation must lie in their assimilation of the facts. As explained in Chapter 6, there is disagreement as to the earth's real predicament, and Earth First!ers have sided emphatically with the debate's pessimists (Scarce 1990:x–xi). Yet, their pessimism does not explain the zeal with which they seek to subvert industrialism. Earth First!ers are predominantly *activists*, and their activism is inspired by the radical philosophy called "deep ecology."

A philosophical system conceived in the 1960s, deep ecology questions western civilization's anthropocentric (human-centred) conception of reality. Deep ecologists assert that citizens in contemporary western democratic states suffer from an existential crisis due to the distorting influence of anthropocentrism. Chellis Glendinning (1995:37) explains, "In Western culture, we live with chronic anxiety, anger, and a sense that something essential is missing from our lives, that we exist without a soul. What could be wrong?" For deep ecologists, the source of our predicament is the systemic separation of our lives from nature. The trappings of modern life—industry, technology, the media and consumerism—have served progressively to divorce the human species from its natural habitat. For both humans and nature, the result has been catastrophic. Mindless of our biological heritage, we have gravely misused the planet. According to deep ecologists, environmental and spiritual recovery requires a "paradigm shift" to a biocentric conception of existence. Deep ecologist and theologian Thomas Berry (Sessions 1995:11,15) draws from this conclusion in calling for a massive rejection of the anthropomorphic mind-set: "The earth as a bio-spiritual planet must become, for the human, the basic reference in identifying what is real and what is worthwhile.... In a new context, the primary educator as well as the primary lawgiver and the primary healer would be the natural world itself." Attuned to the patterns and rhythms of the universe, humans would no longer overconsume or pollute the biosphere. A world-scale paradigm shift would spontaneously solve the light greens' environmental crisis, for it would entail a dramatic realignment from environmentally destructive practices to harmonious living within a biocentric conception of the universe.

At first glance, deep ecology does not seem a likely source of inspiration for the eco-warrior. Although its call for a dramatic reorientation is radical, its emphasis on attunement to cosmic wonder and on the abandonment of our illusions of control over nature, endow it with a mystical quality. Yet, as Martha Lee (1992:11) indicates, deep ecology "demands a reordering of the world," and as such lends itself to the formation of a radical ideology and the pursuit of radical action. The theory clearly indicates the culprit: industrial society—"the plundering processes of the commercial industrial economy" (Hope and Young, 1994:2). Deep ecologists also emphasize the very high stakes involved. Berry (Hope and Young, 1994:2) explains that "never before has the human community been confronted with a situation that required such sudden and total change in life style under the threat of a comprehensive degradation of the planet." In response to this threat, Berry (Zimmerman, 1993:166) calls for "contained vigour of action," and more dramatically, a "reinvent[ion] of the human at the species level." In 1984, Arne Naess and George Sessions moved this philosophical discussion closer to activism by devising a deep ecology platform. Naess's and Sessions's opinions (Sessions 1995:68) that "the flourishing of human life and cultures is compatible with a substantial decrease in human population," that "present human interference with the nonhuman world is excessive," and finally, that "those who subscribe to the foregoing points have an obligation directly or indirectly to try to implement the necessary changes," mark significant steps towards an activist position. As Naess (Sessions 1995:154) himself has submitted:

[T]here are political potentials in this movement which should not be overlooked and which have little to do with pollution and resource depletion. In plotting possible futures, the norms should be freely used and elaborated.

As if in answer to the deep ecologists' call for action, Earth First! was founded in 1980 as a radical alternative to the perceived complacency of mainstream environmental organizations such as the Sierra Club. Earth First!'s slogan—No Compromise in Defense of Mother Earth!—set forth its agenda for the period preceding the imminent demise of industrial society. (The slogan was an intriguing echo of conservative Republican presidential nominee Barry Goldwater's slogan in the 1964 election—"Extremism in Defence of Liberty is No Vice.") "Don't reform," offered Dave Foreman (1991:145), the group's cofounder, "thwart." In the years following the group's founding, Earth First!ers encouraged like-minded radicals to engage in ecotage, or "monkey-wrenching" the industrial machine, on the earth's behalf. According to Foreman (1991:50), ecotage is justified as damage control, "until the machine plows into that brick wall and industrial civilization self-destructs as it must." Clearly, Foreman has accepted deep ecology's assertions that the destruction of western society is imminent, and that industrial civilization is to blame for that destruction.

The Choice

"Smokestacks, strip mines, clearcuts for crackerbox homes, DDT in penguin fat, topsoil eroding to the sea, whale meat on Japanese plates, spotted cat hides on vain rich humans, rhino-horn dagger handles on Yemeni belts, nearly four thousand million years of beauty, diversity, and life chewed up in the space of a human generation or two.

Or goose music, ancient conifer forests, spouting whales, rich complex tropical rain forests, elephants and rhinos and lions, coral reefs, howling wolves, clean air and clean water, nearly four thousand million years of beauty, diversity, and life sailing on through the blackness of space for another four billion years.

The Machine.

Or Life."

Dave Foreman, *Confessions of an Eco-Warrior* (New York: Harmony Books, 1991) 147.

The Earth First! program offered an activist solution to the problems set out in deep ecology theory. It also provided environmentalists with a heroic archetype, the "eco-warrior." A solitary wanderer, the eco-warrior dedicates his life to preservation of the earth. Frequently destitute, he performs his work with stealth, selflessness and a resolute single-mindedness.[1] Edward Abbey (1990:111) explains the eco-warrior's role in *Hayduke Lives!*, a novel based loosely on the Earth First! movement: "The point of his work is to increase *their* costs, nudge them toward net loss, bankruptcy, forcing them to withdraw and retreat from their invasion of our public lands, or wilderness, our native and primordial home."[2] To this end, the eco-warrior subverts the machine. He destroys industrial machinery, pulls up survey stakes, places metal spikes in trees in order to discourage logging and dreams of blowing up dams. He is indeed a warrior, in a battle "for life itself, for the continued flow of evolution" (Foreman 1991:2). Humanity is an ecological disaster, and the sooner it is destroyed, the better for the earth.

Exercise One: Ideological Extremism

To understand how radicals can come to hold extreme beliefs, we need to start at the beginning: the premises upon which their beliefs are based. Consider deep ecology, and imagine you strongly believe in two of its central premises: 1) protecting the ecology is of primary importance; and 2) humans are an ecological disaster. These two beliefs, taken together, lead you to promote ecological interests above human needs. What, then, will be your attitude towards population control? Abortion? Towards such conventionally conceived disasters as famine, plagues, AIDS, and the mass destruction of human life in war? Will these be seen as positive steps in ensuring the earth's survival? Will your premises lead you to promote the end of the human species?

Now imagine defending your views in public. Would a strong negative reaction lead you to reconsider your premises, or would it strengthen your resolve? Can a person who sees the world in black and white be persuaded to see shades of grey? Can extreme beliefs be moderately held, or are moderately held extreme beliefs rapidly abandoned in the face of social pressure to do so?

Earth First!ers openly acknowledge their inspiration both by deep ecology and the novels of Edward Abbey. Yet, as Dave Foreman (1991:25) indicates, Earth First!ers are activists, not philosophers: "Our actions set the finer points of our philosophy." As for the deep ecologists, their gentle indulgence of Earth First!'s tactics is telling. Berry (1995:17) writes of Earth First! that:

> [T]hese are daring ventures that dramatize the stark reality of the situation .... That such tactics ... are needed to force humans to examine and question our behaviour is itself evidence of how deep a change is needed in human consciousness.

So it is that the distinction between radical theory and radical action begins to break down; "Subvert the Dominant Paradigm" is transformed from a deep ecologist's imperative to a slogan scrawled on posterboard, and finally, to an act of ecotage.

The "Engaged Intellectual": Shulamith Firestone

Chapter 5 introduced readers to feminist ideology, including radical feminism. Recall that radical feminists (but not liberal or Marxist feminists) agree that a structure of male domination called "patriarchy" exists, and that it is undesirable. In fact, it is the belief in the centrality of patriarchy that most clearly demarcates radical feminism from other branches of feminism. Radical feminists maintain that patriarchy controls not only formal political institutions, but also personal spheres of family and sexuality. Moreover, they contend that if women are to be emancipated from male domination, if true sexual equality is to be achieved, then patriarchy must be ripped out at its root.

This chapter does not aim to restate the radical feminist ideas presented in Chapter 5, but to examine the ideas of a particularly extreme feminist theorist, Shulamith Firestone, a self-declared radical and a cofounder of the Women's Liberation Movement in the late 1960s. In 1972, she wrote a definitive expression of revolutionary feminism, *The Dialectic of Sex: The Case for Feminist Revolution*, which represents an impassioned incitement to revolution, and serves as an example of the extremes of radical feminism.

From the outset, Firestone's criticism is far-reaching. She tells us (1972:2) that feminists "have to question, not just all of *Western* culture, but the organization of culture itself, and further, even the very organization of nature." In doing so, radical feminists discover that not only politics and culture, but biology also has ensured women's enslavement by men. The structure of present-day society, Firestone asserts, is solidly based on women's biological function as childbearers. She traces the institutions of labour division, family, motherhood and sexuality to their basis in women's biology, and then proceeds to censure those institutions. Although they may be natural, they are nevertheless exploitative, and therefore they must be eradicated if women are finally to gain freedom. Whereas deep ecologists embrace the natural order, Firestone emphatically rejects it.

How does the dissatisfied radical feminist escape the seemingly fixed impositions of nature? Fortunately for women, "[H]umanity has begun to outgrow nature: we can no longer justify the maintenance of a discriminatory sex class system on grounds of its origins in Nature" (Firestone 1972:10). Firestone offers the solutions of revolution, on the one hand, and of science, on the other. New reproductive technologies might soon erase the necessity for women to bear children. "Pregnancy is barbaric," she asserts, and recommends use of both contraceptive and artificial reproduction techniques (implantation of human fetuses in "carrier" mammals) as correctives to nature's intrusions. With the proper technology in the proper hands, women's salvation from their biology is realizable. As Firestone (1972:211) maintains, "Man's difficult triumph over Nature has made it possible to restore the truly natural: he could undo Adam's and Eve's curse to reestablish the earthly Garden of Eden."

Yet, undoing the curse requires the means to undo it. Unless technological tools are placed in the feminist's hands, technology is of no use. At present, Firestone explains, political power rests with male-dominated institutions. Thus, the appropriate antidote is to destroy those institutions. Certainly, the timing is right, as women now have everything to gain by controlling reproductive technologies: "[F]or the first time in some countries, the preconditions for feminist revolution exist—indeed, the situation is beginning to *demand* such a revolution" (Firestone 1972:1). Because of women's unique position in society—their numerical strength and their physical proximity to men—Firestone is confident that a feminist revolution would succeed. And when it does, "[it] will crack through the most basic structures of our society" (1972:38). Even familial ties would be eradicated: "For unless revolution uproots the basic social organization, the biological family—the vinculum through which the psychology of power can always be smuggled—the tapeworm of exploitation will never be annihilated" (1972:12).

What does Firestone perceive to be the outcome of these radical transformations? First, it would be the freeing of women from "the tyranny of their reproductive biology," the gradual obsolescence of parents' bonds with their biological children and the assignment to society as a whole the role of child-rearer (1972: 206–9). Second, it would be economic self-determination for women and children, entailing the realization of a vaguely articulated "cybernetic socialism." Third, it would be the dissolution of mistaken cultural notions of "motherhood" and "childhood," and the total integration of women and children into larger society. Finally, it would be the unrestricted sexual freedom of women and children, and the promotion of loosely defined group marriages.

Firestone's brand of radical feminism promises a revolution in every aspect of existence; as she herself suggests (1972:1), "[I]f there were another word more all-embracing than *revolution* we would use it." However, many feminists would likely refuse to consider this far-reaching solution to patriarchal injustices. Indeed, in achieving the goal of women's liberation set out by feminist ideology, a feminist's response depends largely on her temperament. Liberal feminists want to reform the system; radicals prefer to demolish and reconstruct. But how do such different positions arise from one ideology? In Chapter 5, it was suggested that all branches of feminism agree that sex is an important variable in politics and society, that sex, in effect, acts as a significant class division. (Marxist feminists do not see it as *the* most significant class division.) From this central assumption of feminism, others follow. Pointing out a class-based structure of oppression begs the question of who is the oppressor; radical feminists argue that the oppressor is patriarchy, and that patriarchal oppression is undesirable. Rooting out patriarchy once and for all requires the conscientious radical feminist to dig deep, as Firestone demonstrates.

On Becoming Conscious: The "Hooks" of Radical Theory

Although the internal logic of deep ecology and Shulamith Firestone's radical feminism may be clear, the source of their appeal and influence is less clear. What, then, are the "hooks" consciously used by radical theorists to persuade individuals to form an active, cohesive social movement? Here, Eric Voegelin (1975:127) submits that the political intellectual uses a "catalogue of techniques" aimed at "undermining the authority of institutions and transforming bewildered individuals into a disoriented mass." To this end, radical theorists provide explanations of evil, along with opportunities to raise one's consciousness and theories of historical inevitability.

Beginning in the seventeenth century, critics have noted the aspirations of ideologues to explain evil; and in doing so, to reject existing theological explanations in favour of secular ones. As such, according to Kenneth Minogue (1985:42), ideologies claim their theories are "unusually deep or radical form[s] of criticism." The examples set out in this chapter thus far support Minogue's observation; both deep ecology and Firestone's radical feminism cast their disparaging net over the entire history of western culture. By the very extent of their ambitions, these theories are required to cast wide. A theory seeking to explain evil must start at the beginning, and then explain every instance of abuse throughout human history. Thus, we are led to a second feature of ideological explanation: its propensity to identify "structures." In order for the world's injustices to have had a single cause, the cause must be systemic. The source of women's domination, for example, cannot be traced to individual actors, such as Napoleon, although he may have unwittingly supported a looming, omnipresent patriarchal structure. Similarly, for deep ecologists, the ultimate source of our current ecological crisis cannot be Exxon. Rather, Exxon is portrayed as a single instance of a pernicious, deeply entrenched structure called "industrial society"; it is symptomatic, not causal. "Ideological explanation," concludes Kenneth Minogue (1985: 70), "thus consists in a game of 'hunt the structure.'"

And so, a picture of ideological theory emerges. For ideologues, the source of evil is structural, global and historical. Moreover, it is *identifiable*. Indeed, the source identified, rather than the style of argument, distinguishes one ideology from the next. For radical feminists, it is patriarchy; for deep ecologists, it is a destructive anthropocentric mind-set shared by all industrial societies. We soon will see that for the Nation of Islam, the source of evil is the white race, and for white nationalists, it is Jews. For each movement, though, the nature of the evil is the same; it is total, structural and pervasive.

Yet, there remains a troublesome problem: clearly, not everyone accepts that patriarchy, or humanity, or Jews, or whites, are evil. Such skepticism, when held by fellow members of an "oppressed class," can pose a serious problem for the radical theorist. However, there are devices by which the problem of nonidentification can be circumvented. It can be argued that a true knowledge of the world requires a special sort of awareness. According to ideological theory, that awareness is a raised consciousness. "To be a feminist," submits radical feminist Sandra Bartky (1990:11), "one first has to become one." Without the essential conversion experience, women will never recognize patriarchy, and light green environmentalists will not realize that the economic system within which they operate is fundamentally flawed. With conversion, social reality is "revealed as *deceptive*" (Bartky 1990:17). From this vantage point, Bartky argues, features of social reality are apprehended *as* contradictory, in conflict with one another or disturbingly out of sync with one another (1990:14–15). But outside this vantage point, one does not see the deception. The radical ideological thinker, therefore, offers us the lens of a raised consciousness, a lens that enables us to see structures of oppression which were invisible before. No longer are restrictions on access to birth control, economic differences between blacks and whites and environmental degradation simply widespread and lamentable abuses; rather, they are evidence of the structural imperfection of our current social reality.

Having identified the source of evil, and having attributed the skepticism of non-adherents to the lack of a raised consciousness, the ideology has only to indicate a solution. This step is essential; without conveying the news that change is possible, political action cannot be generated. By its claim that change is not only possible but inevitable, ideological theory does one better. Historical forces that once had sided with the dominant structure finally have turned against it. The structure is cracking, ideologues argue, and the role of the theorist is merely to bring this new reality to our attention (Arendt 1966:469). In this regard, both radical feminism and deep ecology show a predictable commitment to the inevitable end of the dominant structure. Frijtov Capra (1995:24–5), for example, reflects upon the demise of the anthropomorphic paradigm:

> [B]eing based on a framework of concepts and values that is no longer viable, today's dominant culture will inevitably decline and will eventually disintegrate. The cultural forces representing the new paradigm, on the other hand, will continue to rise and, eventually, will assume the leading role.

Ideologies organize facts in such a way that action is demanded, but moderates and radicals disagree about the type of action required to execute ideological imperatives. Moderates seek to save the structure by reforming it. Derisive of the reformers' faintheartedness, radicals seek to topple the structure altogether, maintaining that, at this critical juncture, the whole edifice will collapse with one push. This, in turn, can lead to support for revolutionary violence. James Billington (1980: 25) explains:

> Violence was part of what revolutionaries sought—and was in many ways their ultimate
> form of radical simplification. A thousand hopes and hatreds could be compressed
> into a single act of blood ritual, transforming *philosophes* into *revolutionnaires* .... The
> mark of blood distinguishes real revolution from mythic melodrama about the
> storming of a Bastille or a Winter Palace.

Radical theory therefore plays an important role in creating a radical social
movement. The potential convert is first informed that the world is dominated by a structural evil, the perception of which requires a raised consciousness. She is then told
that political action can eliminate the evil. History is on her side and the toppling of
the structure is inevitable. The ideology comes equipped with an iron-clad logic, and
the pressures to assent to that logic are high. As Hannah Arendt (1966:469–70)
points out: "The purely negative coercion of logic, the prohibition of contradictions,
became 'productive' so that a whole line of thought could be initiated, and forced
upon the mind, by drawing conclusions in the manner of mere argumentation."

RADICAL ACTION: THE NATIONALISMS OF BLACK AND WHITE

The potential for radical, even revolutionary, action brings us to the second pair of
case studies: the Nation of Islam and white nationalism. Despite emphatic appearances to the contrary, the two share certain characteristics which, in turn, help us
illuminate more general features of ideologically induced radicalism. First, both
arose within a political context in which integration was officially endorsed as a goal
of government action. As a result, both groups perceive the existence of a massive,
structural threat to their racial identity. Second, both movements are racist, and their
racism is based on a particular set of political and religious beliefs. Finally, both have
opted out of existing political arrangements, and have fastened upon nationalist ideologies as the most practical means of maintaining racial purity.

The Option of Withdrawal: The Nation of Islam

The 1960s was an explosive era in American domestic politics. Cultural unrest was
widespread among young Americans, protest over the Vietnam War and the military
draft was growing and the national society was subjected to increasingly barbed criticisms from feminists, environmentalists and the New Left. But, if there was a single
dominant issue, it was race. And here there appeared to be a consensual solution to
racial divisions, a solution to be found in the racial-integration philosophy of the civil
rights movement. Integration, however, was not without its critics, some of whom
were to be found within the black community.

In opposition to the growing consensus for racial integration, a calm yet insis-
tent voice called for the opposite solution: territorial separation. "We are a Nation
in a nation," asserted Elijah Muhammad, leader of the Nation of Islam:

> To integrate with Evil is to be destroyed with evil. What we want—indeed, justice for
> us is to be set apart. We want, and must insist upon an area in this land that we can
> call our own, somewhere [where] we can hold our heads [up] with pride and dig-
> nity without the continued harassments and indignities of our oppressors (Lincoln
> 1973:100).

For Muhammad and his followers, American society was both evil and oppressive. Justice for blacks, therefore, required territorial separation, and anything short of that would invite spiritual destruction.

How did the Nation of Islam acquire its views? Undoubtedly, part of the explanation is sociological. C. Eric Lincoln observes (1973) that blacks, from the collective experience of slavery, acquired "an appalling sense of inferiority and even of hatred for their 'Negro-ness.'" Due to the persistence of racial prejudice in American society, black racial consciousness was imposed from without as much as it was discovered within. Yet, where many black leaders such as Martin Luther King Jr. sought to end alienation from American society, the Nation of Islam worked to heighten it. To this end, it censured integration as yet another ploy devised by "White America" to keep blacks enslaved. Muslim ministers chided "integration-mad Negroes" for contentedly eating the crumbs from the tables of whites. In his autobiography, the Black Muslims' best-known spokesman, Malcolm X (1965:344), pointed out the "facts" of blacks' existence in America:

> Twenty-two million black men! They have given America four hundred years of toil; they have bled and died in every battle since the revolution; they were in America before the Pilgrim and long before the mass immigrations—and they are still today at the bottom of everything.

Thus, the Nation of Islam offered an expressive vehicle for blacks' continuing resentment of existing social, economic and political arrangements, and an ideological explanation for those arrangements. Yet, to classify the group only as a response to the social context of the 1960s would be misleading. On the contrary, it was a *movement*, animated by its own doctrines and leaders. Accordingly, an adequate acquaintance with the Nation of Islam requires some discussion of its core beliefs.

Established in the 1930s, the Nation of Islam gained sudden prominence in the 1960s as a religious and political movement promoting black race pride (Lincoln 1973:xxxi). According to the teachings of the Prophet W. D. Fard and later, the Prophet Elijah Muhammad, the "so-called Negro" in America had lost his identity. He had been brainwashed by white society into believing himself to be inferior. Yet, the Prophets argued, America's blacks were not inferior. Rather, theirs had been the superior race since the beginning of time. In *The Message to the Blackman in America*, Muhammad offered the Myth of Yakub as an explanation of blacks' superiority and whites' oppression. According to the myth, the white race had been the product of genetic experiments conducted long ago by the dissatisfied black scientist, Yakub. Seeking to destroy his own race, Yakub leached color from his experimental subjects to create whites—physically pale and morally anemic mutations. The aim of this envious new race of "devils" was to destroy the world's superior nonwhite populations (Muhammad 1965:110). After 6,600 years, this project had almost succeeded; as part of Allah's divine plan, whites had come to dominate the entire world. Very soon, though, the devil race would fall. Muhammad's religious prophecies foretold the "Fall of America," including the return of America's blacks to Islam, "the natural religion of the Black Man" (Lincoln 1973:xxv), and the destruction of the Caucasian devils by Allah. According to the teachings of the Nation of Islam, the white race and its harmful Christianity soon would be destroyed (Lee 1987:55–58).

In the meantime, Black Muslims believed that they were surrounded by their natural enemies. Thus territorial separation, the allocation of "some of this good earth" to the black race, was considered the ideal interim solution to removing blacks from the corrupting influence of whites. Racial mythology was thereby harnessed to the ideological appeal of nationalism. Predictably, however, the territorial solution was not well received by most Americans (Essien-Udom 1963:261). As a second, albeit less desirable, choice, Black Muslim ministers advocated a spiritual, social and economic withdrawal from America. Collusion with the "white devil" establishment was forbidden and contact was to be minimized. Black Muslims were advised not to participate in local or national politics, not to integrate or intermarry, not to purchase goods from whites and not to fill their ears with the brainwashing Christian religion (Essien-Udom 1963:264). They were instructed to obey civil authorities, but only to the barest extent required by law (Essien-Udom 1963:267). Finally, and reflecting the faith that "Allah in His own good time takes the devil off our planet" (Essien-Udom 1963:149), they were instructed to be patient. In the end, the ultimate solution to their race's predicament was a matter of faith, not of politics.

This final stipulation proved politically significant. Because of it, a movement with the potential to grow violent remained passive. "You plead to politics," chided Elijah Muhammad:

> I want to say to you this afternoon politics will not answer your prayers .... Politics will not solve the problem of the Negroes any more than it did for the Hebrews of Israel in Egypt (Essien-Udom 1963:257).

Although the Nation of Islam possessed all the characteristics of a radical movement, and although its demands for land had not been met, the option of revolutionary violence was rejected.[3] Significantly, however, the source of Black Muslims' restraint was a commitment to Allah, not to the American polity. It should also be stressed that passive withdrawal in the face of the integrationist call of the civil rights movement, and in the face of continual harassment from white society, required an iron will. In this sense, passivity can best be seen as a form of radical action.

Although the origins of the Nation of Islam are found in the circumstances of the United States in the mid- to late-1960s, the Black Muslims did not disappear as those circumstances changed. The dream fostered by the civil rights movement of racial integration and equality has been a partial success at best, and the Black Muslims continue to appeal to many who have rejected that dream, or who have been passed over in its pursuit. Nation of Islam leader Louis Farrakhan organized the October 16, 1995, Million Man March in Washington, D.C., an event in which hundreds of thousands of black men rallied in support of racial pride. (Black women were requested by Farrakhan to observe the day by staying home.) It was the largest black rally since Martin Luther King Jr.'s March on Washington during the height of the civil rights movement, and may indeed be the largest ever. The march was billed by Farrakhan as a Day of Atonement for black men who had failed in their responsibility to black women and children.

Farrakhan has been an extremely controversial leader. As we have seen, many aspects of the Black Muslim doctrine are very controversial, and Minister Farrakhan is an adamant and forceful proponent of that doctrine. Farrakhan has been unrepentant in his anti-white and anti-Jewish views, a position that for a long time isolated him from the American mainstream—both black and white—and drove wedges between the black community and some of its traditional political allies. That situation, however, may be changing. In some important ways, Farrakhan and the Black

Muslims are in line with contemporary ideological currents. Like classical liberals and neoconservatives, they advocate self-reliance, business entrepreneurship and the end of the welfare state. While their advocacy of black separatism puts them in an ideological camp all their own, it is no longer an isolated camp. As Jonathan Fredland (1995:A8) observes, even though Farrakhan has not moderated his message of black racism, separatism or anti-Semitism, "the mainstream has come to him." Fredland concludes that "people are wary because Farrakhan cannot be written off as some racist demagogue on the fringes. Instead he is a racist demagogue at the heart of black American life" (1995:A8).

The Revolutionary Option: White Nationalists

In the 1960s, opposition to racial integration, of course, was not restricted to Black Muslims. It also flared up among many whites. A particularly virulent response assumed the garb of white nationalism, and pulled into its orbit not only long-standing racial hostility to the aspirations of blacks, but also equally long-standing anti-Semitism. Whether neo-Nazis or skinheads, members of the Ku Klux Klan or the Aryan Nations, the Heritage Front or Posse Comitatus, white nationalists subscribe to certain tenets that set their movement outside the realm of legitimate political action.

Just as Black Muslims rejected racial integration in the 1960s, today's white nationalists reject the ongoing affirmative action and multiculturalism programs implemented in the 1970s. For white nationalists, affirmative action is "state-sanctioned discrimination against whites," while current levels of non-European immigration and multiculturalism policies mark deliberate attempts by the government to dilute the white race. In Canada, white nationalists contrast the government's tolerance of aboriginal militancy with its labelling of groups such as the Heritage Front as hate organizations. One contributor to *Up Front*, the Heritage Front's national newsletter offered that "[i]f any group within our society currently has a beef with negative stereotyping and its destructive impact it is the White race" (October 1992:16).

White Nationalists and Conservative Ideological Thought: A Comparison

Both white nationalists and many contemporary conservatives oppose official multiculturalism, current levels of immigration and what is perceived to be the excessive influence of government in citizens' lives. Both conservatives (particularly the "religious right") and white nationalists also tend to oppose abortion and gun control. Yet, despite this policy congruence, the reasons behind similar policy positions differ for each group. Many conservatives are likely to oppose abortion for strictly moral reasons. White nationalists, on the other hand, believe it is whites' duty to propagate the race; thus, their opposition to abortion is based on racist assumptions. Similarly, while many conservatives object to gun control legislation because they believe it represents an unwarranted intrusion by government, many white nationalists oppose it because they believe they will need their weapons for the upcoming race war. Where conservatives oppose official multiculturalism because they believe it constitutes an unwarranted intrusion into the private sphere, white nationalists oppose it because they believe it offends their basic assumption that races should not be mixed. Thus, some conservatives may share policy positions with white nationalists, yet reject white nationalist ideology.

Who do white nationalists see as responsible for this unwarranted persecution? On this issue, they are in an awkward position, one that radical feminists and Black Muslims do not face. In support of their claims of system oppression, radical feminists and Black Muslims can point to concrete evidence of historical abuses, as well as to underrepresentation in existing institutions. White nationalists cannot point to similar abuses, and whites are well represented in political and economic institutions. So, when faced with why whites seek to oppress themselves, white nationalists assert that most whites lack race pride and a genuine understanding of the world. If whites truly understood, they argue, if their racial consciousness were raised, they would see their control of political and economic institutions is illusory. Rather, white nationalists claim, such institutions are controlled by the Zionist Occupation Government (ZOG) (Barkun 1994:111). Thus, for the Heritage Front and similar organizations, the cause of whites' present indignities has been historically the same: namely, the Jewish race. Therefore, the basket of conspiracy theories long associated with anti-Semitism is brought into play to explain the seemingly paradoxical oppression of the white majority.

The white nationalist belief in the existence of a worldwide, historical conspiracy of Jews finds expression in the major tenets of a politico-religious doctrine called Christian Identity. According to Michael Barkun (1990:132), Christian Identity provides the white nationalist movement with "a philosophical centre of gravity, explicitly or implicitly acknowledged even by those not immediately identifiable as Identity believers." Loosely based upon a nineteenth-century religious movement called British Israelism, Christian Identity holds that Jews are the devil's offspring; they caused the Fall in the Garden of Eden, and have since been the source of evil in the world. In politics, religion and economics, Jews are seen to have persistently conspired to destroy the white race (Barkun 1994:115–117). This conspiracy theory is not new to white nationalists, nor, for that matter, was it new to British Israelism; it taps a deeply rooted and virulent anti-Semitism that goes back to the time of the Crusades.

As far as white nationalists are concerned, evidence of a Jewish conspiracy is everywhere. By the accounts of such groups as the Heritage Front in Canada, and the Aryan Nations in the United States, Jews are vastly overrepresented in the "establishment"—especially in financial institutions and the media. Domestic politicians are portrayed as puppets of Jewish financiers; the "Jewish lobby" is seen to wheedle massive funding for Israel; and the Jewish media silences those brave enough to speak the "truth" of the Holocaust hoax (*Up Front,* Oct. 1992:15). Worse still, in the eyes of white nationalists, ZOG also controls international organizations like the United Nations.

Not surprisingly, a movement that believes the establishment is controlled by the devil's offspring is not going to trust its government. Indeed, the central beliefs of white nationalists leave them in a position similar to that of Black Muslims. As Michael Barkun explains (1994:24), in their case "every action of the government is seen as sinister, duplicitous and illegitimate." Like the Nation of Islam, white supremacists have advocated physical separation as the only viable solution to the race problem. They seek a "White American Bastion" encompassing the northwest United States and parts of southwestern Canada. This "territorial imperative" was first proposed in 1974 by Richard Girnt Butler, founder of the Aryan Nations, and has since gained steadily in popularity among white racists (Barkun 1994:233).

Ideologies and the Second Coming

In the cases of both the Black Muslims and white nationalists, adherents display a pre-occupation with an imminent apocalypse. The same observation holds to a degree for deep ecologists and radical feminists; although framed in more secular language, each of the latter posits the imminent coming of a decisive catastrophic event: the collapse of industrial society and the overthrow of patriarchy.

The connection between political activism, on the one hand, and religious prophecies of apocalypse and redemption, on the other, has been noted in this century by several scholars. According to such writers as Norman Cohn (*The Pursuit of the Millennium*), Eric Voegelin (*The New Science of Politics*) and Michael Barkun (*Disaster and the Millennium*), the apocalyptic prophecies of many modern radical movements can be attributed largely to western civilization's Christian heritage. These writers have noted the resemblance between modern radical movements and older, more overtly Christian ones. In his landmark study of European apocalyptic movements in the Middle Ages, Cohn submits that radicalism's millenarian style has been evident since the thirteenth century. Similarly, in *The Revolution of the Saints*, Michael Walzer analyzes England's seventeenth-century Puritans as an early instance of radical politics.

To support their observations, Cohn and Walzer point to certain similarities between earlier Christian "millenarian movements" and contemporary ones. Each variety displays similar assumptions. According to Cohn (1970:21), the "millenarian paradigm" holds that "[t]he world is dominated by an evil, tyrannous power of boundless destructiveness—a power moreover which is imagined not as simply human but as demonic." In anticipation of the imminent Second Coming of Christ, millenarian religious movements waited in anxious hope for a millennium in which suffering would be eradicated, the earth would be returned once again to the righteous, and the Kingdom of God on Earth would be restored. The parallels between the basic assumptions of earlier millenarian movements and our four contemporary examples are clear. Indeed, they may shed light on the quasi-religious tones and utterances of the movements' spokespeople. If these authors are correct, then the radical ideological style predates even the coining of the word "ideology" in the eighteenth century. Furthermore, their work suggests that the study of the revolutionary content of Christianity might be a useful undertaking for students of political science.

In pursuit of their objectives, white nationalists have opted for extra-legal activity to a much greater extent than Black Muslims. This difference stems partly from economics. The discipline imposed by the Black Muslim religion encouraged not only race pride but also economic self-sufficiency. Paradoxically, for all its radical doctrines, the Nation of Islam encouraged the adoption of "middle-class values." Indeed, it was so successful in this respect that the movement had to struggle in the 1970s and 1980s with the tendency of its well-to-do members to identify with the economic institutions that were presumably oppressing them. This fortunate coincidence of radical doctrine with economic success does not hold for the Aryan warrior. Frequently impoverished and ostracized as a result of his beliefs, the white nationalist has no stake in the system. Although there have been limited attempts to influence "the system" by legitimate electoral means,[4] most of the movement's rhetoric professes to seek total, violent destruction of the existing order (Barkun 1994:239–41).

Along with the white nationalists' perception that the dominant society has rejected them is their expectation of an inevitable and imminent race war during which racial groups will confront and eliminate each other. The concept of the race war is central to Christian Identity beliefs, and is crucial to an understanding of white nationalists' palpable anxiety about the future of their race. Optimistic adherents of Christian Identity assert that the Nordic race will triumph, and good will prevail over evil. But even optimists believe that a period of tribulation, of acute white suffering, will precede victory (Barkun 1990:130). Worse still, white nationalists believe that without supreme preparedness, a triumph might not come at all due to the enemy's diabolical cleverness. As Barkun (1990:134) observes, "Identity teeters, therefore, on the edge of despair, committed to an inevitable new order but not always certain that it really is inevitable."

Christian Identity's ambivalence on the issue of the survival of the white race has important strategic consequences. In contrast to the Black Muslim movement, adherents of white nationalism actively prepare for war, rather than simply wait for an inevitable victory. Arms must be stockpiled, training must be conducted and committed Aryan warriors must be recruited. In addition, and in contrast to the urban-based Black Muslims, many white nationalists advocate a return to the land and the pursuit of a simple, uncorrupted lifestyle free of ZOG's pernicious influence (Barkun 1990:136). At this critical juncture, they believe, a sufficient number of committed Aryan warriors could well shape the history of the white race. Such an atmosphere lends itself to the creation of martyrs, and to a preoccupation with violence as the means to ensure the survival of the white race.

From Theory Into Practice: The Radical Style

> With a match one has no need of a lever;
> one does not lift up the world, one burns it.
>
> CLAUDE-FRANCOIS MALET

The previous section discussed some of the theoretical hooks by which individuals are drawn to acknowledge the necessity for radical action. This section discusses action itself. However, some reservations apply here. Obviously, the specific doctrines inspiring adherents of our four case studies differ substantially, and for the actors themselves this point is crucial. An eco-warrior is not a radical feminist, and a Black Muslim is not an Aryan warrior. Moreover, although the doctrines of the four movements do not necessarily imply revolutionary bloodshed, their practice may lead to violence. But on this score, the movements are seldom explicit. For example, due to the strength of their faith in Allah's coming, Black Muslims refuse to arrogate His work by bringing on the apocalypse themselves. Shulamith Firestone refers freely to the impending sex revolution, yet is sketchy on practical details. Similarly, deep ecologists call for a drastic reduction of the human population, but provide little guidance as to how that reduction should be achieved. Indeed, only the white nationalist movement articulates a practical plan for a race revolution. In this respect, dedicated Aryan Warriors acknowledge being inspired and advised by *The Turner Diaries* (1980), a detailed revolutionary tale written by William Pierce that called for massive violence in the pursuit of nationalist objectives.

As we have seen, the newly converted radical must first gain a raised consciousness. Finally stripped of illusions about the world, she has been reborn as an eco-warrior, a radical feminist, Black Muslim or Aryan Christian. Very soon, however, she comes to encounter resistance. Not only are her former associates dismayed by the extent of her rapid transformation, she often finds herself rebuffed by skeptical members of her class or group, her exhortations ignored. In his study of the seventeenth-century English Puritans, Michael Walzer (1965:148) captures the radical's uneasy state of mind: "His 'advanced' ideas give him a good conscience; his day-to-day experiences give him bad nerves." As a comfort, however, the radical finds sympathy from fellow companions, who experience similar frustrations. Increasingly isolated from the world, the group's sense of solidarity grows. The outside world comes to be seen as a mine field of hazards devised by supporters of the status quo to ensure complacency. What is worse, the movement's adherents find in television, magazines and newspapers, even in fashion, music and entertainment, a deliberate attempt by the establishment to smear it as extremist, and to turn public opinion against it. Combined with the unshakable logic of radical theory, the convert's bitter experience of the world finally convinces her that the movement alone knows the truth; others are either badly deceived or supporters of a structure whose day of judgment will soon come.

This conclusion, however, is seldom a prescription for mental health. As Stanley Barrett (1987:xi) says, "A person cannot spend his time despising half of mankind, searching for conspiracies in every walk of life and feeding off the flaws in human nature and human institutions without paying the price." The connection between neurosis and radical politics has often been noted. Recall how, in everyday conversation, radical activists are often referred to as "crazy." According to many authors, the connection between psychological disorders and radical politics is not coincidental. In his comprehensive study of the European revolutionary tradition, J. L. Talmon (1955:40) observes that revolutionary movements bring forth "marginal qualities which otherwise may have remained dormant, and bring to the top men of a peculiar neurotic mentality." Talmon's remarks mirror those of Hannah Arendt, Michael Walzer and Eric Voegelin, who maintain that the theoretical and organizational bases of radicalism tend to induce in their leaders and adherents varying degrees of madness.

Eric Voegelin (1952:137) asserts that "once a social environment of this type is organized, it will be difficult, if not impossible, to break it up by persuasion." Moreover, when such a group faces the outside world, its reaction is predictable. According to Voegelin, it perceives the world to be "intrinsically poorly organized." On the bright side, it knows the means by which to remedy the situation. And its radical intervention is certainly timely; without it, the world would be sure to come to final, irredeemable ruin. Voegelin's point is well demonstrated in *The Turner Diaries*: "Until we have thrown the rudder out of its grasp and thrown the System overboard, the ship of state will go careening on its way" (Pierce 1980:52).[5] The movement's membership assumes the heavy mantle of its historical destiny. At this critical juncture, courage is required. Structural change is essential, and much work remains to be done.

By work, the radical does not aim at institutional reform. As we have seen, radical activists are unconcerned with conventional politics, believing conventional participation would mean a sellout to the establishment. In a more practical vein, it would mean certain defeat where, in stable democracies like Canada and the United States, the movement has a slim chance of gaining an electoral victory. Thus, for reasons of both practicality and principle, the radical believes that the only way to change the system is to undermine it. As Edward Shils (Cox 1969:218) has demonstrated, "[E]xtra-constitutionality [is] inherent in [radical] conceptions [of politics]...."

Yet, we have seen that charges of unconstitutionality do not serve as deterrents. Each of the four movements discussed here insists that theirs is not simply a political party; rather, it is a movement. As such, it must rise above the grimy, conciliatory realm of conventional politics, which can produce only incremental change. The practitioners of conventional politics are soon stripped of their ideals (if they had any in the first place) in an effort to compromise with a corrupt system. Thus, only a group that consciously chooses extraconstitutional methods can bring on change while maintaining its overriding ideals. One contributor to *Up Front* declares:

> This is one reason our political opponents fear us so much. They know, that when we speak of achieving political power, we do not propose a simple managerial change, but a complete restructuring of society. Our aim is to change the very relationships that now exist (Jan. 1993:24).

For white nationalists, the strife of pluralistic politics can be eradicated by a single, decisive (and probably violent) act. With varying degrees of commitment to revolutionary means, this belief holds for all four movements. According to deep ecologist Thomas Berry, healing of the planet will ensue only once a massive paradigm shift occurs. For Shulamith Firestone, only a women's revolution will break the spell of patriarchy. And for Black Muslims, the imminent fall of America promises blacks racial redemption. Each movement believes that a single radical act will transform political life forever. By such an act, the entire oppressed class would be mobilized in pursuit of a supremely important goal. Politics would become irrelevant; the endless strife and compromise that previously had required political activity would no longer exist.

Exercise Two: Ideology Versus Politics?

In his well-known essay, *In Defense of Politics,* Bernard Crick contrasts political activity with ideological activism. According to Crick, the differences between the two modes of activity are essential. Where ideologists assert that a society should be governed in accordance with a supreme ideal, Crick submits that the ideal itself must always be open to debate: "The moral consensus of a free state is not something mysteriously prior to or above politics; it is the activity of politics itself" (1962:24). And where ideologists claim their movement will put an end to politics, Crick insists upon the permanent necessity of it:

> Politics, then, like sexuality is an activity which must be carried on; one does not create it or decide to join in—one simply becomes more and more aware that one is involved in it as part of the human condition .... To renounce or destroy politics is to destroy the very thing which gives order to the pluralism and variety of civilized things which enables us to enjoy variety without suffering either anarchy or the tyranny of single truths which become the desperate salvation from anarchy" (1962:21).

Politics, according to Crick (1962: 41) has "limited purposes"; it concerns only the public life of free citizens. Thus, it is not concerned with raising consciousness, or shaping individuals' identities.

Contrast Crick's observations to what you know of radicalism from our four movements. What are the main preoccupations of these movements? Are they comparable to the preoccupations of governments currently holding power in North America? Do they wish to shape or displace conventional politics? Do you think their distaste for conventional politics might be part of their appeal?

This is the model of a postrevolutionary society offered by radical theorists and activists. Yet, would things really turn out that way? What happens when a *movement* gains power and seeks to re-create society in its own image? In Chapter 9, we saw some of the problems that arose when the fascist ideology was applied to Mussolini's Italy. This chapter offers clues to the character of a radical society in certain features of movements themselves. In this respect, Hannah Arendt (1966:377) observes that movements, as opposed to conventional parties, possess characteristics that make them ill-suited to maintaining a healthy society. Moreover, these same characteristics seem irresistibly to pull movements towards totalitarian methods.

As Arendt observes, movements require both a cause and an enemy, requirements rooted in their theoretical bases. Recall that radical theories identify unjust structures, and then indicate the means to eradicate them. Around the explanations and injunctions, the radical movement grows. But because of the intense identification required of activists, movements are difficult to sustain over time. In order to perceive an enemy that is nearly invisible, the radical must be continually anxious, permanently watchful. And in order to dedicate his life to the cause, he must continually renounce his self-interest. Not surprisingly, movements typically extol selflessness as a supreme virtue, and vigilance as a permanent necessity. This formula, Arendt maintains (1965:53), has remained unchanged since the French Revolution.

But if selflessness is extolled as the radical movement's highest virtue, what is its supreme vice? Accordingly to the radical, nonidentification of fellow class members is a delusion, not a vice. As for the enemy, he is not quite human, and thus is capable of neither vice nor virtue. The radical, on the other hand, is fully conscious; as such, he is expected to identify with the group's interest sincerely and completely. For radical movements, therefore, *hypocrisy* is the vice to be most reviled. On this point, Elijah Muhammad was especially explicit. Hypocrites, he charged, "are mockers of believers" (1965:252):

> Being FRIENDS with HYPOCRITES is dangerous. The Holy Qur-an warns you against taking them for friends, and the Holy Qur-an teaches you and me their disbelieving actions so that you may recognize them .... I just hope the day will come that I can weed them out, by the help of Allah, BECAUSE YOU (HYPOCRITES) ARE A GREAT HINDRANCE TO YOUR OWN SALVATION AND THE SALVATION OF OTHERS.

Similarly, albeit less dramatically, Earth First!ers refer to "sellouts," to eco-warriors gone soft, who are now compromisers and beneficiaries of the machine. According to Dave Foreman (1991:29), such individuals have lost both their discipline and will; even though they are aware of the systemic evils faced by the planet, they are too self-interested to continue the struggle.

Thus, if radical movements are to retain a committed core of members, they must continually guard against hypocrisy and self-interest. This is where vigilance is required. At one end, this induces "political correctness," the mild censorship of individual expression where that expression is held to contradict the prevailing ideology. On the other extreme, there is terror—the actual purging of a movement's members. It is, in Arendt's words (1965:51), "the two-edged compulsion of ideology and terror, one compelling men from within and the other compelling them from without," that maintains the radical's discipline. The tendency to become complacent, to relax one's discipline, to institutionalize rather than to pursue a program of permanent revolution, is an abiding problem for movements whose sole basis for existence is a demand for drastic social change.

And what of those who exist outside the movement? It appears that sworn enemies are more easily dealt with than false friends. From a theoretical standpoint, enemies' arguments are easily dismissed as the products of delusion or self-interest. To use a metaphor frequently invoked in radical texts, nonbelievers are *slaves* of the existing order. In *The Turner Diaries* (Pierce 1980:33), the white nationalist revolutionary reveals his attitude towards the masses of whites on whose behalf he worked: "Slavery is the just and proper state for a people who have grown as soft, self-indulgent, careless, credulous and befuddled as we have." "About six months ago," the author confides, "the Organization began treating Americans realistically, for the first time—namely, like a herd of cattle" (1980:101). Thus we arrive finally at radical ideologies' complicity in justifying the use of terror. Taken to their logical limits, these ideologies classify individuals according to social attributes, and then posit those attributes as the determinant of one's humanity. Those who refuse fully to identify with their class are slaves; to eliminate such people is a matter of administration, not murder.

Radical Ideologies

- Radical ideologies are *social constructions*. Indeed, in the limit, adherence to a particular ideology becomes the test of one's humanity. As Bernard Crick (1962:52) points out, "Men who do not act and believe as the ideology says they should are no longer men."

- Radical ideologies offer *normative blueprints* that seek to explain the nature of good and evil. Edward Shils (1969: 219) puts it this way: "Ideological politics are the politics of 'friend-foe,' 'we-they,' 'who-whom.' Those who are not on the side of the ideological politician are, according to the ideologist, against him."

- Radical ideologies offer a *guide to political action*. Having identified the structures responsible for human suffering, they imply that such structures should be overthrown. The action recommended is rapid and total. As an ideologue of the French Revolution suggested, "One does not reach the sublime by gradual steps" (Billington 1980:115).

- To varying degrees, radical ideologies have *formal articulation*. In many cases, certain texts are considered to offer definitive explanations of the world. Elijah Muhammad's *The Message to the Blackman in America* is such a work. Anti-Semites refer to *The Protocols of the Elders of Zion* as proof of a world Jewish conspiracy.

- Radical ideologies have *carriers of the creed*, groups of embattled, intensely dedicated adherents who believe themselves to be fighting for the survival of their particular class, if not the world.

- Radical ideologies display *total scope*. The assumption that the movement should come first leads ideology to permeate all spheres of life, including religion, aesthetics, science, even family and sexuality.

- Radical ideologies exhibit complete *internal consistency* and *attitudinal constraint*. In Kenneth Minogue's words (1985:191), the radical individual must maintain a "a stable and continuous awareness of category membership, a condition not easily distinguishable from the pathology of obsession."

THE APPEAL OF RADICALISM

One of the most striking features of radical ideologies is their durability. Although particular movements often expire quickly, radicalism as a general phenomenon has demonstrated impressive endurance. The work of Hannah Arendt, Kenneth Minogue and J. L. Talmon has shown radicalism to be a persuasive and at times dramatic influence in Europe (and, to a lesser extent, in North America) since the French Revolution. Michael Barkun, Norman Cohn and Eric Voegelin detect something very similar to ideological radicalism at work in human affairs for centuries, and at least since the millennial hopes of early Christianity. We have also seen that when radical doctrines take hold, the price is dear, and it is paid not only by the larger society but also by the individuals who carry them. And yet radical doctrines persist, suggesting they must possess an appeal that spans the fears and hopes of seventeenth-century Puritans, French revolutionaries and Earth First!ers alike. An examination of the four movements discussed here suggests some of the psychological reasons behind radicalism's enduring appeal.

First, it seems that radical movements provide adherents with a sort of family, a sense of camaraderie and shared purpose. Of a recent meeting of the Aryan Nations at Hayden Lake, Idaho, for example, Kevin Flynn and Gary Gerhardt (1989:66) observe that, like an "off-beat blend of Walden Pond and Berchtesgaden, there was insular affection intermingled with the fortress mentality among the people there." Martha Lee (1992:2122) describes a similar affinity among eco-warriors at Earth First! gatherings. As for Black Muslims, there can be no doubt that their collective sense of oppression combined with their frequent meetings and activities at mosques, provide members with a sort of family. In the case of the Nation of Islam, the movement also promotes a sense of dignity. In his autobiography, Malcolm X describes how the Nation of Islam turned his own life around. As E. U. Essien-Udom (1963:337) writes: "The Nation recognizes the needs of Negroes, like other human beings for membership and identity in some community. It insists that Negroes have the capacity to redeem themselves and recover their sense of human worth; that they must take the initiative in their struggle for human dignity." Thus, it appears that two essential human requirements—those of companionship and self-respect—are addressed by radical doctrines. Conventional politics, with its insistence upon the separation of the personal from the public realms, might well fail to satisfy in this respect.

Aside from its appeal to very basic desires for family and dignity, radicalism addresses needs that are both more grandiose and fundamental. First, consider the grandiose. Recall that ideological theory is preoccupied with historical trends, and ideological theorists posit their own age as a crucial historical turning point. Shulamith Firestone's claim, for example, is remarkable. She asserts that, after millennia of oppression, 1972 is the fitting time for a revolution of women. Women around the world are asked to assume the role assigned them by history. With the incitement to undertake radical action, the radical theorist endows activists with a sense of their supreme historical relevance. This observation also holds for the white nationalist movement. Self-proclaimed Aryan warriors clearly believe they have a historical mission. In *The Silent Brotherhood*, Flynn and Gerhardt (1987:32) submit that as a child, the future Aryan martyr, Robert Mathews, acted out "a fantasy; imagining he was the last bulwark between decent society and communist chaos."

As for the fundamental need addressed by radical doctrines, we turn again to the observation that ideologies provide an explanation of evil, thereby addressing our fundamental need to explain suffering. For the communist, the explanation of suffering is economic; for the radical feminist, it is sex-based; and for the Black Muslim and white nationalist, it is based on race. For each, however, the source of evil is this-worldly, identifiable and, ultimately, eradicable. Thus, suffering becomes a problem to be solved, rather than an inescapable condition of life. The ideologue's version of the truth—that, with monumental human effort, the world's ills can be eradicated—is easier to accept than traditional religious beliefs which stress the inherently flawed nature of the world. Radical movements promise the secular means to salvation in this life. With such promises, radical movements cannot help but appeal, especially during periods of social trauma and rapid change.

Given the relatively permanent sources of radicalism's appeal, there is little reason to believe that radical movements will disappear. However, based on the context from which they arise, we might expect some cosmetic changes. Just as radicalism in seventeenth-century England was essentially similar but not identical to radicalism in Jacobin France, so will contemporary movements have different contours from movements earlier in this century. Indeed, in the radical movements of the 1980s and 1990s, there is already evidence of a difference from movements in the 1960s and 1970s. Shulamith Firestone's radical feminism implied a large, highly centralized government as well as intensified efforts at technological development. Other "empowerment" movements such as the New Left and Black Power also embraced the idea that salvation was to be achieved through the efforts of centralized authority. Currently, however, the trend appears to be the opposite. Movements that appear to be on the rise in this decade—white nationalism, self-styled militias, New Agers and radical environmentalists, for example—are hostile to both centralized government and technology, especially nuclear technology. White nationalists, moreover, share with militia movements, and to a certain extent deep ecologists, a concern for globalization and the potential of a monolithic "world government" which would use technology to rob individuals of their freedom. Current radical movements tend to emphasize the imminent coming of a dreadful apocalypse, where prior movements focused more on redemption through political action.

Despite changes in context or details, however, radicalism's essential features remain unchanged. We should not allow Earth First!ers' insistence upon minimal organization to sway us from noting its hostility towards humanity. Nor should we allow the Heritage Front's protests against censorship of their spokespersons' speeches and literature blind us to the fact that the Front and groups like it are inherently opposed to existing political arrangements, *including* the constitutional rights they champion. Indeed, by the very nature of their goals and methods, radicals are enemies of liberal democracies. An understanding of this aspect of radicalism is crucial; in deliberating on issues such as censorship, freedom of speech and even the use of force to subdue such movements, this understanding should serve as our guide.

NOTES

1. The choice of the male pronoun in this case is deliberate. The eco-warrior is a decidedly masculine creation.
2. Edward Abbey's novel *The Monkey Wrench Gang* (New York: Avon Books) inspired the founding of Earth First!
3. The rejection of violence, however, was always tenuous. Malcolm X was more inclined to action than was Elijah Muhammad: "I was convinced that our Nation of Islam could be an even greater force in the American black man's overall struggle—if we engaged in more action. By that, I mean I thought privately that we should have amended, or relaxed, our general non-engagement policy. I felt that, wherever black people committed themselves, in the Little Rocks and the Birminghams and other places, militantly disciplined Muslims should also be there...." (Malcolm X 1965:317).
4. Examples include Heritage Front's attempts to muscle in on the Reform Party of Canada, and the large amount of Christian Identity support for David Duke, Grand Imperial Wizard for the Ku Klux Klan in the United States.
5. Dave Foreman (1991:45) expresses similar pessimism about the prospects of modern society's survival: "There is no hope for reform of the industrial empire. Modern society is a driverless hot rod without brakes, going ninety miles an hour down a dead-end street with a brick wall at the end."

CHAPTER ELEVEN

Ideologies, Identity and Citizenship

WITH JENNIFER STEWART-TOTH

Yet it is also clear that the very notion of community is changing and becoming ever more global in reach. There is a new politics about in the world since 1945 which takes the universal human subject as its subject and the doctrine of universal human rights as its chief demand.

MICHAEL IGNATIEFF

The spirit of global citizenship is almost completely deterritorialized, and is associated with an extension of citizenship as an affirmation of human unity. It is not a matter of being a formal member and loyal participant in a particular political community, whether city or state.

RICHARD FALK

The development of networks that empower citizen activists around the world and facilitate the formation of virtual communities that transcend traditional barriers to understanding might be described as a revolution of consciousness.

NANCY STEFANIK

Ideologies provide models for ordering the political world, and citizenship is one of the more important constructs that define a place for people within those models. Citizenship addresses conceptions of human rights, identity and community, all of which are highly meaningful concepts in contemporary ideological debate. Although citizenship itself is not an ideological construct similar, for example, to conservatism, feminism or liberalism, there is little question that conceptions of citizenship have become the subject of ideological debate. Citizenship, like liberty and equality, is an important organizational and conceptual tool for many ideologies. As we move into the twenty-first century, therefore, citizenship in western democratic states is becoming increasingly contested ideological terrain.

Modern citizenship was constructed upon the foundation of nationalism and within the system of sovereign nation-states that emerged in the eighteenth, nineteenth and twentieth centuries. In contemporary times, to be a citizen means to have membership in a national community, to hold the rights and responsibilities that come with that membership and to participate in the political process in the name of the common good. This, at least, is the formal meaning. But what is happening to citizenship in the late twentieth century? It is not clear, for example, that a common citizenship still implies a common set of political values in countries marked by growing diversity and pluralism. And what is the impact of globalization on conventional notions of citizenship? Of the new political identities associated with environmentalism and feminism? Of "virtual communities" linked by computers and lacking any territorial definition? The constitutive features of modern citizenship—human rights, identity and community—are in flux as their modern setting, the nation-state, is challenged by new transnational identities and movements, by supranational structures such as the European Union and the North American Free Trade Agreement, and by the resurgence of city-states. What happens, then, as the capacity of the nation-state to support citizenship with social programs and economic protection is eroded by globalization and fiscal constraint? Finally, how does citizenship fare in the ideological competition described in the preceding chapters? How do conservative, environmentalist, feminist, liberal, populist and socialist conceptions of the political community shape our contemporary understanding of citizenship? It would be foolish to expect that the traditional meaning of citizenship will remain unscathed by this whirlwind of change.

This chapter explores the impact of ideology on citizenship in the age of globalization. It begins by examining the modern notion of citizenship, which is grounded in the national community. People are born into, or acquire through the process of naturalization, the status of citizen in a territorially bordered state, and it is within that territorial domain that they are able to claim the rights, responsibilities and identity that citizenship brings. But, as suggested above, citizenship is far from a simple concept these days. Notions of identity and community, and thus citizenship, are now contested. Therefore, the chapter will address how political identities will be defined and ordered at a time when the ages-old bases of identity—nationality, ethnicity, language, religion—remain powerful but are challenged by new ideological identities associated with such things as feminism, environmentalism and multiculturalism. This will bring us to the impact of globalization, at one extreme, and laptop computers, at the other.

Here again we will confront a host of questions which defy simple answers. Will the "global village" supersede the territorial communities of the nation-state, and with what impact on conventional notions of citizenship? How do we reconcile American or Canadian citizenship with the emerging notion of the "global citizen"? Will "virtual communities" created by people of common cause and linked by computer technology begin to transcend traditional territorial communities bound together by spatial proximity, but not necessarily by shared interests? Finally, how will the rights of citizenship be defined in an age when universal human rights, grounded in the transnational order, are being advocated, yet when national governments continue to administer rights, often with priorities and concerns at variance with the spirit of universal personhood?

An Illustration of Change

Consider the following scenario: a global network of women, linked by computers, electronic mail, fax machines and telephones, and existing within a media environment shaped by common television and radio programs, newspapers and magazines. Its members act politically to pressure the United Nations and governments around the world to adopt policies for developing countries that pay greater attention to women's health, education and overall economic and social status. Women's groups use the most advanced communications technologies to share ideas and resources, form action plans and pressure political and administrative actors for change.

This is not a futuristic scenario; it describes a global women's network that has been successful in transforming the agenda and criteria for development. The women's network came together by e-mail, airplane, fax, computer and phone, "from Dhaka to Denver to Dakar." Its success was widely reported in 1994, following the International Conference on Population and Development in Cairo. There, the women's network won recognition for the key role of women in development strategies, and for a resolution stating that "eliminating social, cultural, political and economic discrimination against women is a prerequisite of eradicating poverty." In his report on the conference, John Stackhouse writes that "gender equality, at least in international documents, has been established as the bedrock of development and of global population programs" (*Globe and Mail*, September 12, 1994: A8).

Similar networks exist for environmentalists, human rights activists and animal rights activists. They not only exist, but raise intriguing questions about the foundations of political identity. Such networks challenge the traditional communities in which citizens act—in such cases, the community is not territorially bound or limited by national borders, but is a community of interest and concern that is potentially global in scope. They also point to the evolving role and function of the nation-state, which is no longer the sole springboard for political action. National governments are but one locus of political authority, from local to global, that women's groups, environmentalists and others seek to influence.

In order to comprehend the potential transformations of political identities, communities and rights, it is important to remember that the dominant model of modern political organization, the world system of sovereign nation-states and national citizenship, itself represented a fundamental change. It is therefore worthwhile to explore the rise of the nation-state in order to comprehend not only the "real-world" changes that set the stage for the nation-state, but also the impulses of human imagination that have transformed political communities and citizen identities in the past. In this context, and throughout the chapter, it is also important to keep in mind that communities are *imagined* (Anderson 1983). Consider, for example, the imagination required to be a citizen in Canada, where most people will never see, know or meet more than a relatively small circle of their fellow citizens, and some may never travel the breadth of territory that defines their nation. Yet, a Canadian nation exists in the mind of every citizen, one inspired and nurtured by public signs, myths, symbols, holidays, ceremonies and discourse.[1] It follows, then, that there is capacity to imagine communities different from the nation, and thus the potential for other forms of citizenship to emerge which would link members, not of territorial communities, but of communities of mutual cause. But first we must examine how the national community came to be imagined. This takes us into a discussion of the rise of the nation-state and the associated revolutionary changes that occurred in language, communication technology and capitalism.

Exercise One: Global Citizenship

How do you react to the notion of *global citizenship*? Do you think of yourself as a global citizen? If so, in what context? If not, why not? Simply put, is global citizenship something to embrace, or avoid?

Do you think the notion of global citizenship is a product of our times, a creation of global economic transformation and the Internet, or does it have much deeper roots in western democratic states? Can you think of any time in history when the notion of global citizenship would have made sense to people at the time?

What about the future of global citizenship? Do you think it likely or unlikely that more and more people will see themselves as global citizens? To the extent that this does happen, what do think will be the impact on American or Canadian citizenship? Is there any necessary conflict? Is national citizenship necessarily or inevitably weakened as global citizenship takes hold? Or are the two complementary?

THE NATION CONCEIVED

Benedict Anderson's (1983) poetic conception of the birth of the nation teaches us much about the profound meaning of this form of human community. In general, communities fill the fierce human need for connection, for belonging, for meaning in a life marked by knowledge of fatality and the contingency of human existence, by the joys of birth and the sorrows of death. Religious communities have always filled such a need, responding to both the imperatives of mortality and the "obscure intimations of immortality" (Anderson 1883:10–11). Religions constitute systems of meaning that link generations past, present and future. It is no coincidence, then, that the rise of nationalism coincided with the waning of religious worldviews. Anderson (1983:11–12) writes that the eighteenth-century age of Enlightenment, of rationalist secularism, brought a loss of spiritual sustenance in the face of suffering and death:

> Disintegration of paradise: nothing makes fatality more arbitrary. Absurdity of salvation: nothing makes another style of continuity more necessary.

The emergent nation filled the void of meaning, and brought connectedness, belonging, some sense to the cycle of life and death.[2] Nations, in the imagination, linked chance of birth with destiny of nationality.

While the context for the rise of nations and the nation-state was the decline of religious certainty, along with the loss of authority by dynastic realms and divine-right rulers, the vehicle which allowed the collective imagining of new communities was the rise of capitalism which, in turn, produced new mediums of mass communication and print-languages. The importance of language to communities cannot be overstated, for a common language is necessary to communicate the ideas and images of the mind. Thus, ancient religious kingdoms were knit together by "sacred languages" such as Latin, the "media through which the great global communities of the past were imagined" (Anderson 1983:14). However, in the age of the Enlightenment and global exploration, cultural and geographic horizons expanded. Religions became "territorialized," even "relativized," and the primal dominance of sacred languages diminished. For instance, Anderson (1983:19) writes that "the fall of Latin exemplified a larger process in which the sacred communities integrated by old sacred languages were gradually fragmented, pluralized, and territorialized." This decline was linked to the rise of capitalism, a powerful vehicle for change in the capacity of human beings to imagine new communities. In particular, revolutionary changes in the printing industry made possible the mass distribution of books and newspapers which then made tangible the nation and sustained it in the imagination.

Even as the paramount status of sacred languages declined, mass vernacular languages emerged, their growth and formalization spurred by the ongoing search for, and creation of, new markets for the products of capitalism. Print-capitalism produced books and newspapers that allowed hundreds, thousands, millions of people to situate themselves within particular nations, based on a common language and a common set of cultural, social and historical references. This "made it possible for rapidly growing numbers of people to think about themselves, and to relate themselves to others, in profoundly new ways" (Anderson 1983:36). The rise of dominant print-languages in the sixteenth and seventeenth centuries—for example, High German and the King's English—that overlaid many different spoken dialects allowed for the creation of a shared history and experience. These languages also facilitated the adoption of "official languages" by centralizing states, languages which became the key currency of power (Anderson 1983:42–45). "Fraternity, power and time" came to be linked meaningfully in the new imagined communities of nation-states where citizenship reflected horizontal and secular attachments to territory, to the state and to one's fellow citizens.

Modern citizenship thus came to describe the status of individuals in relation to the land, the state and to each other.[3] It reflected the emergence of liberal individualism, and a growing democratic emphasis on liberty and equality. As a formal-legal construct, it means that citizens enjoy rights and have obligations within the territorial boundaries of their nation-states. In western liberal democracies, citizens enjoy such rights as the right to vote, the right to religious freedom and freedom of speech and association. The first responsibility of citizens which comes to mind is the dreaded T-word—the responsibility to pay taxes! The most rigorous calling to which citizens answer is one that asks them to defend their country with their lives. On a daily, more mundane basis, citizens have the obligation to obey laws, an obligation which ensures stability and order. The state, for its part, has the duty to respect the rights of citizens and to ensure order, stability and security.

There are also ideals of citizenship that extend beyond formal-legal definitions of rights and responsibilities into the realm of visions about the nature of the community of citizens, and how it can best function to achieve its goals. Here, in the community of citizens to which one belongs, the spiritual and social expressions of citizenship—commitment, loyalty and service—are practised in the name of the larger good. This more spiritual vision of citizenship bears some resemblance to both the socialist belief that liberty is best realized within a community context and to the conservative emphasis on the organic nature of society. It is the vision which is most likely to be called upon when sacrifice is called for, when the demands of citizenship trump individual self-interest.

Over time, the spatial limits that define the modern community of citizens, that define community membership, have changed enormously. The territorial community within which citizenship was exercised expanded from the walled city-state of medieval times to broader regional communities, and, from the sixteenth and seventeenth centuries onward, to nation-states. As political communities expanded in size, they necessarily became more diverse, and thus the criteria for citizenship became more simplified and more formal in character. In a multiethnic state embracing a wide variety of religious faiths, ethnicity and religion could be the criteria of citizenship only at the risk of civil war. The criteria therefore became reduced to place of birth or length of residence. For instance, an individual is a Canadian citizen because she was born in Canada, or immigrated to Canada, remained in the country and then applied for legal membership in the national community. Her age, sex, ethnicity, language or ideological beliefs are immaterial.[4] And, once achieved, citizenship is virtually impossible to lose. Even heinous crimes do not result in the loss of citizenship; the convicted murderer remains an American or Canadian citizen even though imprisonment may restrict the exercise of that citizenship. What this all means, however, is that as the domain of citizenship expanded in size and shrank in complexity, it also became increasingly disconnected from other dimensions of personality embedded in such elements as race, language, religion and ethnicity. In reaction, there has been an attempt to *deepen* the meaning of contemporary citizenship, to link it to a specific set of political values and social characteristics. This reaction has sparked a very contentious debate to which we shall return later

The past few centuries have seen the rise of the territorially bounded and sovereign nation-state, and with it a model of citizenship defined by nationality, by a particular relationship of citizens to the state and by a sense of loyalty and belonging nurtured by connection to the land and membership in the community. However, the forces that gave rise to the nation-state and modern citizenship—dynamic developments in capitalism, new communications technology and newly politicized identities—have analogies in contemporary times. And, as they did in the past, these forces are transforming traditional forms of political community and citizenship. While the existing system of nation-states will not disappear, the potential for new forms of political community is significant. Given the rise of new ideologies—and the political identities and communities they inspire—in the context of globalization and revolutionary changes in communications technology, changes of profound magnitude in the nature of citizenship are now in play.

GLOBALIZATION

As discussed in Chapter 7, a number of dynamics characterize globalization writ large. The initial and most developed nexus for global activities is international trade and financial transactions, where there is "free circulation of goods and capital without state intervention" (Kymlicka and Lenihan 1994:11). Of course, the technological revolution that continues to produce and refine the infrastructure of high-speed computers, fax machines, modems and other vehicles for twenty-four-hour-a-day communication and trade is foundational to globalization. Another element is the emergence of new social movements—including environmentalism, feminism, human rights activism and the peace movement—discussed earlier. The actors within these global communities have capitalized on the technological revolution in communications, computers and media-broadcast capacities to form "virtual communities" which are emerging as highly responsive political forces. Membership in these communities knows no national boundaries, although the nation-state remains an important but by no means exclusive, site for political action.

In addition to the development of the global market, burgeoning communications capacity and the emergence of political and social forces that are global in reach, Robert W. Cox (1991:335–49) adds two further strokes to the picture of globalization. The first is the "internationalization of the state," whereby states move from a position of "buffer" between domestic welfare and external forces, to being a "conduit" between the forces in the world economy and the domestic economy. The second is the wave of human migration moving from the south to the north, a reversal of the earlier trend of migration patterns during the age of exploration from the fifteenth to the nineteenth centuries. The contemporary movement of populations is a response to structural changes that result from the globalization of production; migrants move to countries with employment opportunities, in particular to urban areas within those countries.

Finally, Peter Drucker (1994:54) argues that globalization is driven by the emergence of new forms of capital. In the "new economy," knowledge is power, and a new social elite emerges—knowledge workers. Drucker writes that these changes, "rather than all the violence of the political surface, have transformed not only the society but also the economy, the community, and the polity we live in." Christopher Lasch (1994:48) also points to the emergence of a new global "elite," whose loyalties are not situated in any particular geographical community: "They have more in common with their counterparts in Brussels or Hong Kong than with the masses ... not yet plugged into the network of global communications."

Globalization has the potential to change fundamental dimensions of human existence—the economic, the social, the psychological, and, of course, the political. As James Rosenau (1989:4) writes: "There are numerous signs that global politics, is, at all levels, undergoing enormous change. New economic, social and political structures are emerging and old ones are being transformed ...." Perhaps the central *political* question that globalization raises is the future of the nation-state. While there is a theoretical consensus that the imperatives of globalization could transform the modern system of nation-states, there is no such agreement about the specific future of the state system or its constituent parts. Indeed, there are contrasting visions of nation-states caught in the midst of the swirling forces of particularism and globalism. Lasch (1994:48–49) describes these forces as follows:

> On one hand, it [the world] is now united through the agency of the market as it never was before. Capital and labour flow freely across political boundaries that seem increasingly artificial and unenforceable .... On the other hand, tribal loyalties have seldom been so aggressively promoted .... It is the weakening of the nation-state that underlies both these developments—the movement toward unification and the seemingly contradictory movement toward fragmentation.

Given the tempest of uncertainty that surrounds the nation-state, it is not surprising that debates rage about its future. At one extreme, the "optimistic" theorists argue that the technological revolution liberates humanity from the parochial, inward-looking nationalism that arose in the nineteenth century. Will Kymlicka and

Donald Lenihan (1994:12) describe this process as one in which the communications revolution "is not only shrinking the world, it is stripping it of the fig leaf behind which it has hidden for two centuries—that of nationalism and the nation-state—and opening the way for a new global culture." Theorists in the "pessimistic" camp agree that much of the nation-state's power will be lost with the technological revolution. However, rather than envisioning a more harmonious world, they argue that a large part of the power that historically accrued to the nation-state will be taken over by a number of disparate forces, or "power-brokers," including transnational corporations, tribal warlords and fundamentalist religious leaders, leading to a volatile and by no means better world order.

In either case, the nation-state will likely be an enduring feature of the world political system, albeit with a significantly modified role. Even Kymlicka and Lenihan (1994:13) argue that there remain national interests—"interests inherently tied to the existence and borders of a particular state"—which the nation-state best defends and advances. In Canada, such interests might include maintaining official multiculturalism in a bilingual framework, performing the international role of peacekeeper or maintaining the system of equalization payments in the federal state. The nation-state has an indispensable role in preserving the integrity of such principles and practices. Michael Ignatieff (1987:984) makes a similar argument but with a different rationale. National citizenship and national governments, he asserts, are important because they are the key vehicles through which national interests are advanced and problems solved in the international arena. Thus, although many policy issues and practices are inevitably caught up in the globalization vortex, nation-states will remain important so long as "national interests" and "national communities" retain their salience.

But nation-states are also challenged by social changes taking place within their boundaries. New social cleavages are emerging in a global era in which knowledge is a burgeoning source of power, and therefore a powerful means of social differentiation. If members of the knowledge elite constitute a new "class," they do so only because the pursuit of their livelihoods depends on the use of information and the trade of professional expertise. They are brokers, bankers, engineers, consultants, scientists, doctors, publicists, publishers, moviemakers, entertainers, journalists, artists, writers, professors. Thus, a distinguishing feature of this contemporary social elite is the heterogeneity of their occupations and political outlooks. While its players often settle in geographic proximity, in "centres of enterprise" like Hollywood or Silicon Valley, they do not form communities in the traditional sense. Rather, their communities are "populated by transients," lacking "the continuity that derives from a sense of place and from standards of conduct self-consciously cultivated and handed down from generation to generation" (Lasch 1994:46).

In opposition to this new cosmopolitan elite, there remains a powerful movement of the "masses" (in Peter Lasch's terms) which stands for the preservation of "middle-class nationalism," for the preservation of a "common ground, common standards, a common frame of reference without which society dissolves into nothing more than contending factions..." (Lasch 1994:49). The masses are differentiated from the new knowledge elite because they continue to engage in more routine jobs in the industrial and service sectors. Their values reflect patriotism, ethnic particularism (even racism) and more conservative moral and religious values, and populist movements provide a powerful form of political expression. In this context,

Michael Ignatieff (1993:6–7) illuminates the emerging social cleavages between cosmopolitans, who take for granted a "post-national state of mind," and the members of national populations who need a sense of belonging—"to be recognized and understood."

It is clear, then, that globalization poses a significant challenge to the nation-state, even though the success of that challenge is by no means predetermined. It is also clear that globalization has the potential to spur the imagination of new forms of political community, ones that are not constrained by the territorial demarcations associated with the nation-state system. And, as a consequence, globalization has significant implications for citizenship. Transformations of the traditional vessel of citizenship, the nation-state, are bound to have implications for citizenship. It is to those implications that we now turn.

Critical Analysis of Globalization

This chapter examines the interaction of globalization and the rise of new ideologies, and the transformation of citizenship that may result from this interaction. In so doing, it taps only a shelf or two in the rich library of literature on globalization; texts on the other shelves bring different perspectives to the study of globalization,[5] including detailed critical analyses of the impact of globalization on the human condition.

For instance, one branch of critical analysis suggests how the welfare of populations living in both the developed and developing world may be harmed in the wake of global capital and the decreasing capacity of nation-states to buffer their domestic populations from the demands of the global economy. The globalization of capital and the market cannot be disconnected from issues of social and political development, and it is therefore imperative to ask how the interests of workers, women and children are affected by these developments. To assume that the impacts of globalization will be uniformly positive would be rash in the extreme.

We must also keep in mind that for a large proportion of the world's population, the technology and knowledge necessary to participate in the global village are not part of everyday life. In fact, two out of every three households around the world have no telephone. The seventy-five percent of the world's population which lives in LCDs (less-developed countries) and LICs (low-income countries) have only five percent of the world's telephones. In most of these countries, there is just one phone for every 100 people, a "teledensity" that is wildly at odds with the situation in the developed world. It is not surprising, then, that corporations, governments and international agencies are now mounting an intense drive to increase the telecommunications capacities of developing countries.

For a discussion of teledensity, see Lawrence Surtees, "Telecom's show of shows," *The Globe and Mail,* September 12, 1995: C1.

CITIZENSHIP IN THE BIG PICTURE

Imagine a framework for understanding the links between territory and citizenship in which there are two dimensions (see figure 11.1). The first is the spatial dimension, reflecting breadth of physical space or distance. The second is the depth dimension, reflecting the capacity for simple or complex, single or multiple layers of citizen identities. The dimensions are related: as the space in which citizenship is operationalized increases, the potential for more, and even conflicting, identities and expressions of citizenship grows. Picture also an inverted pyramid in which the "closest" community is the family. Move up and out, and the base broadens to encompass neighbourhood, city, region, province or state, country and world. At each stop along the way, a new identity can be assumed—for example, daughter or son, neighbour, Calgarian, Albertan, Canadian, world citizen—and laid across preexisting identities.

FIGURE 11.1: Dimensions of Citizenship

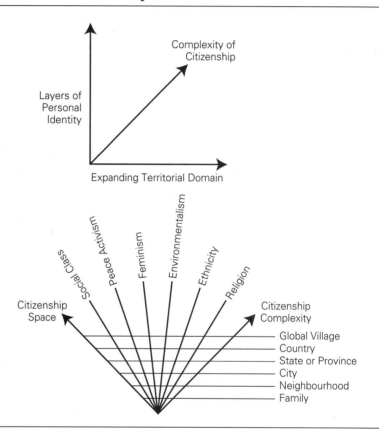

Over time, there has been an expansion of the place to which citizens belong, in which they practise the responsibilities and enjoy the rights of citizenship and to which they give their loyalty. The territorial limits that define communities of citizens have expanded up the pyramid described above, from family and kin to the city and the nation-state. As Murray Bookchin (1992:226) writes:

> [T]he city, initially the Hellenic polis created a new social dispensation: minimally a territorial space in which the 'stranger' or 'alien' could reside with a reasonable degree of protection—later even a measure of participation—that few tribal communities allowed to outsiders, however hospitably they were treated. Two new civilizatory categories—politics and citizenship—began to absorb the largely biosocial forms that held early familial and tribal lifeways together.

The rise of the nation-state from the sixteenth century onward marked a new stage in human organization. Before this, a citizen's allegiances were organized so that the "town was the authentic and most meaningful locus of his personal and public life. He was first and foremost a townsman" (Bookchin 1992:50). With the emergence of the nation-state, national loyalties took precedence over older loyalties to the city: "Larger-than-life institutions, far beyond the reach of the ordinary citizen, began to supplant the civic institutions within which some kind of face-to-face democracy was feasible" (Bookchin 1992:51).

However, the matter of who could be a citizen was not defined by territorial boundaries alone. Indeed, until recently, citizenship was largely an exclusive status. In Aristotle's time, the prerequisite for citizenship in the Athenian polis excluded most people: "The citizen must be a male of known genealogy, a patriarch, a warrior, and the master of the labour of others (normally slaves)" (Pocock 1992:36). Such discrimination in citizenship endured well beyond the times of the ancient polis and into the twentieth century. Women, slaves, native peoples, blacks, the poor and other groups have been excluded from citizenship on the basis of such factors as race, sex and wealth. For example, poll taxes were used to restrict the franchise for the poor and blacks, and women were excluded from the electorates of western democratic states until the first two decades of the twentieth century. Thus citizenship was not equated with territorial residence; many groups deemed neither fit nor worthy were denied the status of citizen, and were relegated to the realm of the household or banished to a life of hard labour.

The struggle for citizenship status came to define many early political movements including the women's movement and the civil rights movement. In Canada, during the years following Confederation in 1867, annual income and property requirements, as well as the exclusion of all women, meant that only about fifteen percent of the population was allowed to vote. In subsequent decades, property qualifications were eliminated and women finally won the federal vote in 1920. Even then, it was not until 1929 that women were declared legal persons in the Persons' Case by the highest constitutional court of the time (the Judicial Committee of the Privy Council in Great Britain), and were thereby allowed to sit in the Senate. Until 1960, Native Canadians could vote in federal elections only if they abandoned their official Indian status; to be an Indian *and* a Canadian was impossible. In the United States and Canada, the debate continues over the legitimate means of ensuring not only formal, legal equality of citizenship status, but also real equality of political participation and representation. This debate reflects some of the themes addressed in Chapter 2; is the formal equality of political rights sufficient, or must the equality of rights be reinforced by some measure of economic equality if it is to have any meaning?

We have seen, then, the extension of citizenship to cover larger and larger pieces of territory, and to include more and more people within the territorial domain. Citizenship is thus more inclusive in two respects. We now face a number of questions. First, will these forms of expansion stop at the territorial limits of the nation-state? What is the likely impact of new transnational political communities that sweep across the territorial boundaries of the nation-state? And what is the likely impact of newly politicized identities, such as those associated with feminism and multiculturalism? Do they form the base for more expansive conceptions of citizenship?

Nation-States and Other Spaces

Territorial boundaries are but one way to construct spaces—communities—within which citizenship is made meaningful. There are other ways, and the system of rules that governs the behaviour of citizens need not be constrained by territorial boundaries alone. Recent Canadian debate demonstrates, for example, that it is possible to conceive of systems of aboriginal self-government for non-reserve-based First Nations, in which a particular system of justice or social services applies to all members—citizens—regardless of where they live. Separate-school boards exist in many Canadian provinces for denominational and public education systems. Moreover, the spaces in which citizens operate can be seen as fluid, and demarcated by various boundaries. Federal states are an example of the possibilities for multiple and overlapping identities and loyalties; one can be a Texan or an American, depending upon the issue at hand and the context in which it is raised. Finally, systems of rule can be completely unrelated to territory, as in traditional authority systems based on kinship. John Ruggie (1993:149) describes such systems as ones in which "territory was occupied ... but it did not define them." Thus, the modern system of nation-states is distinguished by the fact that collectivities of citizens are defined by "fixed and mutually exclusive enclaves of legitimate dominion" (Ruggie 1993:151). However, in this age of globalization, the system of states is at the very least growing more complex, and at the most being transcended and transformed. In Ruggie's model, the organization of states along territorial lines is not in decline as much as other forms of organization are being added. For instance, in the economic realm, there are microeconomic trade links which have created "nonterritorial 'regions'" in the world economy:

> Conventional spaces-of-places continue to engage in external economic relations with one another, which we continue to call trade, foreign investment and the like, and which are more or less effectively mediated by the state. In the non-territorial global economic region, however, the conventional distinctions between internal and external once again are exceedingly problematic, and any given state is but one constraint to corporate global strategic calculations .... This nonterritorial global region is a world, in short, that is premised on what Lattimore described as the "sovereign importance of movement," not of place (1993:172–73).

Furthermore, the decline of territorial divisions as the central organizing principle in the modern world-system is about, to some degree, the relative decline of national governments as the locus of political action. This is true not only because of global economic forces which weaken the capacity of national governments to control domestic economies, and not only because of serious public debt crises. True, states are losing the capacity to defend nations from the imperatives of global capitalism as they retreat from the role of coordinating and distributing large social welfare programs. Moreover, many of the "security" threats to western industrialized states—resources scarcity, pollution, illegal immigration—appear beyond the control of the state. However, another dynamic at work is the politicization of formerly nonpolitical identities and the creation of new communities for which the nation-state is not central to political action. National governments are becoming less vital for political action by groups such as feminists and environmentalists, as well as scores of nongovernmental organizations (NGOs). Governments have traditionally been an important source of funding for the activities of such groups, but will be less so in the future as funding is slashed to control public debt. Moreover, political and social action might be aimed at national governments—for example, by lobbying for policy changes—but it can be independent of those governments, as well, as in the case of war- and famine-relief efforts by NGOs. States, of course, are still the agents for one important source of individual and collective identity—that of the nation— and still provide many of the essential instruments for political action. The nation-state remains the forum for deciding "who makes the laws, what the laws say, and who will administer them" (Hart 1995:49). But it seems possible, and even likely, that they will grow less important in an era of globalization, when the logic of national boundaries is reduced and when many nation-states are no longer closely associated with unique religious, ethnic or linguistic communities.

The decline of national (and state/provincial) governments as sites for political activity, and as a source of funding, has been reinforced by the apparent disenchantment of citizens with large state bureaucracies, and by the ability of NGOs to respond in an efficient way to global crises. International NGOs have taken on an increasingly important role in promoting human rights in general and the rights of women in particular, and in establishing international programs for education, health, development of essential services, environmental protection and care for civilians in times of war, famine and epidemic. To illustrate, it is interesting to note that a report on a two-day Canadian conference on reform of the United Nations included proposals for a world tax on the one trillion dollars of speculative currency transactions that occur daily around the globe, a tax that would be used to finance U.N. development and peacekeeping initiatives. There was also a proposal to allow people to bypass governments and petition the U.N. directly for a resolution of grievances.[6] As journalist Michael Valpy (1995) points out, the proposal for the global tax, as well as one for a "Blue Planet Global Lottery" in which revenue from lottery tickets sold on international airline flights would be used for environmental and sustainable development projects, reflects

> …the eroding control the national governments exercise over economic activity ….
> In the past, foreign aid and international organizations were financed from the tax revenues of national governments. With the diminution of nation-state powers, new mechanisms of financing are being sought, new means of collecting and distributing the surplus generated by the global economy.

The Blue Planet lottery proposal would bypass national governments in favour of administration by a nonprofit foundation. The driving force behind the project is a coalition between the international airline industry and groups active in the environmental and development communities. So, not only is globalization an independent variable in the decline of territorialism and national governments, but the simultaneous rise of newly politicized identities and social movements reinforces its effects. Both, moreover, contribute to the decline of the centrality of states as the focus of political action.

Where, then, do we locate *citizens* in the global era? In this context we must first ask whether it is appropriate to speak of the decline of the nation-state in favour of a global political community when, in fact, there are no authoritative world political institutions. As discussed above, we often hear of the potential for the evolution of existing global institutions into more powerful centres of political power. Indeed, it is not unusual to hear calls for world governmental institutions even in the midst of devolution and decentralization by national governments no longer capable of sustaining vast social welfare programs and the administrative infrastructure needed to support them. For instance, one private initiative, the Commission on Global Governance, has called for United Nations institutions to assume authority for international taxation, and for the U.N. to be a more active and representative assembly. In early 1995, the secretary-general of the United Nations, Boutros Boutros Ghali, envisioned the U.N. as shifting over time from "interstate dialogue to transnational co-operation" to become a "true democratic assembly for the planet" (Thorsell 1995:D5). Yet the fact remains that international organizations in which we would participate *as citizens* are at best embryonic at the present time.

Nation-states, therefore, continue to play a crucial role in world political organization. They remain the linchpins between individual citizens and the public realm. And the nation-state is a particular kind of community and institutional complex that is not easily replaced. For example, it must be kept in mind that many of the vehicles for citizen participation in governance—voting, running for office, distributing campaign pamphlets during an election—remain bounded by national, subnational and local political units which are territorially grounded. Nonetheless, participation at the national level may offer fewer opportunities in the future to influence decisions as globalization limits the power of nation-states, and the legitimacy of their decisions—on human rights, development, trade, international relations, monetary and fiscal policy—is increasingly located in the transnational realm. This in turn creates the new citizenship dilemma, for there is no global polity and institutional arena in which citizens can participate, leaving the forum primarily to corporate actors and groups (communities) which transcend the territorial boundaries of nation.

Exercise Two: Forms of Political Participation

Step back for a moment from our traditional conception of political participation, which focuses on the state, government and political parties. New kinds of political activity—the letter-writing campaigns of Amnesty International, the protests on the high seas by Greenpeace, the "Take Back the Night" rallies to protest violence against women—show us the potential of new political "resources, repertoires of action, and identities" (Magnusson 1994:528). New political movements not only transcend the political arena of the nation-state, they also bring new meanings and forms to political participation. But are these new forms likely to be as satisfying or as effective? Are they likely to engage a broader or narrower cross section of the population? Are they likely to complement or supplant more conventional forms of political participation?

Of course, at a mundane level, the logic of capitalism allows for a shared community of consumerism on a global scale. That great divide—language—can be overcome when trademarks, brand names and franchise outlets are recognizable around the world. The global supermarket is open for business. Stuart Hall (1991:27–30) writes:

> Global mass culture is dominated by the modern means of cultural production, dominated by the image which crosses and recrosses linguistic frontiers much more rapidly and much more easily and which speaks across language in a much more

immediate way .... It is dominated by television and film, and by the image, imagery, and style of mass advertising .... Global mass culture ... remains centered in the West and it always speaks English.

However, it is hard to integrate the shared experience of consumption into the traditional conception of citizenship—as identity, loyalty and service in the name of the national community.

Going beyond the mass culture of consumerism, David Elkins (1994:3) argues that the process of globalization is part of an ongoing transformation of consciousness which began in the sixteenth century and beyond, in the age of European exploration, imperialism and settlement, and then quickened in this century with the spread of independence of colonies from empires. These developments mean that "almost all nations of the world are learning about almost all other nations." Elkins (1994:7) writes:

Globalization defined as wider awareness of condition into other parts of the globe should heighten the sense of awareness of differences in culture and life-chances. But it should also encourage and underwrite the awareness of "people like me" who live in other places. Furthermore, opportunities to travel and visit "people like me" can only strengthen the multiple identities which challenge national loyalties.

So, we might find citizens of the future developing a global consciousness by living in a world community. But, paradoxically, the dynamic of globalization may also evoke an urge to define who belongs to the community, to attach some specificity to expanding notions of citizenship. Elkins (1993:8) recognizes that communities will be confronted with the questions of "where people may reside and still be part of our community. More pointedly, where can people be and still be citizens of here?"

Perhaps it is not surprising, given these multiple responses to globalization, that there is a parallel movement towards local or grass-roots practices of citizenship, in which participation takes place in communities where, it seems, a difference can be made. Local-level participation allows citizens to influence decisions that have an impact on their day-to-day lives. Cities as arenas for political action could therefore be revitalized in the global age. Richard Knight (1989:16) maintains that cities became "simply places of opportunity" in the age of nation-states, losing their authenticity as polities. Now, he sees a growing awareness, most apparent in Europe, of the need to strengthen local and regional authorities to balance the flow of power to the supranational level: "the reinforcement of local governments—governance closest to the citizen and with which citizens can most easily identify—is a natural corollary and complement to the development of a global society" (1989:16).

It is clear that there is deep tension as globalization overlays the modern system of nation-states. We find that citizens are located in multiple and overlapping political spheres: local, provincial, national, global. As we move the discussion from where citizenship is operationalized to a consideration of its meaning, it is clear that traditional concepts of rights, identity and community, grounded as they are in the territory and institutions of nation and state, and in rights and responsibilities, cannot simply be transplanted to the global arena in which there is no single or authoritative institutional structure or system that creates a focus for citizen loyalty and arena for participation. Thus, the meaning of citizenship in the age of globalization must evolve.

Human Rights in the Global Era

Globalization has its most clearly perceived impact on conceptions of citizenship with respect to human rights, which have become more universalized over the last half century. Universal rights claimed by both individuals and collectivities increasingly derive their legitimacy from the transnational realm, although they are administered by nation-states (Soysal 1994:18). Rights claims are grounded more and more frequently in international conventions and agreements, including, for instance, the United Nations' Universal Declaration of Human Rights. Yasemin Soysal (1994:7) writes:

> The notion of human rights as a codification of abstract concepts of personhood, has become a pervasive element of world culture. Continual invocation of human rights establishes and advances universal contiguities and thus legitimates claims for rights and identities of "persons," from within or without national limits.

In turn, this universalization of rights alters the relationship between citizens and the state, making the link between them "more and more instrumental and routine rather than charismatic and sentimental" (Soysal 1994:165).

Indeed, Soysal argues for a "postnational" model of citizenship to provide for the incorporation of migrant "guestworkers" (all noncitizen migrant populations) into the social and political order of host European countries. In the model of post-national citizenship, "national belonging, or a formal nationality, is no longer imperative for this role of citizen. Rights, participation, and representation in a polity are increasingly matters beyond the vocabulary of national citizenship" (1994:165). This model can be pushed further to accommodate the growth of new ideologies, and the identities, communities and calls for political action that flow from them. Universal rights complement this model of multiple identities because the formerly preeminent identity—nationality—may recede in importance. Thus, individuals can choose among multiple identities, including traditional identities of nationality or ethnicity, and new identities—feminist, environmentalist, multiculturalist. Of course, from these new identities, communities can be constructed on a global scale. Nation-states might retain their importance for many, but would be less important for those groups where national identity is but a background while other identities (feminist, environmentalist, multiculturalist) take on primary meaning (depth). This cosmopolitan view of the global village paints a picture of a community of humankind, joined by transnational interests and values in a postnational era in which discrimination and exclusion based on traditionally defined territorial definitions of nationhood are less and less legitimate.

However, the postnational model of citizenship does not go unchallenged. Michael Ignatieff (1993) argues that nations offer not only security and protection to citizens, but also recognition and understanding. In his view, nationalism is about being with "my people," about fitting into the ebb and flow of everyday life and shared history. Ignatieff (1993:7) considers the possibility of cosmopolitan cities, "gigantic, multi-ethnic melting pots which provided a home for expatriates, exiles, migrants, and transients of all kind." But such cities, and their spirit of tolerance, are a luxury available, for the most part, to the developed West, because they rely on the "rule-enforcing capacities of nations." When such order breaks down in the flames of ethnic and religious warfare, there is no possibility for a postnational age. Security of nation, therefore, is a precondition for cosmopolitan attitudes and peaceful coexistence. Consequently, nations continue to be the source of security and civility for citizens (Ignatieff 1993:9). A postnational rejoinder is that the very logic behind the openness and fluidity of the globalization of identities demands more open defini- tions of who belongs.[7] Still, there is dissonance between the powerful forces of the abstract, universal rights of personhood, on the one hand, and the explosion of claims to nationhood and sovereignty, inspired by the equally powerful principles of national sovereignty and self-determination, on the other.

It is helpful, then, to refine the debate by recognizing a distinction between nations built upon the foundations of a dominant ethnic, linguistic and religious heritage common to a majority of the population, and nations built in the civic tra- dition, founded by people of different ethnic backgrounds who share a commitment to building a nation but not a common ethnicity. Recall the distinction made in Chapter 7 between *ethnic* and *civic* nationalism. In the former case, citizenship tends to be defined in exclusive terms: one can live in the nation-state but not be a mem- ber of the nation. In the latter case, citizenship is defined in more inclusive terms: with rare exceptions, those who live within the nation-state are thereby citizens. There is little question that civic nationalism is more compatible with the dynamics of globalization than ethnic nationalism. What is less clear is which form of nation- alism will predominate as we move into the twenty-first century. Paradoxical devel- opments—the opening up of traditional national citizenship as more and more groups seek to define themselves with the claim of "nation"—illustrate the tension that is an essential part of the evolution of citizenship in the global era. Furthermore, while the advancement of universal human rights—the formal-legal dimension of citizenship—continues, we are left wondering about the other meaningful dimen- sions of citizenship: identity and community.

The Evolution of Identity and Community

The expansion of the spatial limits that define citizenship is intimately linked to the increasing potential for much greater depths of citizen identity. Citizens defined in terms of nationality or, in the case of federal states, by national and provincial loyal- ties, can now cloak themselves in other identities that emerge from such develop- ments as the women's and environmental movements. Their common cause may transcend the national loyalties that formerly defined the limits of common citizenship.

The blossoming of new social and political identities, and their associated com- munities, finds roots in the extension of the status of citizenship from a very limit- ed, exclusive group—traditionally, male property owners—to an inclusive status that, in western democracies, includes with few exceptions, all adults. Stuart Hall (1991:44) argues moreover that the relative decline and erosion of the power of the nation-state is accompanied by a decline in the centrality of national identities, and "a fragmentation and erosion of collective social identity." Hall defines the "great collective social identities"—class, race, nation, gender and the West—as "those which we thought of as large-scale, all-encompassing, homogeneous, as unified col- lective identities which could be spoken about almost as if they were singular actors in their own right but which, indeed, placed, positioned, stabilized and allowed us to understand and read, almost as a code, the imperatives of the individual self..." It is not that these categories have disappeared as a way of organizing society, but that their usefulness as "codes of identity" is challenged by recognition of the multiple and complex possibilities for individual and collective identities.

On the Importance of Territory and Sovereignty

This chapter considers future possibilities for citizenship defined not only by territory, nation and nation-state, but also by other sources of identity and community. However, this exploration should not lead us to conclude that territory and the status of nation-state are becoming artifacts of the nineteenth and twentieth centuries. Indeed, to live in Canada is to experience the passion and vision inspired by its citizens' claims to territory and self-determination.

Since the 1960s, sovereigntist leaders of the province of Quebec have sought popular support from Quebeckers for separation from Canada and the establishment of a sovereign country, Quebec. At the same time, First Nations across Canada, including the Cree in northern Quebec, have asserted claims to land and the right to self-government after enduring more than a hundred years of political domination by the federal government, as well as discrimination by, and alienation from, mainstream society. Not surprisingly, these conflicting visions for the same territory generate high levels of tension within Quebec and the rest of Canada. The sovereigntists claim the right to include all the existing territory of Quebec in their vision of a sovereign nation, while the Cree argue that they are sovereign within their territory in northern Quebec, and claim the right to determine their future. Meanwhile, federalists in both Quebec and the rest of Canada fight to preserve the integrity of the country.

The Quebec sovereigntist vision was eloquently expressed in September 1995, through the preamble to Bill 1, An Act Respecting the Future of Quebec. It reads, in part:

"Because we inhabit the territories delimited by our ancestors, from Abitibi to Iles-de-la-Madeleine, from Ungava to the American border, because for 400 years we have cleared, plowed, paced, surveyed, dug, fished, built, started anew, discussed, protected and loved this land that is cut across and watered by the St. Lawrence River;...

"Because the heart of this land beats in French and because that heartbeat is as meaningful as the seasons that hold sway over it, as the winds that bend it, as the men and women who shape it; ...

"Because it is this land alone that represents our pride the source of our strength, our sole opportunity to express ourselves in the entirety of our individual natures and our collective heart; ...

"We, the people of Quebec, declare it is our will to be in full possession of all the powers of a state; to levy all our taxes, to vote in all our laws, to sign all our treaties and to exercises the highest power of all, conceiving, and controlling, by ourselves, our fundamental law ... We, the people of Quebec, through our National Assembly, proclaim: Quebec is a sovereign country."

The position of the Quebec Cree has been expressed with equal force by Matthew Coon Come, Grand Chief of the Grand Council of the Crees of Quebec:

"We Crees have lived in the James Bay area since the last Ice Age. We have always identified ourselves as one people with our own language, laws, beliefs and systems of land tenure and governance. We Crees gave our lands a name—*Eenou Astchee*—long before there was a Canada or a United States .... I am speaking up to defend Cree rights. *There will be no annexation of ourselves or our territory to an independent Quebec without our consent.* There is an obvious and undeniable logic here: If Quebec has the right to leave Canada, then certainly the Cree people have the right to keep their territory in Canada, if that is our choice .... We Crees do not think of borders as sacred. We are part of the land. There is no other place in the world where everything, every hill, every stream, every fork in the river is named in Cree. *Eenou Astchee* is the centre of Cree civilization, and it is inconceivable that we would cease to care for it."[8]

Territory and sovereignty are the very heart and soul of the Parti Québécois' quest for a new country, and of First Nations' demands for self-determination. Rarely do we hear such passion in public life as that expressed by peoples seeking self-determination. This quest continues to grip the human imagination. However, we are reminded on a daily basis that this grip can become a brutal iron fist, when nationalism and secessionism, sparked by ethnic, religious and cultural differences, explode in flurries of violence and warfare. Thus, while the boundaries of modern citizenship are expanding with the rise of new political identities and communities, territory and nation-state status are still of profound importance to those peoples who seek them.

The new ideologies discussed in previous chapters give rise to opportunities for identities and political practices not bound by national loyalties, opportunities reinforced by the ability of citizens around the world to link up in common cause, regardless of their current place of residence. Robert Cox (1994: 53) writes that movements associated with feminism, environmentalism and the search for peace "evoke particular identities .... They exist within states but are transnational in essence." In his description of the emergence of new forms of citizenship, David Elkins (1994:6) refers to this process as the "unbundling" of the old hierarchy of identities that put loyalty to, and identity with, the nation-state at the top. Elkins argues that this hierarchy of identities could be replaced by "multiple" hierarchies that are different for each individual. Identity need not be dominated by a single construct, but rather can reflect multiple selves, fluid in relative importance. Hand in hand with the possibilities for multiple identities are the possibilities for multiple loyalties. Such developments signal a diminution of the homogeneity that characterizes mass society, and allow the individual greater freedom. The potential for multiple identities and loyalties, in turn, clearly affects the meaning of citizenship.

Multiculturalism: A Postmodern Response to Globalization and Citizenship?

Frederick Buell (1994:127) argues that globalization has undercut the "territorialization of culture" so that even national cultures have come to exist apart from, across and even without territories. As a consequence, there is a "decentering" of formerly national cultures in Canada, the United States and Britain, where the dominant culture is "dislocated from its locus and forced to stop considering itself the culture of reference" (Derrida 1978:86). In such countries, it is now less tenable to equate national cultural identity with the nation-state. As Stuart Hall writes (1991:21), "The notion of a national formation, of a national economy, which could be represented through a national cultural identity, is under considerable pressure." The process of decentering is one in which dominant monolithic cultures are displaced from their equation with national culture by cultural pluralism in a more "up-for-grabs world" (Buell 1994:143).

Indeed, multiculturalism, as a policy of "cultural intervention," represents a reconfiguring of national culture to accommodate changes in the world system. Buell (1994:144) writes that the debate over multiculturalism can therefore be seen as part of a larger transformation in the world system, which he describes as "the movement from a globally disseminated nationalism, which reinforced the construction of national identities as objects of faith and focuses for social organization, to a period of globalism, in which the stereotypical national culture has become increasingly strained, fractured and demystified, and more complex and heterogeneous forms of local culture have been developed to negotiate the larger system." For example, in the United States, the ideal of the country as the land of immigrants, "a nation of nations," erupted in the 1960s, even as America championed the idea of national self-determination in the world. This was brought about through a powerful movement by blacks to protest racism and inequality at home, a movement inspired by the spirit of an "oppositional" form of cultural nationalism, and one that shattered "the boundaries of American identity" (Buell 1994:144). The philosophy that informs multiculturalism constructs one "space" in which the bases of identity converge with the principles of citizenship. Here, citizenship is defined by the community's capacity to accommodate social diversity, while still inspiring the loyalty, sense of belonging and willingness to serve that inform traditional conceptions of citizenship.

In policies of multiculturalism, rights and identity meet; claims to the right to be different, and to protect cultures, are asserted as inalienable, universal rights. For instance, education in one's own language and with respect for cultural practices are claimed as human rights in transnational discourse (Buell, 1994:154). In the deterritorialized field of universal rights, legitimized in the transnational sphere, rights have been expanded to include culture, language and development.

And yet, some critics argue that a policy of multiculturalism actually inhibits development of citizenship virtues that extend beyond rights, including a sense of loyalty and commitment to the laws and values of the larger nation-state. Canadian writer Neil Bissoondath (1993:376) argues that the official policy of multiculturalism in Canada encourages the remembrance of "Old World feuds"—ethnic, religious and political—that "frequently override loyalties to the new country .... In stressing the differences between groups, in failing to emphasize that this is a country with its own ideals and attitudes that demand adherence, the policy has instead aided in a hardening of hatreds." Furthermore, Bissoondath (1993:373–74) charges that the Canadian multicultural policy "simplifies culture": "Our approach to multiculturalism thus encourages the devaluation of that which it claims to wish to protect and promote. Culture becomes an object for display rather than the heart and soul of the individuals formed by it." Still others argue that the politics of identity are incompatible with the broad, horizontal attachments that characterize national citizenship. It is not surprising that the current attack on multiculturalism in the United States includes claims for restoration of the national culture, the decline of which also signals, to critics, the loss of "national power as well as identity" (Buell 1994:143).

The invention of incredible technological ways of linking the world, in combination with new social movements, means that opportunities now exists for the construction of "spaces of people" that transcend the borders of territorially based communities. The communities created by people who discover and act on shared identity and interests—via e-mail, fax or phone—are the result of voluntary psychological and emotional investments, and so, like interpersonal relationships, can be deeply meaningful. David Elkins (1994:8) argues that participants in such communities are likely to be less prejudiced or "parochial," and more able to embrace a global community. Thus, while traditional notions of citizenship linked to nation-states will certainly endure, the emergence of new ideologies discussed in this book might also be seen as new mobilizing vehicles for citizenship. And, like the ideologies, new orientations to citizenship can emerge at the local, provincial/state, national, transnational and global levels. This shift involves the search for a holistic view of local, national and global issues, one that includes not only the search for new identities but also for a renewed sense of community. It takes us, in turn, to issues of intergroup relations and citizen empowerment.

THE FUTURE OF POLITICS IN THE GLOBAL AGE

Still to consider is whether meaningful loyalties and the sense of belonging that inspire citizenship within the nation-state can be sustained within other kinds of political communities. The blood-and-belief ties that link nations to territory—language, ethnicity and religion—evoke profound bonds and constitutive identities. But new political identities and their collectivities are based on membership by choice. As noted in earlier chapters, such identities can be donned and doffed. The question is, can they inspire the same powerful loyalties and sense of belonging and commitment to community that inform national citizenship? Conversely, might new communities, because they are chosen, inspire deeper loyalty and commitment?

It cannot be automatically assumed that the social identities inspired by feminism, environmentalism and multiculturalism will be sufficient to mobilize most people to political action.[9] For example, and as noted in Chapter 5, feminism offers both an identity and a way of seeing the political world. Depending on the choice of the person involved, these can be shallow or deep, a mere diversion or a guide to every choice and action, a social engagement on the Internet or a cry for political change to the very foundations of society. Furthermore, in the age of the Internet, when mediating social forums—"virtual communities" of strangers who share concerns, cares, interests—become increasingly important, what becomes of common political action? Of public discourse? Do public forums and a common good become less compelling? It seems possible that these new forums for social and political interaction can enhance the practice of direct democracy—for example, via electronic petitions delivered to politicians on the Internet or televoting. On the other hand, there is also the possibility that political activity could become limited to communities of common interest, with little concern for, or commitment to, a larger public good. In short, we are witnessing both the fragmentation of old communities and the building of new communities, and it is by no means clear whether, on balance, deconstruction or construction will prevail.

Citizenship and Politics in the Global Age

Stuart Hall (1991:33) contributes a valuable model for making sense of the tension inherent in globalization and new political identities. In his model, the responses to globalization are multifaceted. First, there can be an impulse to return to the earlier world-system of nation-states, an order he describes as "an older, corporate, enclosed, increasingly defensive one which has to go back to nationalism and national cultural identity in a highly defensive way, and to try to build barriers around it before it is eroded." There is much evidence of this reaction in the world today, in the hatreds of ethnic warfare between and within nation-states. A second outcome or reaction is that of the the cosmopolitan or "global, post-modern" individual who is trying to "live with, and at the same moment, overcome, subsume, get hold of, and incorporate difference." The third response emerges from a space Hall calls the "local." Hall (1991:34) writes that there are two impulses behind the local dynamic. First, it can be a response to the overwhelming enormity and complexity of politics on a global scale. This reflects a move to the local in territorial terms, and echoes our earlier discussion of the revitalization of cities. Second, and more important for our understanding of how the new ideologies and their politics fit into the politics of the global era, we must recognize another form of local politics that flows from "the most profound cultural revolution" of the twentieth century. It is the process by which groups at the margins have struggled to "come into representation ... in art, in painting, in film, in music, in politics, and in social life generally." Hall writes (1991:34) that in this space, "new subjects, new genders, new ethnicities, new regions, new communities, hitherto excluded from the major forms of cultural representation, unable to locate themselves except as decentred or subaltern, have acquired through struggle, sometimes in very marginalized ways, the means to speak for themselves for the first time. And the discourse of power in our society, the discourses of the dominant regimes, have been certainly threatened by this decentred cultural empowerment of the marginal and the local." Hall does not argue that the formerly marginalized have become dominant or even equal, but that, paradoxically, "marginality has become a powerful space. It is a space of weak power but it is a space of power, nonetheless" (Hall 1991:34).

Exercise Three: Citizenship and Ideologies

A number of quite different ideologies have been discussed in previous chapters. Some of these may be compatible with conventional notions of citizenship, embedded within the territory and institutions of nation-states, whereas others may be more problematic. How would you sort out the following ideologies with respect to their fit with conventional notions of citizenship: conservatism, environmentalism, feminism, liberalism, nationalism, populism, socialism? Which pose the greatest challenge, and which are the most compatible?

Groups at the margins, including the nations that came into existence in the postcolonial era, feminists, and cultural and political movements by blacks and indigenous peoples, have uncovered their stories from the "bottom up" (Hall 1991: 35). The social and political movements that grow from the margins, from the local, necessarily go through a stage of defensive self-definition and politicization, when belonging and identity with the group are foundational—the politics of identity. Yet, Hall argues, such an essentialism is impossible to defend in this age of fluid and multiple identities. Thus, politics in the age of globalization is "the politics of recognizing that all of us are composed of multiple social identities, not of one. That we are all complexly constructed through different categories, of different antagonisms, and these may have the effect of locating us socially in multiple positions ...." (1991:157). However, if political identities must be understood as multiple and complex, derived from the various spaces in which individuals live, there is, at the same time, the emergence of a global consciousness from which many political problems—environmental degradation, poverty, discrimination, violence—have come to be understood as problems common to the universal human condition.

Thus, Roland Robertson speaks of the possibility for the earth's ecology and the future of the human species to be central to "the politics of the global-human condition in the coming decades." Interestingly, Robertson (1991:81) suggests that such a politics could be "'institutionalized' as 'merely' a female issue; but yet it could, alternatively, come to be a powerful basis for *feminism*." Robertson argues that the way in which women participate in the global discourse will be crucial to the outcome of "politics of the global-human condition." And the strength of the international women's movement indicates that it *is* moving from the margins to the centre stage of global politics, gaining sufficient strength to influence policy at the local and the global levels. Therefore, some of the best possibilities for opening up the vistas of citizenship on a global scale lie in the movements related to the new ideologies of feminism and environmentalism.

The emergence of new ideologies and their related social movements may therefore bring about a metamorphosis in ways of conceiving citizenship. William Harman (1988:117) writes that the "ecological movement, peace movement and women's movement are now more clearly recognized to be different drops in a single wave of transformative change." He describes the changing consciousness that these movements embody as a major shift in the "underlying paradigm of western industrial society." Yet, at the same time, as a global consciousness is promoted, there also emerges, from local spaces, a challenge to global mass culture. Robert Cox (1991:349) argues that the emergence of a political culture grounded in popular social movements is one way that citizens can offset the dominance of the global capital imperative. Such movements work best at the local level. He writes (1991:349):

> They will in many cases be local responses to global problems—to problems of the environment, of organizing production, of providing welfare, of migration. If they are ultimately to result in new forms of state, they will arise from the practice of non-state popular collective action rather than from extensions of existing administrative types of control.

This point is taken up by Richard Falk (1993:47) in his description of the impact of new ideological movements in the 1980s:

> The real arena of politics was no longer understood as acting in opposition within a particular state, nor the relation of society and the state, but ... consisted more and more of acting to promote a certain kind of political consciousness transnationally that could radiate influence in a variety of directions, including bouncing back to the point of origin. Amnesty International and Greenpeace are emblematic of this transnational militancy with an identity, itself evolving and being transformed, that can't really be tied very specifically to any one country or even any region but may also be intensely local in its activist concerns ...

Theories of globalization, especially regarding its meaning for nation-states and citizens, contain foundational assumptions about human nature and the social capacities of human beings. The vision of global citizenship is informed by positive assumptions about the human capacity for meaningful social connection with billions of unknown fellow citizens. Yet theories that emphasize the rebirth of cities and local movements as the locus of citizenship suggest that the meaning and practices of citizenship can only be operationalized in a profound way in local communities, although often in the name of solving global problems. This global-local dynamic permeates theories about where and how citizenship will be practised in the future. At the same time, the emergence of new ideologies, political identities and conceptions of community are giving new meaning to citizenship. It must be reiterated that the modern forum for citizenship—the nation-state—and the rights and responsibilities, as well as the identities and loyalty inspired by the nation-state, are not dead. Rather, old and new political identities—of religion, ethnicity, gender, nationalism, environmentalism, culture, language, sexual orientation, human rights activism—and their communities, whether grounded in territory or transcending territory in new spaces, give us different ways of conceiving citizenship. Like the ideologies from which they flow, these new orientations challenge traditional conceptions of identities and loyalties based on national territories and states. The transformations described above reflect the interplay of established and dynamic forces in history, as newly politicized identities and communities overlay existing ones, creating multiple arenas for the practice of politics.

While most of this chapter has explored new frontiers for our understanding of citizenship, it is important to remember that some of the current political debates in the nations of the western world hark back to decades-old arguments between those on the political left and those on the political right about what are the appropriate socioeconomic rights for citizens. Earlier this century, central questions about citizenship focused on the proper balance of individual and social responsibility, and on the appropriate role of government in the lives of citizens. A resurgence of this debate, in terms of challenges to the modern welfare state, attests to the enduring importance of the oldest political ideologies—liberalism, socialism, conservatism. The questions of central importance now being revisited revolve around the degree to which citizens should be collectively responsible for the well-being of their fellow citizens, and the role that government should play in society.

To understand this debate in terms of citizenship, it is helpful to review T. H. Marshall's theory of citizenship, in which he traces the evolution of the rights of modern citizenship from civil to political to social. The individual's right to liberty, free speech, property ownership and equality before the law—products of the eighteenth and nineteenth centuries—marked the first stage in Marshall's model of citizenship; the right to political participation came next. Social rights—welfare, security, education—were first developed in the early part of the twentieth century, and they represent the final block in Marshall's model of citizenship. In this model, citizenship is the bulwark against class inequality in society, and with its complete realization all citizens can be "full members of a community" (Marshall 1964:84). Marshall includes social rights in the model of citizenship because he argues that civil rights—the right to be free and to own property—are grounded in the principles of a liberal, free-market ideology. They give the "legal capacity to strive for the things we would like to possess but do not guarantee the possession of any of them ...." Similarly, the right to free speech has little meaning if "from lack of education, you have nothing to say that is worth saying, and no means of making yourself heard if you say it" (1964:88).

Although strong national communities arose from the bonds of shared political and civil rights in the nineteenth century, the class system and social inequality in Marshall's Britain remained intractable. By the late nineteenth and early twentieth centuries, such inequality came to be challenged as the working classes claimed social rights, which "imply an absolute right to a certain standard of civilization that is conditional only on the discharge of one's general duties of citizenship," not on one's wealth or economic status (Marshall 1964: 96). As workers' incomes grew and the gap between economic classes diminished, as direct, progressive income tax was developed and as workers became the new target for mass consumption, the working class was closer to the "good life" than it had ever been. Social rights came to be a claim of citizenship, and states began to redistribute income via taxation in the form of income transfers, as well as through public education, health care and housing subsidies.

In the years following the Second World War, a broad consensus developed around the welfare state that endured until the late 1970s and early 1980s, when a growing neoconservative ideological current gathered momentum and challenged the large-state foundation upon which the edifice of the welfare state had been constructed. Today, there is no plank in that edifice that is not threatened with the saw of government spending cuts. The current ideological current, reinforced by economic globalization, tells governments in the developed world that the economic imperatives of the international economy are preeminent over the provision of domestic social services for citizens. As Ian Culpitt (1992:1) argues, there is now an "eclipse of citizenship entitlements and social rights":

> An essential aspect of this attack on the welfare state has been the complete rejection of those social ideals of citizenship rights and obligations which were encapsulated in the political and social structures of welfare states. The champions of the new corporate state ... have criticized the welfare state because it is regarded as a 'coercive bargain between strangers which abridged the liberties of both rich and poor, while infantilizing the poor.' This neo-conservative critical stance has spurned any emphasis on collective responsibility, or obligation, and has stressed the threat that its proponents believe the welfare state poses to individual liberty.

For their part, neoconservative critics of the welfare state claim that it has weakened rather than strengthened citizenship. The welfare state has promoted "passive" or "private" citizenship by emphasizing entitlements, and by neglecting any obligation or responsibility in public life (Kymlicka and Norman 1994:355). In ideological terms, neoconservatives argue that the welfare state fails to uphold or promote "(negative) freedom" or "(desert-based) justice." Furthermore, it is economically inefficient, and creates a culture of dependency among the poor that fails to improve their life chances (Kymlicka and Norman 1994:355). Those on the political right argue for a focus on economic responsibility among individuals, for privatization of social assistance and for a market-based approach to running governments that would not only contribute to greater individual freedom but would also eliminate government overspending and reduce public debt. Thus, both sides argue for the virtues of citizenship, while disagreeing strongly on what citizenship should entail.

Not surprisingly, the neoconservative arguments, which claim political ascendency in the 1990s, are challenged by those on the left who maintain that such an individualistic conception of citizenship destroys the political community. Will Kymlicka and Wayne Norman write (1994:357–58):

> They believe that the dependent are kept out of the mainstream of society because of a lack of opportunities such as jobs, education, and training, not because of any desire to avoid work. Imposing obligations, therefore, is futile if genuine opportunities are absent, and unnecessary if those opportunities are present, since the vast majority of people on welfare would prefer not to be .... So, while the left accepts the general principle that citizenship involves both rights and responsibilities, it feels that rights to participate must, in a sense, precede the responsibilities.

The contemporary debate between the political right and left on the future of the welfare state illuminates the enduring importance of traditional ideologies in defining the rights of citizenship in western societies, as well as the dominant values that define the community.

IN CONCLUSION...

The forces of globalization and the increasing importance of new ideologies discussed in this book generate a storm of change that rocks our understanding of citizenship. Of course, historically, citizenship has been an evolving political construct, taking on new form with expansion of the territorial places in which citizenship is practised, and with the extension of rights and membership in the community, regardless of gender, ethnicity, religion or socioeconomic standing. The meaning of citizenship continues to evolve. Increasingly, we think of human rights as universal, thus not delimited by national borders. At the same time, new political identities and communities blossom, grounded not in territorial proximity, but in common interest, and linked by the technology of global communications.

The revolutionary changes associated with globalization—the free movement of investment and capital, the emergence of high technology and the knowledge elite and the migration of people—evoke multiple and sometimes conflicting responses. It is clear that a global consciousness is emerging in policy areas that do not respect territorial borders: environmental issues, human rights issues, development and health issues. Such a consciousness is associated with the rise of the ideologies of feminism, environmentalism, as well as the peace and development movements, and indigenous people's movements. Here, we find new sources of political identity and new forms of political community. Traditional nation-states are but one forum, from the local to the global, in which these citizens participate.

This chapter identifies the currents of change and resistance that flow through all periods of great transformation in human history. Globalization is a powerful source of that change, but it is not a democratic phenomenon. As mentioned earlier, a majority of the world's people lack access to the knowledge and technology to participate in the new communities. There is much talk of the global village, yet the traditional sources of identity and community—territory, nationhood and sovereignty—continue to inspire and incite. Challenges to globalization take many forms, including resistance to the universalization of rights in the transnational order, and the demand for recognition and sovereignty of peoples defined by ethnicity, culture or religion. Feminism and environmentalism give us new models for understanding political identity, community and participation. Yet, the traditional ideologies of liberalism, conservatism, socialism and populism remain powerful forces for ordering communities. One way to understand these currents is to consider them from the perspective of citizenship. Citizenship, is, after all, an essential political construct, constituted by definitions of human rights, identity and community. Both traditional and new ideologies contain visions about rights, identity and community—about citizenship. It is not surprising, therefore, that citizenship has become increasingly contested ideological terrain as the century closes.

NOTES

1. In the case of the Québécois, a separate nation, Quebec, is imagined.
2. Benedict Anderson emphasizes that nationalism should be understood in the context of the large cultural systems from which it arose; specifically, religious communities and dynastic realms. Nationalism did not replace religion, but arose out of and against religious communities and dynastic realms.
3. There are many excellent studies of the development of modern citizenship. See, for example, Murray Bookchin, *Urbanization Without Cities: The Rise and Decline of Citizenship* (Montreal: Black Rose Books, 1992); Derek B. Heater, *Citizenship: The Civic Ideal In World History, Politics, and Education* (U.K.: Longman Group, 1990); Michael Ignatieff, "The Myth of Citizenship," *Queen's Quarterly* 94 (Winter 1987), 966–85; William Kaplan, ed. *Belonging: The Meaning and Future of Canadian Citizenship* (Montreal and Kingston: McGill–Queen's Univ. Press, 1993); James H. Kettner, *The Development of American Citizenship: 1608–1870* (Chapel Hill: Univ. of North Carolina Press, 1978); Susan Moller Okin, "Women, Equality, and Citizenship," *Queen's Quarterly* 99 (Spring 1992), 56–71; and J.G.A. Pocock, "Ideal of Citizenship Since Classical Times," *Queen's Quarterly* 99 (Spring 1992), 33–55.
4. It should be recognized, of course, that the criteria for *immigration* are much more complex than the criteria for *citizenship*. For example, individuals who apply to immigrate to Canada are selected according to a number of criteria. Business-class immigrants must have entrepreneurial capacity, and are required to start a business that will create at least one job for a Canadian. Criteria for independent immigrants include language skills in one of Canada's two official languages, age, education, employability and health status. Under the family reunification program, an immigrant living in Canada can apply to sponsor immediate family members as immigrants to the country. For humanitarian reasons, the refugee program accepts individuals who claim refugee status in Canada and who are determined to be in need of a safe haven. Once immigrants have acquired legal permanent resident status and have lived in Canada for three years, they can apply for Canadian citizenship. Criteria for Canadian citizenship includes knowledge of one of Canada's two official languages, some knowledge of Canada's geography, history, political process, and the rights and responsibilities of citizenship, and finally, respect for the laws of the land.
5. See, for instance, Richard Stubbs and Geoffrey D. Underhill, eds. *Political Economy and the Changing Global Order* (Toronto: McClelland and Stewart, 1994)
6. Canadian Press, Talks prompt hopes of overhaul of U.N., *Calgary Herald*, 27 March 1995: A3.
7. The implications of globalization for the movement of people are indeed profound, especially for the "affluent, underpopulated settler societies" (Elkins 1993:10). Anderson (1983:13) describes the migration phenomenon as one in which "inequality and misery are in all senses 'closer' to privilege and wealth than ever before in human history." Thus, there is a mass wave of migration from the periphery to the western, industrialized core, a reversal of the direction of migration in the age of exploration. David Elkins predicts resistance to the idea of open borders, resistance grounded in the increasingly obsolete justifications of national sovereignty and "national way of life." On the same subject, an article in *The Atlantic Monthly* (1994:43) envisions "the coming anarchy," when "nations break up under the tidal flow of refugees from environmental and social disaster ... wars are fought over scarce resources ... armed bands of stateless marauders clash with the private security forces of the elites."
8. From remarks made by Matthew Coon Come, Grand Chief of the Grand Council of the Crees of Quebec, to the Canadian Club, March 13, 1995. Cited in The Crees of Quebec, on sovereignty, *The Globe and Mail*, 30 March 1995: A29.
9. While the women's movement and the environmental movement have a significant number of committed and vocal activists, only a small percentage of the total population engages in such high levels of political participation.

CHAPTER TWELVE

The Politics of Ideological Diversity

WITH BORIS DEWIEL

Do I contradict myself? Very well then I contradict myself,
(I am large, I contain multitudes.)

WALT WHITMAN

A foolish consistency is the hobgoblin of little minds, adored by little statesmen and
philosophers and divines. With consistency a great soul has simply nothing to do.

RALPH WALDO EMERSON

May God us keep from single vision and Newton's sleep!

WILLIAM BLAKE

The central fact that confronts the student of politics is that people tend to disagree about fundamental political questions. Given the fact of ideological diversity that this book describes, how can we make sense of this range of beliefs? How can it be that so many intelligent, well-informed people can disagree so often, and so fundamentally, about public issues—issues that by definition involve the things we have in common?

Three strategies for dealing with the phenomenon of ideological diversity suggest themselves. In the first approach, we can choose to hold fast to our own ideological precommitments, and seek to discredit alternative visions; this is the strategy of ideological combat, with the winner taking all. The second approach is to try to make competing ideologies mutually compatible, by removing from each its most contentious parts. This strategy could be called neutralization, or perhaps, syncretism, the search for a middle way. The third approach, the one that will be explored in this chapter, is to accept ideological diversity as a fact of life, and try to understand how it can be that others may *legitimately* disagree with our own cherished beliefs and values.

This chapter will suggest that politics is pluralistic. That is, (a) there are many legitimate ways of seeing the world, and (b) each of these views captures something true and important about political problems, but (c) each also leaves out important things. There are reasons to believe that we will always be faced with a range of contending ideologies, that no single ideology will ever capture everything true and good about political life. Rather than try to pick the "right" ideology, or to create one anew, students of politics should try to understand the ways in which each ideology succeeds in expressing important things about our common lives, but fails to satisfy some of our other shared values. The aim of this discussion is to help the reader to think like a citizen, who is prepared to make critical choices between legitimate alternatives, rather than like an ideologue, who believes there is a single right answer to all political problems.

Because this chapter suggests a certain way of seeing ideological conflict, its tone may be less descriptive than that of previous chapters, and will be characterized by an attempt to persuade. It will be for the reader to decide whether there is something to be said for this way of seeing political life, or whether another strategy is better.

The discussion will begin by suggesting that the belief in final answers to political questions is itself a notion with roots in our own political history; then moves to an examination of the difference between pluralism, the idea that there is more than one right answer to political questions, and relativism, the idea that there are no wrong answers. Next, a few concrete political issues will be illustrate how different ideologies help cast their own kind of light onto some of the controversies of our day. These examples will show how a pluralist approach can be helpful to the student of politics by promoting a sympathetic understanding of ideological controversies; that is, an understanding of the way participants in debate themselves see the problems. Whether pluralism can be taken a step further, to provide a normative framework and a guide to political action—that is, whether pluralism can be an ideology—will be the subject of the final section.

THE BELIEF IN FINAL ANSWERS

If there is a single writer whose work has been animated by the idea of the pluralism of values and the diversity of ideological beliefs, it is the Oxford historian of ideas, Isaiah Berlin. Throughout his celebrated career, Berlin has argued again and again that there is more than one true answer to the fundamental questions of politics. Many resist Berlin's pluralistic vision because it is part of the modern worldview to believe that all political problems should be, in the end, resolvable. In the same way that scientists still search for a Grand Unified Theory of physics, many of us believe that with enough information and expertise, every political issue can be finally solved by finding the single set of true principles to guide public life. Berlin (1969:x) traces this idea back to the ancient Greeks, who originated the idea that if something is truly good, it must be consistent with all other truly good things, so that all good things taken together form a perfect whole. It is this doctrine which pluralism would have us reject.

In an age dominated by the marvels of science, however, the pluralist view may seem out of place. Science is the realm of facts and logic, and both factual and logical statements are ruled by the law of noncontradiction: if a statement is true, then any contradictory statement, by implication, must be false. Since we know this law holds in the factual and logical realm, many have come to believe that the way to find final answers is by reducing political questions to technical ones. That is, once political leaders, guided by the electorate, decide on the broad goals of public policy, the rest can be left to experts with the appropriate scientific training. Since science is the realm of indisputable facts, the experts who design public policies need not trouble themselves with questions of values. These can be left to philosophers and poets. With this division of labour, we have become accustomed to seeing public-policy problems as resolvable by the techniques of science—and scientific questions can have only one true answer. In an age that places its faith in science, therefore, it is hard not to believe in final solutions.

Unfortunately, this optimism about scientific public policy has not been fulfilled. The greatest problem has been that it is not so easy to separate facts and values. The philosopher Hilary Putnam describes this problem when he writes:

> It is all well and good to describe hypothetical cases in which two people "agree on the facts and disagree about values," but in the world in which I grew up such cases are unreal. When and where did a Nazi and an anti-Nazi, a communist and a social democrat, a fundamentalist and a liberal, or even a Republican and a Democrat, agree on the facts? Even when it comes to one specific policy question, say…education, … unemployment, or … about drugs, every argument I have ever heard has exemplified the entanglement of the ethical and the factual.

In short, in the philosophy of the social sciences, the fact-value dichotomy, on which the idea of scientific or technocratic public policy relies, has become problematic. It is no longer accepted that troubling questions of value can be separated from technical issues, or that technically trained experts can find the single best route to politically given goals. While this has raised a range of issues in the field of policy analysis (Hawkesworth 1986), the problem here is to figure out what this means for our understanding of the diversity of political ideologies.

The question we must ask is this: Does the law of noncontradiction apply to statements about values? Is it true that for a particular public goal to be genuinely valuable, conflicting goals must therefore be false ones? For example, if it is true that freedom and equality sometimes come into conflict, must it therefore be true that one is a legitimate value and the other is not? Our intuition tells us that this is not so, and that the law of noncontradiction does not apply to assertions about values. And if facts and values are inevitably entangled in political issues, then perhaps there is something to Isaiah Berlin's ideas about the diversity of legitimate ways of life. Maybe the reason we are confronted by a range of political ideologies is that our underlying values are various and conflicting, and cannot be reduced to some basic consensus. Each ideology may be thought of as involving a vision of the political good. If these political ideals are many, and some are incompatible with others—in other words, if we cannot have all good things at once—then competing ideologies must inevitably arise.

Consider again the definition of ideology expressed in Chapter 1: an ideology is a socially constructed system of political beliefs with formal articulation, scope, internal consistency and durability, which provides a normative framework and a practical guide for political action. Here the value-laden nature of ideologies is clear. Since by definition, each ideology involves an evaluative outlook, the question is whether we have any convincing reason to think that all legitimate values must be finally resolvable into a single, coherent vision of "The Good." Berlin's message is that we have no reason to believe this. Furthermore, he argues, we have a great deal of evidence—from our understanding of history, our knowledge of other cultures and our self-understanding of modern democratic nations—pointing to the diversity of true ideals around which public life may be legitimately organized.

If so, ideological diversity will be a permanent fact of modern life. The American political philosopher John Rawls (1987:4) agrees:

> This diversity of doctrines—the fact of pluralism—is not a mere historical condition that will soon pass away; it is, I believe, a permanent feature of the public culture of modern democracies. Under the political and social conditions historically associated with these regimes, the diversity of views will persist and may increase.

Our optimism about a final, singular answer to political questions may therefore turn out to be in vain. This conclusion need not be accepted for pluralism to be useful as a heuristic device; that is, as a tool to aid understanding. A provisional or hypothetical pluralistic attitude can be useful to help us understand others, even while we continue to hold out hope for final solutions. But in its pure form, pluralism would have us accept diversity and ideological conflict as a permanent characteristic of modern life.

As a practical matter, it is obvious that perfect solutions to political problems are often beyond our grasp. Not all legitimate goals can be realized in full. For example, freedom and equality are both among our ultimate ideals, but we cannot have a maximum of both. To achieve perfect equality, we must deny certain freedoms; to allow perfect freedom, a degree of inequality must be permitted. While the precise relationship between equality and freedom depends on the way these terms are defined by political theorists, it is difficult to believe that there need never be a conflict between the two ideals. In reality, in public policy, as in private life, there is a cost to our choices. This is what economists call "opportunity cost." In choosing to devote ourselves fully to any one of our goals, we must give up hope of achieving some others—we pay a price in terms of forgone opportunities.

This mundane fact of life is usually thought to be due to the scarcity of basic resources, especially time and money, but Berlin's point is deeper. There is a permanent obstacle, which is not based on practical contingencies, that makes it impossible to achieve all our ends together. The deep problem is not just that our ultimate goals require the same resources, but that they actually conflict with one another. Berlin writes (1991:13):

> The notion of the perfect whole, the ultimate solution, in which all good things coexist, seems to me to be not merely unattainable—this is a truism—but conceptually incoherent .... Some among the Great Goods cannot live together. That is a conceptual truth. We are doomed to choose, and every choice may entail an irreparable loss.

Competition for the resources needed to achieve our goals is only the most superficial aspect of pluralism. The more significant problem is that our ideals themselves often are not compatible with one another. Berlin (1969:171) argues that there is no hierarchy of values; he denies that we can have a single scale with which we can measure all values. Different values are incommensurable, so there is no objective solution when legitimate values conflict.[1] "Should democracy in a given situation be promoted at the expense of artistic achievement; or mercy at the expense of justice; or spontaneity at the expense of efficiency; or happiness, loyalty, innocence at the expense of knowledge and truth?" (Berlin 1969:xlix–l). Scarcity of resources is an aggravating problem, but in the end it is not the cause of our inability to design perfect public policies—or to live perfect lives. The problem is in the inherent conflicts among our values themselves. This is Berlin's deep insight.

But why must these value differences come to be expressed as ideologies? Why study ideologies when the underlying conflicts involve our values themselves? Why can we not just address the conflicts of values directly, without involving ourselves in the intricacies of ideological conflict? The answer, again, is that facts and values are inevitably entangled. In political debates, statements that look as though they are about purely factual matters almost always have hidden evaluative presumptions, as will be illustrated below. And if we cannot talk about the facts involved in policy questions without raising questions of value, neither can we get very far by talking about value questions outside the context of actual political problems. While political philosophers may want to argue about values in the abstract, the entanglement of fact and value means that theirs is a highly artificial way to talk. In practice, it is difficult to understand value conflicts except as they take shape in actual political controversies.

In short, while it is possible to speak abstractly about our values and the conflicts among them, the entanglement of facts and values means that we cannot get very far in this way. Instead, we must consider peoples' differences as we find them. For some purposes, we might want to talk about cultural differences, and consider the conflicts between legitimate ways of life. But for the purposes of this discussion, we must confront underlying value conflicts as they take shape in the form of contending ideologies. Specifically, we should try to understand how different but legitimate values are raised in regard to social issues by those on different sides of actual policy debates.

Before turning to this task, the question may be raised as to whether pluralism is just a restatement of value relativism—the idea that everyone, or perhaps every culture, has a unique evaluative outlook, and that because of this, no one may ever legitimately question anyone else's values. Relativism, most reflective people will agree, is an unsatisfactory political position. As an argument, it fails because it is internally contradictory: the prohibition against judging others is asserted as an overriding moral truth, but it is itself a judgment. Philosophers call this the self-reference problem. More generally, relativism robs us of the ability to make the kind of political judgments that we need to make. A consistent relativist cannot condemn nazism, for example, or the genital mutilation of children. The question is, can a pluralist make these kinds of judgments?

Relativism, the Self-Reference Problem and Special Pleading

In philosophy, these three terms are associated with the problem of understanding others' values and beliefs.

"Relativism" is a term that encompasses a range of ideas, beginning with the simple observation that people in various cultural or historical circumstances tend to have different ideas, mores and beliefs. Sometimes, this basic fact is taken to mean that there are no moral standards that apply to all human beings. This idea is called *ethical relativism*, and implies that our own moral beliefs apply only to us. Thus, ethical relativism suggests that morality is subjective. A related idea, called *conceptual relativism*, holds that our beliefs about what is true or false depend on our cultural or historical situation, so that *all* factual knowledge is subjective.

The "self-reference problem" arises when someone expresses skepticism about values or beliefs, but in so broad a statement that it applies to all human beings in all situations, *including the person making the statement.* Suppose Jane declares that all human beliefs are necessarily false. Does this not imply that her own beliefs about skepticism are false? This dilemma is called the self-reference problem. Jane's skeptical assertion is so broadly stated that it applies to her own ideas, which means that she has contradicted herself.

"Special pleading" is the attempt to make an exception for oneself in order to avoid the self-reference problem. For truly universal statements, no exceptions can possibly exist, because that is what it means to be universal. In such cases, special pleading is always a fallacy. If Manual claims that all human knowledge is false—except for his own insights about knowledge—he is involved in special pleading. For students of political ideologies, the self-reference problem and the fallacy of special pleading mean we should avoid the idea that all knowledge is ideological in the pejorative sense of being groundless or illusory.

RELATIVISM VERSUS PLURALISM

The problem with the idea that all values are subjective, and therefore relative, is that it takes the force out of the idea of value itself. Relative values are values without substance, values reduced to mere preferences. The idea that values are subjective and relative is behind what the prominent Canadian philosopher Charles Taylor (1991) has called the "malaise of modernity," the devaluation and debasement of modern life.[2] Relativism leaves each of us as a moral universe unto ourselves, with no common values between us, and it has contributed to the lonely detachment and alienation of modern life.

Pluralism, on the other hand, need not lead to this kind of debasement. The central difference between a relativist and a pluralist is that the relativists say that each person (or cultural group) has a unique set of values. A pluralist, by contrast, says we share the same set of values, but that these values are complex and often conflicting. The pluralist points out that human beings seem to share the ability to appreciate what is valuable in others' ways of life. For example, an honest, reflective conservative can understand and appreciate, in the abstract at least, the values and outlook of a liberal, because they share the same moral universe. Where a relativist might say that the liberal and conservative live in separate political worlds, a pluralist would say they live in the same world—but that the world is morally complex. This means that we all have, at least on the level of sympathetic imagination, a common moral outlook. Each of us knows the value of liberty, or equality, or fraternity, and so on, even though we know that painful choices must sometimes be made between them. In short, relativists deny that we share the same values, while pluralists believe that our values are shared, though in practice we make different choices between competing "goods."

Again, this way of expressing things is highly artificial. In practice, we do not detach ourselves from our situation in order to make pure moral judgments. Instead, facts and values are entangled within our ways of seeing the world. We are rarely faced with an essential moral choice about the direction our lives should take; instead, our commitments are expressed every day in the way we live our lives, and in our understanding of problems that confront us. It is this embeddedness that creates the appearance of cultural relativism, but this appearance is misleading. The evident variety of values embedded in diverse ways of life does not mean that one's morality is nothing more than a reflection of one's culture or history. It means only that our *common* values themselves are diverse. When confronted by people from different cultures, we have the resources to understand what is valuable, and what is not, about their way of life. We have the common moral resources that allow us to have an ethical appreciation for others' ways of life. Cross-cultural understanding is possible; in the age of global travel, it happens all the time.

A pluralist, in short, can believe that many incompatible things are genuinely good, while still recognizing that there are a great range of things that are not, and many more that should be condemned as evil. There are many valuable ways of life, but this does not imply that anything goes. Thus, a pluralist, without contradiction, can condemn nazism or genital mutilation, whereas a relativist cannot.

But how do we know that strangers live in the same moral universe as ourselves? One kind of proof is the simple fact that we recognize them as human beings. Our idea of humanity itself implies a being with moral knowledge. Berlin (1969:xxxi) points out that anyone who is out of touch with the factual world—an individual who cannot tell the difference between true and false—is properly thought of as abnormal, or even insane. More important, we make the same judgment about anyone who cannot tell the difference between right and wrong. These sorts of persons are tragically lacking in what we think of as the basic elements of humanity. In other words, recognizing others as being human means we understand them as having recognizable human values.

Furthermore, we know that, with a bit of work, communication with strangers is possible. In order to understand others, we must, as a matter of methodological necessity, assume that they have more or less the same values that we do.[3] Otherwise, we could have no hope of understanding them. "[T]he possibility of understanding ... depends upon the existence of some common values, and not on a common 'factual' world alone" (Berlin 1969:xxxi). Because we know we can communicate with others, we can conclude that values are shared, and thus are neither subjective nor relative.

> Moral categories—and categories of value in general—are nothing like as firm and ineradicable as those of, say, the perception of the material world, but neither are they as relative or as fluid as some writers have .... tended to assume. A minimum of common moral ground ... is intrinsic to human communication (Berlin 1969:xxxii).

In short, pluralism posits a shared moral universe, but one that is internally complex. The pluralist stance is a demanding one because it asks the student of politics to be of two minds at once. On one hand, we often have our own ways of seeing particular issues; on the other, we must acknowledge that contradictory views may also be of value. But for those who can do so, this dual-mindedness is a useful ability, both for scholars and for citizens of modern democracies. Pluralists approach those who have different views in the same way that enlightened tourists encounter foreign cultures, with an appreciation for what is good about other ways of life and a cautious disapproval for what is not. When their travels are over, enlightened tourists return to their own way of life with a renewed understanding of what is valuable about it, but also with ideas about how their own beliefs and way of life could be improved. Students of political ideologies, if they are sympathetic, critical and honest, can learn the same kinds of lessons.

POLITICAL CONTROVERSIES IN A DIVERSE WORLD

To demonstrate the pluralist approach to political controversy, this section will discuss a small selection of political issues, each of which involves fundamental disagreements about values and political goods. The issues explored are abortion, affirmative action policies and the provision of social welfare.

Abortion

Few issues are more contentious and polarized today in the United States and Canada than the issue of abortion. Two sides, each with an absolute stand based on a firm moral conviction, confront each other with distrust and often hostility. On one side are the defenders of women's right to choose. On the other are those who defend the rights of the unborn. One way to understand this controversy is to point out the differences in each side's view of the value of human life. The question is, what is a human life, and when does life begin? While this looks at the outset like a matter of factual definition, we will see that this is a paradigm case of the entanglement of facts and values, and of the fundamental ideological disagreement that results from essential value conflict.

The defence of a woman's right to choose whether to continue a pregnancy follows from an ideal of human life centred on the value of autonomy: a life worth living is one in which each of us has control over our own life. A corollary of autonomy is reflective self-understanding, because a choice, to be meaningful, must be one that is taken with full understanding of the alternatives available. This kind of knowledge presupposes rational consciousness and full awareness of one's circumstances. In other words, the ideal of autonomy is built on the assumption of moral self-consciousness. This self-awareness is presumably garnered gradually as we grow up, so that in the very early stages of life we are not yet fully autonomous, and therefore not yet fully human. In short, by this view, a fetus is not yet a human being. When the value of autonomy of a pregnant woman comes in conflict with the value of the not-yet-human fetus, the balance of values is clearly in favour of the mother's choice, according to supporters of abortion rights.

This view is not without its deficiencies. For example, it is hard to see the moral difference between a very late abortion—say, for the purposes of illustration, an hour before birth—and the death of a one-hour-old baby. And if a very late abortion seems too close to infanticide, the question becomes one of where to draw the line. More generally, the argument for autonomy may prove too much, because few people would argue that a newborn baby is self-aware and autonomous, but no one thinks that its death is not a tragedy. This suggests that supporters of abortion rights do not entirely devalue the unborn, but that at early stages at least, if a conflict of values aris-es, the mother's freedom takes precedence. At the extreme, where the fetus is little more than a zygote, the ideal of autonomy, with its corollary of self-awareness, seems to favour the woman's right to choose.

For opponents of abortion, human life is defined differently. It is something inherently valuable, often defined in religious terms as a God-given gift, or a divine spark. Thus, the unborn is considered to have full human value from its beginning at conception. This position may also prove too much; for example, it is sometimes pointed out that opponents of abortion often tend to be proponents of capital pun-ishment. If life is inherently valuable, this sounds like a contradiction.[4] However, the point remains that if human life is defined in this way, to abort a fetus is to kill a child, which no mother has a right to do. Opponents of abortion, it should be noted, do not deny the value of the mother's freedom. They say instead that, in the great majority of cases, by the time she has become pregnant, the woman has exhausted her freedom of choice.

There are undoubtedly a range of refinements made to these arguments, and there are surely other points to be made that do not follow directly from the posi-tions as outlined here.[5] But this summary is enough to demonstrate that what looks like a factual argument—When does life begin?—is actually a conflict of values. Furthermore, for impartial or undecided observers, perhaps it is not hard to see something to sympathize with in either position. On one hand, women should not be forced to bear children against their will; on the other, it is not hard to think of an abortion as a tragic event. We seem to have moral intuitions favourable to both sides of the debate. Perhaps in this case, as a pluralist might conclude, *both* sides are right. If so, there may never be an adequate answer to the controversy over abortion.

This will be an unsatisfactory answer for those who believe in politics as the route to ultimate solutions. This is exactly the pursuit that a pluralist like Isaiah Berlin would have us give up, but many will want to resist his thesis. It is easier to agree, for the present, that since final solutions to questions like abortion are not yet clear to everyone, as a first step we should try to understand the controversy as its participants do. For this task, a provisional kind of pluralist stance may be helpful, whereby we suspend judgment in order to gain a greater understanding. For the student of polit-ical ideologies, then, pluralism can provide a starting point for a sympathetic exam-ination of contentious issues, of which the abortion debate is an example. We can conclude, at the least, that each side can make a *prima facie* case for its moral posi-tion, and that proponents of each side have some plausible reasons for genuinely believing themselves to be right. The abortion debate, in other words, may turn out to be a paradigm case of the ideological diversity that results from the pluralism of values. And until a better solution comes along, the most even-handed analytical stance is to presume, as a working hypothesis, that the ideological positions on both sides are founded on legitimate, but conflicting values.

However, while a pluralist attitude may help us to better understand the debate, it gives us little hope of resolving it. Indeed, pluralism suggests that many political controversies *do not have* an ultimate solution. Yet, as the example of the abortion issue shows, often the state cannot help but favour one side or the other, because to refuse to prohibit an activity is to allow it to continue. Later, we will see what kinds of policies a pluralist might favour, but at that point it will be suggested that pluralism itself begins to look like an ideology with its own controversial implications. For the moment, if pluralism is taken merely as a heuristic device rather than as an ideology unto itself, we can see the abortion debate as arising from an underlying conflict of deeply held values, the resolution of which is not yet in sight.

Affirmative Action

Where the abortion debate is so highly charged that contending ideological groups have arisen specifically around that issue, other controversies more often draw supporters for various positions from existing ideological camps on the right or left of the political spectrum. For the purposes of illustration, affirmative action will be used to show how reform liberals and conservatives might think about the question of inequality in the work force. This is not to say that every liberal or every conservative must see the issue the way it is outlined here, for we know from earlier chapters that each ideology contains a range of views. Instead, our more modest aim is to sketch a pair of opposing positions that are roughly consistent with the general ideology of each group. Since a thorough analysis of the issue is not possible in this chapter,[6] the more limited question will be addressed, as to how the problem might be defined by individuals with different ideological orientations. Again, what looks like a factual matter of statistical distributions will turn out to involve contentious evaluative judgments.

The brute fact that women and minorities are not equally represented in all sectors of the work force is not disputed. For many liberals, this is sufficient proof that something is seriously wrong with our society. Among reform liberals, the argument is sometimes made that equality should be the overriding liberal value.[7] The egalitarian ideal of human nature, they say, is one in which all persons should have equal status. Therefore, the social roles which confer status onto individuals should be impartially distributed. If certain social roles bring with them more power, money, and so on, then all persons should have an equal chance at these roles. Because our careers in the work force convey status, power and wealth in exactly this way, there is no acceptable reason to accept less than equal distributions of people in various job categories. External characteristics such as sex or skin colour are considered irrelevant to the ideal of equality. This is not so much an empirical assumption as the expression of an evaluative ideal about human nature; facts and values are entangled in the reform liberal conception of human nature. For the reform or egalitarian liberal, since we have statistical evidence of inequality in the workplace, we have positive proof that a social problem exists. Affirmative action policies are one kind of response to this manifest social inequality.

By contrast, conservatives do not value equality to the same extent that reform liberals do. Rather than describe them as valuing inequality for its own sake, it is fairer to say that conservatives, when forced to choose,[8] rank equality less highly than other goods, including peace and order, which they associate with established social hierarchies. In other words, conservatives do not grant equality the same presumptive status in policy debates as reform liberals do, and thus are more willing to accept unequal distributions in the work force. For example, a conservative might be more apt to believe that there is something immutable about men that makes them tend to be more aggressive than women and therefore more often driven to succeed in the workplace, whereas women are more likely to be better nurturers, and less likely to want to partake in the competitive struggle for career advancement. But this is not just a factual assertion; instead, it exemplifies the entanglement of fact and value. Traditional male and female roles are not only descriptions of the way things are, but of the way they should be.

In other words, conservatives are more likely to accept traditional sex roles in the workplace and in the home. The conservative sees these roles, and the resulting gender-based division of labour, as valuable in themselves, as part of a time-honoured way of life. If so, for conservatives, statistics about workplace distributions are simply evidence that the world is unfolding as it should. Furthermore, as long as significant numbers of women share the conservative outlook, or for other reasons of their own choose not to participate in the paid work force, the statistical story does not prove very much.

Again, this brief description does not come close to exhausting the issue. For one thing, the debate can become much more ominous when we turn to questions of race rather than gender. For another, a radical or Marxist feminist might accept that men and women are different, but argue that we should therefore work towards changing the status of different social roles, perhaps by paying women who work in the home. But this quick summary may be enough to show how contrasting ideals of human nature, based on different evaluative judgments, can lead to incompatible conclusions about the existence of a social problem. What one side sees as conclusive proof that something should be done, the other sees as the natural unfolding of events.

This does not mean that reform liberals and conservatives live in different moral worlds, or that they have nothing to say to each other. Rather, it is to say that the moral resources they hold in *common*—at least insofar as is necessary for one side to understand the other's position—are rich enough to allow a range of legitimate views of social life. As well as ideological conflict, the brief description here shows that there are also areas of agreement on some of the questions surrounding issues like employment equity. For example, neither side denies that people should have the right to find their own place in the world. Given the contrasting ways each side defines the proper social order, and each person's place within it, this may seem like a superficial kind of agreement. But it does show that the goal of social mobility does not seem to be disputed. That is, almost everyone seems to agree that merit, ambition, individual talent and hard work should make a difference to one's life chances. For example, conservatives are willing to allow that individual women, like Margaret Thatcher, may have what it takes to transcend traditional roles, but still believe that most women are better suited to traditional social roles. The point is that, besides conflicts of values, ideological debates take place within a broader context of evaluative agreement. If this were not so, there would be no reason to discuss things in the first place. Indeed, strictly speaking, if no commonalties existed, communication between opposing sides would not be possible.

We should not, however, minimize the differences between reform liberals and conservatives. The goal of this discussion is not to try to resolve the debate over issues like affirmative action in favour of one side or the other; it is to illustrate the pluralist view of conflicts of this sort. The point is, if we work hard to put our own ideological preconceptions on hold for a while, and try to cast the arguments of each side into the most favourable possible light, differences in judgments about competing values begin to emerge on each side. If we do this work well enough, the pluralist would say, we will begin to see that there is no apparent solution to fundamental ideological conflicts of this sort. This conclusion might be taken as provisional; if so, we can continue to hope that a final solution will emerge. Alternatively, we can conclude more boldly, with the likes of Berlin and Rawls, that ideological conflict is a permanent feature of modernity. Either way, in the here and now, we will have to deal with the tensions between contending ideologies, and a good first step in doing so is to develop a sympathetic understanding of what's at stake on either side.

The Provision of Welfare Benefits

No one today argues that the poor should be allowed to starve. Anyone making such a claim would be thought less than human, and would be excluded from the public debate. In this way, political discussions are based on some minimum of shared assumptions about human nature. Those who do not share this basic view are thought to be beyond the pale, and are in effect shunned from the public conversation.

But within this minimal framework of understanding of what it means to be human, there is still considerable room for disagreement. On the question of the role of the welfare state—one of today's most prominent political issues in Canada and the United States—the debate ranges very widely. For the purposes of this discussion, it is again necessary to try to narrow the focus to one of the core issues. The attempt might be made to address the question in terms of individualism versus collectivism, but this distinction may not do justice to the debate. The problem is that every ideology, given our definition, is about a theory, or an ideal, of how we ought to live together. Instead, we would do better to ask, regarding the question of welfare provision, how opponents differ in their ideal of the individual's responsibility to, and expectations from, the group.

On the right side of the political spectrum are critics of the welfare state,[9] who could be characterized as believing in the ethic of self-reliance. The ideal here is a society in which every able-bodied person contributes to the public good by doing their best to take care of themselves. The ethic of self-reliance implies that those whose circumstances are beyond their own control, and those who cannot support themselves, must be provided for by public beneficence. The question remains whether the best public means is state agencies (Olasky 1992), but the point is that these opponents of the welfare state do not advocate abandonment of the poor.

In this conception, the ideal community is one in which members take care of the things that are their own responsibility, and present the minimum possible burden to their neighbours. Institutions of community life, such as churches, family, voluntary associations and so on, tend to be revered by these opponents of the welfare state (Berger and Neuhaus 1977). Their fear is that with the growth of the welfare state, community institutions are crowded out of the public sphere. The critique of the welfare state, from this point of view, is not a rejection of the idea of community in favour of atomistic individualism, but a concern that the growth of government inadvertently undermines community.

This is not to say that this vision is without a conception of individual human flourishing. This ideal is seen as a process of self-creation. Anything that interferes with this process is not just a waste of time and resources, it is actually harmful to people. The unconditional provision of welfare benefits, it is claimed, is an interference of just this sort. People need basic resources, but if welfare benefits begin to undermine the ethic of self-reliance, welfare will be harmful to its recipients. Again, this is less a question of empirical investigation, and more the assertion of an ethical ideal. Dignity, by this ideal, cannot be provided by others. Dignity is the product of self-creation.

Support for welfare benefits is usually associated with the left side of the ideological continuum.[10] Rather than self-reliance, the ideal of human life in this view is more altruistic. "The essence of altruism is the belief that one ought *not* to indulge a sharp preference for one's own interest over those of others" (Kennedy 1976:1717). The altruist says that as long as there is human suffering in the world, it is irrelevant whether it is my suffering or yours. We should take whatever measures necessary to alleviate the problem. By this view, no distinction should be made about individual circumstances; help should be given unconditionally wherever it is needed.

Furthermore, since the altruist is completely impartial with regard to individual differences when neediness occurs, the question of social subunits, like families or neighbourhoods, is not given much relevance. Family status or religious affiliation should not matter; the sole important issue is the fact of deprivation. Social institutions like the church or the family may even be seen as the source of illegitimate differentiation and social hierarchy, typified by the patriarchal household. Rather than natural and necessary elements of community life, they may be viewed as the source of social divisions—instead of bringing us together in broad solidarity, these institutions create unnecessary distinctions between people and keep us apart. In this sense, supporters of the welfare state may even be more individualistic than advocates of self-reliance, because these supporters are likely to see each person as having an individual claim on state resources, and to deny that this claim should be mediated through community groups. But each side of this debate has a view of the individual in relation to the community. Neither is about individuals alone, or solely about forms of collectivism. Each is an ideal of social life, of people living in groups.

Once again, the caveat must be made that this is not a complete picture of the welfare debate. This cursory outline is merely an effort to show how different evaluative judgments can lead to very different views of a social problem, and completely divergent ideas about appropriate political responses. And again, each side has an intuitively strong case to make. We can easily agree that poverty is an awful condition, which in a perfect world would not exist and that personal circumstances should be irrelevant to the fact of human suffering. But many of us will also agree that self-reliance is part of what we think of as a worthy life. This is not to say that a dependent person is completely unworthy—after all, we are all dependent on others in all sorts of ways—but only that it is better not to unnecessarily burden our fellow citizens, and that complete helplessness is a tragic condition.

All of this may seem perfectly obvious, and the solution may be thought to be equally clear. We should design welfare policies that do the least violence to either ideal. To some extent, the debate over social welfare spending can be seen to involve just this kind of search for a policy instrument that encourages self-reliance while minimizing deprivation. Welfare benefits, it is often said, should not be a safety net that catches people and traps them, but a trampoline that helps the unfortunate bounce back onto their feet. But at the same time, the debate over welfare is about larger visions of the good life, and these are not so easy to reconcile. All sides agree that something should be done for the destitute, but beyond this simple statement, the area of agreement on actual policy responses quickly diminishes. For example, there is not even indisputable agreement about how much poverty exists in society. This might look like a purely factual matter, but we have to make evaluative judgments as soon as we try to define "poverty." Is it a question of inequality in society, so that we should measure the differences in wealth? Or is poverty about the inability to meet basic needs, so that we should look for measures of actual deprivation? These different definitions, based on different judgments about values, lead to diverse conclusions about how many poor people exist in society. Here again, the definition of the problem involves evaluative decisions, and these will inevitably vary depending on our ideological outlook.

Some policy analysts have made exactly this point, and then concluded that policy decisions should therefore be more democratic; that is, the political system should be responsive to a wider range of social interests. M. E. Hawkesworth (1988) reaches this conclusion by arguing that political questions necessarily involve "essentially contested concepts." This term originated in an essay by William Gallie (1956), and it became popular among theorists on the left as a way of criticizing the legitimacy of policy decisions. Gallie's original point was "to show that there are disputes ... which are perfectly genuine: which, although not resolvable by argument of any kind, are nevertheless sustained by perfectly respectable arguments and evidence" (1956:169). Among the short list of characteristics he gave of these kinds of disputes, the first was that they involve evaluative judgments (1956:171). In short, Gallie's insight was what here has been called pluralism.

The problem for those, like Hawkesworth, who think that more democracy is the answer, is that democracy itself is an essentially contested concept. In fact, it was for Gallie a paradigm case for such concepts. "The concept of democracy which we are discussing is internally complex in such a way that any democratic achievement (or programme) admits of a variety of descriptions in which its different aspects are graded in different orders of importance" (Gallie 1956:184). Therefore, when the term is used in policy debates, we must be careful to see whether contentious evaluative judgments are being introduced in an unexamined way. In other words, the demand for more democracy may serve to bring participatory, egalitarian values into the debate, but in such a way that they are hidden from discussion. Moreover, democracy means different things to different people—that is why it is an essentially contested concept. Finally, if pluralism is a permanent characteristic of modern democracies, as Gallie's thesis suggests, then collective decisions will become *more* difficult as we expand the range of issues and interests to be addressed. The call for more democracy does not get us very far towards a solution, and only raises more areas of contention.

However, the point can be taken another way. Perhaps it is to admit that under democratic conditions, there is no end in sight to controversies over abortion, affirmative action, basic welfare provision and so on. If so, we should look for ways to accommodate pluralism within democratic states. The alternative strategy, for the ideologically minded, is to believe that our own views are right and that conflicting ones are just plain wrong. This, says the pluralist, is much too simplistic a view of modern life, one that captures neither its richness nor its difficulties. Worse, the hardening of ideological positions cannot help but lead to the breakdown of public discussion because the strategy on each side must be to depict the other as morally or intellectually deficient. Pluralism, as we have seen, recognizes our intractable differences, but points out that these differences in judgment take place against a background of shared understanding. The alternative strategy is to deny that one's opponents understand things properly. That is why, in today's public debates, people on the right often assume that others are softheaded, while those on the left think their opponents are mean-spirited. Both accusations are attempts to undermine the legitimacy of others' points of view, a way of implying that those who disagree with us are deficient in some essential human faculty. The suggestion here is that pluralism, by contrast, is a more democratic approach because it provides the grounds for continuing public debate about issues, even while expressing skepticism about final resolutions. Democratic politics, it is sometimes said, is a like a conversation; the pluralist adds, it is a conversation without end.

Exercise One: Debating Political Controversies

Below is a list of controversial political propositions. From this list, or using issues that are currently controversial in your area, pick two or three that you would like to debate. Normally in formal academic debates, participants do not know which side of the question they will be assigned to defend, so for each issue chosen you will have to prepare arguments on either side. Try to imagine the ideological position that proponents on either side might likely adopt. What are the values and political ideals that might be raised by each side? Given these values, what are the best factual arguments in favour of either side?

- We do not spend enough on national defence.
- We should spend more on foreign aid.
- Taxes should be higher.
- We should have more government ownership of industries.
- Capital punishment should be reinstated.
- Punishing criminals is less important than rehabilitation.
- Handguns should be outlawed.
- Jobs are more important than environmental protection.

IS PLURALISM AN IDEOLOGY?

The discussion thus far has attempted to show that there is something to be said for pluralism, the idea that more than one ideological approach to political questions may be genuinely valuable, and that conflicts between ideologies are something we must learn to live with. Two versions of this thesis have been suggested. The weak or provisional version suggests that pluralism can be used as a heuristic device, as an attitude that lets us discover through sympathetic imagination how participants in ideological debates themselves understand the issues. Pluralism in this form does not require that we accept that there will never be resolutions to these debates, only that each side can make at least a *prima facie* case by appealing to some of our shared values, and that no clear solution is yet apparent.

A stronger version of the idea of pluralism would be to conclude that the idea of final solutions to political controversies is itself false, and that the ideal of a perfect social order, in which everyone agrees about goals and means, is a myth—not because every proposed solution is false, but because more than one is genuinely true and good. Pluralism in this form might include the argument that the belief in final solutions is itself something that can be explained as an ideological falsehood. This explanation might point to our misplaced faith in science as a solution to policy questions, or the psychological discomfort that arises when we try to hold two opposed notions in mind at once. It might be argued, in other words, that the distaste for pluralism arises from what psychologists call cognitive dissonance. Nevertheless, the argument would go, the evidence of history, of cross-cultural comparison and of our own self-understanding shows that the discomfort of cognitive dissonance is something we should learn to live with, in order to be better citizens of modern, complex democracies. The alternative is to be an ideologue, and to see public discussions about politics degenerate into ever more bitter acrimony.

In this stronger sense, pluralism might be considered an anti-ideology, at least against those who think their own ideology is exclusively true. However, as soon as a pluralist begins to participate in debates against the supporters of other ideologies, we must ask whether pluralism has become an ideology unto itself. And if that is true, then pluralism may begin to look self-contradictory. On one hand, the pluralist wants to say that there are many legitimate ideologies, and that there is no overriding way to resolve the disputes that must inevitably arise between them. The pluralist denies that we can have a super-ideology within which all political disputes can be resolved. On the other hand, pluralism as an ideology itself may begin to look like a kind of super-ideology, one which somehow seeks to accommodate all other ideological points of view, if not resolve their conflicts. The ideological pluralist seems to be flirting with self-contradiction.

The pluralist might try to avoid this logical problem, perhaps by arguing that as an ideology it is exceptional in some way—perhaps in that pluralism, unlike other ideologies, can accept the truthfulness of other ideologies while still making its own qualifications about the nature of political life. The logical problem would then turn to whether the pluralist is involved in special pleading. But even if we leave these sorts of problems to the philosophers, it is not hard to imagine how pluralism could become politically controversial.

In order to understand this point, recall the definition of ideology used in this book: an ideology is a socially constructed system of political beliefs with formal articulation, scope, internal consistency and durability, each of which provides a normative framework and a practical guide for political action. If we suppose that pluralism may in time come to fulfill the criteria of scope, consistency, durability and so on, what would it look like as a normative framework and a guide to political action? Given a pluralist understanding of the world, what are the sorts of policy implications we might draw from it? Answering this question will illustrate the sorts of political opposition that might arise to pluralism as an ideology, and show what might be at stake politically.

For this discussion, let us assume that the best justification for state action is the common good. The state, by this view, is the voice of the people speaking in unison, united in their understanding of the proper ends and means of public policy. Immediately, pluralism looks like a challenge to state action in many areas because its claim is that there is no singular common good, or at least that the common good is complex and sometimes internally contradictory. In other words, we will never have complete justification for state action except in areas where no legitimate controversy exists. Therefore, pluralism could quickly become an ideological obstacle to those who would like the state to increase its activities.

To illustrate the point, let us accept, in regard to the specific political controversies discussed above, that the following conclusions are consistent with an ideological kind of pluralism:

1. The state should neither prohibit nor abet abortions. If there are legitimate values on both sides of the debate, then the state should neither force women to continue their pregnancies, nor should it force opponents of abortion to subsidize the procedure. Subsidies, where necessary because of poverty, should be given voluntarily by supporters of women's right to choose.

2. Affirmative action policies should be voluntary.

3. The state should allow a plurality of modes of welfare provision. This should include the encouragement of community groups, such as churches and neighbourhood associations, to provide benefits to the needy. But those who prefer other kinds of institutions should be free to organize their own collective groups. The state should be involved only as needed to encourage these organizations, and as the provider of last resort.

Once again, the caveat must be made that these are cursory conclusions, meant to illustrate how a pluralist ideology *might* look. If we accept that these positions follow from a pluralist understanding of social life, the reasons some people might have for opposing it become apparent. Neither proponents nor supporters of abortion rights will be happy, advocates of affirmative action will be outraged and defenders of the traditional welfare state will be worried about the fate of the programs and institutions they have worked hard to create. The general trend of pluralism as an ideology seems to lead in one direction, that there are limitations on the justified intervention by the state into social life.

The strongest opposition to ideological pluralism will come from those who believe that the state should be a community. This is an ideal that goes back as far as Aristotle, who believed that humans are essentially political animals, and that therefore social and political life in their highest form are the same thing. His ideal form of government was the city-state, or *polis*, in which citizens collectively decide public issues in an ongoing process of participatory democracy, as it is sometimes called today. This ideal has been revived in recent years by theorists who are broadly categorized as communitarians.[11] In general, these writers are troubled by what they see as the disintegration of modern life, as people pursue their own selfish ends instead of working towards the common good. This, they say, leads to alienation and the breakdown of holistic community life. Pluralism, communitarians would object, is a symptom of the central problem of our time. As an ideology, it is a deceptive justification for exactly the difficulty we should be seeking to overcome. Rather than a truthful account of our common values, pluralism is rationalization of private interests by those who want to justify their own selfish preferences and privileges.

By now, the political stakes over pluralism as an ideology should be clear, and readers must decide for themselves whether there is nonetheless something worthy in the idea. In answer to the question of whether pluralism is an ideology, we can conclude that if it is not yet so, it could easily become one. More specifically, pluralism might be thought of as a refinement of liberalism, exemplified by writers like Isaiah Berlin (1969; 1991), Charles Larmore (1987) and Joseph Raz (1986; 1994). This becomes clear when we realize that pluralism emphasizes the necessity of making hard choices between competing goods. This entails a certain kind of liberty, the freedom to choose among legitimate alternatives. As such, like other ideologies, pluralism may be seen as having its own core values.

All of this may be taken by the student of political ideologies as a kind of warning about the difficulty of arriving at the foundational truths of politics. On one hand, pluralism is a way to make sense of the diversity of ideologies; on the other, it can become an ideology unto itself, and perhaps one with its own limitations. As such, pluralism will be criticized by those with different ideological orientations. It will become, in other words, another aspect of political life about which reasonable people may disagree, one of many that continue to crowd the ideological landscape as we move into the twenty-first century. This is not a conclusion that a pluralist would want to dispute.

NOTES

1. Charles Larmore (1987), in *Patterns of Moral Complexity*, a book about the inevitability of value conflict, suggests that moral theory must make room for human judgment, but that no moral theory can predetermine the proper answers to question of this sort.

2. Charles Taylor is not a pluralist in the sense used here, despite his advocacy of the notion of "deep diversity," the idea that there are "a plurality of ways of belonging" in the world (1993:183). Like other leading communitarians, he tends to identify the community with the nation-state (Friedman 1994:298), and it is not clear that this must necessarily be so. Taylor believes that all social questions about the good life, to avoid being marginalized, must be thought of as political questions (1991:18). In a world of permanent legitimate diversity, it seems doubtful that social life can be thoroughly politicized in the way communitarians like Taylor would prefer. Instead, we would expect to see a diversity of communities arise based on shared commitments, with political questions centred on finding a *modus vivendi*, a way for them to respectfully coexist (Larmore 1987).

3. This argument is similar to Donald Davidson's "principle of charity." See Antony Flew (1984:84).

4. This kind of problem, whereby categorical assertions in regard to one policy issue are in conflict with the ideals asserted in reference to another, often arises in ideological disputes. For an example on the other side of the current debate, the feminist pro-choice slogan, "Keep Your Laws Off My Body," seems to contradict another feminist motto, "The Personal is Political."

5. For example, there are the issues raised by feminists about male attempts to control women's bodies.

6. A more thorough analysis of the underlying evaluative assumptions behind this debate is available in M. E. Hawkesworth (1988:95–122). The central difference between her view and the one proposed here is that she begins with a pluralistic analysis by uncovering the value assumptions on each side of the debate, but then shifts gradually to a critique of one side in favour of the other. Here, the analysis will be more consistently pluralistic.

7. For example, Will Kymlicka (1989:13) argues that any liberal theory worthy of the name must start from the "egalitarian plateau" whereby the interests of each person are considered as equal, an idea he takes from another egalitarian liberal, Ronald Dworkin (1983:24).

8. Remembering the entanglement of facts and values, we should note again that talking abstractly about the choice between competing values is a highly artificial way of describing things, more suitable to political philosophy than to practical politics.

9. This is not to imply that there are no critics of the welfare state on the political left. See, for example, Frances Piven and Richard Cloward (1971). Moreover, as Chapter 3 pointed out, there are conservatives who support welfare benefits, perhaps in part for the reason Piven and Cloward suggest: to regulate the poor.

10. An exception is Canada's "red Tories," conservatives who supported a limited welfare state.

11. The best-known communitarian theorists are Alasdair MacIntyre, Michael Sandel, Michael Walzer and Charles Taylor. See Stephen Mulhall and Adam Swift (1992) and Jeffrey Friedman (1994).

REFERENCES

_____. The maths and morals of Ross Perot. 1992. *The Economist,* May 16, 32.

_____. Hardship divides women's world. 1995. *The Globe and Mail,* Aug. 26, pp. A1, A6, A7.

Abbey, Edward. 1975. *The Monkey Wrench Gang.* New York: Avon Books.

_____. 1990. *Hayduke Lives!* Toronto: Little Brown and Co.

Akzin, Benjamin. 1964. *State & Nation.* London: Hutchinson Univ. Library.

Allcock, J. B. 1971. Populism: A Brief Biography. *Sociology* 5, 371–87.

Allen, Charlotte. 1995. A Conservative's Lament. *Utne Reader* (March–April), 91–94.

Allen, Richard. 1973. *The Social Passion.* Toronto: Univ. of Toronto Press.

Almond, Gabriel, and Sydney Verba. 1965. *The Civic Culture.* New York: Little Brown Press.

_____. 1980. *The Civic Culture Revisited.* Boston & Toronto: Little, Brown.

Alter, Peter. 1989. *Nationalism.* London: Edward Arnold.

Amidon, Stephen. 1994. The closing of the liberal mind. *The Sunday Times,* Nov. 6, pp. 10–12.

Anderson, Benedict. 1983. *Imagined Communities: Reflections on the Origin and Spread of Nationalism.* New York: Verso. 2nd ed. pub. 1991.

Arendt, Hannah. 1958. *The Human Condition.* Chicago: The Univ. of Chicago Press.

_____. 1966. *The Origins of Totalitarianism* (3rd ed.). New York: Harcourt, Brace & World, Inc.

_____. 1968. *Totalitarianism.* New York: Harcourt Brace Jovanovich.

_____. 1969. *On Revolution* (7th ed.). New York: Viking Press.

Argersinger, Peter H. 1974. *Populism and Politics: William Alfrid Peffer and the People's Party.* Lexington: The Univ. Press of Kentucky.

Armstrong, Luanne. 1993. Connecting the circles: Race, gender, nature. In *Canadian Women's Studies—Women and the Environment.* (Spring). North York: Univ. of Toronto Press.

Ashford, Nigel. 1981. New conservatism and old socialism: the neo-conservatives. *Government and Opposition* 16:3, 353–69.

Audry, Colette. 1985. Socialism tomorrow. In Milos Nicolic (Ed.), *Socialism on the Threshold of the Twenty-first Century* (pp. 29–42). London: Verso.

Avakumovic, Ivan. 1975. *The Communist Party in Canada: A History.* Toronto: McClelland & Stewart.

Bailey, Ronald. 1993. *Eco-Scam: The False Prophets of Ecological Apocalypse.* New York: St. Martin's Press.

Balcerowicz, Leszek. 1991. Problems with the definition of socialism in today's world. In Ota Sik (Ed.), *Socialism Today? The Changing Meaning of Socialism* (pp. 65-74). London: Macmillan.

Baldwin, Marshall, Charles Cole, and Carlton Hayes. 1956. *History of Europe.* New York: Macmillan Company.

Ball, Terence, and Richard Dagger. 1991. *Political Ideologies and the Democratic Ideal.* New York: Harper Collins.

_____. 1995. *Political Ideologies and the Democratic Ideal* (2nd ed.). New York: Harper Collins.

Baradat, Leon P. 1994. *Political Ideologies: Their Origins and Impact* (5th ed.). Englewood Cliffs, N.J.: Prentice-Hall.

_____. 1988. *Political Ideologies: Their Origins and Impact* (3rd ed.). Englewood Cliffs, N.J.: Prentice-Hall.

Barber, Benjamin R. 1994. *Strong Democracy: Participatory Politics for a New Age.* Berkeley: Univ. of California.

Barkun, Michael. 1974. *Disaster and the Millennium.* London: Yale Univ. Press.

———. 1990 . Racist apocalypse: Millennialism on the far right, *American Studies* 31.

_____. 1994. *Religion and the Racist Right.* Chapel Hill: Univ. of North Carolina Press.

Barney, Gerald O., P. H. Freeman and C. A. Ulinski. 1981. *Global 2000: Implications for Canada.* Toronto: Pergamon Press.

Barrett, Stanley R. 1987. *Is God A Racist? The Right Wing in Canada.* Toronto: Univ. of Toronto Press.

Bartky, Sandra. 1990. *Femininity and Domination.* New York: Routledge.

Bashevkin, Sylvia B. 1985. *Toeing the Lines: Women and Party Politics in English Canada.* Toronto: Univ. of Toronto Press.

Beauvoir, Simone de. 1953. *The Second Sex.* New York: Knopf.

Bell, Daniel. 1955. *The New American Right.* New York: Criterion Books.

_____. 1985. The revolt against modernity. *The Public Interest* 81 (Fall), 42–63.

Bell, David V. J. 1995. Political culture in Canada. In Michael S. Whittington and Glen Williams (Eds.), *Canadian Politics in the 1990s* (pp. 105–28). Toronto: Nelson Canada.

Bell, Edward. 1993. *Social Classes and Social Credit in Alberta.* Montreal & Kingston: McGill-Queen's Univ. Press.

Bellah, Robert, and Phillip E. Hammond. 1980. *Varieties of Civil Religion.* San Francisco: Harper & Row.

Bellah, Robert. 1985. Populism and individualism. *Social Policy* 16:2 (Fall), 30–33.

Berger, Peter L., and Richard John Neuhaus. 1977. *To Empower People: The Role of Mediating Structures in Public Policy.* Washington: American Enterprise Institute.

Berlin, Isaiah. 1969. *Four Essays on Liberty.* Oxford: Oxford Univ. Press.

_____. 1991. *The Crooked Timber of Humanity.* London: Fontana.

Betcherman, Lita-Rose. 1975. *The Swastika and the Maple Leaf.* Toronto: Fitzhenry and Whiteside.

Bill 1, *An Act Respecting the Future of Quebec,* preamble. (1995). Cited in The time has come: The PQ appeals to Quebecers with history and emotion. *Maclean's* 108 (Sept. 18), p. 20.

Billington, James H. 1980. *Fire in the Minds of Men: Origins of the Revolutionary Faith.* New York: Basic Books, Inc.

Birch, Anthony H. 1989. *Nationalism & National Integration.* London: Unwin Hyman.

Bissoondath, Neil. 1993. A question of belonging: Multiculturalism and citizenship. In William Kaplan (Ed.), *Belonging: The Meaning and Future of Canadian Citizenship* (pp. 368–87). Montreal & Kingston: McGill-Queen's Univ. Press.

Bloom, Allan. 1987. *The Closing of the American Mind.* New York: Simon and Schuster.

Bloom, William. 1990. *Personal Identity, National Identity and International Relations.* Cambridge: Cambridge Univ. Press.

Bookchin, Murray. 1989. *Remaking Society.* Montreal: Black Rose Books.

_____. 1991. *The Ecology of Freedom* (rev. ed.). Montreal: Black Rose Books.

_____. 1992. *Urbanization Without Cities: The Rise and Decline of Citizenship.* Montreal & New York: Black Rose Books.

Boucher, David. 1983. *The Feminist Challenge: The Movement for Women's Liberation in Britain and the USA.* London: Macmillan.

Boyer, Patrick. 1992. *Direct Democracy in Canada: The History and Future of Referendums.* Toronto: Dundurn Press.

_____. 1992. *The People's Mandate: Referendums and A More Democratic Canada.* Toronto: Dundurn Press.

Boyle, Christine. 1983. Home rule for women: Power-sharing between men and women. *Dalhousie Law Journal* 7, 790–809.

Bramwell, Anna. 1989. *Ecology in the 20th Century: A History.* New Haven & London: Yale Univ. Press.

_____. 1994. *The Fading of the Greens: The Decline of Environmental Politics in the West.* New Haven & London: Yale Univ. Press.

Breuilly, John. 1994. *Nationalism and the State.* Chicago: Univ. of Chicago Press.

Brown, Courtney. 1994. Politics and the environment: Nonlinear instabilities. *American Political Science Review* 88:2, 292–303.

Brugger, Bill and Dean Jaensch. 1985. *Australian Politics: Theory and Practice.* Sydney: Allen & Unwin.

Buell, Frederick. 1994. *National Culture and the New Global System.* Baltimore & London: John Hopkins Univ. Press.

Bunch, Charlotte. 1984. Lesbians in revolt. In Alison M. Jaggar and Paula S. Rothenberg (Eds.), *Feminist Frameworks: Alternative Theoretical Accounts of the Relations between Men and Women*, 2nd ed. (pp. 144–48). New York: McGraw-Hill Inc.

Bus, Wlodzimierz. 1991. Socialism: The very concept under scrutiny. In Ota Sik (Ed.), *Socialism Today? The Changing Meaning of Socialism* (pp. 47–57). London: Macmillan.

Caldicott, Leonie, and Stephanie Leland (Eds.). 1983. *Reclaim the Earth*. London: Women's Press.

Caldwell, L. 1985. Binational responsibilities for a shared environment. In C. Doran and J. Sigler (Eds.), *Canada and the United States: Enduring Friendship, Persistent Stress*. New York: Prentice Hall Press.

Canovan, Margaret. 1981. *Populism*. London: Junction Books.

Capra, Fritjof. 1982. *The Turning Point*. Toronto & New York: Bantam.

—— and Charlene Spretnak. 1984. *Green Politics*. New York: E. P. Dutton.

Carlyle, Thomas. 1956. *Sartor Resartus*. New York: E. P. Dutton and Sons.

Carson, Rachel. 1962. *Silent Spring*. Boston: Houghton Mifflin.

Clement, Wallace, and Glen Williams (Eds.). 1989. *The New Canadian Political Economy*. Montreal & Kingston: McGill-Queen's Univ. Press.

Cockburn, A., and J. Ridgeway (Eds.). 1979. *Political Ecology*. New York: Times Books.

Cohen, Carl (Ed.). 1972. *Communism, Fascism and Democracy: The Theoretical Foundations*. New York: Random House.

Cohn, Norman. 1970. *The Pursuit of the Millennium* (rev. ed.). New York: Oxford Univ. Press.

Collard, Andree, and J. Contrucci. 1988. *Rape of the Wild*. London: Women's Press.

Commoner, Barry. 1990. *Making Peace With The Planet*. New York: Pantheon Books.

Connelly, Owen. 1967. Foreword to Robert Sobel, *The French Revolution: A Concise History and Interpretation*. New York: Ardmore Press.

Converse, P. E. 1964. The nature of belief systems in mass publics. In D. E. Apter (Ed.), *Ideology and Discontent* (pp. 206–61). New York: The Free Press.

Conway, J. F. 1984. The nature of populism: A clarification. *Studies in Political Economy* 13 (Spring), 137–144.

Coon Come, Matthew. 1995. The Crees of Quebec, on sovereignty. *The Globe and Mail*, March 30, p. A29.

Copleston, Frederick C. 1983. On the relationship between ideology, philosophy, and politics. In Anthony Parel (Ed.), *Ideology, Philosophy and Politics* (pp. 17–36). Waterloo: Wilfrid Laurier Press.

Cott, Nancy. 1987. *The Grounding of Modern Feminism*. New Haven: Yale Univ. Press.

Cox, Robert. 1991. The global political economy and social choice. In Daniel Drache and Meric S. Gertler (Eds.), *The New Era of Global Competition: State Policy and Market Power*, pp. 335–349. Montreal & Kingston: McGill-Queen's Univ. Press.

——. 1994. Global restructuring: making sense of the changing international political economy. In Richard Stubbs and Geoffrey R. D. Underhill (Eds.), *Political Economy and the Changing Global Order* (pp. 45–49). Toronto: McClelland and Stewart.

Coyne, Andrew. 1995. Look in the dictionary under liberalism and it says, anything goes. *The Globe and Mail* (March 13), p. A16.

Crane, David. 1992. *The Next Canadian Century: Building a Competitive Economy*. Toronto: Stoddart Publishing Co. Ltd.

Crawford, Alan. 1980. *Thunder on the Right: The "New Right" and the Politics of Resentment*. New York: Pantheon Books.

——. 1980. Right-wing populism. *Social Policy* 11:1 (June), 2–9.

Creighton, Donald. 1980. *The Passionate Observer: Selected Writings*. Toronto: McClelland and Stewart.

Crick, Bernard. 1973. *In Defence of Politics* (rev. ed.). London: Penguin Books.

Crisp, L. F. 1955. *The Australian Federal Labour Party, 1901–1951*. London: Longmans, Green, & Co.

Cronin, Thomas E. 1989. *Direct Democracy: The Politics of Initiative, Referendum, and Recall.* Cambridge: Harvard Univ. Press.

Culpitt, Ian. 1992. *Welfare and Citizenship: Beyond the Crisis of the Welfare State?* London: Sage Publications.

Dalton, Russell J. 1984. Cognitive mobilization and partisan dealignment in advanced industrial democracies. *Journal of Politics* 46, 264–84.

Davis, Susan E. (Ed.). 1988. *Women Under Attack: Victories, Backlash and the Fight for Reproductive Freedom.* Boston: South End Press.

Delmar, Rosalind. 1986. What is feminism? In Juliet Mitchell and Ann Oakley, *What is Feminism: A Re-Examination* (pp. 8–33). New York: Pantheon Books.

Denfeld, Rene. 1995. *The New Victorians: A Young Woman's Challenge to the Old Feminist Order.* New York: Allen & Unwin.

Denitch, Bogdan. 1990. *The Socialist Debate: Beyond Red and Green.* London: Pluto Press.

Derrida, Jacques. 1978. Structure sign and play in the discourses of the human sciences. In *Writing and Difference* (pp. 84–92). Trans. Alan Bass. London: Routledge and Kegan Paul; quoted in Frederick Buell (1994). *National Culture and the New Global System.* Baltimore & London: John Hopkins Univ. Press.

Devall, Bill, and George Sessions. 1985. *Deep Ecology: Living as if Nature Mattered.* Salt Lake City: Peregrine Smith Books.

Diamond, Irene, and Gloria Fenman Orenstein. 1990. *Reweaving the World.* San Francisco: Sierra Club Books.

Dickerson, Mark O., and Thomas Flanagan. 1994. *An Introduction to Government and Politics* (4th ed.). Scarborough, Ont.: Nelson Canada.

Dickerson, Mark O., Thomas Flanagan and Neil Nevitte. 1995. *Introductory Readings in Government and Politics* (4th ed.). Scarborough, Ont.: Nelson Canada.

Die Grünen (The German Greens). 1983. *Programme of the Green Party.* Trans. Hans Fernback. London: Heretic Books.

Dobbin, M. 1991. *Preston Manning and the Reform Party.* Toronto: Lorimer and Company.

Dobson, Andrew. 1990. *Green Political Thought.* London: Unwin Hyman.

Dolbeare, Kenneth M., and Linda J. Medcalf. 1988. *American Ideologies Today: From Neopolitics to New Ideas.* New York: Random House.

dos Santos, Theotonia. 1985. Socialism: ideal and historical practice. In Milos Nicolic (Ed.), *Socialism on the Threshold of the Twenty-first Century* (pp. 180–45). London: Verso.

Downs, Anthony. 1957. *An Economic Theory of Democracy.* New York: Harper and Row.

Draper, Theodore. 1969. *The Rediscovery of Black Nationalism.* New York: The Viking Press.

Drucker, Peter. 1994. The age of social transformation. *The Atlantic Monthly* 274 (Nov.), 53–80.

Dubiel, Helmut. 1986. The spectre of populism. *Berkeley Journal of Sociology* xxxi, 79–91.

Dworkin, Ronald. 1983. In defence of equality. *Social Philosophy and Policy.* Vol. 1.

Eccleshall, Robert. 1977. English conservatism as an ideology. *Political Studies* 25 (1), 62–83.

_____. 1984. Conservatism. In Robert Eccleshall et al., *Political Ideologies: An Introduction* (pp. 79–114). London: Hutchinson Publishing.

Echols, Alice. 1989. *Daring To Be Bad.* Minneapolis: Univ. of Minnesota Press.

Eckersley, Robyn. 1988. Green politics: A practice in search of a theory?" *Alternatives* 15(4), 52–61.

_____. 1992. *Environmentalism and Political Theory.* Albany: State Univ. of New York Press.

The Economist. 1995. In Greenpeace's corporate blueprint. Reprinted in *The Globe and Mail,* Aug. 23, p.A9.

Elgin, Duane. 1981. *Voluntary Simplicity.* New York: William Morrow and Company.

Elijah Muhammad. 1965. *Message to the Blackman in America.* Chicago: Muhammad Mosque of Islam No. 2.

Elkins, David J. 1994. The second magellanic age: Territory and political authority in the 21st century. Paper presented at "Redesigning the State: The Politics of Mega Constitutional Change," Canberra, Australia, July 27–29.

_____. 1995. *Beyond Sovereignty: Government à la Carte in the 21st Century*. Toronto: Univ. of Toronto Press.

Elshtain, Jean Bethke. 1981. *Public Man, Private Woman: Women in Social and Political Thought*. New Jersey: Princeton Univ. Press.

Engels, Friedrich, and Karl Marx. 1848. *Communist Manifesto*. London: Allen & Unwin (1954).

Erikson, Erik H. 1954. *Identity And The Life Cycle*. Indiana Univ. Press.

Errington, Jane. 1993. Pioneers and suffragists. In Sandra Burt, Lorraine Lode, and Lindsay Dorney (Eds.), *Changing Patterns: Women in Canada* (pp. 59–91). Toronto: McClelland and Stewart.

Essien-Udom. E. U. (1961). *Black Nationalism*. Chicago: Univ. of Chicago Press.

Everett-Green, Robert. 1995. "There's no place like 'home page,'" *The Globe and Mail*, p. A.12.

Evernden, Neil. 1985. *The Natural Alien: Humankind and Environment*. Toronto:Univ. of Toronto Press.

Eysench, H. J. 1954. *The Psychology of Politics*. London: Routledge & Kegan Paul Ltd.

Falk, Richard. 1993. The making of global citizenship. In Jeremy Brecher, John Brown Childs, and Jill Cutler (Eds.), *Global Visions: Beyond the New World Order* (pp. 39–50). Montreal, New York, London: Black Rose Books.

Faludi, Susan. 1991. *Backlash*. New York: Crown Publishers Inc.

Ferguson, Marjorie. 1992. The mythology about globalization. *European Journal of Communication* 7:1 (March), 69–94.

Finkel, Alvin. 1992/93. Populism and gender: The UFA and social credit experiences. *Journal of Canadian Studies* 27:4 (Winter), 76–97.

Firestone, Shulamith. 1972. *The Dialectic of sex*. New York: Bantam Books, Ltd.

_____. 1984. The dialectic of sex. In Alison M. Jaggar and Paula S. Rothenberg (Eds.), *Feminist Frameworks: Alternative Theoretical Accounts of the Relations Between Men and Women* (2nd ed.) (pp. 136–44). New York: McGraw-Hill Inc.

Flanagan, Thomas. 1994. The Politics of the Millennium. Unpublished paper, Univ. of Calgary.

_____. 1995. *Waiting for the Wave: The Reform Party and Preston Manning*. Toronto: Stoddart Publishing Co. Ltd.

Flew, Antony (Ed.). 1984. *Dictionary of Philosophy* (2nd rev. ed.) New York: St. Martin's Press.

Flynn, Kevin, and Gary Gerhardt. 1989. *The Silent Brotherhood: Inside America's Racist Underground*. New York: The Free Press.

Foreman, Dave. 1985. *Eco-Defense: A Field Guide to Monkeywrenching*. Tucson: Ned Ludd Books.

_____. 1991. *Confessions of an Eco-Warrior*. New York: Harmony Books.

Fredland, Jonathan. 1995. Minister Louis Farrakhan: He has a dream, *Calgary Herald*, Oct. 15, p. A8.

French, Marilyn. 1992. *The War Against Women*. New York: Summit Books.

Fried, Albert. 1970. *Socialism in America*. Garden City: Anchor.

Friedman, Jeffrey. 1994. The politics of communitarianism. *Critical Review*. Vol. 8, No. 2.

Fulford, Robert. 1984. The world according to the X-Files, *The Globe and Mail*, Nov. 2, p. A14.

Futrelle, David. 1995. Libertarians on the march. *Utne Reader* (July–Aug.), 20–2.

Gallie, W. B. 1956. Essentially contested concepts. *Proceedings of the Aristotelian Society*. Vol. 56.

Gellner, Ernest. 1983. *Nations and Nationalism*. Oxford: Basil Blackwell.

Gentile, Giovanni. 1972. The philosophic basis of fascism. In Carl Cohen (Ed.), *Communism, Fascism and Democracy: The Theoretical Foundations* (pp. 340–43). New York: Random House.

_____. 1973. The origins and doctrine of fascism. In Adrian Lyttleton (Ed.), *Italian Fascisms from Pareto to Gentile* (p. 32). London: Jonathan Cape.

Geoghegan, Vincent. 1984. Socialism. In Robert Eccleshall (Ed.), *Political Ideologies: An Introduction* (pp. 115–149). London: Hutchinson Publishing.

German Greens (Die Grünen). 1983. *Programme of the Green Party*. Trans. Hans Fernbach. London: Heretic Books.

Gershoy, Leo. 1957. *The Era of the French Revolution, 1789–1799: Ten Years that Shook the World.* Toronto: D. Van Nostrand Company.

Gerth, H. H., and C. Wright Mills (Eds.). 1958. *From Max Weber: Essays in Sociology.* New York: Oxford Univ. Press.

Gibbins, Roger. 1985. *Conflict and Unity: An Introduction to Canadian Political Life* (1st ed.) Toronto: Methuen.

—————— and Sonia Arrison. 1995. *Western Visions.* Peterborough: broadview press.

—————— and Michelle Honkanen. 1995. Environmentalism and the politics of mega-constitutional change. In Brian Galligan and Peter Russell (Eds.), *Redesigning the State: The Politics of Constitutional Change.* Sydney: The Federation Press.

Giddens, Anthony. 1990. *The Consequences of Modernity.* Stanford, California: Stanford Univ. Press.

——————. 1993. Dare to care, conserve and repair. *New Statesman & Society* (Oct. 29), 18–20.

Gillespie, Ed, and Bob Schellhas (Eds.). 1994. *Contract With America.* New York: Random House.

Goldsmith, E. 1972. *A Blueprint for Survival.* London: The Ecologist.

Gompers, Samuel. 1925. *Seventy Years of Life and Labor.* New York: A. M. Kelley.

Gonick, Cy. 1992. Socialism: past and future. In Jos. Roberts and Jesse Vorst (Eds.), *Socialism in Crisis? Canadian Perspectives* (pp. 199–24). Winnipeg: Fernwood Publishing.

Goodin, Robert E. 1992. *Green Political Theory.* Cambridge: Polity Press.

Goodwin, Barbara. 1982. *Using Political Ideas.* Chichester: John Wiley & Sons.

Grant, George. 1965. *Lament for a Nation.* Toronto: McClelland and Stewart.

Grant, Judith. 1993. *Fundamental Feminism: Contesting the Core Concepts of Feminist Theory.* New York: Routledge.

Gray, Alexander. 1946. *The Socialist Tradition: Moses to Lenin.* London: Longmans.

Gregor, James. 1968. *Contemporary Radical Ideologies.* New York: Random House.

——————. 1979. *Young Mussolini and the Intellectual Origins of Fascism.* Los Angeles: Univ. of California Press.

Griffin, Roger. 1991. *The Nature of Fascism.* New York: Routledge.

——————. (Ed.). 1995. *Fascism.* New York: Oxford Univ. Press.

Griffin, Susan. 1978. *Women and Nature: The Roaring Inside Her.* New York: Harper and Row.

Hagopian, Mark N. 1978. *Regimes, Movements and Ideologies.* (pub. data N/A)

Hall, Stuart. 1991. The local and global: globalization and identity. In Anthony D. King (Ed.), *Culture, Globalization and the World-System: Contemporary Conditions for the Representation of Identity* (pp. 19–40). London: Macmillan.

——————. 1991. Old and new identities, old and new ethnicities. In Anthony D. King (Ed.), *Culture, Globalization and the World-System: Contemporary Conditions for the Representation of Identity* (pp. 41–68). London: Macmillan.

Hallowell, John H. 1950. *Main Currents in Modern Political Thought.* New York: Henry Holt and Company.

——————. (Ed.). 1975. *Voegelin, From Enlightenment to Revolution.* Durham, N.C.: Duke Univ. Press.

Hardin, Garrett. 1968. The tragedy of the commons. *Science* 162, 1243–48.

Harrington, Michael. 1989. *Socialism: Past and Future.* New York: Arcade Publishing.

Harrison, J. F. C. 1979. *The Second Coming: Popular Millenarianism 1780–1850.* London: Routledge and Kegan Paul.

Harrison, Trevor. 1995. *Of Passionate Intensity: Right-Wing Populism and the Reform Party of Canada.* Toronto: Univ. of Toronto Press.

Hart, Michael. 1995. Globalization and governance. *Policy Options* 16 (July/Aug.), 49–53.

Hartmann, Heidi. 1984. The unhappy marriage of Marxism and feminism: Towards a more progressive union. In Alison M. Jaggar and Paula S. Rothenberg (Eds.), *Feminist Frameworks: Alternative Theoretical Accounts of the Relations Between Men and Women* (2nd ed.) (pp. 172–189). New York: McGraw-Hill Inc.

Hartz, Louis. 1955. *The Liberal Tradition in America.* Toronto: Longmans.

_____. 1964. *The Founding of New Societies.* New York: Harcourt, Brace and World.

Hawkesworth, M. E. 1988. *Theoretical Issues in Policy Analysis.* Albany, N.Y.: SUNY Press.

Hayek, Friedrich A. von. 1972. *The Road to Serfdom.* Chicago: Univ. of Chicago Press.

_____. 1989. *The Fatal Conceit: The Errors of Socialism.* Chicago: Univ. of Chicago Press.

Hayes, Carlton J. H. 1926. *Essays on Nationalism.* Reprinted 1966. New York: Russell & Russell.

———. Marshall Whithed Baldwin, and Charles Woolsey Cole. 1956. *History of Europe.* New York: Macmillan Co.

Hayes, Carlton J. H. 1960. *Nationalism: A Religion.* New York: Macmillan Co.

Heidegger, Martin. 1993. *Basic Writings.* San Francisco: Harper Collins.

Held, David, and Anthony McGrew. 1993. Globalization and the liberal democratic state. *Government and Opposition* 28:2 (Spring), 261–88.

Heywood, Andrew. 1992. *Political Ideologies: An Introduction.* London: Macmillan.

Hibbert, Christopher. 1981. *The Days of the French Revolution.* New York: Morrow Quill.

Hicks, John D. 1931. *The Populist Revolt: A History of the Farmers Alliance and the People's Party.* Lincoln: Univ. of Nebraska.

Hitler, Adolph. 1972. *Mein Kampf* and selected speeches. In Carl Cohen (Ed.), *Communism, Fascism and Democracy: The Theoretical Foundations* (pp. 374–90). New York: Random House.

Hobbes, Thomas. 1651. *Leviathan.* Cambridge: Cambridge Univ. Press (1991).

Hofstadter, Richard. 1955. *The Age of Reform: From Bryan to F.D.R.* New York: Alfred A. Knopf.

Hobsbawn, Eric. 1977. Some reflections on "The Break-up of Britain." *New Left Review* 105 (Sept.–Oct.), 3–24.

_____. 1990. *Nations and Nationalism Since 1780.* Cambridge: Cambridge Univ. Press.

Hood, Elizabeth F. 1984. Black women, white women: Separate paths to liberation. In Alison M. Jaggar and Paula S. Rothenberg (Eds.), *Feminist Frameworks: Alternative Theoretical Accounts of the Relations Between Men and Women* (2nd ed.) (pp. 189–202). New York: McGraw-Hill Inc.

Horowitz, Gad. 1966. Liberalism, conservatism, and socialism in Canada: An interpretation. *Canadian Journal of Political Science and Economics* 32: 2, (May), 143–71.

Huber, Hartwig. 1995. The immortal principle. In Roger Griffin (Ed.), *Fascism* (pp. 365–66). New York: Oxford Univ. Press.

Hudelson, Richard H. 1993. *The Rise and Fall of Communism.* Boulder: Westview Press.

Hughes, Colin A. 1980. *The Government of Queensland.* St. Lucia, Queensland, Australia.

Ignatieff, Michael. 1987. The myth of citizenship. *Queen's Quarterly* 94 (Winter), 966–985.

_____. 1993. *Blood and Belonging: Journeys Into the New Nationalism.* Toronto: Viking.

Inglehart, Ronald, 1977. *The Silent Revolution.* Princeton, N.J.: Princeton Univ. Press.

_____. 1990. *Culture Shift,* Princeton, N.J.: Princeton Univ. Press.

Irving, David. 1995. Laying it on the line. In Roger Griffin (Ed.), *Fascism* (pp. 335–37). New York: Oxford Univ. Press.

_____. 1995. The bicycle thief. In Roger Griffin (Ed.), *Fascism* (pp. 335–37). New York: Oxford Univ. Press.

Jackson, Robert J., and Doreen Jackson. 1990. *Politics in Canada: Culture, Institutions, Behavior and Public Policy* (2nd ed.). Scarborough, Ont.: Prentice-Hall Canada, Inc.

Jaggar, Alison M., and Paula S. Rothenberg. 1984. *Feminist Frameworks: Alternative Theoretical Accounts of the Relations Between Men and Women* (2nd ed.). New York: McGraw-Hill Inc.

Jamison, Andrew et al. 1991. *The Making of the New Environmental Consciousness: A Comparative Study of the Environmental Movements in Sweden, Denmark and the Netherlands.* Edinburgh: Edinburgh Univ. Press.

Jay, Richard. 1984. Nationalism. In Robert Eccleshall et al., *Political Ideologies* (pp. 185–215). London: Hutchinson Publishing.

Johnson, Lawrence E. 1991. *A Morally Deep World.* Cambridge: Cambridge Univ. Press.

Kamenka, Eugene. 1993. Nationalism: Ambiguous legacies and contingent futures. *Political Studies* XLI, 78–92.

Kanji, Mebs, and Neil Nevitte. 1995. North American reactions to environmentalism. A paper presented to "Border Demographics and Regional Interdependency: A Trinational Symposium." Western Washington Univ., Bellingham, Washington.

Kedourie, Elie. 1960. *Nationalism*. New York: Praeger.

Kellas, James G. 1991. *The Politics of Nationalism and Ethnicity*. London: Macmillan.

Kennedy, Duncan. 1976. Form and substance in private law adjudication. *Harvard Law Review* 89: 1685–1778.

Keynes, John Maynard. 1936. *General Theory of Employment Interest and Income*. London: Macmillan.

Khosla, Punam. 1993. *Review of the Situation of Women in Canada*. Toronto: National Action Committee on the Status of Women.

King, Dennis. 1989. *Lyndon LaRouche and the New American Fascism*. Toronto: Doubleday.

King, Ynestra. 1989. The ecology of feminism and the feminism of ecology. In Judith Plant (Ed.), *Healing the Wounds: The Promise of Ecofeminism* (pp. 18–28). London: Green Print.

Kinsella, Warren. 1994. *Web of Hate: Inside Canada's Far Right Network*. Toronto: Harper Collins.

Kitchen, Martin. 1976. *Fascism*. London: Macmillan.

Knight, Richard V. 1989. Redefining cities. In Richard V. Knight and Gary Gappert (Eds.), *Cities In a Global Society* (pp. 15–20). Newbury Park, London, New Delhi: Sage Publications.

Kobach, Kris W. 1993. *The Referendum: Direct Democracy in Switzerland*. Aldershot, England: Dartmouth Publishing.

Koenig, Louis W. 1971. *Bryan: A Political Biography of William Jennings Bryan*. New York: G. P. Putnam's Sons.

Kogan, N. 1968. Fascism as a political system. In S. J. Woolf (Ed.), *The Nature of Fascism* (pp. 11–18). London: Weidenfeld and Nicolson.

Kohn, Hans. 1944. *The Idea of Nationalism*. New York: Macmillan.

———. 1962. *The Age of Nationalism*. New York: Harper & Brothers.

———. 1965. *Nationalism: Its Meaning and History* (rev. ed.). Princeton, N.J.: D. Van Nostrand Company.

Kymlicka, Will. 1989. *Liberalism, Community, and Culture*. Oxford: Clarendon.

——— and Donald G. Lehihan. 1994. Whither the nation-state? Finding a niche in the global village. *Policy Options* 15, (July–August), 11–14.

——— and Wayne Norman. 1994. Return of the citizen: A survey of recent work on citizenship theory. *Ethics* 104 (Jan.), 353–81.

Lane, Robert E. 1962. *Political Ideology: Why the American Common Man Believes What He Does*. New York: The Free Press.

Lapham, Lewis H. 1995. Reactionary chic: How the nineties right recycles the bombast of the sixties left. *Harper's Magazine*. Vol. 290. No. 1738 (March), pp. 31–42.

Laqueur, Walter. 1979. *Fascism: A Reader's Guide*. London: Penguin Books.

Larmore, Charles E. 1987. *Patterns of Moral Complexity*. Cambridge: Cambridge Univ. Press.

Larrain, Jorge. 1979. *The Concept of Ideology*. London: Hutchinson Publishing.

Lasch, Peter. 1994 . The revolt of the elites. *Harper's Magazine* 289 (Nov.), 39–50.

Laycock, David. 1990. *Populism and Democratic Thought in the Canadian Praries, 1910 to 1945*. Toronto: Univ. of Toronto Press.

Lee, JeeYeun. 1995. Beyond bean counting. In Barbara Findlen (Ed.), *Listen Up: Voices from the Next Feminist Generation*. USA: Seal Press.

Lee, Martha. 1987. *The Fall of America*. Ottawa: National Library of Canada.

———. 1992. Environmental apocalypse: A case study of Earth First! Unpublished paper.

Lefebvre, Georges. 1947. *The Coming of the French Revolution*. Princeton, N.J.: Princeton Univ. Press.

Leonhard, Wolfgang. 1970. *Three Faces of Marxism: The Political Concepts of Soviet Ideology, Maoism, and Humanist Marxism*. Trans. by Ewald Osers. New York: Holt, Rinehart and Winston.

Lenz, Elinor, and Barbara Myerhoff. 1985. *The Feminization of America*. Los Angeles: Jeremy P. Tarcher, Inc.

Lévesque, René. 1968. *An Option for Quebec.* Toronto: McClelland and Stewart.

Levi, Primo. 1995. The deadly trunk of fascism. In Roger Griffin (Ed.), *Fascism* (pp. 391–92). New York: Oxford Univ. Press.

Levine, Andrew. 1988. *Arguing for Socialism: Theoretical Considerations.* London: Verso.

Lichtheim, George. 1970. *A Short History of Socialism.* London: Weidenfeld and Nicolson.

Linz, Juan. 1995. The latecomer. In Roger Griffin (Ed.), *Fascism* (pp. 299–300). New York: Oxford Univ. Press.

Lipset, Seymour Martin. 1950. *Agrarian Socialism* (rev. ed.). New York: Anchor Books.

———. 1960. *Political Man.* New York: William Heinemann.

——— and Earl Raab. 1970. *The Politics of Unreason: Right-Wing Extremism in America, 1790–1970.* New York: Harper and Row.

———. 1988. Neoconservatism: Myth and reality. *Society* 25 (5), 29–37.

———. 1990. *Political Man: The Social Bases of Politics.* Garden City, N.Y.: Doubleday & Co.

Locke, John. 1690. *Two Treatises on Government.* Reprinted 1978. Ann Arbor: Univ. of Microfilms International.

Lorber, Judith. 1994. *Paradoxes of Gender.* New Haven: Yale Univ. Press.

Lyttleton, Adrian (Ed.). 1973. *Italian Fascisms from Pareto to Gentile.* London: Jonathan Cape.

Macdonald, Douglas. 1991. *The Politics of Pollution: Why Canadians Are Failing Their Environment.* Toronto: McClelland and Stewart.

MacIntyre, Alisdair. 1984. *After Virtue: A Study in Moral Theory* (2nd ed.). Notre Dame, Ind.: Univ. of Notre Dame Press.

MacRae, D. G. 1961. *Ideology and Society.* London: Heinemann.

Maddox, William S. and Stuart A. Lilie. 1984. *Beyond Liberal and Conservative: Reassessing the Political Spectrum.* Washington: Cato Institute.

Magleby, David B. 1984. *Direct Legislation: Voting on Ballot Propositions in the United States.* Baltimore: Johns Hopkins.

Magnusson, Warren. 1994. Critical social movements: De-centering the state. In James Bickerton and Alain-G. Gagnon (Eds.), *Canadian Politics* (pp. 515–41). Peterborough: broadview press.

Malcolm X [with Alex Haley]. 1973. *The Autobiography of Malcolm X.* New York: Ballantine Books.

Manes, Christopher. 1990. *Green Rage: Radical Environmentalism and the Unmaking of Civilization.* Boston: Little, Brown and Company.

Manning, Preston. 1992. *The New Canada.* Toronto: Macmillan Canada.

Manthorpe, Jonathan. 1995. China ensures it will be targeted. *Calgary Herald* (Aug. 25), p. A1–2.

Marchak, M. Patricia. 1988. *Ideological Perspectives on Canada* (3rd ed.). Toronto: McGraw-Hill Ryerson.

Marsh, James L. 1991. *Radical Fragments.* New York: Peter Lang.

Marshall, Peter. 1992. *Nature's Web: An Exploration of Ecological Thinking.* London & Sydney: Simon & Schuster.

Marshall, T. H. 1964. *Class, Citizenship and Social Development: Essays by T. H. Marshall.* New York: Doubleday and Co.

Marx, Karl. [1845] 1978. Theses on Feuerbach. In *The Marx-Engels Reader* (2nd ed.). Ed. Robert C. Tucker. New York: Norton.

——— and Friedrich Engels. 1848. *Communist Manifesto.* London: Allen & Unwin (1954).

———. 1867. *Das Kapital.* Ed. by Friedrich Engels.

Matas, Robert. 1993. B.C. eyes strict recall rules: 50% of voter support could force by-election, committee proposes. *The Globe and Mail,* Nov. 24, p. A1.

McAllister, Ian. 1991. Party elites, voters and political attitudes. *Canadian Journal of Political Science* XXIV, 2:237–68.

McAuley, Mary. *Soviet Politics 1917–1991.* Toronto: Oxford Univ. Press.

McKenna, George. 1973. *American Populism*. New York: G. P. Putnam's Sons.

McKibben, Bill. 1989. *The End of Nature*. New York: Random House.

McLaughlin, Corinne, and Gordon Davidson. 1994. S*piritual Politics: Changing the World From the Inside Out*. New York & Toronto: Ballantine Books.

McLellan, David, and Sean Sayers (Eds.). 1991. *Socialism and Democracy*. London: Macmillan.

Mellor, Mary. 1992. Green politics: Ecofeminist, ecofeminine, or ecomasculine? *Environmental Politics*. Vol. 1, No. 2 (Summer), 229–51.

Merchant, Carolyn. 1980. *The Death of Nature*. New York: Harper and Row.

Michels, Robert. 1962. *Political Parties*. New York: The Free Press.

Mill, John Stuart. 1961. *The Early Draft of John Stuart Mill's Autobiography*. Ed. Jack Stillinger. Urbana, Ill.: Univ. of Illinois Press.

_____. 1993. *Utilitarianism, On Liberty, Considerations of Representative Government*. Ed. Geraint Williams. Vermont: Charles E. Tuttle.

Miller, David (Ed.). 1994. *The Blackwell Encyclopedia of Political Thought*. Cambridge: Blackwell Publishers.

Miller, S. M. 1985. Challenges for populism. *Social Policy* 16:1 (Summer), 3–6.

Millett, Kate. 1970. *Sexual Politics*. New York: Doubleday and Co. Inc.

Minogue, Kenneth. 1985. *Alien Powers: The Pure Theory of Ideology*. London: Weidenfeld and Nicolson.

Mises, Ludwig von. 1981. *Socialism: An Economic and Sociological Analysis*. Indianapolis: Liberty Classics.

Mitchell, Juliet, and Ann Oakley. 1986. *What is Feminism: A Re-Examination*. New York: Pantheon Books.

Morgan, Robin. 1977. *Going Too Far: The Personal Chronicle of a Feminist*. New York: Random House.

Morton, W. L. 1944. Direct legislation and the origins of the Progressive movement. *Canadian Historical Review* 25, 2: 279–88.

_____. 1950. *The Progressive Party in Canada*. Toronto: Univ. of Toronto Press.

Mosse, George L. 1995. A third way. In Roger Griffin (Ed.), *Fascism*. New York: Oxford Univ. Press.

Mouffe, Chantal. 1988. The civics lesson. *New Statesman and Society* 1:18, (Oct. 7), 28–31.

Mulhall, Stephen, and Adam Swift. 1992. *Liberals and Communitarians*. Oxford: Blackwell.

Mussolini, Benito. 1972. The doctrine of fascism. In Carl Cohen (Ed.), *Communism, Fascism and Democracy: The Theoretical Foundations* (pp. 328–39). New York: Random House.

_____. 1975. *The Corporate State*. New York: Howard Fertig.

Nash, George H. 1976. *The Conservative Intellectual Movement in America Since 1945*. New York: Basic Books.

Nash, Roderick. 1989. *The Rights of Nature: A History of Environmental Ethics*. Madison: Univ. of Wisconsin Press.

Nasrullah, Amber. 1995. Manning hopes meeting sparks tax revolt: Electronic "town hall" on cable TV discusses cuts, limits on federal spending. *The Globe and Mail* (Feb. 13), p. A3.

Nevitte, Neil, and Roger Gibbins. 1990. *New Elites in Old States: Ideologies in the Anglo-American Democracies*. Toronto: Oxford Univ. Press.

Newman, Peter C. 1995. E-cash: A looming financial revolution. *Maclean's* (June 26), p. 30.

Nisbet, Robert. 1985. The Conservative renaissance in perspective. *The Public Interest* 81, 128–141.

Oakeshott, Michael. 1991. The masses in representative democracy. In Timothy Fuller (Ed.), *Rationalism in Politics and Other Essays*. Indianapolis: Liberty Press.

Olasky, Marvin. 1992. *The Tragedy of American Compassion*. Washington: Regnery.

O'Sullivan, Noel. 1983. *Fascism*. London: J. M. Dent & Sons.

Paehlke, Robert. 1989. *Environmentalism and the Future of Progressive Politics*. New Haven: Yale Univ. Press.

Pal, Leslie A. 1993. *Interests of State: The Politics of Language, Multiculturalism, and Feminism in Canada.* Montreal & Kingston: McGill-Queen's Univ. Press.

Palmieri, Mario. 1972. The philosophy of fascism. In Carl Cohen (Ed.), *Communism, Fascism and Democracy: The Theoretical Foundations* (pp. 344–61). New York: Random House.

Pamyat. 1995. Patriots of the World Unite! In Roger Griffin (Ed.), *Fascism* (pp. 374–76). New York: Oxford Univ. Press.

Parekh, Bhikhu. 1973. Social and political thought and the problem of ideology. In Robert Benewick, R. N. Berki, and Bhikhu Parekh (Eds.), *Knowledge and Belief in Politics: The Problem of Ideology* (pp. 57–87). New York: St. Martin's Press.

Parel, Anthony. 1983. Ideology and philosophy. In Anthony Parel (Ed.), *Ideology, Philosophy and Politics.* Waterloo: Wilfrid Laurier Press.

Patsouras, Louis, and Jack Ray Thomas (Ed.). 1981. *Varieties and Problems of Twentieth-Century Socialism.* Chicago: Nelson-Hall.

Pepper, David. 1986. *The Roots of Modern Environmentalism.* London & New York: Routledge.

Pierce, William L. 1980. *The Turner Diaries.* Arlington: The National Alliance/National Vanguard Books.

Piven, Frances Fox, and Richard A. Cloward. 1971. *Regulating the Poor: The Functions of Public Welfare.* New York: Vintage.

Plamenatz, John. 1970. *Ideology.* London: Pall Mall Press Ltd.

Pocock, J. G. A. The ideal of citizenship since classical times. *Queen's Quarterly* 99 (Spring), 33–55.

Polanyi, Michael. 1960. *Beyond Nihilism.* Cambridge: Cambridge Univ. Press.

Popper, Karl R. 1963. *The Open Society and Its Enemies.* Princeton: Princeton Univ. Press.

Porritt, Jonathon. 1984. *Seeing Green: The Politics of Ecology Explained.* Oxford: Blackwell.

Porter, Gareth, and Janet Welsh Brown. 1991. *Global Environmental Politics.* Boulder: Westview Press.

Putnam, Hilary. 1990. *Realism with a Human Face.* Cambridge: Harvard Univ. Press.

Qualter, Terence H. 1986. *Conflicting Political Ideas in Liberal Democracies.* Toronto: Methuen.

Rae, Douglas. 1989. *Equalities.* Cambridge: Harvard Univ. Press.

Rawls, John. 1987. The idea of an overlapping consensus. *Oxford Journal of Legal Studies.* Vol. 7, No. 1.

Raz, Joseph. 1986. *The Morality of Freedom.* Oxford: Clarendon Press.

_____. 1994. Multiculturalism: A liberal perspective. *Dissent* (Winter), 1–13.

Reed, Evelyn. 1984. Women: Caste, class or oppressed sex? In Alison M. Jaggar and Paula S. Rothenberg (Eds.), *Feminist Frameworks: Alternative Theoretical Accounts of the Relations Between Men and Women* (2nd ed.) (pp. 132–36). New York: McGraw-Hill Inc.

Reform Party of Canada. 1992. Party Caucus Issue Statement 36. Calgary, July 16.

_____. 1993. *Reform Party of Canada 1993 Blue Sheet: Principles, Policies and Election Platform.* Calgary.

Rieff, David. 1993/94. A global culture? *World Policy Journal* X:4 (Winter), 73–81.

Rifkin, Jeremy. 1991. *Biosphere Politics: A New Consciousness for a New Century.* New York: Crown Publishers.

Riker, William H. 1982. *Liberalism Against Populism: A Confrontation Between the Theory of Democracy and the Theory of Social Choice.* Prospect Heights, Ill.: Waveland.

Ritter, Paul. 1995. The expansionary spirit of a rejuvenated people. In Roger Griffin (Ed.), *Fascism* (pp. 143–45). New York: Oxford Univ. Press.

Robertson, Roland. 1991. Social theory, cultural relativity and the problem of globality. In Anthony D. King (Ed.), *Culture, Globalization and the World-System: Contemporary Conditions for the Representation of Identity* (pp. 69-90). London: Macmillan.

_____. 1992. *Globalization: Social Theory and Global Culture.* London: Sage Publications.

Robin, Martin. 1992. *Shades of Right: Nativist and Fascist Politics in Canada, 1920–1940.* Toronto: Univ. of Toronto Press.

Rocco, Alfredo. 1972. The political doctrine of fascism. In Carl Cohen (Ed.), *Communism, Fascism and Democracy: The Theoretical Foundations* (pp. 315–316). New York: Random House.

_____. 1973. The *Politica* Manifesto. In Adrian Lyttleton (Ed.), *Italian Fascisms from Pareto to Gentile.* London: Jonathan Cape.

Rokeach, Milton. 1960. *The Open and the Closed Mind.* New York: Basic Books.

Rootes, C. A. 1992. Environmentalism: Movements, politics and parties. In *Environmental Politics,* (Fall), Vol. 1, No. 3. London: Frank Cass and Company.

Rose, Hillary. 1986. Women's work: Women's knowledge. In Juliet Mitchell and Ann Oakley, *What is Feminism: A Re-Examination* (pp. 161–183). New York: Pantheon Books.

Rosenau, James. 1989. Global changes and theoretical challenges: Toward a postnational politics for the 1990s. In Ernst-Otto Czempiel and James N. Rosenau (Eds.), *Global Changes and Theoretical Challenges: Approaches to World Politics for the 1990s* (pp. 1–20). Lexington: Lexington Books.

Rosenberg, Alfred. 1972. The myth of the twentieth century. In Carl Cohen (Ed.), *Communism, Fascism and Democracy: The Theoretical Foundations.* New York: Random House.

Rossiter, Clinton (Ed.). 1961. *The Federalist Papers.* New York: NAL Penguin, Inc.

Roszak, Theodore. 1978. *Person/Planet.* Garden City, N.Y.: Doubleday.

Rowbotham, Sheila. 1973. *Hidden from History: 300 Years of Women's Oppression and the Fight Against It.* London: Pluto Press Ltd.

_____. 1992. *Women in Movement: Feminism and Social Action.* New York: Routledge.

Rudé, George. 1988. *The French Revolution.* London: Weidenfield and Nicolson.

Ruff, Norman J. 1993/94. Institutional populism in British Columbia. *Canadian Parliamentary Review,* 16:4 (Winter), 24–32.

Ruggie, John Gerard. 1993. Territoriality and beyond: Problematizing modernity in international relations. *International Organization,* 47 (Winter), 139–74.

Sabine, George H., and Thomas L. Thorson. 1973. *A History of Political Theory* (4th ed.). Hinsdale, Ill.: Dryden Press.

Sale, Kirkpatrick. 1984. Mother of all: An introduction to bio-regionalism. In S. Kumar (Ed.), *The Schumacher Lectures,* Vol. II. London: Blond & Brigg.

_____. 1991. *Dwellers in the Land: The Bioregional Vision.* Philadelphia: New Society Publishers.

Salutin, Rick 1995. *The Age of Improv: A Political Novel of the Future.* Toronto: Harper Collins.

Sandel, Michael J. 1982. *Liberation and the Limits of Justice.* Cambridge: Cambridge Univ. Press.

Sargent, Lyman Tower. 1990. *Contemporary Political Ideologies: A Comparative Analysis* (8th ed.). Pacific Grove: Brooks/Cole Publishing Company.

Scarce, Rik. 1990. *Eco-Warriors: Understanding the Radical Environmental Movement.* Chicago: The Noble Press.

Schwantes, Carlos A. 1989. *The Pacific Northwest: An Interpretive History.* Lincoln: Univ. of Nebraska.

Schwartz, Edward. 1980. Populism: A tradition in search of a movement. *Social Policy* 10:5 (March/April), 14–20.

Sessions, George (Ed.). 1995. *Deep Ecology for the 21st Century.* Boston: Shambhala.

Seton-Watson, Hugh. 1977. *Nations and States: An Enquiry into the Origins of Nations and the Politics of Nationalism.* London: Methuen.

Shafer, Boyd C. 1955. *Nationalism: Myth and Reality.* New York: Harcourt, Brace and Company.

_____. 1972. *Faces of Nationalism: New Realities and Old Myths.* New York: Harcourt Brace Jovanovich.

Shalom, Steve Rosskamm (Ed.). 1983. *Socialist Visions.* Boston: South End Press.

Simpson, Jeffrey. 1994. *Faultlines: Struggling for a Canadian Vision.* Toronto: Harper Perennial.

_____. 1994. So far, the Reform Party's performance in the Commons is not surprising. *The Globe and Mail,* Oct. 14, p. A32.

Skidmore, Max J. 1993. *Ideologies: Politics in Action* (2nd ed.). Toronto: Harcourt Brace Jovanovich.

Smith, Anthony D. 1976. Neo-Classicist and Romantic elements in the emergence of nationalist conceptions. In Anthony D. Smith (Ed.), *Nationalist Movements* (pp. 74–87). London: Macmillan.

———. 1979. *Nationalism in the Twentieth Century.* London: Martin Robertson.

———. 1983. *Theories of Nationalism.* London: Duckworth.

Smith, Rogers M. 1994. Unfinished Liberalism. *Social Research* 61:3 (Fall), 631–70.

Snyder, Louis L. 1968. *The New Nationalism.* Ithaca: Cornell Univ. Press.

Sobel, Robert. 1967. *The French Revolution: A Concise History and Interpretation.* New York: Ardmore Press.

Sommers, Christina Hoff. 1994. *Who Stole Feminism?* New York: Simon and Schuster.

Sorel, Georges. 1914. *Reflections on Violence.* New York: B. W. Huebsch.

Soysal, Yasemin Nuhoglu. 1994. *Limits of Citizenship: Migrants and Postnational Membership in Europe.* Chicago: Univ. of Chicago Press.

Stackhouse, John. 1994. A victory for women's rights. *The Globe and Mail,* Sept. 12, p. A8.

Stefanik, Nancy. 1993. Sustainable dialogue/sustainable development: Developing planetary consciousness via electronic democracy. In Jeremy Brecher, John Brown Childs, and Jill Cutler (Eds.), *Global Visions: Beyond the New World Order* (pp. 263–72). Montreal & New York: Black Rose Books.

Steinfels, Peter. 1979. *The Neoconservatives: The Men Who Are Changing America's Politics.* New York: Simon and Schuster.

———. 1979. Neoconservatives and the fear of equality. *Dissent* 26 (2), 169–182.

Sternhell, Zeev. 1994. *The Birth of Fascist Ideology: From Cultural Rebellion to Political Revolution.* Princeton: Princeton Univ. Press.

Stromberg, Roland. 1990. *European Intellectual History Since 1789.* Englewood Cliffs, N.J.: Prentice-Hall.

Stubbs, Richard, and Geoffrey D. Underhill (Eds.). 1994. *Political Economy and the Changing Global Order.* Toronto: McClelland and Stewart.

Surtees, Lawrence. 1995. Telecom's show of shows. *The Globe and Mail,* Sept. 12, p. C1.

Switzer, Jacqueline Vaughn. 1994. *Environmental Politics: Domestic and Global Dimensions.* New York: St. Martin's Press.

Sydenham, M. J. 1965. *The French Revolution.* London: B. T. Batsford.

Sykes, Charles J. 1992. *A Nation of Victims: The Decay of the American Character.* New York: St. Martin's Press.

Symmons-Symonolewicz, Konstantin. 1968. *Modern Nationalism: Towards a Consensus in Theory.* New York: The Polish Institute of Arts and Sciences in America.

———. 1970. *Nationalist Movements: A Comparative View.* Meadville, Pa.: Maplewood Press.

Talmon, J. L. 1960. *The Origins of Totalitarian Democracy.* New York: Frederick A. Praeger.

———. 1960. *Political Messianism: The Romantic Phase.* London: Secker & Warburg.

Taylor, Charles. 1991. *The Malaise of Modernity.* Concord, Ont.: Anansi.

———. 1993. *Reconciling the Solitudes: Essays on Canadian Federalism and Nationalism.* Montreal: McGill-Queen's Univ. Press.

Therborn, Goran. 1985. Leaving the post office behind. In Milos Nicolic (Ed.), *Socialism on the Threshold of the Twenty-first Century* (pp. 225–50). London: Verso.

Thorne, Melvine J. 1990. *American Conservative Thought Since World War II: The Core Ideas.* New York: Greenwood Press.

Thorsell, William. 1995. If the centre cannot hold, will we invent a new centre? *The Globe and Mail,* Feb. 11, p. D5.

Todd, Dave. 1994. Fight against child labour falters. *The Globe and Mail,* Nov. 26, p. A5.

Togliatti, Palmiro. 1976. *Lectures on Fascism.* New York: International Publishers.

Tokar, Brian. 1992. *The Green Alternative: Creating an Ecological Future* (rev. ed.). San Pedro: R. & E. Miles.

Tong, Rosemarie. 1989. *Feminist Thought: A Comprehensive Introduction.* Boulder: Westview Press.

Tocqueville, Alexis de. 1984. *Democracy in America.* Ed. Richard D. Heffner. New York: Penguin.

Trebilcot, Joyce. 1984. Sex Roles: The argument from nature. In Alison M. Jaggar and Paula S. Rothenberg (Eds.). *Feminist Frameworks: Alternative Theoretical Accounts of the Relations Between Men and Women* (2nd ed.) (pp. 114–120). New York: McGraw-Hill Inc.

Trudeau, Pierre Elliott. 1968. *Federalism and the French Canadians.* Toronto: Macmillan.

Turner, Henry (Ed.). 1975. *Reappraisals of Fascism.* New York: Franklin Watts.

Tyndall, John. 1995. Spiritual AIDS In Roger Griffin (Ed.), *Fascism* (pp. 197–98). New York: Oxford Univ. Press.

Valois, George. 1995. Empty Portfolios. In Roger Griffin (Ed.), *Fascism* (pp. 197–98). New York: Oxford Univ. Press.

Valpy, Michael. 1995. Using a global lottery to protect the earth. *The Globe and Mail,* March 30, p. A2.

Vickers, Jill, Pauline Rankin, and Christine Appelle. 1993. *Politics As If Women Mattered.* Toronto: Univ. of Toronto Press.

Viguerie, Richard A. 1981. *The New Right: We're Ready to Lead.* USA: The Viguerie Company.

Voegelin, Eric. 1952. *The New Science of Politics.* Chicago: Univ. of Chicago Press.

_____. 1975. *From Enlightenment to Revolution.* Ed. John H. Hallowell. Durham: Duke Univ. Press.

Vogel, David. 1993. Representing diffuse interests in environmenal policymaking. In Kent Weaver (Ed.), *Do Institutions Matter?* (pp. 237–71). Washington D.C.: The Brooking Institution.

Wagner, Richard. 1995. The redemptive mission of German culture. In Roger Griffin (Ed.), *Fascism* (pp. 97–98). New York: Oxford Univ. Press.

Walzer, Michael. 1965. *The Revolution of the Saints: A Study in the Origins of Radical Politics.* London: Lowe and Brydone Ltd.

_____. 1983. *Spheres of Justice: A Defense of Pluralism and Equality.* New York: Basic Books.

Ward, Barbara.1959. *Five Ideas That Changed the World.* New York: W. W. Norton.

Waring, Marilyn. 1988. *If Women Counted: A New Feminist Economics.* San Francisco: Harper.

Warren, Donald I. 1976. *The Radical Center: Middle Americans and the Politics of Alienation.* Notre Dame, Ind.: Univ. of Notre Dame Press.

Watkins, Frederick M. 1964. *The Age of Ideology—Political Thought, 1750 to the Present.* Englewood Cliffs, N.J.: Prentice-Hall.

Webb, James. 1974. *The Occult Underground.* LaSalle, Ill.: Open Court.

Weimann, Gabriel, and Conrad Winn. 1986. *Hate on Trial.* Oakville: Mosaic Press.

Wente, Margaret. 1995. The end of affirmative action. *The Globe and Mail,* June 3, p. D7.

Will, George F. 1988. Snap, crackle and populist. *Newsweek,* Feb. 29, p. 76.

_____. 1993. *Restoration: Congress, Term Limits and the Restoration of Deliberative Democracy.* New York: Macmillan.

Williams, Geraint. 1991. *Political Theory in Retrospect.* Aldershot, England: Edward Elgar.

Wolf, Naomi. 1993. *Fire With Fire.* Toronto: Random House.

Worsley, Peter. 1969. The concept of populism. In Ghita Ionescu and Ernest Gellner (Eds.), *Populism: Its Meanings and National Characteristics* (pp. 212–50). London: Weidenfeld and Nicolson.

Wright, Anthony. 1986. *Socialisms: Theories and Practices.* Oxford: Oxford Univ. Press.

Young, John. 1990. *Sustaining the Earth.* Cambridge: Harvard Univ. Press.

Young, Stephen C. 1992. The different dimensions of green politics. *Environmental Politics,* Vol.1, No.1 (Spring), 9–44.

Young, Walter. 1968. *The Anatomy of a Party: The National CCF, 1932–1961.* Toronto: Univ. of Toronto Press.

Youngdale, James M. 1975. *Populism: A Psychohistorical Perspective.* Port Washington, N.Y.: Kennikat Press.

Zimmerman, Michael E. et al. 1993. *Environmental Philosophy: From Animal Rights to Radical Ecology.* Englewood Cliffs, N.J.: Prentice-Hall

INDEX